W9-AGZ-245

Privatization

Theoretical Lenses on Public Policy

Series Editor, Paul A. Sabatier

Privatization

An International Review of Performance

Graeme A. Hodge

Monash University, Melbourne Australia

A Member of the Perseus Books Group

Theoretical Lenses on Public Policy

All rights reserved. Printed in the United States of America. No part of this publication may be reproduced or transmitted in any form or by any means, electronic or mechanical, including photocopy, recording, or any information storage and retrieval system, without permission in writing from the publisher.

Copyright © 2000 by Westview Press, A Member of the Perseus Books Group

Published in 2000 in the United States of America by Westview Press, 5500 Central Avenue, Boulder, Colorado 80301-2877, and in the United Kingdom by Westview Press, 12 Hid's Copse Road, Cumnor Hill, Oxford OX2 9JJ

Find us on the World Wide Web at www.westviewpress.com

Library of Congress Cataloging-in-Publication Data
Hodge, Graeme A.
    Privatization : an international review of performance / Graeme A. Hodge.
        p.   cm. — (Theoretical lenses on public policy)
    Includes bibliographical references.
    ISBN 0-8133-6682-8 (hc.) — ISBN 0-8133-6681-X (pb.)
    1. Privatization—Comparative method.   I. Title.   II. Series.
HD3850.H59   1999
338.9–dc21   99-37926
                                                                                                        CIP

The paper used in this publication meets the requirements of the American National Standard for Permanence of Paper for Printed Library Materials Z39.48-1984.

10   9   8   7   6   5   4   3   2   1

Contents

v

Tables and Figures

Figures

Acknowledgments

As with all major projects, a longer list of people have contributed positively toward this book than will be possible to thank here. My thanks go to my work colleagues at both Monash University and Monash Mt. Elisa Business School, including Alex Owen, Graeme Macmillan, Phillip MacLeod, Rob Hyndman, and Bill Russell, and to the library staff at the Monash Library. A big thank-you to all of you. Whether smoothing the journey through willing and positive conversations, gathering literature, or through unstinting explanations and clarifications on many meta-analytic or mathematical modeling issues, I acknowledge your assistance and contributions.

Most of all, I would like to note with much thankfulness and appreciation the ever-present support and love of my wife Stephanie. Always willing to assist and nurture, I dedicate this work to her. To my sons, Anthony, Christopher, and Michael, I thank you from my heart. For all the times when you graciously allowed Dad to continue working on "his project," I appreciate your patience.

Graeme A. Hodge

Acronyms

ANOVA	analysis of variance
ARIMA	auto-regressive integrated moving average (ARIMA) transfer function technique
CCT	compulsory competitive tendering
CTC	competitive tendering and contracting
DAO	Dissertation Abstracts Online
GBE	government business enterprise
GDP	gross domestic product
GDR	German Democratic Republic
GNP	gross national product
IMF	International Monetary Fund
IT	information technology
LDCs	less developed countries
NCPA	National Center for Policy Analysis
OECD	Organisation for European Cooperation and Development
PAIS	Public Affairs Information Service
PSRC	Public Sector Research Centre (NSW)
PSBR	Public Sector Borrowing Ratio
R&D	research and development
RMIT	Royal Melbourne Institute of Technology University
RoE	return on equity
RoS	return on sales
SOE	state-owned enterprise
TFP	total factor productivity
TQM	total quality management
USGAO	United States Government Accounting Office
USSR	Union of Soviet Socialist Republics

PART I

Concepts Underpinning Privatization

1

Introduction

The 1990s are a significant time of change for governments throughout the world. One major economic and social issue in many countries is that of reforming organizations across the public sector. These reforms have been driven by several considerations. Citizens are certainly looking to get more for less from government as a whole. There is increasing pressure from all fronts for reduced funding. Simultaneously, there are also significant community expectations for marked improvements in government practices in terms of economic efficiency and service delivery. Many improvements expected of the public sector are modeled on those of the private sector. For example, a greater customer focus is expected across government. Old methods and procedures are being increasingly challenged, and service delivery practices and standards are being subjected to review.

These drivers of reform are leading to a renewed questioning of not only the practices of government but its structures, processes, and service delivery mechanisms. The very roles and responsibilities of government are being opened up. In providing services, there is now a requirement to benchmark and to openly demonstrate competition and efficiency.

This review follows these pressures for change and the imperatives that are inherent within them. This book aims not to provide a fashionable statement of current trends in service provision, but a careful and measured review of empirical findings in contracting out and the sale of government enterprises. Such a considered review is in keeping with the simultaneous requirements of the public sector both to review service delivery improvement options, and to be held accountable to the public in adopting those changes that clearly do lead to enhanced performance.

Government uses a significant proportion of the resources of a nation. For example, projected government outlays as a proportion of the U.S. gross domestic product (GDP) were around 33.1 percent in 1998, and for Organisation for Economic Cooperation and Development (OECD) countries around 39.2 percent on average.[1] Of this, a significant part is related to the provision and production of goods and services.

WAVES OF REFORM

In the past two decades a series of reforms have flowed through the business sector and through government. In most cases, these reforms have been international in significance. Although their objectives have varied, each has in one way or other claimed to be able to increase productivity and enhance the effectiveness of operations. These reforms have spawned an industry of expert publications including books, manuals, and guidelines—all aiming to ensure that the busy executive is brought up to date with the latest imperative that, if you believe the sales pitch, is now urgently required for the ongoing success of their business.

Whilst clearly not a comprehensive listing, some of these reform waves since the mid-1970s have included the following:

- performance measurement
- management by objectives
- performance budgeting
- program budgeting
- systems analysis
- managerialism
- customer focus/customer service
- total quality management (TQM)
- decentralization/centralization
- corporatization/commercialization
- privatization
- benchmarking
- contracting out
- competitive tendering
- worlds best practice
- business process reengineering
- reinventing government

Layered on top of these reforms have been various others. At the business level, we have seen an increased emphasis on strategic planning, whilst reforms at the level of the work team have included initiatives such as quality circles and outdoor team training. Ongoing microeconomic reforms at the individual level have continued.

Many appear to have led to real improvements in productivity. Articles in industry magazines and newspapers tell of successes. Indeed, few would argue against the need to adopt "best practice" or to "improve quality." However, experience has also taught the seasoned manager that each reform has also been accompanied by other impacts that, once experienced, may in the longer term have slowed down the wholesale application of the reform across all areas of the business. The cumbersome requirements of much of the TQM reform work has, for example, led to a significant slowdown in the pace of this particular reform and in the initiation of other reform movements such as reengineering. In some instances, reforms may have entirely petered out after a flurry of initial enthusiasm and energy. The promise of program budgeting, compared to the meager benefits it delivered, is a case in point here.

In hindsight, we might conclude that whilst the goals of a reform were usually desirable, the mechanisms themselves were often far from perfect. The promised benefits of the reform were theoretical—the actual implementation impacts were not.

A salutary lesson from these waves of reform has been the need to be cognizant of the differences between the structure of beliefs on the one hand, and the empirical knowledge gained to date on the other. The belief that through the improvement of management processes, solutions to complex public policy problems will evolve (managerialism) appears to have differed from the knowledge of the United Kingdom community whose welfare has been managed. The political belief in the superiority of the private sector in terms of efficiency and effectiveness apparently differs from the reality of the United Kingdom's privatized operations. Here, if we believe the press reports, there have clearly been "winners" and "losers." Senior managers (many of whom were privatization supporters), businesses, and investors have nearly always won. Customers served have not received the improvements promised. Indeed, in privatizations around the world, even World Bank research has indicated that customers have gained nothing or have lost more often than not.[2]

Traditionally, the functions of government included seven areas:[3]

1. provision of economic infrastructure
2. provision of various collective goods and services
3. resolution and adjustment of conflict groups
4. maintenance of competition
5. protection of natural resources
6. provision of minimum access by individuals to the goods and services of the economy, and
7. stabilization of the economy.

These functions are argued as having considerable persistence over time, and broad political support or acceptance.

The mechanisms for intervention by government are fourfold. These encompass the provision of goods and services through budget funding, the provision of subsidies to people, the direct production of goods and services, and regulation through law.

The current economic environment has been accompanied by community demands for improvements in services offered by the public sector, both in terms of the types of services and sophistication of services. A healthy unwillingness to accept standards of service below those offered by best practice companies elsewhere throughout industry is appearing.

With increased pressures on government budgets, the community is therefore demanding more for their money, in levels of service and service efficiency.

Importantly, the capital requirements of capital intensive growth sectors such as telecommunications and airlines has also well outstripped the capacity of governments to support such growth, at least within the limits of the public sector borrowing ratio currently in operation.

As a result of these pressures, governments worldwide are searching for mechanisms to better enable service provision goals to be met. Managerialism, or the pursuit of results through mechanisms such as management by objectives, performance measurement, and performance pay, has been a part of the response to this issue. The increased complexity of the environment within which government services are provided, and the sophistication of the services themselves, point inevitably to a long debated question: What is the role of government in service provision?

Part of this debate has involved questioning whether or not the public sector needs to produce the full range of services itself, as it has done in the past. Osborne and Gaebler's theme of "steering not rowing" encompasses this thrust.[4] Here, the emphasis is increasingly on the public sector making policy decisions as to which services will be funded by government and the quality levels desired for these services. The private sector may actually produce these goods and services. Such a reliance on the private sector to provide services that were previously the domain of the public sector has been termed "privatization" by some authors,[5] but is this really the case? How is privatization best defined and interpreted? I shall take a closer look at these questions in Chapter 2.

Internationally, it is clear that much activity has been occurring in the area of privatization. For example, several high-profile political campaigns incorporating privatization as a central plank have been conducted throughout the 1980s. These have included New Zealand, the United Kingdom, South America, Canada, and Europe as well as some less developed countries (Boston 1988, Moore 1992, Kikeri, Nellis, and Shirley 1992). Simultaneously, these have been accompanied by the strains of conservative politics through the Reagan and Thatcher eras. Although privatization strategies have typically been defined as part of the liberal (or right) ideology, it has not simply been a response limited to conservative governments. In governments as diverse as the Conservative Party in the United Kingdom and the Labour Party in New Zealand, the use of the private sector to provide public services has been adopted by both persuasions.[6] Privatization is evidently not simply a one-sided political movement, but enjoys more widespread support.

In the words of Professors Bishop and Kay from the United Kingdom,[7] privatization is the result of a changed intellectual climate. They describe it as "a shift from concern for market failure to concern for regulatory failure." From an historical perspective, one could not help in the 1950s but be impressed "on the one hand, by the obvious failure of the capitalist economies in the great depression of 1929–33, and on the other, by the successes of governments in mobilizing resources to fight the second world war." The increased importance of nationalized industries was over time, however, accompanied by a tendency for such industries to regard themselves as "the high custodians of the public interest." According to Bishop and Kay, then, the failure of nationalized industries was due to the absence of financial control, and to the managerial culture that emerged. This culture was "predominantly engineering driven, stressing and achieving high technical standards." Financial and marketing capabilities were relatively weak.

Against this background, the emergence of privatization in the U.K. was, in Bishop and Kay's view, the result of policy failures in two areas. The first area related to industrial relations. Privatization emerged as a mechanism to satisfy the desire by the British Conservative Party to stem excessive public sector union power. The second area related to fiscal management—the requirement to fund public investment without increasing the public sector borrowing ratio.

From a global perspective, this changed intellectual climate has also been further bolstered by the failure of centrally planned economies, and the relative success of Western capitalist democracies.[8]

AIMS OF THIS BOOK

In this book, I will draw out existing knowledge of privatization activities within the context of a formal performance framework. I will aim to answer the following questions:

1. What are the most common privatization activities, and to what extent do these occur?
2. What are the theoretical underpinnings forming the conceptual basis for the improved provision of public services through the private sector?
3. What is the evidence from existing studies of privatization over the past twenty years? (What can we learn from the statistical findings of studies investigating the improved provision of public services through the private sector, and from studies of the sale of government enterprises? Does privatization usually improve service provision, and at lower cost, or are such generalities misleading and inappropriate? Alternatively, has privatization been found to generally succeed in some areas, but not others?)
4. On the basis of specific case studies, what are the perspectives of performance from the key stakeholders of public services? What are their conclusions as to the efficacy of privatization activities?
5. To what extent is the conclusion as to the effectiveness of privatization of public services dependent on our definition of performance?

IMPORTANCE OF CAREFULLY REVIEWING PRIVATIZATION

The importance of reviewing the performance of privatization does not simply stem from its high profile and frequent appearance in the daily press. It is more fundamental than that. We could view this question from several perspectives. First, the shear magnitude of the privatization effort worldwide is substantial. Over 6,800 state-owned enterprises (SOEs) have reportedly been privatized worldwide in the decade of the 1980s.[9] Substantial amounts of capital are also involved. On a global scale, the end of the 1980s saw governments around the world receiving between US$40 billion and US$60 billion each year from the sale of assets.[10] Specific nations have also seen massive capital flows. In the United Kingdom, the sale of British enterprises throughout the 1980s yielded about US$55 billion in sales revenues,[11] and slightly more during the 1990s.[12] In New Zealand proceeds were around US$6 billion by the end of 1992,[13] whilst during the 1990s, Australia saw proceeds totaling US$37 billion up until 1998.[14] Clearly, large amounts of capital are involved. It is critical that these privatization actions be based on a full understanding of past experience.

Second, the privatization bandwagon has often been proclaimed with substantial fanfare, with many election manifestos having privatization as a central plank. In some cases, the initial energy has not been followed through. The reasons for this are worthy of analysis.

Third, significant community concerns appear to have been emerging simultaneously with this worldwide privatization trend. This has been evident in both the United Kingdom throughout the privatization program of the Thatcher Conservative government,[15] and in New Zealand over the Labour government privatization actions.[16] As a consequence, this has lead to vociferous debate over the efficacy of planned privatization activities. In Britain, the accusing catch cry of "selling the family silver," first coined by former Conservative Prime Minister Harold Macmillan in 1985, has characterized one such concern.[17] Privatization is also a key issue of public policy debate in most countries, and as such it spans several academic disciplines. Economics, finance, political science, and social science are just some of the areas contributing to the debate. A judgment of the performance of privatization activities is likely to therefore require a multidisciplinary approach. In other words, a holistic assessment is likely to be needed in which it is important for all disciplines to make a contribution.

Fourth, with the potential for significant private wealth gains to be made, many interest groups are keen to participate in privatization activities. Professional services in fields such as accounting, finance, management consulting, and share market services are said to have been rewarded with revenues of around US$1.36 billion through the 1980s.[18] Clearly, such interest groups have much to gain from promoting moves towards increased privatization. Moreover, it is evident that groups such as this do not directly represent the community's interests on this question.

The fifth reason why a careful review of the effectiveness of privatization activities is a high priority is that there does not appear to have been, at least to date, a significant effort put into the development of a strong body of knowledge in this area. Much has been written, but what do we learn from the measurements? On first appearance, the driving force to date behind continued privatization activities appears to have been political ideology, rather than spectacular results from careful research and evaluation studies. The privatization lubricant has been a belief in superior private sector efficiency.

The sixth issue concerns the wide spread of services delivered by many privatized agencies. Some of the groups served by large enterprises are the least articulate and most vulnerable of our society. The vulnerability of such groups makes it particularly important to articulate any areas of trade-off that might be occurring throughout the privatization process and, where necessary, protect their interests. The social impact that privatization activities have had on the number of disconnections from utilities such as gas or water is a case in point.

The topic of privatization is also important for another reason. Much work has been undertaken to articulate the factors that lead to strong enterprise performance in private sector firms.[19] Less work has been undertaken on public sector services. In particular, there appears to have been little work on where privatization actions appear to generally be successful, and when they are less so. Most analyses have also had significant limitations to date. Moreover, these limitations may not be widely appreciated, perhaps because of the relative power of various interest groups during the promotion of privatization activities.

Lastly, privatization activities to date have been substantially a one-way process. Few cases of privatized companies being renationalized, for example, have been recorded. If the process is effectively one-way, it is critical to make the best possible decision for the community, and to base this decision on the best available information to date.

The objective of this book is therefore to undertake a careful integrative review of the available empirical evidence and determine lessons from experience. Its scope is necessarily broad, since privatization actions have covered a wide array of services and types of transaction.

A substantial amount of the data adopted in this analysis has been gathered from other studies. The use of this secondary data is of course subject to the nature of the meta-analysis, which will be detailed later. The assumptions and limitations inherent within this data are limitations of this study.

STRUCTURE OF THE BOOK

This book broadly comprises three sections. In the first section, the concepts and beliefs underpinning privatization are presented. Thus, following this introductory chapter, the concept of privatization is formally defined, including a wide array of definitions. The objectives sought through privatization activity are then articulated, both those explicit through policy statements and unseen, implicit goals. Chapter 2 then closes with an outline of the occurrence of privatization as a worldwide activity. The extent of global privatization both geographically across countries and over time is covered. The final part of this first section, Chapter 3, deals with the theoretical foundations supporting privatization. Several models behind privatization are outlined and for each of these perspectives, some critical observations and analysis are undertaken.

The second section of the book establishes a broad evaluation framework upon which to build our assessment of privatization performance. Thus, in Chapter 4, the meaning of performance is explored. Three perspectives are adopted to build this performance assessment framework—the major relevant theoretical models, the privatization objectives listed in Chapter 2, and the expectations of the community regarding public sector activities. These perspectives are then combined. Having established a framework to help us measure the performance of privatization activities, Chapter 5 looks at some of the available quantitative research methods that might assist in reviewing privatization performance. The traditional narrative review of past empirical research studies is discussed and its shortcomings are presented. The philosophy of meta-analysis is introduced, and a range of disciplines in which the meta-analytic approach has already contributed is outlined. It is concluded that this approach is one that could also make a contribution to the field of privatization.

The third section of this book, in which our empirical knowledge of privatization is analyzed, is the largest part. It begins with Chapter 6. Here the search undertaken to gather privatization data is outlined, along with the selection of those studies that formed the basis of the meta-analysis. In this chapter, privatization as contracting out is analyzed, and the characteristics of the contracting studies themselves are then presented. An analysis of the effectiveness of contracting out public sector services is then covered in Chapter 7. Firstly, a traditional narrative review is presented. For the case of economic performance in refuse collection services, some evaluation issues are highlighted. The changes in economic performance measured in studies of contracting out are then analyzed using the meta-analytic review technique, including the possible influence of several moderator variables. Several conclusions are then drawn from these findings. A review of the social dimension of performance follows, firstly for the case of service impacts, and then for employment and other impacts. Findings developed through the narrative review are contrasted against those made through the meta-analytic perspective. The performance of privatization in terms of democratic process issues, legal issues, and political issues is then investigated.

Chapter 8 looks at the collection of empirical findings, viewing privatization as the sale of enterprises. The available global evidence analyzing the performance of privatized companies is described. In Chapter 9, these empirical measurements are subjected to a meta-analytic review as well as to the more traditional narrative review perspective. Again, conclusions are drawn along with the practical implications. In Chapter 10, the policy implications of these research findings are discussed for both privatization as contracting out and as the sale of enterprises.

Having already thrust the reader face-to-face with the term "privatization" numerous times throughout this introductory chapter, it is with some degree of circumspection that the journey goes back a few steps. What exactly is privatization? This is the question for the next chapter.

2

Privatization Patterns

Privatization is being adopted all around the world. It promises improvements to a sloppy and lethargic state-owned enterprise (SOE) sector. What's more, it delivers on these promises. Why be left behind when the move towards privatization has already developed into a stampede? The benefits are as obvious as the urgency to reform. Or that is what we are told. But to what extent are these assertions, so often heard from reformers, actually true?

In this chapter, I will take the first step in developing an answer to this question. I will firstly canvass the definition of privatization and establish the objectives of privatization activities. To the extent that such objectives have been explicitly documented in the literature, these are outlined in this chapter, as well as other nonexplicit privatization objectives. The occurrence of privatization activities is then documented—both across international geographical regions, and over time, throughout the past twenty years. This will enable me to begin evaluating some of the above comments as well as establishing a basis for my later empirical observations on performance.

DEFINING PRIVATIZATION

Privatization as a modern political construct is often traced back to the comments of Peter Drucker. He first coined the term "reprivatize" in the late 1960s. Drucker argued that "the best we get from government in the welfare state is competent mediocrity," and that "more often we do not even get that; we get incompetence."[1] "Government," he concluded, "is a poor manager."[2] In his view, government was good at making decisions, but not good at executing them. Therefore, Drucker contended, government ought to "reprivatize," and separate decisionmaking in areas of public policy from the execution of service provision. It ought, in Drucker's mind, to return as many activities as possible to the private sector.

The earliest privatization program to punctuate recent history was that of General Pinochet in Chile in 1974, who of course was to have his dictatorship marked indelibly into time for his violent repression of all political opposition as well as the military coup staged to bring him to power.[3] Following this, the term privatization has had a wide array of meanings.

Three decades later, privatization is now truly international. Governments of all persuasions are seriously considering it as a reform mechanism and many are adopting it with vigor. It is certainly one of the key considerations in enabling public services to be delivered more effectively and more efficiently. High-profile campaigns have occurred throughout several regions such as the United Kingdom, New Zealand, and Europe, and as was noted previously, through governments of several persuasions (Letwin 1988, Hartley and Parker 1991).

But what is privatization? How can we interpret the movement? At the one extreme, privatization has been broadly regarded as having "come to symbolize a new way of looking at society's needs, and a re-thinking of the role of government in fulfilling them."[4] Privatization, accordingly, has been regarded as "the act of reducing the role of government, or increasing the role of the private sector, in an activity or in the ownership of assets." At this broad level, then, it "includes all reductions in the regulatory and spending activity of the State" (Starr 1989, p. 22). Privatization is therefore unashamedly a policy movement initiated from political origins and objectives. Such a shift of activities or functions from the state to the private sector has seen support with the rise of conservative governments in Britain and the United States, but has by no means been limited to these.

Using this broad philosophy, many activities could be identified as being part of privatization.[5] These are shown in Table 2.1.

Clearly, a wide range of possible activities could be construed as privatization. But it is more than just an action. Indeed, as Starr (1989, p. 43) points out, privatization as policy is also a signal about the competence and desirability of public provision. It is an overall message calling into doubt the nation's capacity and need for collective provision.

Several commentators offer a slightly narrower definition of privatization to the above table, and refer to only the first three groups of activities.[6] Of course, not all authors agree on the validity of including each element as a part of privatization. Load shedding, for example, evokes strong reactions from some who see it as false privatization,[7] and who argue correctly that under the load shedding concept, there is no guarantee that the private sector actually continues to provide the service, once shed. Not surprisingly, therefore, many others see privatization as narrower still— simply as the sale of public enterprises (or denationalization) or as a shift from public to private provision of goods through, for example, contracting out while maintaining public funding. Under this philosophy "privatization is the transfer of assets and/or service functions from public to private hands. It includes therefore activities that range from selling State Owned Enterprises to contracting out public services with private contractors."[8] This latter definition will be adopted in this book.

Although it follows the mainstream of international references, it is recognized that viewing privatization as including both the sale of public enterprises and the

TABLE 2.1   Definition of Privatization Activities

Group	Activities
Denationalization	Selling the whole enterprise (i.e., divestment) Selling complete parts of the enterprise Selling a proportion of the enterprise Selling to the workforce "Giving" to the public "Giving" to the workforce Liquidation
Load shedding	Encouraging exit from state provision Withdrawal Encouraging alternative institutions
Privatization of production	Contracting to the private sector Franchising Payment of grants to private suppliers Distribution of vouchers to private consumers Diluting the public sector Subsidize private sector arrangements that undermine public sector provision
Deregulation/liberalization	Right to private substitution/competition Curbing state powers Repealing monopolies Encouraging small-scale trials Buying out existing interest groups Deregulation via voluntary associations
Privatization of finance	Charging for previously nonpriced goods and services (i.e., user pays) Voluntary provision of services

SOURCES: Based on Heald 1984 and Pirie 1985.

contracting out of public services could be quite different from the common meaning attached to privatization in some countries, such as Australia or New Zealand. There, this term is usually taken to mean simply the sale of government agencies or sale of assets—that is, a far narrower definition.

This book focuses on contracting out and enterprise sales as two influential modalities of privatization in contemporary public sector reform. Having developed this definition, it is recognized that the dimension of ownership, although a key characteristic of privatization, is only one of several important dimensions to be considered in practice. Ideally, we need to be able to consider the effects of each of these dimensions separately.

Competition as a part of the privatization philosophy is a case in point. The possible inclusion of increased competition within the definition of privatization

FIGURE 2.1   Competition and Ownership of Service Delivery Enterprise

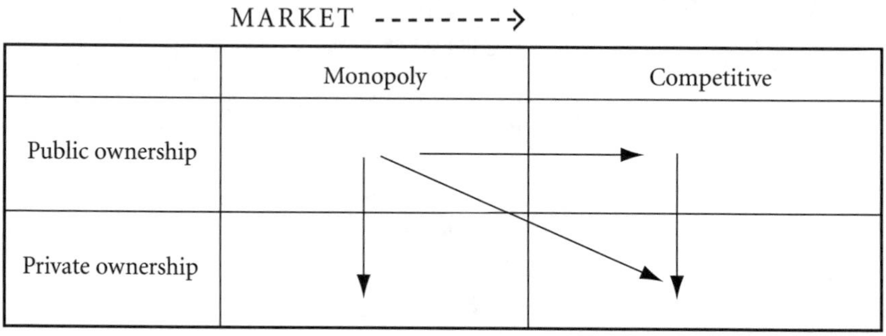

MARKET - - - - - - - ->

	Monopoly	Competitive
Public ownership		
Private ownership		

SOURCE: Hartley and Parker 1991.

is another source of difference between definitions. Some authors, such as Barnekov and Raffel (1990), argue that the introduction of competition through the removal of controls on private provision (i.e., deregulation) is sometimes considered to be part of privatization, whilst others (Wiltshire 1990, Hartley and Parker 1991) expressly exclude competition in their definitions. The conceptual framework provided by Hartley and Parker assists here in better understanding the role of competition.

The first part of the taxonomy draws out the distinction between a public enterprise with and without competition, or alternatively, private enterprise with and without competition. This is shown in Figure 2.1.

As we move from left to right and increase competition, an improvement in enterprise performance would normally be expected, ceteris paribus, according to Hartley and Parker.

FIGURE 2.2   Ownership of Service Delivery Enterprise and Payment for
               Services

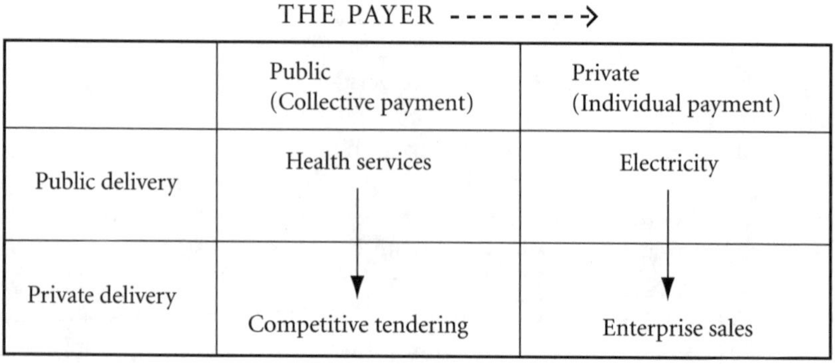

THE PAYER - - - - - - - ->

	Public (Collective payment)	Private (Individual payment)
Public delivery	Health services	Electricity
Private delivery	Competitive tendering	Enterprise sales

SOURCE: Hartley and Parker 1991.

Likewise, on the issue of ownership, a distinction can be drawn between ownership of the production capability (the deliverer) and the payer providing the finance (Roth 1987a). In Figure 2.2, an example of each privatization path is given.

This framework allows us to separate out the effects of a public enterprise reform through a change in ownership as well as market deregulation or other activities.[9] In any event, either change from public to private service delivery is termed privatization.

PRIVATIZATION OBJECTIVES

The objectives of privatization, however defined, are intimately bound up with the political, social, and economic agenda of government. They are as much tied to our beliefs about the role of the state as other more specific objectives. To assert otherwise, and to relate privatization to solely economic issues, for example, would be to both grossly underestimate the breadth of the privatization agenda and misunderstand the role of government issue. The context of privatization is inherently ideological. This section will review the explicit objectives documented for privatization. Privatization as the sale of a government enterprise will firstly be covered, and against this broader set of objectives, the fewer and more specific objectives documented for the narrower view of privatization as "contracting out" will then be outlined.

OBJECTIVES WHEN SELLING AN ENTERPRISE

Interestingly, it has been widely argued that there were no specific explicit objectives documented early in the British privatization program.[10] Whitfield (1992), for instance, argues that following the general aim of increased industrial efficiency, privatization originated as a political and financial strategy, and importantly, that "the economic rationale was appended later." Nonetheless, there is no doubt that since the early Thatcher years, the common general aim of privatization programs worldwide has had a central theme of improved economic efficiency. As Nellis (1991) comments, the "overriding reason [for privatization] is to increase the efficiency with which the enterprise's resources are used." In his view, other rationales were secondary to this objective.

Having made this observation, a review of the objectives of privatization that have been reported in the literature is useful in broadening our understanding of the privatization philosophy. The explicit objectives documented by reformers are much wider than simply economic in nature.

In his measured analysis of the British privatization experience, Ernst (1992) viewed the objectives of this program as falling into two broad headings—economic and political. Table 2.2 summarizes some of the objectives formally documented by governments, providing a range of explicit reasons for privatizing. This table adopts a split of political and economic objectives, along with categories for consumer service objectives, and others.

TABLE 2.2 Summary of Explicit Privatization Objectives from the Perspective of Governments

Category	Explicit objective(s)	Reference
Economic		
Efficiency	• "privatization accompanied by deregulation and competition will lift GDP by billions of dollars annually"	Moore (1990)
	• "provide the financial spur to improved performance"	Moore (1990)
	• improved efficiency	Wiltshire (1987)[a]
	• maximize corporate performance	Liberal and National Parties (1996)
	• "more efficient use of the State's total resources"	Carney (1993)
Increase competition	• "private authorities will be better able to compete"	Wiltshire (1987)
	• "authorities will be able to attract high quality managers"	Wiltshire (1987)
	• "maintaining the staff commitment to the company"	Wiltshire (1987), Public Accounts Committee (1982)
	• increased competition . . . and exposure to capital market disciplines	Liberal and National Parties (1996)
Political		
Funding autonomy	• "the organisation has the opportunity to raise capital when and how it requires"	Moore (1990)
	• "SOE's require substantial capital injections . . . which the State cannot afford"	Boston (1988)
	• "access to capital markets will make it easier to pursue effective investment strategies"	Wiltshire (1987)
	• "authorities will be released from the constraints on financing"	Wiltshire (1987)
Reduce public debt	• "reduce the country's international indebtedness"	Boston (1988)
	• reduce government debt	Liberal and National Parties (1996)
	• "reduce State debt"	Carney (1993)
Maximize sale proceeds	• "achieving a good return for the Exchequer"	Wiltshire (1987), Public Accounts Committee (1982)
	• "maximisation of net sale proceeds"	Wiltshire (1987), Department of Trade and Industry (1986)

participation	"employees"	
	"wide ownership of shares both among employees and among local customers"	Wiltshire (1987), Public Accounts Committee (1982)
	"ensuring the widest possible spread of share ownership"	Wiltshire (1987)
	"achievement of wide share ownership with a substantial take up of shares by employees"	Wiltshire (1987), Department of Trade and Industry (1986)
	ensure wider share ownership throughout Australia	Liberal and National Parties (1996)
Freedom from government intervention	"authorities will be free from government intervention . . . and fluctuating political pressures"	Wiltshire (1987)
Consumer		
Better services and lower prices	"privatization in conjunction with deregulation and competition will hand back significant benefits to the consumers of GBE services"	Moore (1990)
	"The main prize, if competition can be increased is for the consumer"	Moore (1985), cited in Ernst (1992)
	"the benefits of greater efficiency are systematically passed on to customers in the form of lower prices and better services"	Wiltshire (1987)
	"greater incentive to ascertain the needs and preferences of customers, and to tailor services and tariffs accordingly"	Wiltshire (1987)
	improved quality of services	Wiltshire (1987)
	"lower prices" to consumers	Liberal and National Parties (1996), Carney (1993)
Other		
Environmental protection	"provide a clearer strategic framework for the protection of the water environment"	Wiltshire (1987)
Transfer to private sector	"securing successful transfer of the company to the private sector"	Wiltshire (1987), Department of Trade and Industry (1986)
National company	"preserving the firm as an independent British company"	Wiltshire (1987), Public Accounts Committee (1982)

ᵃ Each of these explicit government objectives sourced against Wiltshire (1987) are also presented by Whitfield (1992).

SOURCE: Hartley and Parker 1991.

What can be learned from this table? Several observations are pertinent. Firstly, on the basis of this representative information available from an array of sources, a surprisingly wide spectrum of goals appears to have been stated explicitly by governments for privatization. Perhaps this is a symptom of a more fundamental issue? If privatization is indeed the result of the deeply held ideological belief that, for example, the private sector was inherently more productive than the public sector, then it would not be surprising that many objectives could be marshaled together as a plausible set. The objectives in this case would all stem from the primary ideology, rather than any more specific cause-effect relationship in the context of improving government services. The sale of government policies to the electorate would be the primary concern here rather than performance improvements. The interpretation that privatization has arisen as a result of ideology is supported by the observation that in the United Kingdom the objectives of privatization were not revealed to the public in a cohesive and comprehensive way until several years into the privatization program of the Thatcher government. There is certainly no doubt on the one hand that, with the wide array of objectives being pursued by government, the goalposts could be seen as shifting as the political debate proceeded. As Wiltshire (1990, p. 196) commented, different objectives seem to have had different priorities at different times in the United Kingdom.

Secondly, it is clear that some of the explicit goals conflict, though this is rarely documented formally. The classic example here is the often mentioned conflict between the objective of increasing competition and the desire to maximize the proceeds of the sale. Clearly, the greater the competitive pressures forced on the agency to be sold, the lower the potential price for the sale.

Thirdly, it is apparent that in some of the more recent commentaries of Moore (1990) and Carney (1993) in Australia, and Boston (1988) in New Zealand, fewer objectives appear to have been nominated by government. The reasons for this are uncertain, but may include the government's unwillingness to make explicit political goals such as maximizing the proceeds from the sale of assets. Indeed, explicit and clear objectives for proposed actions of government play only one small part in the broader political process. It may also include the government's uncertainty as to the actual economic efficiency and effectiveness results likely to be achieved, in the context of experience over the past decade.

Fourthly, some explicit objectives are surprising. An example here is the aim of providing a clearer strategic framework for protecting the water environment in the United Kingdom.

Lastly, it is interesting that one of the explicit objectives has been the successful completion of the privatization process itself. In other words, privatization is deemed to be successful simply if the company is transferred to the private sector.[11]

But is it these explicit objectives from government that are important in understanding privatization, or the unspoken and purposely implicit objectives that are more important here? Many authors argue for the latter, saying that it is the less visible, implied objectives that are more critical. Privatization is simply a tool being used in the pursuit of a range of other goals, in their view.

Table 2.3 summarizes the range of implicit objectives attributed to privatization actions by various authors. Again, I use the categories of economic, political, consumer, and other goals.

Again, what can be learned here? Recall that the most commonly noted explicit goals included those of economic efficiency, funding autonomy (or access to capital), share ownership, and benefits to the consumer. On the other hand, the most commonly suggested implicit goals related to fiscal management (including revenue raising), benefits to the consumer, and a reduction in the power of trade unions. Other implicit goals included more flexible labor markets, new markets for private capital, the clarification of government/industry relationships, rewarding political colleagues, and placating financing bodies or credit ratings agencies. Clearly, these two sets of objectives have much in common, but several of the implicit objectives suggested by analysts are not well advertised. All need consideration in the review of performance.

To both of these listings of objectives—both those explicit from government and those implicit—a further set could be added. These relate to the case of privatization in less developed countries (LDCs). In this case, an expanded agenda is being pursued. As Inotai (1992) remarks, "privatization is not a goal but an element of economic transformation . . . the entire economy as such is being privatized." Thus, in addition to all previously mentioned objectives such as efficiency, lower costs to the consumer, and reducing public debt, the objectives in Table 2.4 have also been suggested as relevant.

Viewing privatization objectives for both developed and less developed countries, a vast array of possible objectives appears to exist. Indeed, one wonders whether, with such a breadth in objectives, privatization is really about pursuing any one or two specific aims, or whether it is more a political tool—with the consequence that these objectives are essentially statements of hope and assertion.

Nonetheless, it has been determined that privatization does have some common objectives, however these are sourced. The extent to which these more common objectives have been met in practice will be investigated in the meta-analysis later in this book.

All of this is not to say that everyone agrees on which objectives of privatization usually command priority. Yarrow (1986, p. 363), a key academic contributor in the field, for instance, concludes that:

> The principle objective of privatization should be to increase economic efficiency. In the absence of efficiency gains, the public finance goals of the policy are generally misguided and their pursuit may actually damage efficiency. Similarly, privatization is usually a poor policy instrument for the attainment of such goals as reducing trade union power, widening share ownership, and redistributing income; in each case, it is dominated by superior policy instruments.

TABLE 2.3 Summary of Implicit Privatization Objectives from the Perspective of Representative Analysts

Category	Implicit Objective(s)	Reference
Economic		
Efficiency	• "the case for denationalisation is built substantially around the efficiency argument"	Ernst (1992)
	• "increase the efficiency with which the enterprises resources are used. . . . This goal takes precedence over all others because unless efficiency levels are raised the achievement of the other goals listed would either be impossible or illusory. . . . The overriding reason for transferring the ownership of an enterprise from public to private hands is economic"	Nellis (1991)
	• "increasing efficiency and productivity"	Whitfield (1992)
	• "reducing the costs of production" and "reducing corporate taxation"	Whitfield (1992)
	• increase allocative efficiency (i.e., "the production of the goods and services that the public want")	Chin and Webb (1987)
	• increase productive efficiency (i.e., "the production of these services at least cost")	Chin and Webb (1987)
Increase competition	• "extending the scope for market forces and increasing competition"	Whitfield (1992)
More flexible labor market	• "achieving a more flexible labour market"	Whitfield (1992)
	• "create a more flexible labour market"; "enabling business to operate more freely"	Whitfield (1992)
New markets for private capital	• "open new markets for private capital"	Whitfield (1992)
	• "creating new markets for private capital in the finance, production and maintenance of services and the urban infrastructure"	Whitfield (1992)
	• "wider share ownership"	Hartley and Parker (1991)
Political		
Fiscal management	• reduce the public sector borrowing ratio, and improve scope for tax cuts	Ernst (1992)
	• raise revenues	Nellis (1991)
	• "increase government revenue"	Whitfield (1992)

	• make private sector responsible for needed enterprise investments	Nellis (1991)
Smaller government	• "reduce the size of the public sector"	Hartley and Parker (1991)
Create share owning democracy	• extending share ownership within the workforce, and amongst the public • create popular capitalism • "wider share ownership"	Ernst (1992) Nellis (1991) Hartley and Parker (1991)
Reduce trade union power	• "debilitate the industrial and political strength traditionally held by trade unions in nationalised industries" • "demolish the moral and philosophical legitimacy of collectivist solutions to social and economic problems in Britain" • "reduce the strength of the trade union movement" • "reduce the monopoly power of public sector trade unions"	Ernst (1992) Ernst (1992) Whitfield (1992) Hartley and Parker (1991)
Reward political colleagues	• to reward political loyalists	Nellis (1991)
Consumer		
Consumer sovereignty	• "economic freedom," rather than being captive to a producer dominated system • "increasing consumer choice" • "consumer benefits" including "greater efficiency, better services, lower prices and wider choice" • "consumers are expected to benefit"	Ernst (1992) Whitfield (1992) Wiltshire (1987) Hartley and Parker (1991)
Other		
Placate external bodies	• to placate the demands of external financing agents	Nellis (1991)
Clarify the government-industry relationship	• decrease the administrative burden of the state bureaucracy • "clarifying the government-industry relationship"	Nellis (1991) Wiltshire (1987)

[1] NOTE: Not all of Whitfield's implied objectives of privatization are listed. Some suggested objectives, such as "creating social fragmentation," and "increasing private ownership of key assets in the economy to make the achievement of socialism more difficult and less tangible" were omitted.

TABLE 2.4   Additional Privatization Objectives for Less Developed Countries

Additional Objective(s) for LDCs	Author—Reference
• "balance or replace a weak private sector"	Kikeri, Nellis, and Shirley (1992)
• "produce higher investment ratios"	"
• "transfer technology to strategic sectors"	"
• "to generate employment"	"
• "develop local capital markets"	Leiberman (1993)
• "democratisation of capital"	"
• "encourage the return of flight capital"	"
• "attract direct foreign investment and new technology"	"
• "increase domestic and international business confidence"	
• controlling corruption currently endemic in some public services	Russell (1994)

Of course, these discussions about privatization objectives have assumed that known, definable, and clear objectives are indeed being pursued when privatization programs are underway. Inasmuch as privatization is a part of the political process, this contention may not be accurate. Kay's oft used quotation illustrates the point here:

> Shortly before the flotation of British Telecom, I talked to a friend who is deeply experienced in the ways of Whitehall. 'Tell me,' I asked him, 'what privatization is really about. Is it about raising revenue, or improving the efficiency of privatized industries, or what?' He thought for a moment, and said, 'The mistake in that question is to suppose that privatization is actually about anything. It is a political imperative, pursued for itself. If any arguments for it can be found, or any benefits from it can be perceived, a grateful government will seize on them as rationalisations; these are not objectives. The policy is the policy because it is the policy. There is fundamentally no more to it than that.' (Kay 1985)

This perspective, that the fundamental objective of privatization is simply the successful transfer of assets to the private sector, is interesting. It may be one that is gaining prominence at the end of the twentieth century as Western governments renew the debate as to what business they should and should not be in. As Leiberman (1993) puts it, privatization should simply aim to "get government out of business to the fullest extent possible." To date, however, it has rarely been explicit in government statements of objectives, with only one exception to this noted in Table 2.2.[12]

OBJECTIVES WHEN OUTSOURCING

If the narrower definition of privatization as contracting out or outsourcing is adopted, a somewhat different set of objectives has been documented historically.

In this case, the objectives have almost universally related to economic efficiency. Thus, objectives such as increased efficiency and economy have occasionally been presented.[13] More usually, however, the objective of outsourcing public sector services has simply related to cost savings.[14] As Chandler and Feuille (1991) note, "the primary rationale for contracting appears to be cost savings rather than increases in the quality of services or some other factor."

In recent times, there has been a concerted move to view activities such as outsourcing and contracting out in a more sophisticated way. As part of this, the specification of objectives of contracting out has been explored more thoroughly. Jones (1993), for instance, confirms in his review of global contracting out experience that "the major goal of contracting is to save money." He then adds that there can be other goals. These might include saving scarce management time, obtaining expertise not always available in small organizations, and retaining flexibility by not renewing contracts in low priority areas or letting new contracts in others. More recent reports such as PA Consulting (1997) also investigate the reasons for outsourcing and suggest that up until the early 1990s, cost reductions and headcount reductions were indeed the most highly valued benefits of outsourcing. In the last few years, this appears to have changed, however, with a greater ability to focus on core business, and better access to specialist skills now being rated more highly than cost savings and service quality improvements when outsourcing.[15] Deloitte and Touch Consulting Group (1997) also confirm this trend based on surveys on information technology outsourcing, reporting that access to skills and technology have replaced cost and service as the driving rationale for outsourcing.[16]

The objectives of privatization as contracting out or outsourcing appear to have become a moving target. The extent to which this has occurred as a result of organizations now viewing contracting out in a more sophisticated way, or as a result of a changed organizational rationale learning from unmet early expectations of sizable cost reductions, is uncertain. Nonetheless, the primacy of cost reductions as an early commercial driver of this activity is clear.

Few broader types of objectives were specified for outsourcing in the literature. Paddon (1993a) was one of the few exceptions to this, nominating the objectives of outsourcing as firstly to transfer services from in-house to the private sector, and secondly to introduce internal markets as a discipline.

Clearly, the range of objectives for this type of privatization activity is much narrower than was the case for privatization as the sale of equity.

OCCURRENCE PATTERNS: SELLING ENTERPRISES

To understand the significance of transferring major assets that were previously owned by a national government, a particular context is required. The relative government ownership of various industries as of 1998 in countries throughout the world is indicated in Figure 2.3.[17] Relative ownership levels, although only indicative, are instructive. Denmark, which at this time had almost all relevant

FIGURE 2.3   Industry Ownership in Selected OECD Countries

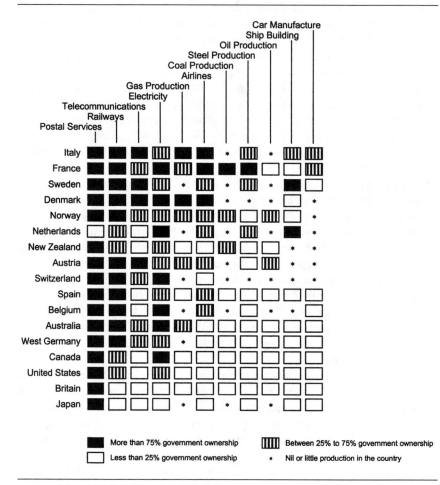

SOURCE: Adapted from Public Bodies Review Committee 1991.

industry sectors predominantly under public ownership, is at one extreme. Sweden, France, and Italy also had strong government ownership across nearly all sectors. At the other extreme was Japan and Britain. For these two nations, only the postal sector was under government ownership, with all other sectors being overwhelmingly private sector owned.

The level of activity in privatization in terms of the sale of enterprises or assets can be judged against this background. Surprisingly, little definitive information is available documenting the extent of privatization globally, and estimates differ wildly.

Kikeri, Nellis, and Shirley (1992) discuss the privatization record of state-owned enterprises (SOEs) up until 1991, and state that some 6,800-plus sales have taken place around the world. They argue that the vast majority (66 percent) of these privatizations have been within the former German Democratic Republic, other Eastern European countries (12 percent), or Latin American and Caribbean countries (12 percent).[18] Interestingly, the OECD itself is listed with only 170 privatizations of SOEs, or 2 percent of the total. Although clearly significant, the OECD number represents only a small fraction of the total number initially quoted.

In the case of some of the developing countries listed, the changes to ownership of SOEs have been massive. Since 1973, Chile is reported to have liquidated some 501 of its 524 SOEs, reducing ownership of production assets from 39 percent of GDP in 1973 down to 12 percent in 1989. Likewise, since 1984, Mexico is reported to have privatized more than 400 of its 1,115 SOEs.

For many of the other developing countries in this survey, however, this spectacularly high level of privatization requires cautious interpretation. Although the number of SOEs privatized may have been high, the actual significance of this change in ownership levels may have been more modest. As an example, in Guinea, some seventy of the ninety-eight privatizations involved "the liquidation of virtually defunct retail outlets and small non-operating enterprises."

Other estimates of the extent of global privatization activity differ markedly from that of Kikeri, Nellis, and Shirley (1992). Nellis (1991), for instance, estimates in the absence of any worldwide stocktake of privatizations that "several thousand—perhaps around 3,000—privatizations have taken place since 1980." No data to support this estimate were presented, though. Wolf's commentary on the Treuhand approach to privatization in Eastern Germany suggests another figure around this magnitude.[19] By the end of August 1991, Wolf notes that 3,400 businesses had been sold by the Treuhandanstalt, but these were the easier ones, and it still had another 10,000 still on its hands. Clearly, many of these must have been of minor significance.

Likewise there has been little consolidated information on a global scale regarding the types of enterprises that have been privatized. One of the few exceptions to this was presented in Organization for Economic Cooperation and Development (1994). This information related solely to privatizations in Central and Eastern European countries. The levels of privatization indicated here differed wildly from previous estimates, with large privatizations being estimated at some 11,193 worldwide, and transactions relating to small privatizations numbered at some 128,706.[20]

There is certainly no doubt that the financial implications of these privatizations have been significant. Consolidated figures on the proceeds from privatizations are not available, aside from the previously mentioned statement from Mason (1991, p. 31) that governments around the world received £25 billion during 1990 from the sale of assets—about the same as in the previous year, but down from £39 billion in 1988. Clearly, massive flows of resources are involved. Indeed, in the words of the editor for the *Privatization International* newsletter, these figures were "a remarkable demonstration of the continuing appeal of privatization."

In a counter view to this and aiming to dampen the fervor of advocates, Aharoni (1988) comments that apart from Britain and Chile, "significant privatization is still rare," and that furthermore "in most countries privatization has been token." Aharoni's comment of the late 1980s is obviously a little dated a decade further on. Nonetheless, apart from the major privatization programs of New Zealand and Australia, his measured comments still stand strong in an international context.

How then to summarize the global characteristics of privatization activities? It might be useful to reflect on the massive influence of ownership changes within the centrally controlled economies of the GDR and Eastern European countries. Indeed, we have observed that in terms of privatization transactions, the most common enterprise to have been privatized to date is likely to have been either small retail shops or small industrial firms, or perhaps units within a larger enterprise in such economies. This contrasts the higher profile and better publicized cases of privatization under Thatcher's conservative government in the United Kingdom, or others such as the Labour government privatizations of New Zealand and some recent privatization activities within Australia, where major government enterprises were sold.[21] Table 2.5 indicates examples illustrative of the privatization sales undertaken in these countries.

OCCURRENCE PATTERNS: OUTSOURCING

Turning now to outsourcing public sector services as one of the perspectives of privatization, what do we currently know about its occurrence? This technique is increasingly the subject of political platforms. Looking to American experience, Jones (1993) reports that "some people dream of contracting out to the private sector to create an 'enabling' authority where a very small group of in-house staff uses the competition among private contractors to get the most value for money and to keep the bureaucracy small." He notes that Lakewood in California has only eight city workers to serve a population of some 60,000, and that likewise, one Dallas suburb with a population of 2,500 has no city workforce at all, apart from a solitary secretary to handle the paperwork for the contractors who supply all the services. These examples give an impression of a brave new contractual world in which efficient practices and commercial principles guarantee citizens the maximum capacity for service flexibility and effectiveness. But how widespread are these practices in reality and how do they measure up?

Viewed overall, the practice of providing public sector services through the private sector is not as widespread as it first appears. An early U.S. survey from Florestano and Gordon (1980) relating to 89 municipalities under 50,000 population indicated that "although a variety of public services are provided by private

TABLE 2.5 Examples of Enterprise Privatizations in the United Kingdom, New Zealand, and Australia

Country	Agency	Year	Proceeds (UK£, NZ$, Aust$, in millions)
United Kingdom[1]	Cable & Wireless	1981	UK£22
	Amersham International	1982	71
	Britoil	1982	549
	Associated British Ports	1983	22
	Enterprise Oil	1984	392
	Jaguar	1984	294
	British Telecom	1984	3,916
	British Gas	1984	5,434
	British Airways	1987	900
	Rolls Royce	1987	1,363
	British Airports Authority	1987	1,225
	British Steel	1988	2,420
	10 water authorities	1989	2,183
	12 electricity companies	1990	5,200
	Unipart	1987	30
	British Airways Helicopters	1986	13.5
	National Bus Company	1986	250
	Royal Ordnance	1986	201
	Vickers Shipbuilding	1986	60
	Inmos	1984	95
	Sealink	1984	66
New Zealand[2]	New Zealand Steel	1988	NZ$327
	Petro Corp	1988	801
	PostBank	1989	678
	Air New Zealand	1989	660
	Rural Bank	1989	550
	Shipping Corporation	1989–90	34
	Government Print Office	1990	35
	State Insurance	1990	735
	Tourist Hotel Corporation	1990	74
	Telecom	1990	4,250
Australia[3]	AUSSAT	1991–92	Aust$504
	2 airlines	1992–96	1,850
	4 airports	1996–98	3,338
	4 banks	1991–98	10,314
	Telstra	1997–98	14,330
	12 electricity generators/distributors	1992–98	23,272
	Totalizator Agency Board	1994–95	609
	5 gas pipelines/companies	1992–97	1,577
	5 state insurance offices	1992–96	1,767

SOURCES: 1. United Kingdom: Bishop and Kay (1992); 2. New Zealand: Mascarenhas (1991); 3. Australia: Reserve Bank of Australia (1997).

contractors, the majority of services are not provided in this manner." They found that of the municipalities surveyed, three-quarters provided less than one-third of their governmental services through contracts with private providers. The largest dollar volume in public services provided by private contractors was in solid waste collection, street construction, and professional services such as architectural, engineering, and legal services.

Ferris and Graddy (1986) also provided data on the relative extent of contracting out government services. Their data, which included contracting with all types of external organizations, were broadly consistent. It suggested that 57 percent and 69 percent of jurisdictions relied solely on public sector in-house service provision in the areas of residential waste collection and street repair, respectively. Again, a high reliance on in-house services was also evident for 86 percent of jurisdictions who provided public safety police patrols and fire safety services. At the other extreme, the data also showed some areas where there was clearly a large reliance by jurisdictions on contracting with external organizations as the sole supplier of services. These services included vehicle towing (77 percent of jurisdictions), day care (73 percent), and hospital services (71 percent).

In the United Kingdom, and more recently in Australia, the introduction of compulsory competitive tendering for local government services has occurred. This has resulted in a greater number of the services being delivered by the private sector. Table 2.6 indicates the proportion of the various blue-collar services tendered that are won by the public and private sectors in the U.K.

As commented then by Paddon (1993a), and later by Jones (1993), these figures show that although a share of local government contracts goes to the private sector, local government in the U.K. still wins most. In terms of the value of con-

TABLE 2.6   Contracts Awarded for Blue-collar Services in the United Kingdom

Service	*Percent of Number of Contracts Awarded*		*Percent of Value of Contracts*	
	Public Sector	*Private Contractors*	*Public Sector*	*Private Contractors*
Building cleaning	54.1	45.9	83.3	16.7
Refuse collection	72.1	27.9	75.2	24.8
Other cleaning	71.1	28.9	80.6	19.4
Vehicle maintenance	78.6	21.4	88.5	11.5
Catering (educ/welfare)	91.6	8.4	97.2	2.8
Catering (other)	76.1	23.9	82.3	17.7
Ground maintenance	67.3	32.7	81.5	18.5
Sport & leisure	82.4	16.6	84.4	15.6
Average for all services	69	31	83.9	16.1

SOURCE: Paddon 1993a.

tracts awarded, some 16 percent is now in the hands of private sector producers, and 84 percent is in-house.

In Australia, a 1989 survey of contracting out in the local government arena again revealed that at the national level the large majority of services actually provided by local government areas were not being contracted out.[22] At the high end, the proportion of councils contracting out the collection of household garbage, for instance, was just above one-half (55 percent) at this time, and did not vary markedly across regions. Significant variation was evident in the proportion of councils contracting out any one particular service state to state or across metropolitan, provincial, or rural regions. Thus, for road construction and the operation of caravan parks, the practice of contracting out varied by a factor of around three state to state and across regions, with rural areas contracting out the least. At the other extreme, services such as social work and the operation of public libraries at that time saw little contracting out (at 1 percent and 2 percent, respectively) irrespective of state or region. Overall, estimates of the proportion of local or state government expenditure contracted out have varied from around 4 percent to 18 percent for the early 1990s.[23]

In Victoria, the adoption by the Kennett government of a compulsory competitive tendering policy for all local government services with a requirement of 50 percent of turnover to be competitively tendered has resulted in an upsurge of contracting arrangements.[24] The driving force has been government insistence on targets rather than any spontaneity by local governments to move in this direction. Currently around one-half of local government's operating expenditure is now provided by external contractors in Victoria.[25]

PRIVATIZATION TRENDS OVER TIME

There is little doubt that the role of the private sector in providing services traditionally under the public sector wing is currently increasing. Globally, the world witnessed the failure of many centrally planned economies in the 1980s. The USSR, several Eastern bloc countries (such as the Czech Republic, Poland, and Romania), and developing countries (including for instance Mexico, Chile, and Venezuela) all illustrate this trend. In each of these cases, increased private ownership was a priority for reforming government. The relative success of Western economies throughout the 1980s was recognized, and following the end of the cold war, economic models and techniques were borrowed.[26] These global trends provided a key plank to support the belief worldwide that private ownership within a capitalist economy is fundamentally beneficial.

In the U.S., early work by Poole and Fixler (1987) suggested a growth trend in contracting out the provision of public services. They cited a comparison by the U.S. National Center for Policy Analysis (1985) comparing surveys a decade apart, in 1972 and 1983. This comparison reported growth in contracting out over this decade ranging from 43 percent for the case of refuse collection to 3,644 percent in the case of data processing. Although early, these figures support later international findings confirming the growth of privatization.

Other indicators of the increasing role of the private sector in public sector services include the trend to open up to competition the provision of local government services. Local government reform in Britain has been followed by New Zealand and Australia. Data on the growth in the use of the private sector to provide public services has been difficult to gauge, with many different snapshots of contracting out or tendered services being produced for a variety of services—each with a different purpose, survey design, and service definition. Nonetheless, some sparse comparisons are possible.

In Britain, Adonis (1992) reported increased private sector success in winning contracts in the early 1990s. Comparing the first tranche of contracts awarded in August 1990 to those offered in January 1992, the private sector increased its share from 14 percent to half of those offered in the area of refuse collection and street cleaning.

In Australia, similar trends have been observed with most reforming conservative governments reinvigorating the potential for private provision through contracting out as well as enterprise sale initiatives. The most striking of these was the previously noted Kennett government's policies in Victoria, under which targets were set at 20 percent, 30 percent, and 50 percent of local government services to be subject to competitive tender by mid-1995, 1996, and 1997 respectively.

In terms of the sale of enterprises, the decade of the 1980s also saw privatization grow in a spectacular way. A frenzy of privatization activity has dominated newspaper headlines and commanded a high public profile following early British asset sales. No specific and comprehensive time series data are available on the growth of international asset sales, however. Nonetheless, the speed and hence perceived priority for change is shown in the numerous divestitures in countries such as Mexico and New Zealand.

Having made these observations, there is also a need to separate judgments on the rise of privatization as a reform policy from the obvious razzmatazz of newspapers and political advertising. Two contexts are useful here—an historical perspective and a rhetorical perspective.

Historically, our history over centuries might be seen in terms of a few steps as part of the bigger picture, and many smaller recurring steps. At the big picture level, the relationship between the public sphere and the private can be traced back to the beginnings of civilization. Indeed, there has always been a tension between what is held to be public and what private.[27] Over the past three centuries, the mercantile role of government, in which it had an involvement in all trade transactions, was replaced by Adam Smith's laissez-faire society. The primary message of Adam Smith was that the state should only be responsible for defense, a system of laws, and providing public goods—otherwise government should not interfere with economic life.[28] The pursuit of free markets, however, saw undesirable impacts as well as wealth increases to some. Child labor, poor public health, and inadequate housing were some of these. The state was gradually seen to be responsible for its citizens' welfare, and electoral advantage was also bolstered by the economic stabilization ideas of Keynes. The rise of the welfare state brought increased living standards and saw the growth of major public enterprises, often in place of failed embryonic private markets. Even up until the mid-1970s, nationalizations were still being witnessed in the United Kingdom in order for the government to take the "commanding heights" of the economy. Such action, it was deemed, was necessary to ensure that the public good was not left to the vagaries of the market, which experience had shown, through depressions, was a rather unstable and flawed system. Increasing financing pressures and a reducing political support base saw the more recent period of economic rationalism evolve. These notions, along with policies tied to individual rationality and a maximum role for market mechanisms, also implied a minimum role for government.

But how do these historical observations help here? The assistance comes firstly in recognizing the continuing and inevitable tensions between the public and private domains. The depressions of both the 1890s and 1929 as well as other times in our history led to strong and emotional debates around the inherent benefits or otherwise of private ownership versus government intervention in the economy. These important debates continue today. Other, perhaps smaller, recurring steps can also be found looking at the history of contracting in the public sphere, which, for many Western countries, is not new at all.[29] Mathew, the private tax collector from the Bible; the cleaning of street lamps in eighteenth-century England; or the railways of the nineteenth century all testify to this. Again, the arguments for and against the use of private contractors for public sector services can be traced back over a century and half. Importantly, the great debates around cost advantages, quality, and accountability, for example, were all well rehearsed at the turn of the last century in Australia, for one, and led to a swing away from the use of private contractors towards the use of government-supplied labor for construction work.[30] Furthermore, repeated swings of this private/public pendulum occurred over subsequent decades in the light of evolving experience and political demands. Such trends and swings are likely to have been the case in other Western countries as well. Evidently, what is new here is not contracting per se, but the elevation of contracting out services to a first order policy issue and its appearance as a solution in its own right to the problems of public policy.

These observations bring us to the perspective of rhetoric. Is there a separation of the rhetoric from the reality? To an extent, yes. We might look at the United States as an example. Despite the strong global spread and supportive tone on the growth in privatizations through asset sales, the actual sale of public agencies has not always been as aggressive as the political rhetoric. As Wettenhall (1993, p. 47) notes for the case of the U.S., "America presents to the world an image of itself as the citadel of capitalist virtues and private enterprise." It nevertheless continues to make considerable use of public enterprise, "with little if any indication that either it (the public authority) or the public enterprise functions for which it carries responsibility are in retreat." During the Reagan era an antistatist ideological stance was particularly pronounced. He continues, arguing that "notwithstanding the rhetoric, it is apparent that there was not much outright privatization of public enterprises during the Reagan era," and that "so-called privatizing activity in the U.S. has focussed largely on the contracting out of activities which are not central to the functions of public organisations (rather than the disposal of the organisations themselves)."

A parallel can also be drawn here with the implementation of much heralded privatizations in developing countries. Here, initial impressions gained from glowing and positive headlines suggesting major successes and promising almost certain improvement have been dampened by some commentators. Frydman and Rapaczynski (1993), for instance, have argued that in the case of developing countries, "despite ardent support for the concept, not much privatization is actually taking place, and what does occur is often much more ambiguous than originally expected."

3

Theoretical Foundations for Privatization

This chapter outlines some of the major theoretical models and conceptual frameworks underpinning privatization. In a broad sense, privatization has arisen through the confluence of two of the major political legacies of the 1980s. Harvard's John Donahue reminds us that, firstly, we have witnessed a renewed cultural enthusiasm for private enterprise and the adoption of market-based mechanisms. Secondly, a deficit-induced imperative to limit government spending has also been growing steadily year after year.[1]

But on what theoretical grounds might it be hoped that privatization will provide a solution in the context of these trends? Those models put forward to date provide a basis for an analysis of privatization and articulate potential areas in which performance gains could be available. These models ought to also enable performance measures to be developed on which the effectiveness of privatization activities may be judged.

MODELS UNDERPINNING PRIVATIZATION

Several distinct conceptual bases have been suggested as underpinning privatization reforms. The most often voiced bases fall in the arena of economics. The driver here is the objective to increase economic efficiency as a means of increasing the well-being of citizens. Those intellectual foundations upon which privatization stands in the field of economics are many, but would include the key ideas of public choice theory, agency theory, and transaction cost analysis[2] as well as property rights theory and governance structures.[3] To these we might also add a few other influential reform concepts such as measurement issues and the notion of managerialism or new public management. Each of these concepts directly appeals to our rational desire for efficiency improvements through better organizational performance and control.

On top of these models is the plausible idea that privatization does not have an economic rationale at all. It may be more a political mechanism aiming to facilitate the achievement of noneconomic goals such as a redistribution of power away from unions, or vote winning for governments at elections. Alternatively, it may simply be more a symbolic statement from an incoming political party about the role of government than a reform having a strict economic rationale. Each of these foundations deserves some attention.

PUBLIC CHOICE THEORY

Public choice theory has had an enormous impact on public administration practices and ongoing reforms over the past two decades.[4] It has as its fundamental tenet the notion that self-interest dominates human behavior—the idea that humans are essentially rational utility maximizers and are inherently selfish. The idea that economic interests provide the primary motivation and lubricant of human behavior also forms the foundation of the theories of property rights and agency theory, as well as transaction cost analysis. In the words of Self (1994), "public choice theory starts from the assumption that individuals are rational egoists; further, that this assumption is as true of political as of market behaviour.... It then argues that individuals can express their personal preferences much more efficiently through market exchanges than via political participation." Hence,

> just as businesses supposedly seek to maximise their profits, government officials are believed to maximise their budgets while politicians seek to maximise their votes. . . . Any suggestion that politicians are significantly concerned with societal well being or the common good, or that they and their advisers are guided by fundamental ethics precepts, is generally dismissed. Indeed, public choice theorists have tended to reject concepts like "public spirit," "public service," the "public interest" and even "social justice" either on the grounds that they have little, if any, meaning or relevance or because they are often used to give legitimacy to the demands of sectional interest groups. (Boston 1991, p. 3)

Public choice ideas have been exceedingly influential in supplying supporting frameworks to legitimize and provide an intellectual underpinning to political reforms. The implications of such notions are that the role of the state should be reduced, that functions such as regulation, policy advice, and the delivery of services should be undertaken separately, and furthermore, that service delivery should, where possible, be privatized through either contracting out or sale.

Thus, those supporting moves towards a greater use of the private sector argue that, in line with the predictions of the public choice theoretical ideas, government organizations are often captured by those who traditionally supply the services of the organization, and that in the absence of the profit motive, bureaucrats in government maximize the size of their own bureau rather than maximizing benefits to customers or citizens. In other words, bureaucrats look after their own interest, not the public interest. Proponents point out that organizations need to buy services from external sources through a contract in favor of using in-house staff. In an age where corporate planning objectives, targets, and activity-based costing are becoming the norm, they argue that the role of government nowadays should be viewed as establishing high-level objectives and developing policies, rather than actually delivering the services per se. In the parlance of Osborne and Gaebler, government ought to "steer not row."[5]

Several serious criticisms of the public choice theory exist. We will focus on two of the most cogent criticisms here.

Firstly, and fundamentally, the behavioral assumptions adopted in the theory have serious flaws. The assumption is that the individual is simply a competitive and self-interested rational utility maximizer, or as Stretton and Orchard (1994, p. 126) describe it, "homo economicus." Self-interest has a strong influence on human behavior. However, it is a significant distortion to assert that it is the only motivation. The existence of a large voluntary sector in the community, and the development of groups that promote interests on a public or community scale, suggest that both individuals and politicians are influenced by a wide range of values. As well as the self-interested desire for material income, the motivations of many individuals include generosity, adherence to a moral code including an acceptance of various obligations to others, and an interest in rewards other than money. Individuals are in varying degrees clearly cooperative as well as competitive, and altruistic as well as selfish, as Self (1994) puts it. Voters are also swayed by group or party loyalties, by ideology and by beliefs about which party will do the most for national prosperity and welfare. Bureaucrats are as much concerned with notions of public interest, personal integrity, pride in their work, professional standards, and simply doing a good job, as in their own self-interest. Boston (1991, p. 13) puts it cogently:

> In short, human beings are not merely economic beings, but also political, cultural and moral beings who inhabit an economic system which is profoundly influenced by, and in a sense dependent upon, the attitudes, habits, beliefs, aspirations, ideals, and ethical standards of its members. Any theory which ignores these broader contextual factors, social relations and normative commitments is at best incomplete, and at worst misleading and damaging.

Added to this critique of the behavioral assumptions of the public choice school are the early motivational concepts of scholars such as Maslow (1954), Herzberg (1966), or Alderfer (1972). These ideas suggest that for large sectors of the developed world, economic factors are likely to have become much less important as drivers of human behavior once basic existence needs have been satisfied.[6] More important sources of happiness and well-being than simple economic activities would most likely include family life, friendship, intellectual development, self-reliance, self-esteem through social affiliation and relatedness, and job challenge. To the extent that this is true, human beings are likely to behave very differently from the economic rationality and acquisitiveness assumed under homo economicus. As Lane (1991) concludes, "the economists' idea that work is the sacrifice or disutility that earns for workers the benefits or utilities of consumption is . . . quite false."

The second common criticism voiced against public choice theory concerns lack of empirical validation. Boston (1991) notes that "the predictive power of public choice theory has been found wanting in many areas of social and political life" and lists numerous examples of the lack of empirical support for the theory. He quotes several observers as having noted that the deregulation and liberalization policies of the OECD run counter to the predictions of public choice models that assume that it is in the electoral interests of politicians to promote tight regulation. At the personal level, politicians are just as apt to want to do that which they believe to be "the right thing" as to do that which is the most popular, apparently.

Likewise, Self (1994) argues against public choice ideas on empirical grounds. He argues that the notion that governments that minimize their responsibilities will therefore be more impartial between groups and interests is quite wrong. He cites the case of nineteenth-century governments, which although small in scope were strongly biased towards the interests of property and capital. Any reading of history teaches us that it took the growth of more balanced political forces to improve the appalling conditions of industrial workers and peasants. Arguing even more strenuously, Stretton and Orchard (1994, p. 46) state that "after twenty years or so of empirical research none of the original and distinctive elements of public choice theory can be said to be proven." It is therefore indeed ironic, as Boston (1991) notes, that the intellectual ascendancy of this theory comes at a time when its explanatory power is declining.

In view of its theoretical, conceptual, and empirical shortcomings, public choice theory must be regarded as at best a partial and limited model for some areas of human behavior.

AGENCY THEORY

The manner in which organizations function can be viewed from several perspectives. We might view an organization, for instance, as a bureaucracy with its rules, authority, and hierarchy; as a community with its values, relationships, and networks; or as a market with its incentives and prices from independent buyers and sellers.[7] Building on the market model, we could also view the delivery of services through an organization as a series of contracts. This is the assumption of agency theory, where the owners of a company are not the managers, and where ownership is separated from control. The principal (owner) therefore enters into a contract with managers (the agents) to deliver services. The agent agrees to deliver these services in an acceptable way, for the agreed reward. However, since the principal and the agent have interests that may diverge, some monitoring is necessary for control purposes. This theory focuses on finding the optimal way of establishing and operating such contracts, whilst meeting the requirements of the principal. In operating according to these contracts, agency costs such as incentives, monitoring costs, and bonds are incurred (Boston 1991, Spicer et al. 1991).

Several criticisms have emerged to challenge the validity of agency theory. Boston (1991), for example, notes three. Agency theory firstly fails to recognize that an unequal power distribution exists for many contracts in the real world. It also assumes that the agent alone is opportunistic—and not the principal—an assumption of dubious veracity. Thirdly, this theory cannot handle complex social and constitutional relationships that can occur.

The application of agency theory to government services may be subject to serious inaccuracies to the extent that these criticisms are true. Such concerns deserve attention through empirical evidence.

TRANSACTION COST ANALYSIS

Williamson's theory of transaction cost analysis used five main concepts as a basis for explaining the development of large firms in capitalist economies.[8] These concepts, according to Boston (1991, p. 7), include uncertainty, small-numbers bargaining, asset specificity, bounded rationality, and opportunism. These concepts are explained by Boston as follows:

> Uncertainty refers to the inability of economic agents to foresee or control changes in their environment. The concept of small numbers bargaining explains the privileged position (i.e., in terms of experience, expertise, skills, and specialisation gained over potential competitors) which the parties to a long term contract generally enjoy. As a result of these advantages, few other firms may be in a position to compete when the contract comes up for renewal. The closely related notion of asset specificity refers to the specific skills or assets acquired through undertaking a particular task or operation. For example, an employee who works in a specialised area in a firm will acquire a range of skills that may be difficult for an employer to replace. This gives the employee added bargaining power. Bounded rationality refers to the fact that individuals generally have limited information and cognitive capacity. Finally, opportunism is the tendency of individuals to pursue their own self interest and to take advantage of other workers or market participants.

Williamson's argument, then, is that firms aim to minimize the costs of transacting their business. He suggests that this aim can often be achieved by vertical integration, that is, by taking over either the firms to whom they sell, or else their suppliers. He sees large firms in capitalist economies as being the result of these firms aiming to minimize transaction costs. It is another paradox that Williamson's ideas, which seek to explain why firms expanded, now underpin the move to reduce the core size of firms.

The validity of this theory has also been contested. On the one side it has been seen to contribute to better understanding alternative governance structures.

Balanced against this are criticisms including limited predictive and explanatory power, and the looseness in defining the core "transaction cost" concept.[9] Added to these criticisms is also the fact that the actual growth of large firms over the past century can be attributed mainly to the pursuit of market power and to the various mechanisms of government support, rather than transaction costs per se. In this light, the theory offers only a limited explanation of the development of large firms.

Importantly, it also suffers from the criticisms leveled at the key assumption of "homo economicus," the concept forming a common foundation for the theories of property rights, agency theory, and public choice as well as transaction cost theory.

The area of governance structures is a branch of transaction cost theory. This area of theory deals with alternative forms of organization structure, the contracting processes employed to undertake services, and the resulting transaction costs. It dates back to the early work of Coase (1937).[10]

MANAGERIALISM/NEW PUBLIC MANAGEMENT

Throughout the 1980s, various sets of ideas came together to provide the basis for a managerialist approach to public administration. Although the subject of some controversy during evolution and introduction,[11] there is now substantial agreement, at least according to authors such as Hughes (1992, p. 293), as to just what constitutes managerialism. He sees managerialism in terms of five broad thrusts. Firstly, objectives are set and overall strategy is determined. Programs are then devised to meet these objectives, and each program is organized and budgeted. Performance at all levels is then measured in terms of the efficiency of achieving objectives. Lastly, the achievement of objectives in terms of effectiveness is assessed. Phrases such as "let the managers manage" and "managing for results" have often been used to encapsulate the managerialist philosophy of public sector service provision.

These managerialist concepts have more recently been married together with public choice theory and institutional economics to produce a new public management doctrine.[12] The central tenets of this new doctrine significantly extend the principles noted above, emphasizing management skills, quantified performance targets, devolution, the separation of policy, commercial and noncommercial functions, the use of private sector practices such as corporate plans and short-term contracts, monetary incentives, and cost-cutting. Importantly, the new public management also emphasizes a preference for private ownership, and the use of contracting out and contestability in the provision of public services.

Not everyone sees managerialism in this way, however. Pollitt (1993, p. 1), for example, sees managerialism as more fundamental than just a set of techniques or practices. To him, it is a belief system. It is an ideology "at the core of which burns the seldom-tested assumption that better management will prove an effective solvent for a wide range of economic and social ills." He concludes that this cluster of beliefs and practices is an ideology, which has become steadily more prominent in policies adopted by right-wing governments towards their public services. In Pollitt's view, the logic of managerialism stems from the rise of governments such as those of Thatcher and Reagan who came to power on the basis that government had become too big.[13] Cuts in government functions and privatizations were consequent policies. After being in government for some time, a choice was then made to improve productivity of the services in preference to cutting services altogether or continuing the privatization of services, with many looking increasingly more complex or messy. Pollitt's line of argument leads him to conclude that improving the productivity of public services has been a popular political option, and that managerialism itself has encouraged "the popularity of management solutions to what were previously conceived of as political problems." Managerialism is viewed as being quite distinct from simply better administration. It is seen as "the acceptable face of new right thinking concerning the State."

There is no doubt that managerialism has seen wide support through its inherent attractiveness. Indeed, Pollitt comments that "better management sounds sober, neutral, as unopposable as virtue itself" and that "the productivity centred logic has a power of its own."[14] Several benefits of this managerialist thrust are noted. These include enhanced partnerships with the private sector, greater cost consciousness in the knowledge of actual costs of delivering activities and products, and economic savings. He also points out several serious criticisms of managerialism. Overall, he concludes that "the attempt to impose a largely generic and neo-Taylorian model of management on the public services seems to have been either an act of culpable ignorance on the part of those concerned or an exercise in (possibly unwitting) ideological imperialism, or some mixture of the two" (Pollitt 1993, p. 144). Whilst other authors see this case as having been overstated,[15] one indisputable result of the managerialist approach has been a shift towards a greater private sector involvement in the provision of public services.

PROPERTY RIGHTS THEORY

The theory of property rights argues that private ownership of the assets of a company results in superior profitability and effectiveness. The logic is best summed up by Starr (1989, p. 28), who outlines the case as follows:

> The theory of property rights explains differences in organisational behaviour solely on the basis of the individual incentive created by the structure of property rights (Alchian 1965, Demsetz 1967, Furubotn and Pejovich 1972, 1974, De Alessi 1987). Property rights, in this view, specify the social and economic relations that people must observe in their use of scarce resources, including not only the benefits that owners are allowed to enjoy but also the harms to others that they are allowed to

cause. A right of ownership actually comprises several rights, chiefly the rights to use an asset, to change its form, substance or location, and to transfer all or some of these rights. Thus, the key issues for the theory are, first, to whom are property rights assigned, and, second, how, if at all, are they attenuated? . . . The more individuals stand to gain from tending to their property, the better it will be tended. Conversely, the more attenuated and diluted their property rights, the less motivated individuals will be to use property under their control efficiently.

In this theory, the major focus is on incentives for performance improvement, principally at the level of the individual decisionmaker. This logic has a certain simple appeal on first view. A critical analysis of the theory on conceptual grounds tempers this view, however.

Starr's analysis, for instance, notes three shortcomings. Firstly, the theory implies that in comparing the performance of different organizations, ownership effects dominate the other sources of variation. Hence, many sources of performance variation are not recognized, including for instance organizational characteristics such as size, hierarchy or leadership, task characteristics, goal ambiguity, or economic incentives unrelated to property rights such as contractual incentives. Secondly, the property rights theory implies that the market is the standard for assessing the performance of the organization. It implies that since public organizations do not always measure against this standard, their performance is less than that of those organizations that do. Put another way, since the shareholders cannot sell their equity, and since the community as owners are not rewarded through the production of a residual financial profit, the performance of the public organization is, by definition, less than it might otherwise be. Thirdly, the property rights theory assumes that "the market for corporate control is highly efficient, and that the chief reason corporations are acquired is for their management's poor performance." Additionally, it does not recognize the sometimes considerable monitoring power of the state, the public, and the press. These latter two criticisms also have weight. In the former case, the acquisition of a company can be motivated just as much by a desire for market control, or by the need for access to working capital, as for reasons relating to performance. Likewise, monitoring mechanisms on public corporations are far from perfect, but battles during annual general meetings by disgruntled shareholders in private companies also testify to the notion that performance monitoring by private sector owners also leaves much to be desired from the perspective of smaller shareholders.

On empirical grounds, the property rights theory has enjoyed considerable support, although not unanimous over all service sectors. Such empirical support has normally been on the basis that there is a significant association between the type of ownership of a firm (whether public or private) and the performance of firms measured in financial or efficiency terms. Davies's early review of the evidence (Davies 1981) lists several analyses supporting the theory, as does De Alessi (1980), who assesses the evidence as overwhelming in favor of the theory. On the other hand, Becker and Sloan (1985, p. 11) find that "the property rights paradigm does not fit the hospital industry very well," and that once factors other than ownership are held constant, "profitability is no higher for the for-profit hospitals than for their non-profit counterparts."

To citizens, though, the strength of empirical research support or otherwise is not the central issue. The simple logic that privately owned property is better tended than publicly owned property guarantees the popularity and continued appeal of this notion. To many, it is obvious that private ownership is superior to public ownership.

MEASUREMENT ISSUES

Measurement issues can also form an important intellectual foundation underpinning efficiency reforms if we go by the case of New Zealand.[16] Public agencies often have multiple and complex goals. As well as being financially responsible, agencies are expected to act in the community interest, and to reflect a wide range of government social and economic policies. Measuring the actual performance of such an agency is therefore not a simple matter. The performance of a public sector agency has, by definition, multiple dimensions. An agency can, for example, be assessed in terms of its financial performance, as well as its effectiveness, efficiency, and economy. Additional to these performance dimensions, however, are the dimensions of democracy with inherent values of equity and collectivity, and political electability.[17] This multidimensional nature of public agency performance results in several significant challenges in assessing agency performance and subsequently improving performance.

The first is that it is difficult to readily measure performance in a clear and unambiguous way. With multiple and complex goals, measurement is a complex task that can be accomplished only imperfectly. Unlike commercial businesses, performance results in the public sector cannot be aggregated up to a single valid measurement of agency performance. Performance measurement difficulties are significantly reduced for government trading enterprises that operate commercially in areas such as power generation or in water and sewerage services. Here, performance can be addressed largely through accepted financial measures such as the return on assets or return on equity. This is common to both the private and public sectors. Secondly, a challenge exists in simply defining the customer. The equitable treatment of patients in hospitals (following time spent on a waiting list) and the position of prisoners in prisons are two examples of the need for a more sophisticated stakeholder approach to viewing government services than the simple business-customer model. Thirdly, the interpretation of the performance information itself is usually not straightforward. Paradoxically, those things that are easiest to measure are usually the less important activities. Workload (or demand) indicators and level of service indicators, for example, can be accurately established. These measurements are, however, usually less important than assessing the actual effectiveness of the program from the perspective of providing benefits to the community—according to the objectives established for the program. Lastly, an additional challenge in measuring performance in the public sector concerns the concept of ownership of performance measurements. In some areas, several agencies may contribute towards outcomes for the community. For instance, police, transport accident commission, road and traffic authorities, emergency services associated with on-site trauma, medical support and transport, hospitals, community groups, and educators are some of the contributors to the general aim of reducing road accident trauma. None of these contributing agencies, however, would be wholly responsible for the overall level of road trauma occurring over any one particular time period. In any single year, all agencies would have partial ownership of the road trauma outcome in the community.

Such complexities result in an inability to accurately measure agency performance through traditional public program evaluation and effectiveness measurement techniques. Nevertheless, to the extent that the measurement of agency performance might become a more manageable task, and to the extent that interpretation of performance might become clearer, privatization of an agency may be seen as beneficial.[18]

HISTORICAL/CONTINGENCY THEORY

Added to these models is the plausible idea that privatization does not have an economic rationale at all, but is more simply a political mechanism aiming to facilitate the achievement of noneconomic goals. In other words, it is simply a tool in the political kit bag available for use when deemed expedient. One example of this might be the redistribution of power away from unions, who are seen to be overly influential, back towards the elected government. Another plausible example of this might be the redistribution of power away from the unions towards a coalition of major business interests and government. The role of financial interests is likely to be largely invisible to the community in this case. Under this concept, the role of the noneconomic objectives of privatization would depend on the influence at any point in time of particular historical contingencies. Thus, as was the case in the late 1970s with severe industrial unrest throughout the U.K.—this period later being referred to by Thatcher as the winter of discontent—the privatization mechanism could be adopted to weaken the influence of the union movement on the public sector in the United Kingdom.[19]

More generally, we could adopt the postulate suggested by Wettenhall (1983) that privatization is the direct result of combinations of both ideological and pragmatic contingencies within a fluctuating political and ideological environment of history throughout this century. In other words, privatization is essentially a reaction to a complex political and social environment at any one point in history, and may have any one or more of several noneconomic aims. Tables 2.2 and 2.3 in Chapter 2 presented many of the explicit and implicit noneconomic objectives possible. These dimensions included public sector debt reduction, funding autonomy, encouragement of public share ownership, freedom from political interference, consumer benefits, reduced trade union power, placating external financing bodies, and reducing endemic corruption within the public sector. Such objectives may have greater or lesser priority at any point. Governments seek, for any unique set of circumstances, to balance up the political imperatives. As noted earlier, one of these aims may also be the objective of simply completing the privatization transaction itself. Ideology aside, it is often useful, from the perspective of electability, for governments to demonstrate that action has been taken to improve perceptions of a problem. Kay's 1985 quotation in Chapter 2 musing that "the policy is the policy because it is the policy" well illustrates this notion.

Simms (1982) is another who sees privatization as a response of governments to various combinations of both ideological and pragmatic considerations in history.[20] This idea is illustrated with four categories of conservative-government involvement in Australian economic enterprise. Firstly, the whaling and aluminum industries were evacuated *after* they had become profitable and suitable purchasers had appeared, both ventures having outlived their developmental function. Secondly, in the case of airlines and post–World War II shipping, either no suitable purchaser appeared or the citizenry demonstrated its liking for the public operator, so that solutions were devised that simply prevented unrestrained competition between public and private operators. Thirdly, conservative governments continued to favor public ownership of natural monopolies (for example, the Snowy Mountains Scheme or the Overseas Telecommunications Commission) which private enterprise would have been unable to provide. And fourthly, virtually completing a circle, public enterprises were always justified wherever their function was to provide the "demonstration effect" apparent in whaling, aluminum, oil-refining, and similar cases.

The downfall of communism and demise of centrally planned economies in several countries throughout the past two decades may be seen as the most prominent and overwhelming endorsement of capitalism. Such events have no doubt been interpreted by the voting community as glowing evidence of the superiority of Western capitalism and the values that support it, including individual economic freedom and private ownership. There is a leap in logic here, however. The first part of the argument is reasonable—the relative success of Western economies may well illustrate that Western economies are stronger and have responded better to world economic conditions. The consequential glowing endorsement of private ownership as a general philosophy is a stretch of faith, however. The more appropriate extension of this logic would be that the typical Western economy—which is overwhelmingly mixed and includes both private and government ownership—is stronger and more robust than the centrally planned economy.[21] The central issue for our current deliberations on privatization is not the superiority or otherwise of a centrally planned economy versus a capitalist economy. The real question is at what point should the line be drawn between public and private ownership in today's mixed economy?[22]

PART II

Performance Evaluation Framework

4

Performance Framework for the Assessment of Effectiveness

This brief chapter establishes a conceptual framework upon which the performance of privatized activities or enterprises may be assessed. The framework will be developed in an heuristic fashion. In concept, I will be attempting in this chapter to develop a useful conceptual framework by combining knowledge of the theoretical models discussed previously, the objectives specified for privatization, and the underlying principles and values associated with traditional public sector work. These three parts, providing the origin of the framework, are shown in Figure 4.1.

Firstly, a series of performance dimensions are gleaned from the models underpinning privatization as summarized in Chapter 3. For each performance dimension, some potential performance indicators are presented for illustration. Secondly, a range of illustrative indicators are presented for each of the privatization objectives listed earlier in Chapter 2. These two performance domains have been implied by governments, by privatization advocates, or by privatization analysts.

Outside these indicators, a broader range of performance information is also relevant and deserves to be pursued. This third domain represents performance in terms of the values of service provision traditionally sought through public sector activities. Such values include, for example, equity and democracy.

Together these three dimensions provide a conceptual framework that could form the basis for judging the performance of privatization actions. To the extent that performance evaluation results are available on each dimension, conclusions ought to be possible through a traditional narrative review or a meta-analysis. Conversely, to the extent that no results are presently available on a dimension, reliable empirically based conclusions on performance are unlikely to be possible at present.

PERFORMANCE DOMAIN BASED ON PRIVATIZATION MODELS

Chapter 3 outlined several models that together formed a series of theoretical bases for privatization actions. The basic tenets of each of these models, along

FIGURE 4.1   Three Domains of Performance Including Indicators from
(A) Underlying Models, (B) Privatization Objectives, and
(C) Traditional Public Sector Values

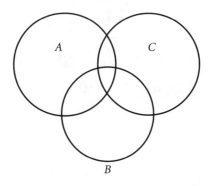

with some of the major implications of the models, are presented in Table 4.1.
Also given are possible indicators that could potentially signal any performance
improvements.

From this table it is evident that there are few indicators of performance that
are common across all models underpinning privatization. The profitability or
cost-reduction performance indicators are directly applicable to public choice
ideas, transaction cost economics, property rights theory, and to an extent to notions of measurement. Other common linkages between directly measurable indicators of agency performance and other theories appear to be surprisingly
weak, however.

PERFORMANCE DOMAIN BASED ON PRIVATIZATION OBJECTIVES

In Chapter 2, we also noted a range of objectives for privatization, as suggested by
both governments and interested observers and analysts. The objectives included
the domains of economics, politics, consumer benefits, and others. The various
objectives within each of these dimensions are shown in Table 4.2, with those related to fiscal management listed separately as well.

PERFORMANCE DOMAIN BASED ON PUBLIC SECTOR ACTIVITIES

The third area in which judgments about the performance of a privatization ini-
tiative might be made is the broadest. It is the area over and above the agency's
performance assessed purely on the basis of either models underpinning privatization, or the objectives of privatization policy.

TABLE 4.1 Possible Performance Dimensions and Illustrative Indicators, from Models Underpinning Privatization

Theory	Central Tenets	Implications of Theory	Possible Performance Indicators/Information
Public choice	• Business maximizes profits • Government managers maximize their budgets • Politicians maximize their votes	• Reduce the role of the state • Separate regulation, policy, and service delivery • Privatize service delivery	• Successful withdrawal of the state from previous service provision role • Increased profits by an entity following privatization (by reduced expenses, and/or increased revenues)
Agency theory	• Agents undertake services for the principal • Monitoring is needed (bonds, incentives, and monitoring costs)	• Monitoring costs increase if an agent (with own objectives) delivers	• Monitoring costs
Transaction cost analysis	• Through uncertainty, asset specificity, small-number bargaining, bounded rationality, and opportunism, firms aim to minimize the costs of transacting their business	• Firms take over either suppliers or client firms (i.e., vertically integrate) to minimize business costs	• Service cost reductions
Managerialism/ new public management	• Setting objectives, devising programs, and then measuring the achievement of these objectives • Public choice tenets above	• Separate policy, commercial, and noncommercial functions	• As for Public choice

(continues)

TABLE 4.1 *continued*

Theory	Central Tenets	Implications of Theory	Possible Performance Indicators/Information
Property rights theory	• Private ownership of company assets results in superior profitability and effectiveness • The more direct and unattenuated are the rights to property, the better the assets will be used	• Increased private ownership increases performance	• Profitability of entity • Effectiveness
Measurement issues	• Performance measurement of public sector agencies is complex, due to goal multiplicity, adoption of the customer model, interpretation of performance information, and performance indicator ownership	• Reduce goal multiplicity • Encourage explicit service standards to defined customer groups • Reduce performance dimensions to dollar values for easier monitoring • Increase performance indicator ownership	• Improved goal clarity • Improved measurement of financial and other quantitative performance • Increased measurement of performance
Historical/contingency theory	• Ideological and pragmatic considerations drive privatization decisions • Objectives may have greater or lesser priority at any one point in time • Privatization itself may be an objective, for reasons of electability	• Ideological and pragmatic reasoning in the political process has more weight than the economic or social goals espoused • Few general rules on the impact of privatization are possible because of the different contexts into which privatization may be thrust, and because objectives are contingent on situation • Successful completion of the privatization transaction itself	• Political success at elections • Decision criteria/reasoning in context (e.g., business development goals or employ-ment levels in specific geographic regions)

TABLE 4.2 Possible Performance Dimensions and Illustrative Indicators, Based on Privatization Objectives

Domain	Objective	Illustrative Performance Indicators
Economic	• Economic efficiency • Increased competition • More flexible labor market • Develop/create market for private capital • Balance/replace weak private sector • Produce higher investment ratios	• Degree of cost minimization • Number of new entrants in market • Labor productivity • Size and composition of capital market • Investment ratios
Fiscal management	• Funding autonomy • Reduce public sector debt • Maximize sale proceeds • Create scope for tax cuts	• Reduced call on public purse • Public sector borrowing ratio effect • Dollar proceeds • Defined scope and cuts
Political	• Employee share participation • Create a "share owning democracy" • Freedom of government enterprise from government • Reduce trade union power • Reward political loyalists • Transfer assets (i.e., smaller government) • Transfer technology to strategic sectors • Generate employment • Encourage the return of flight capital • Attract direct foreign investment/technology • Increase domestic and international business confidence • Control corruption in public sector utilities	• Number and profile of employee owners • Number and profile of share-owning citizens • Extent to which new agencies have more freedom • Cases of "jobs for the boys" or cronyism • Extent of asset transfers • Number and profile of employment generated • Extent to which foreign investment/technology is attracted • Business confidence surveys • Degree of corruption
Consumer	• Better services • Lower prices • Increased choice	• Survey results • Survey results • Number and profile of suppliers
Other for	• Environmental protection • Placate external financing agencies (e.g., IMF) • Clarify government-industry relationship • Placate credit-rating agencies	• Environmental standards/case studies • Degree and extent of external agency requirement privatization • Alteration in credit rating

The performance of government agencies can, from first principles, be assessed in terms of at least five different dimensions.[1] These dimensions include economics, democracy, legality, professionalism, and politics. Of course, other frameworks are also possible. Punch (1990), for instance, talks about the need to make judgments on the performance of public sector activities in terms not only of economy, efficiency, and effectiveness, but also efficacy, equity, and electability. Alternatively, Fels and Xavier (1990) present a narrower range of five dimensions covering economy, efficiency, and effectiveness, as well as financial and equity grounds in their discussion of SOE performance. All of these dimensions of performance are relevant to an assessment of the performance of a public sector agency.

One particular issue is central to considerations about more broadly defining performance following privatization. This concerns the extent to which private enterprises within an economy operate under different values from public sector activities. Pollitt (1993), for example, presents several value differences between what he refers to as the public service orientation and the generic private sector model. He highlights the differences between the equity of the market in the case of the private sector, and the equity of need in the case of the public sector.[2] Likewise, he differentiates between the search for market satisfaction on the private side, and the search for justice on the public side. The market model, where the individual customer is sovereign and competition is the operating mechanism, is seen as quite distinct from the political (public sector) model, where collective choices are made through the voices of citizens in the polity, and collective action is the mechanism. The former is viewed as closed, the latter as open. The pressure for change is seen in the private sector to be the exit of a customer out of the buying decision, compared to voice as a pressure for change in the public arena. These are outlined in Table 4.3.

Clearly, the processes of government and of private business have fundamentally different values underpinning them.[3]

TABLE 4.3   Value Differences Between the Traditional Public Service
             Orientation and the Generic Private Sector Model

Private Sector Model	*Public Sector Model*
1 Individual choice in the market	1 Collective choice in the polity
2 Demand and price	2 Need for resources
3 Closure for private action	3 Openness for public action
4 The equity of the market	4 The equity of need
5 The search for market satisfaction	5 The search for justice
6 Customer sovereignty	6 Citizenship
7 Competition as the instrument of the market	7 Collective action as the instrument of the polity
8 "Exit" as the stimulus	8 Voice as the condition

SOURCE: Pollitt (1993, p. 155).

TABLE 4.4   Summary of Broader Performance Dimensions for Public Sector Activities

Performance Domain	Objectives [1]	Values [2]
Economic	Economy Economic efficiency • allocative • technical • dynamic Financial	Choice in the market Search for market satisfaction Customer sovereignty Increased competition and ability to exit the market
Democratic	Effectiveness Equity (Including professional opinions and standards)	Openness for public action Equity with respect to needs Needs-based resource distribution Citizen role (voice) in collective action
Legal	Legal	
Political	Political electability	Collective choices through polity Search for justice

[1] Objectives were drawn from the following authors: Hodge (1993a, p. 26), Punch (1990), and Fels and Xavier (1990).
[2] See Pollitt (1993).

All the various broader dimensions noted in this section on the nature of public sector activities can now be combined into a single table. The framework shown in Table 4.4 is the result.

The inclusion of Pollitt's values in this table is enlightening. It serves as a reminder that discussions on privatization in terms of equity, operating mechanisms, and citizen/customer satisfaction require extreme care. Moreover, such discussions need to be conducted within the context of Pollitt's public and private sector orientations. The values underlying the economic dimension clearly contrast those underlying the democratic dimension. As well, the political dimension can also be viewed separately based on this table. Each of these broader dimensions will need to be included in any assessment of the performance of privatization, along with those dimensions drawn from theory or from nominated objectives.

COMBINED PERFORMANCE FRAMEWORK

Ideally, all of the previously noted performance dimensions should be part of an assessment of a privatized enterprise or activity. Such a framework would be extensive, however. To illustrate the breadth of dimensions necessary in an assessment of privatization actions, I have constructed a final overall summary, shown in Table 4.5. The categories of performance here have been grouped in like areas

TABLE 4.5   Framework Summarizing Performance Dimensions for Assessing Privatization

Performance Domain/Category	Illustrative Performance Indicators
Economic	
Economy	Input costs (including labor flexibility)
Economic efficiency	
• allocative	Price levels for quality of services
• technical	Total factor productivity
• dynamic	Level of innovation/entrepreneurship
Financial	Rate of return
"Scorekeeping" integrity	Auditor criticism
Increased competition	Number and profile of market competitors
Private capital market development	Size and profile of capital market
Enhanced weak private sector	Size of private sector
Produce higher investment	Investment levels
Fiscal management	Reduced public sector debt levels, scope for tax cuts, level of sale proceeds
Social	
Consumer benefits	
• Better services	Consumer service quality levels/survey results
• Lower prices	Service prices
• Increased choice	Number of service providers available to individuals
Social outcomes/impacts	
• equity and need	Various, such as number of electricity or telephone disconnections for non-payment, price trends

Democratic

Openness of processes for public action — Extent to which openness is reduced; treatment in public debate

Equity of processes with respect to needs — Extent to which democratic processes accompany and follow privatization

Needs based resource distribution decision processes

Enhanced citizen role in collective actions and choices — Extent to which citizen roles in collective actions are enhanced, opinions of professional associations, violations of professional "standards"

Equity in professional debate

Legal

Court verdicts
Appeals
Ombudsman criticism

Political

Electability — Election results, public opinion surveys

Creation of share owning democracy — Number of share owners in community, and employees

Freedom of agency from government — Extent to which agency is freed of political influence

Reduced trade union power — Reduction in trade union influence

Reward to political loyalists — Cases of "payback"

Transfer assets (i.e., smaller government) — Size of government (e.g., percent GNP)

Transfer technology to strategic sectors — Case study examples

Generate employment — Employment growth

Encourage the return of flight capital

Attract direct foreign investment/technology — Case study examples

Increase domestic/international business confidence — Business surveys

Control corruption in public sector utilities — Demonstrated reduction in corruption

Placate external financing bodies or credit rating agencies — Availability of external financing, or adjustments to credit ratings

Clarify government-industry relationships — Case study examples as much as possible, albeit that groupings are to an extent arbitrary. In this final table, five summary dimensions are shown along with some illustrative performance indicators for each.

Of course some of the development of this conceptual framework is by its nature arbitrary. One example of this concerns the categorization of consumer benefits. This type of impact could logically be included in its own right, as say a "customer" category. Alternatively, it could be included as part of the "economic efficiency" category. As a third alternative, it could be included as part of "social impacts," as in Table 4.5.

The similarity of the social performance dimension and that of democracy is also acknowledged. For the research in this book, the "democracy" performance dimension has been taken to mean the process of community involvement in government. The "social performance" category has been taken to mean the outcomes of privatization actions on citizens.

A common but key thread crossing each of these five dimensions in the evaluation framework is that of accountability. In each dimension of performance, the question could be asked, To what extent has privatization enhanced or else reduced accountability? I shall return to this question later.

5

Review Methodology

Much learning involves the cumulation of results across studies undertaken to date to establish "facts." By reviewing multiple studies, the relevant findings can be weighed up, study results interpreted, and an overall picture formed. The development of this overall, integrated picture leads to an expansion of our existing knowledge of the subject. If only a few empirical studies have been completed, a review of research findings to date may be straightforward. In many cases, however, the conclusion often reached has been uncertainty as to "the truth of the matter," accompanied by a call for more research in view of the scarcity of empirical evidence.

Nowadays, many areas of business and management research do not have a few empirical research studies potentially available for review, but hundreds. Increasingly sophisticated and inclusive research information systems, and the internationalization of telecommunications networks have both resulted in an explosion of empirical research information at the fingertips of the researcher. This is an interesting point to ponder. One might think that the research community would more often reach a resolution on a particular issue if it were to be reviewed now. The contrary is the case, however (Hunter and Schmidt 1990, p. 13). Most traditional review studies have not concluded with resolution, but with a call for yet more research to be done on the question.

In this chapter, I will explore the question of how to synthesize many different research findings in order to form a reliable picture of the evidence on an issue. This chapter first presents the two most common methods for reviewing and integrating literature in a field of study. A critique is made of both the traditional narrative review technique and the vote-counting method of review. I then contrast these techniques with the alternative meta-analytic perspective and suggest that the latter approach is more robust and reliable for this type of problem. It is concluded that this approach would be a useful one to adopt for reviewing the performance findings within the field of privatization.

I then look at some of the more important dimensions of the meta-analytic approach, along with the implications these have for the current privatization performance review.

INTEGRATING RESEARCH STUDIES

Traditional Narrative Review Technique

There are a variety of methods potentially available to integrate together a number of research findings. By far the most commonly applied technique is the traditional narrative review. Alternatively called the qualitative, literary, or literature review, it aims to look at all studies at face value and find overarching theories that reconcile the findings (Hunter and Schmidt 1990, p. 468). Each study is presented in the review, and its scope, methodology, findings, and limitations are noted within the context of a critical verbal appraisal. By reviewing multiple studies, therefore, the relevant findings can be weighed up, study results interpreted, and an overall picture formed. The development of this overall, integrated picture leads to an expansion of our existing knowledge of the subject.

Some examples illustrate the point that integrating the findings of even a small number of studies may not necessarily be straightforward. Glass, McGaw, and Smith (1981, p. 19) cite Miller's classic work in 1977 where the findings of five reviews of the efficacy of psychotherapy and drug therapy were reviewed. These five reviews integrated the findings from fourteen studies and were completed within a period of about five years. Largely the same body of literature was available for review. The reviews came to conflicting resolutions, with some concluding that the combination of both psychotherapy and drug therapy together were quite clearly superior to drug therapy alone, whilst others concluded that no firm conclusions could be reached. Of particular interest in Miller's work was the manner in which the various reviewers interpreted the studies. In several cases, the same study was claimed by the reviewers to support opposing hypotheses. Thus, for instance, one reviewer listed three particular studies as supporting the hypothesis that drug therapy plus psychotherapy treatment was superior to drug therapy alone, whereas two other reviewers saw these same three studies as supporting precisely the opposite hypothesis. In fact, from the summary of Miller's results presented by Glass, McGaw, and Smith, it is evident that eight of the fourteen studies were reviewed by more than one reviewer. Importantly, of these eight studies, only two out of the eight were listed by the reviewers as consistently supporting one hypothesis. In other words, in six of the eight cases, different narrative reviewers saw the same studies as supporting opposite hypotheses. This observation is critical to the technique of narrative review. Clearly, different reviewers see the same empirical results quite differently.

Another example further illustrates this contention. Glass, McGaw, and Smith (1981) cite the experiment conducted by Cooper and Rosenthal (1980) in which forty people reviewed the research findings of seven studies. Two groups were formed, one employing the traditional narrative review technique, whilst the other employed a simple statistical technique. The results were strikingly different between the two groups. In the first group, 75 percent of the reviewers concluded that there was no relationship between the variables being studied. In the latter group, 31 percent of reviewers concluded that the variables were not related. Thus, these two groups of researchers integrating findings from the same seven studies formed very different impressions about what the studies revealed. The integration of findings from dozens, or even hundreds, of studies is likely to be substantially more difficult.

These comments are likely to have central relevance to the integration of research findings within the privatization field as well. Take the evidence on the relative efficiency of public versus private production, for instance. The conclusions by Borcherding, Pommerehne, and Schneider (1982) and Millward and Parker (1983) are two of the classic international narrative reviews in this regard. On the one hand, Borcherding's team found that in forty of the fifty-two cases reviewed, private supply was "unequivocally more efficient" than public supply. Only one year later, however, Millward and Parker concluded that none of the cost studies supported the proposition that public firms have a lower productivity or higher costs than private firms in the case of producing electricity. In this area, they argued that "there is no systematic evidence that public enterprises are less cost effective than private firms." With strong political beliefs forming part of the foundation for privatization, the phenomenon of opposing interpretations of the same empirical evidence is likely to occur in the areas of contracting out and enterprise sales. Thus, perhaps it is not surprising that we find U.S. authors such as Ted Savas[1] arguing vigorously that contracting reform is the obvious way forward, whilst others such as Dexter Whitfield[2] from the U.K. conclude with equal conviction exactly the opposite.

Several different explanations are possible as to why different conclusions may be drawn from the same apparent evidence. The first is the fact that even if the definition of privatization is consistent between studies and reviews, the performance dimension adopted by any one reviewer can slant the reviewer's conclusions. Drawing on the evaluation framework developed in Table 4.5, it is possible for one reviewer to speak in the language of economic efficiency, whilst others may speak in the quite separate languages of social policy objectives, democratic processes, or political values. A second explanation concerns the potential influence of the confounding variables, so that, for example, one reviewer talks of contracting out including a simultaneous review of service specifications as well as a change in the ownership of production, whilst another talks of contracting out as only including the transfer of the means of production, with service levels remaining the same. Third, authors may refer to different service types, such as electricity production, manufacturing, health services, refuse disposal, cleaning, or a wide range of services.

A further and more profound explanation concerns the research methodology adopted for the review process itself. It arises from the theme begun earlier in this section, that the narrative review approach may result in conclusions that are clearly not as reliable as is traditionally assumed. The reasons for this lie in the method. The findings of previous studies may be integrated in either a systematic or unsystematic manner, using strategies that may be either explicit or implicit (Shannon and Athanasou 1992). Hunter and Schmidt (1990) suggest that when, as is often the case, findings vary across studies being reviewed, the reviewer usually resolves this dilemma in one of three ways.

Firstly, the reviewer may not even attempt to integrate the findings, but simply provide synopses of studies strung out in dizzying lists.[3] Moreover, such lengthy narrative reviews may, in the end, simply rely on overall qualitative impressions gained through viewing the morass of findings.[4]

Secondly, the reviewers may simply base their conclusions on a smaller number of studies—usually deemed to be those of the best design or analysis. Although this is a very common review technique, some caution with this approach is necessary. Glass (1976) explains why, arguing that "a common method of integrating several studies with inconsistent findings is to carp on the design or analysis deficiencies of all but a few studies—those remaining frequently being one's own work or that of one's students or friends—and then advance the one or two acceptable studies as the truth of the matter."

Although this quotation has a cheeky overtone for emphasis, it is nonetheless clear that in a traditional narrative review, the reviewer may indeed reject all but a few of the studies as being deficient in one way or the other, and then take notice of those one or two studies deemed to be acceptable. This approach fails to use much of the available information by basing review conclusions wholly on the acceptable studies and neglecting the remainder. Such a review may even base final conclusions on unrepresentative studies.

The third approach taken by reviewers is to actually attempt the task of mentally integrating findings—but run the real risk, already alluded to above, of doing an inadequate job.

A further aspect of the narrative review is the requirement of reviewers to describe to the reader the sampling, measurement, analytical methods, and findings of each of the studies under review. Both Hunter and Schmidt (1990, p. 498) and Glass, McGaw, and Smith (1981, p. 13) point out that published reviews often violate these reporting precepts. Both report Jackson's pivotal work in 1978 in which a random sample of thirty-six integrative reviews were drawn from the leading journals in education, psychology, and sociology for analysis. Hunter and Schmidt reported that:

> Jackson's (1978) analysis of 36 review articles in quality journals found that only four of the 36 reported major aspects of the search for relevant studies; only seven indicated whether or not the full set of located studies on the topic was analysed; just over half of the 36 reported the direction and magnitude of the findings of any of the primary studies; and only three cited the mean, range, or another summary of the magnitude of the primary study's findings.

Whether or not the reviewer in question took a systematic approach to the review and did not report this, or else did not take a systematic approach at all is not the issue. In either case, without this information reported, the reader of the review cannot sensibly interpret or intelligently assess any conclusions made.[5]

Traditional Vote-counting Technique

In an effort to bring comprehensive reviews to some sort of clear conclusion, a vote-counting technique has evolved as a popular way of integrating many findings. The aim is to allow the reader to get an overall impression of what the literature says. Examples of this approach include Weimer and Vining (1989) and Richardson (1987), as well as others. In this method, the reviewer firstly examines each of these research studies. The findings from each are then classified into one of three categories; the relationship between the dependent variable and the independent variable is either significantly positive, significantly negative, or else is not significant. The number of studies with findings in each of the three categories is then tallied, and the "votes" for each category are counted. The most popular category is deemed in the narrative sense to be the winner. In other words, the most popular category of result automatically provides the resolution. For example, Weimer and Vining (1989, p. 174) present a table indicating which studies have research findings suggesting the private sector is more efficient than the public sector, which results find in favor of the public sector, and which studies do not favor either or have inconclusive results.

The vote-counting review procedure has, however, been criticized on several counts. This method does not address the problem that the effects may have different consequences under different conditions—in other words, any potential variation between studies is lost. This is a major shortcoming, as one important reason to undertake a review in the first place is to shed some light on why findings do vary between studies. As Hunter and Schmidt (1990, p. 470) note, reviewers using the voting method treat all studies alike. They completely ignore the fact that studies with different sample sizes each logically have quite a different meaning for "significant."[6]

This integration procedure also suffers a more serious shortcoming: It can lead to false conclusions. As Hunter and Schmidt (1990, p. 469) point out, Hedges and Olkin (1985) have shown that for any set of studies for which the statistical power is less than about 0.50, the probability of a false conclusion using the voting method actually increases as the number of studies increases. Hence, the more studies reviewed using the voting method, the greater the chance of a false resolution being reached! It is no wonder that Hunter and Schmidt conclude that the traditional voting method is fatally flawed both statistically and logically.

It is ironic, therefore, that although researchers tend to take much care in establishing and reporting results of their own primary research, the same accuracy and care does not often appear to be pursued when integrating research findings across multiple studies. Hunter and Schmidt quote Gene V. Glass, the originator of the term "meta-analysis" in 1976, in the following terms:

The results of hundreds of studies can no more be grasped in our traditional narrative discursive review than one can grasp the sense of 500 test scores without the aid of techniques for organising, depicting, and interpreting data. . . . What is needed are methods that will integrate results from existing studies to reveal patterns of relatively invariant underlying relations and causalities, the establishment of which will constitute general principles and cumulative knowledge.

They continue with their own comments: "In many areas of research, the need today is not additional empirical data, but some means of making sense of the vast amounts of data that have been accumulated" (Hunter and Schmidt 1990, p. 34).

In order to develop a more reliable approach to the problems of reviewing multiple empirical findings, we need look no further than the methodological lessons learned through the 1970s and 1980s in the research fields of education, medicine, and psychology.

Other Methods of Integrating Research Findings

Several other techniques are available to integrate multiple research findings in a quantitative way. Hunter and Schmidt (1990) provide details of another eight possible review techniques that may be adopted to integrate findings from multiple studies. These exhibit varying degrees of sophistication and rigor. Table 5.1 provides a summary of these approaches to research integration, listed broadly in order of efficacy.

Since this work, an assessment has been undertaken of the consistency and behavior of the three main streams of meta-analysis. Johnson, Mullen, and Salas (1995) argue that the three major streams of meta-analysis now in operation include those from Hedges and Olkin (1985), Rosenthal (1991), and Hunter, Schmidt, and Jackson (1982). In comparing the adoption of these three frameworks, they note that the results from the Hunter et al. method often differ from the other two frameworks. They also observe that whereas the former two methodologies produce results that are consistent with conventional (statistical) expectations, the Hunter, Schmidt, and Jackson approach violates these expectations. On this basis, they argue that the latter method should be used only with caution. In this book, the Rosenthal approach has been adopted. Rosenthal's approach is well documented, and is highly accessible to all researchers irrespective of statistical background. His approach adopts as its measure of the magnitude of a relationship, the correlation coefficient "r."

THE META-ANALYTIC APPROACH

Introduction

Earlier in this chapter it was concluded that in many areas of research, the need at this time was not so much for more primary research studies, but for some means

TABLE 5.1   Summary of Alternative Approaches to Integrate Multiple Research Findings

Title of Method	Explanation	Comments
Traditional methods		
1. Traditional narrative	The methods and findings of studies are reviewed through a critical verbal appraisal.	Very commonly applied, but unsystematic and haphazard.
2. Traditional voting	Studies are categorized as in support, against, or neutral in respect to an hypothesis.	Statistically unreliable, and can lead to false conclusions. Only uses part of the available information.
3. Cumulation of 'p' values across studies	P values (significance levels) are combined.	Although most sets of studies will give a combined 'p' value that is significant, nothing is known about the magnitude of the effect or variation in its effect sizes.
Statistically correct vote-counting methods		
4. Vote-counting methods yielding only significance levels	The "sign test" or proportion of studies can be tested against that expected under the null hypothesis.	Does not provide an estimate of effect size when the null hypothesis is false.
5. Vote-counting methods yielding estimates of effect sizes (counting positive significant findings, counting positive results, or counting positive and negative significant results)	Effect sizes and associated confidence intervals around these estimates can be established from the proportion of positive results or positive significant results.	Substantial uncertainty because methods are based on only part of the information that should be present.

(continues)

TABLE 5.1 *continued*

Title of Method	Explanation	Comments
Meta-analytic methods		
6. Glassian meta-analysis methods	A systematic quantitative technique for integrating research findings. This approach emphasizes effect sizes rather than significance levels, and does not assume equal effect sizes across studies.	Seen as incomplete. Criticized for the inclusion of all studies irrespective of methodological quality, the inclusion of multiple effect sizes from one study, and because of other statistical issues.[1]
7. Study effects meta-analysis	An improvement on the Glassian meta-analysis, which includes only one effect size estimated from each study, and which seeks to exclude from the analysis studies with deficiencies that are likely to distort study outcomes.	Similar to Hunter and Schmidt's work, indicated in methods 9 and 10 below.
8. Homogeneity test based meta-analysis	Uses statistical testing (chi square) to attempt to find moderator variables, by testing whether findings differ by more than would be expected from sampling error alone.	Assumes (falsely) that variance is due only to sampling error, and has an over reliance on statistical testing and significance levels. Less useful than Glassian methods.
9. Validity generalization (Schmidt-Hunter) meta-analysis	Introduces more accurate effect size estimates (weighted estimates), statistical corrections for effect estimates, and hypothesis tests to determine whether effect size variance is due solely to artifacts.	Cannot always correlate study characteristics with study effect sizes.
10. Psychometric meta-analysis (Schmidt-Hunter)	Extends the validity generalization techniques for analyzing effect sizes, and provides correction factors for additional artifacts.	

SOURCE: Adapted from Hunter and Schmidt 1990
[1] These are detailed in Hunter and Schmidt 1990, p. 480.

of making sense of the vast number of accumulated study findings. This is indeed the aim of meta-analysis. Furthermore, Glass, McGaw, and Smith (1981) argue that when reviewing multiple research findings, it is not uniformity in integration definitions and techniques that is important here. It is "clarity, explicitness, and openness" that are sought.

Researchers have been attempting to summarize relationships in many areas of science for decades.[7] Snedecor (1946) included in his early classic statistics text-book an example of how to combine six correlation coefficients available from studies. This example showed how to combine estimates of the magnitude of a relationship, and also tested how heterogeneous these estimates were as a group. Other major figures in the history of mathematics also contributed to this field. Fisher (1932) and Pearson (1933) described procedures for combining probability levels from multiple experiments. Using these techniques, an estimate could be made of the probability that a series of correlation coefficients measured in several studies could have arisen if there was in reality no relationship in the population. Further developments in statistical techniques for summarizing and contrasting studies continued over the next four decades.

Although several statistical procedures were available over this period of time, there was no corresponding revolution in how we conducted reviews of the literature or summarized domains of research.[8] Gene Glass and his colleagues changed this. He first coined the phrase "meta-analysis" in 1976.[9] Glass and his team employed meta-analytic procedures, and were able to provide a dramatic demonstration of the effectiveness of psychotherapy, according to Rosenthal (1991). This showed the power of the technique and provided a major impetus, pushing the use of meta-analysis into common research practice.

Meta-analysis is quite distinct from other types of analysis. Glass, McGaw, and Smith (1981, p. 21) explain that:

> Primary analysis is the original analysis of data in a research study. It is what one typically imagines as the application of statistical methods.
>
> Secondary analysis is the re-analysis of data for the purpose of answering the original research question with better statistical techniques, or answering new questions with old data. . . . Secondary analysis is an important feature of the research and evaluation enterprise.
>
> Meta-analysis is nothing more than the attitude of data-analysis applied to quantitative summaries of individual experiments.

It is, as Glass (1976, p. 3) originally put it, "the analysis of analyses. . . . The statistical analysis of a large collection of results from individual studies for the purpose of integrating the findings. . . . It connotes a rigorous alternative to the casual, narrative discussions of research studies." The meta-analysis approach is based on the central desire to "discipline research synthesis by the same methodological standards that apply to primary research."[10] It is therefore an alternative perspective to enable the integration of research findings, rather than the application of a single technique.

Stages of the Meta-analytic Review

The meta-analysis approach generally contains five stages (Cooper 1989a). He explains these stages as follows.

The first stage is problem formulation. Here, the researcher asks the question of whether a relationship or association between two variables exists, decides how to distinguish studies that are relevant for inclusion in the review from those that are not relevant, and focuses on the operational definitions of variables of interest.

Stage two is data collection. Here studies, both published and unpublished, are located. Numerous possible sources may be tapped for relevant studies, with each likely to have their own particular bias. An important part of this stage is therefore recognition of potential biases, and the definition of ways to ensure that studies are included in the review in a way that will enable such possible biases to be recognized explicitly.

Data evaluation is stage three. Each individual research study is assessed in terms of its research quality. Methodological adequacy is judged, and the various research methods are categorized. The development of independent hypothesis tests is central to this stage. Here, a decision is made as to the individual unit to be adopted in the meta-analysis. The researcher, the study, the sample, or the hypothesis are all possible alternatives for the individual unit.

The fourth stage is analysis and interpretation. Here, the findings from the individual research studies are synthesized into a unified statement about the research problem. Statistical methods are used to ensure that results from separate studies are combined in a way that allows the reviewer to distinguish between systematic patterns and chance fluctuations, and that enables the size of a relation to be estimated. Differences between the sizes of relations in different studies are also estimated.

In stage five, the results of the review are presented. The report written in this stage represents the final part of the meta-analysis, and is no less important than the written report accompanying a primary research study.

Characteristics of Meta-analysis

Thus, meta-analysis can be seen to have the following general characteristics, drawing on the work of Glass, McGaw, and Smith (1981, p. 22):

1. Meta-analysis is quantitative. It uses numbers and statistical methods in a practical way, namely, for organizing and extracting information from large masses of data.
2. Meta-analysis does not prejudge research findings in terms of research qual-

ity. The findings of studies are not ignored a priori. Methodological weaknesses are recorded and their possible relationship with the study findings are examined as an empirical question.

3. Meta-analysis seeks general conclusions from different studies relevant to an issue.

Meta-analysis should not be seen simply as a replacement for the traditional literature review. Rather it is a complimentary tool that can build on the concepts and the various threads of arguments that come out of traditional literature reviews. It aims to investigate the apparently common threads and consistent findings of the studies, and articulate both the extent to which conflicting findings actually do exist, and the extent to which any overall conclusions are possible.

Looking at the perspective of the meta-analyst, two comments are pertinent. Firstly, inadequacies in the data clearly cannot be overcome through meta-analytic techniques. It is, however, possible to use meta-analysis to aid conclusions, and better advise what the overall findings of the literature are. For example, we could determine whether moderating variables appear to influence the results found from a statistical perspective rather than simply from speculation. Secondly, because both results from many studies and the context of each of these studies are being combined, it is also possible to draw conclusions that were not actually part of any one particular study. There may not be any one study that, for instance, has tested whether the results for privatization of activities (as contracting out) produces different results in terms of effectiveness for local government operations compared to federal government operations. Possible differences in effectiveness can, however, be tested to some extent within a meta-analysis.

In other words, by documenting the context in which all studies were undertaken, new knowledge can be gained of the conditions under which findings appear to either be consistent or conflict.

Applications of Meta-analysis

A range of fields have seen the application of meta-analysis. These applications vary from the fields that formed the early foundations of the techniques, including education, psychology, and medicine, to applications in business, commerce, and law. Table 5.2 illustrates several examples of meta-analysis over these fields.

Although many applications exist in these areas, indeed hundreds of meta-analyses now exist in the literature,[11] no applications of meta-analysis were noted in the field of public administration. Likewise, no applications were noted in the privatization arena.

STATISTICAL CHARACTERISTICS: THE EFFECT SIZE CONCEPT

With statistical information available for a series of studies, how could the effectiveness of, say, contracting be assessed? A few statistical concepts are now introduced.

TABLE 5.2   Illustrations of Meta-analysis Applications in Several Fields

Research Field	Application	Study
1 Education	Relationship between educational achievement and class size	Glass and Smith (1979)
2 Education	Relationship between educational gain and type of homework	Cooper (1989b)
3 Psychology	Relationship between expectancy of researcher and experimental outcome	Rosenthal and Rubin (1978)
4 Medicine	Relationship between alternative drug treatments and depression	Anderson and Tomenson (1994)
5 Psychiatry	Relationship between drug treatments and behavior of hyperactive children	Ottenbacher and Cooper (1983)
6 Business/ Management	Relationship between strategic planning and financial performance	Boyd (1991)
7 Business/ Management	Relationship between various determinants and financial performance	Capon, Farley, and Hoenig (1990)
8 Marketing	Relationship between various determinants and international tourism demand	Crouch (1992)
9 Product development	Relationship between various determinants and the success of new products	Montoya-Weiss and Calantone (1994)
10 Law	Relationship between authoritarianism and juror's perceptions of defendant culpability	Narby, Cutler, and Moran (1993)

We wish to test for the existence of a relationship between variable X and variable Y. For this thesis, Y is the performance characteristic, such as the cost of service provision, and X is the sector in which the service is provided, normally the contract arrangement being either contracted out or being provided under traditional government means. We postulate that there is a relationship—that indeed the cost of provision is lower when the service is contracted out than when it is not. To check whether such a relationship exists, we undertake a formal statistical test on a sample of measurements. The key to understanding the meta-analysis concept, as Rosenthal (1991, p. 14) explains, is that in doing this statistical test on any one data sample, the answer comes in two parts:

1. an estimate of the magnitude of the relationship (the *effect* size), and
2. an indication of the accuracy or *reliability* of the estimated effect size (as in a confidence interval placed around the estimate).

Thus, formally, this relationship can be seen as follows:

Test of Significance = Size of Effect × Size of Study

In carrying out a formal test of significance, it is evident that a researcher may obtain a "statistically significant" result (i.e., relationship) if a small effect is present but the size of the study is large. Alternatively, if a large effect is actually present but a small study is undertaken a significant result may again occur. Notice that both studies would have been reported as significant but that both would have been investigating quite different effect sizes.

This meta-analysis, in line with common meta-analysis practice, uses the effect size as its common piece of information. It therefore focuses on the *sizes of relationship* found in each study in the literature, not the size of the study undertaken. The sample size does not influence the effect size per se. However, knowing the sample size provides useful information that helps determine a confidence interval around the effect size estimate. The use of the effect size as the basis of study when reviewing international findings means that a review can be undertaken of all samples large and small, and not simply those that were reported as statistically significant.

For studies reporting sufficient statistical information, at least one type of effect size can usually be calculated. In this privatization research, the effect size adopted was the correlation coefficient "r," in line with the work of Rosenthal (1991). Where, for example, studies adopted a student's t test to determine statistical significance of the relationship between service provision cost and contracting out arrangement, the effect size "r" can be computed as follows:

$$r = \sqrt{t^2/(t^2 + df)}$$

Where

df = the number of degrees of freedom, typically the number of data points
less the number of parameters estimated in the econometric equation.

For each correlation coefficient calculated, Fisher's transformation must be
computed to ensure that the transformed effect size "z_r" is normally distributed.[12]
This transformation can be undertaken as follows:

$$z_r = 1/2 \log_e [(1 + r) / (1 - r)]$$

In all discussions of effect sizes in this research, we shall deal with this "corrected" effect size z_r.

In some instances, several effect sizes, with Fisher corrections applied, were
available from each of the studies for different service types. As a general rule,
only one effect size was used for any one service measurement. Where multiple
measurements of the same service were taken, the available effect size estimates
were averaged to provide one estimate for the analysis. Many of the studies analyzed several services and were able to provide separate effect size estimates for
each service. As well as effect sizes for each service type, an average effect size and
confidence limits on this estimate are also possible.

A number of statistical tests were relevant. Empirical work in this research
adopted three main tests. The first was a simple sign test to clarify whether the
proportion of either positive or negative empirical findings may have arisen simply by chance. The second statistical test undertaken was one that determined the
degree to which the empirical results under consideration were homogeneous or
heterogeneous. In other words, we are searching for the potential existence of
other sources of variation as well as just sampling error amongst the various effect
sizes. Do different types of services appear to have reported different effect sizes
for instance? The third statistical test was aimed at investigating the long held
concern in social science research that the research reports available for review
and analysis may have been biased, comprising mostly those that had found significant results. Perhaps there are file drawers full of research conclusions that
have gone unreported?

The details of each of these statistical tests are provided in Appendix A. Each
was applied in the meta-analysis, the results for which are reported in Chapters 7
and 9.

THE APPLICATION OF META-ANALYSIS TO
PRIVATIZATION PERFORMANCE

Meta-analysis will be applied to the major two definitions of privatization—the
contracting out of services to the private sector, and the sale of enterprises to the
private sector. The aim of the analysis is to address the questions:

- What is the general relationship between performance and privatization when defined as the contracting out of public sector services?
- What is the general relationship between performance and privatization when defined as the sale of an enterprise providing public sector services?

We are therefore seeking an answer to the question, What is the general relationship between performance and sector providing the service?

In considering this question, many definitions of performance are possible. Understandably, not all performance criteria are amenable to meta-analysis. Most areas of performance have not typically been subject to quantitative statistical analysis, and consequently could not, by definition, be subject to a meta-analysis. Studies of corruption under private and public service provision, for example, have usually been undertaken on a case study basis and have adopted a narrative analysis. Likewise, comments on political, democratic, legal, and social performance dimensions have all, to a large extent, comprised case study observations and narrative analysis. These dimensions will therefore be subject more to a traditional narrative review, but complemented by meta-analytic observations where possible.

In undertaking a traditional narrative review of some performance dimensions, these dimensions will be subject only to an analysis of findings considered to be representative of the empirical literature, rather than quoting extensively from all findings in a comprehensive manner. Remember that whilst the author's judgment is necessary to choose which reports are representative, particularly knowing that no literature review can include all reports ever written analyzing empirical experience, this is no different from a typical literature review. It is different only to the extent that this review is being qualified explicitly, in recognition of the uncertainties associated with a narrative review process.

PART III

Empirical Knowledge of Privatization Performance

6

Performance Data for Privatization as Contracting Out

In the last chapter it was argued that there is a need nowadays, with so much accumulated research, to synthesize these studies in order to provide a more informed overall picture of research findings for an area. It was suggested that such a careful synthesis would usually require the use of meta-analytic techniques to assist in contrasting and comparing the various findings available. The central thrust of this meta-analytic approach was the desire to collect research findings as data, and then study this data in a quantitative way to form a picture of what the research findings say. An attitude of data analysis is then applied to these collected findings in a structured and, importantly, transparent way. So, how was the data gathered, and what parameters best describe these research studies and findings? In this chapter, I aim to answer these questions.

SEARCHING FOR DATA

In establishing a comprehensive set of reports on contracting-out public sector services, we are continually seeking answers for the question, What does the literature look like? Our first discovery is that it is voluminous. Although the vast majority of reports on the subject are discussions and commentaries, there is still a reasonably large body of studies claiming to report empirical results. The corollary to this, however, is that what one finds in the literature can depend to a large extent on where one searches for evidence, and whether one seeks results to support and legitimize particular conclusions already formed.

The literature search for this project was undertaken through the following databases:

1. ABI/INFORM Global
2. Public Affairs Information Service (PAIS)
3. Dissertation Abstracts Online (DAO)

These international computer databases together covered some 1,400 journals and magazines, and 800 journals respectively, as well as some 6,000 nonserial publications and university theses.[1] The geographical coverage of these databases was international, with reporting of periodical articles, as well as monographs, government documents, pamphlets, reports of public and private agencies, microfiche, and newspapers. A broad range of disciplines was also covered including humanities, social sciences, science, and engineering. Of course, despite the global coverage claimed by these databases, it is recognized that in practice, information from the United States is probably far more accessible than other countries. It should also be noted that these databases are only three from a significant list of sources that might have potentially been adopted as the basis of this study.[2]

A wide variety of search terms were employed to search these databases in order to maximize coverage, and some 4,200 abstracts were read initially.[3] Around 20 percent of these were selected as promising candidates for subsequent follow-up. In the research undertaken for this book, a period of around two decades spanning 1971 to 1995 was covered for all databases, with coverage of the dissertations going back further than this. Bibliographies of all major reviews and the majority of other references were also searched for the potential existence of additional empirical findings. Additionally, listings for both Australian and British theses were searched, and suggestions from personal contacts were investigated.[4] Throughout all searching, reports sought were limited to those in English. A database was established in order to keep track of all reference titles and relevant details for subsequent analysis.[5] This database assisted the study in keeping track of reports being retrieved, the presence or absence of empirical results, and summaries of findings.

All in all, some 299 references directly relating to performance results for contracting/contracting out/privatization through contracts were identified. Abstracts of all references were reread, and the retrieval of all articles was followed up. Success was achieved in retrieving 232 of these. Of these, nearly one-half presented discussions, concepts, or professional arguments for or against contracting services. They did not, however, present any empirical results from actual contracting experience. These aside, 129 references were listed as potential sources of empirical evidence on the effectiveness of contracting out and competitive tendering. All of these reports presented some form of empirical result on the effectiveness of contracting or competitive tendering. Most presented their own experience. Those presenting the findings of others were included where the measurements were unique and were not covered elsewhere.

As part of our larger search for evidence on privatization, around the same number of references were also found for each of the categories of enterprise sales (292) and property rights (214), as well as one further category of general reviews and discussion of the relationship between public and private sector business effectiveness (266). The total number of reports in the database developed for this research was 1,071.

FIGURE 6.1   Possible Levels of Reviewing Literature

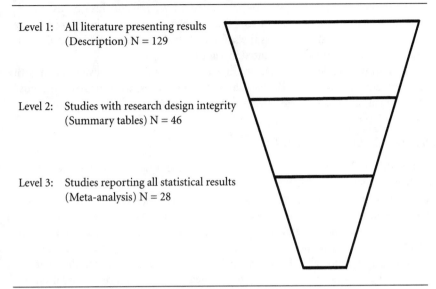

Level 1:   All literature presenting results
(Description) N = 129

Level 2:   Studies with research design integrity
(Summary tables) N = 46

Level 3:   Studies reporting all statistical results
(Meta-analysis) N = 28

In addition to the formal literature search through the international databases noted, an attempt was also made to retrieve any unpublished studies that might have been completed on contracting out in the local government sector of the Australian state, South Australia. A letter was sent to all 118 local government bodies in South Australia requesting a copy of results from any evaluation (no matter how primitive or approximate) that may have been undertaken of contracting out or competitive tendering. Replies from a handful of councils were received and of these, no actual study results were forwarded. On this basis, it is concluded that the number of statistical analyses that have not been published, but instead have been kept in the "bottom of a file drawer," appeared to be small in this area of research.

It is possible to review the empirical evidence presented from the 129 references collected on three levels. First, the sample of 129 references quoting empirical results could be reviewed. The studies found in the literature cover a whole range of sophistication, however. Some findings appear to have been based on only a back-of-the-envelope guestimate and to have been published with the enhancement of corporate image in mind. Other studies were more carefully designed and formally researched. A second level of review that could be adopted in this book would be to take particular note of only those studies that were undertaken on a more rigorous and scientific basis.

The third level is that of the meta-analysis. Here, an attempt is made to combine all findings in a statistical way, such that these findings can be both combined and contrasted. Only studies that have presented results in a complete and open manner in the statistical sense can be used in this phase. Using this technique, greater certainty ought to be achievable for general conclusions and possible causal factors. Moderating factors that might not all appear in any one single study can also be analyzed across the sample of studies to assess their possible impact. These three levels are indicated in Figure 6.1.

The narrative review by its nature may refer to studies at all levels, albeit with greater weight being put on those studies with higher research integrity and those reporting all statistical results.

STUDY SELECTION PROCESS

For a study to be included in the meta-analysis, the usual requirement was that it address a general hypothesis. Secondly, it was necessary that it report sufficient statistical information. In the general field of meta-analysis, it may also sometimes be a requirement that the studies to be included be of a particular research design, or that they contain specific statistical controls. For this study, such requirements for inclusion were not adopted. Thus, if a study researched the effectiveness of contracting, and it reported sufficient statistical information, it was included. For our case, "sufficient information" was taken to mean that the quantitative relationship between contracting (to either the public or private sector) and performance was explicit, with the statistic used to test significance being reported. Alternatively, some other estimate of the variability of the effectiveness such as a χ^2 or F statistic, for example, may have been reported instead.

A listing of all studies initially viewed as possibly having relevant empirical findings is shown in Table 6.1. This table indicates, for each report, whether it could be included in the meta-analysis or not. Most could not. The most usual reason for exclusion was that insufficient statistical information was reported. In several cases, raw data were presented, and it was possible to analyze these data from first principles to ensure sufficient statistical information for inclusion.[6] Several studies also reported findings which had been covered by others.[7] Results of any one research study were included only once.

After exclusions, twenty-eight studies were available for the meta-analysis. Some of the major characteristics of these studies are indicated in Table 6.2, which shows that the reports cover the period 1976 to 1994, and refer to a wide range of services. In line with earlier observations, the countries studied are mostly the United States and Britain, with a few other countries such as Australia as well. By far the most common performance indicator adopted was some type of cost measurement. Again, the most common analysis method adopted was the multiple regression technique. Hence, authors would usually measure changes in several independent variables (including the type of contract arrangement in place), whilst observing the dependent variable service cost. By measuring the extent to which changes in cost were consistently correlated with changes in contract arrangement, the effectiveness of contracting arrangement on "cost" could be estimated.

TABLE 6.1 Empirical Studies Reviewed

Author (Primary)	Other Authors	Year of Publication	Reference Number	Comments on Inclusion in Meta-Analysis	Included?
Albin, S.		1992	378	No statistical details provided in case study.	Yes
Ambrosio, J.		1992	192	Anecdotal evidence: no statistical details.	No
Anonymous		1993	154	No statistical details.	No
Ascher, K.		1987	9	Paired t test completed by author, from data presented by Ascher.	Yes
Baer, T.		1991	157	No statistical details provided.	No
Bails, D.		1979	714		Yes
Baquet, D.	Gottlieb, M.	1991	771	Case study: no statistical variation data presented.	No
Beauris, V.		1993	746	Case study: no statistical variation data presented.	No
Berenyi, E.B.	Stevens, B.	1988	510		Yes
Berglund, D.D.		1992	586		Yes
Biggs, B.L.	Kralewski, J., and Brown, G.	1980	818	The raw data is not amenable to inclusion in the meta-analysis.	No
Buck, D.	Chaundy, D.	1992	1,021	Reanalysis of DMT data.	Yes
Burnett, M.		1984	415	No statistical details provided.	No
Carver, R.H.		1989	256		Yes
Centre for Public Services		1995a	981	The raw data is not amenable to inclusion in the meta-analysis.	No
Centre for Public Services		1995b	980	The raw data is not amenable to inclusion in the meta-analysis.	No
Chandler, T.	Feuille, P.	1991	60	Raw data only presented. Insufficient statistical information.	No
Chandler, T.D.		1994	358	Different hypothesis tested.	No
Cubbin, J.	Domberger, S., and Meadowcroft, S.	1987	196	No variance data presented.	No
DeHoog, R.		1985	739	No variance data presented.	No
Dixon, R.B.		1992	205	No details apart from raw data were presented.	No
Doherty, E.		1989	144	No statistical details provided.	No
Domberger, S.	Meadowcroft, S., and Thompson, D.J.	1987	503		Yes
Domberger, S.	Meadowcroft, S., and Thompson, D.J.	1986	502		Yes
Domberger, S.	Meadowcroft, S., and Thompson, D.J.	1988	427	No additional statistics provided in reanalysis.	No
Domberger, S.		1994	983	Review only: no statistical results presented.	No
Domberger, S.	Rimmer, S.	1994	987	Review only: no statistical results presented.	No
Domberger, S.	Hall, C., and Li, E.	1994	872	Review only: no statistical results presented.	Yes
Donahue, J.D.		1989	219	Review only: no statistical results presented.	No

(continues)

TABLE 6.1 Continued

Author (Primary)	Other Authors	Year of Publication	Reference Number	Comments on Inclusion in Meta-Analysis	Included?
Douglas, M.		1994	996	No variance data presented.	No
Edwards, B.	Moch, A.	1992	204	No statistical details provided.	No
Edwards, F.R.	Stevens, B.J.	1978	104	Insufficient statistical data presented.	No
Ernst, J.		1995	1,012	Case study results on accountability not subject to quantification.	No
Escott, K.	Whitfield, D.	1995	982	No details of statistical variance provided.	No
Evatt Research Centre	Hall, C., and	1990	289	Raw survey data presented.	No
Farago, S.	Domberger, S.	1994	303	No details of statistical variance provided.	No
Feldman, T.R.		1987	594		Yes
Ferris, J.M.		1988	1,019		Yes
Finder, A.		1993	777	Case study: no statistical results presented.	No
Florestano, P. S.	Gordon, S. B.	1980	11	Raw opinion data presented only.	No
Folz, D.H.		1985	596		Yes
Freund, D.		1988	892	Insufficient statistical data presented.	No
Fryklund, I.		1994	174	No statistical data presented.	No
Gewirtz, N.		1987	591	Not possible to summarize into an effect size.	No
Greene, J.D.		1994	533	t tests recalculated by present author where statistics not reported.	Yes
Halper, M.		1993	190	No statistics presented.	No
Harding, R.W.		1990	588		Yes
Hartley, K.	Huby, M.	1986	1,023	No statistical estimates provided.	No
Hatry, H.P.	Brounstein, P.J. and Levinson, R.B.	1993	450	No statistical results provided.	No
Hensher, D.		1989	831	t tests recalculated by present author using raw data presented.	Yes
Hensher, D.		1987	811	Insufficient statistical information.	No
Hirsch, W.Z.		1991	976	No empirical statistical results presented.	No
Holcombe, R.G.		1991	390		Yes
Holmes, P.A.		1985	276	No details of statistical tests provided.	No
Hubbard, G.		1993	191	Raw data presented.	No
Jensen, P.	Fernandez, P.	1994	281	No statistical findings.	No
Jensen, R.		1990	6	Insufficient statistics information.	No
Juneau, L.		1992	156	Anecdotal evidence: no statistical details.	No
Kemper, P.	Quigley, J. M.	1976	10		Yes
Kitchen, H.M.		1976	126		Yes
Knipe, D.		1993	7	Insufficient statistical information.	No
Kobrak, P.		1995	1,025	Results on corruption/accountability cases not subject to quantification.	No
Kostro, C.		1994	351	No statistical details presented.	No

Author	Co-author(s)	Year	No.	Comment	Selected
LGIU (Local Government Information Unit)		1994	978	No statistical details presented.	No
Loh, L.	Venkatraman, N.	1992	208	The whole firm's performance (overall) was researched.	No
Malka, S.		1990	755	No statistical data presented.	No
Mangan, T.	Carlini, J.	1991	158	No statistical details provided.	No
Martin, D.L.	Stein, R.M.	1993	930		Yes
McDavid, J.C.		1985	8	No statistical variance information provided.	No
McDavid, J.C.	Schick, G.K.	1987	466	No statistical variance information provided.	No
McEntee, G.W.		1985	3	Insufficient statistical information.	No
Mehay, S.L.	Gonzalez, R.A.	1993	449		Yes
Mehay, S.L.	Gonzalez, R.A.	1985	1,026	Included in 449 (above).	No
Mennemeyer, S.T.	Olinger, L.	1989	893	No relevant statistical variance information presented.	No
Messier, G.		1993	757	No statistical variance information presented.	No
Miller, T.	Dickerson, H., and Greenstein, I.	1984	278	19 sites studied: no statistical variance information presented.	No
Milne, R.		1987	740	Insufficient statistical information presented.	No
Moore, S.		1986	610	No statistical variance information presented.	No
Morgan, D.R.		1992	482	Insufficient statistical information presented.	No
Musgrove, K.E.		1988	590	Client opinion data on costs omitted. Data on quality levels included.	Yes
NSW Treasury		1993	302	No statistical variance information presented.	No
Osborne, D.	Gaebler, T.	1993	779	Information is anecdotal in style: no statistical data presented.	No
Pack, R.		1992	563		Yes
Paddon, M.		1993b	963	No statistical variance information presented.	No
Parker, D.		1990	969	Review only: no statistical results presented.	No
Peak, D.A.		1994	559	Hypothesis different to meta-analysis hypothesis.	No
Perry, J.L.	Babitsky, T.T.	1986	275	Insufficient statistical information presented.	No
Peterson, N.M.		1984	975	No statistical variance information presented.	Yes
Pommerehne, W.	Frey, B.	1977	203	No statistical data presented.	No
Proust, E.		1995	1,022	No statistical information presented.	No
Rehfuss, J.A.		1991	159	No statistical variance information presented.	No
Rimmer, S.	Webb, G.	1990	1,011	No statistical variance information presented.	No
Robinson, M.	Wilson, S.	1994	169	Insufficient statistical details provided.	No
Roehm, H.S.	Castellano, J., and Karns, D.A.	1989	274	Raw survey data presented.	No
Rose, P.		1994	436	Raw data provided only.	No
Rothenburg Pack, J.		1989	461	No statistical results provided.	No
Savas, E.S.		1993	172	No statistical variance information presented.	No
Savas, E.S.	Grava, S., and Sparrow, R.	1991	1,010	No variance infomation presented.	No
Savas, E.S.		1992a	761	Averages presented only.	No
Savas, E.S.		1981	627	No statistical variance information presented.	No

(continues)

TABLE 6.1 Continued

Author (Primary)	Other Authors	Year of Publication	Reference Number	Comments on Inclusion in Meta-Analysis	Included?
Savas, E.S.		1977b	200	No variances presented.	No
Savas, E.S.		1980	731	Results reanalyzed by Stevens (ref 509/510).	No
Savas, E.S.		1992b	997	No statistical variance information presented.	No
Savas, E.S.		1977a	641	No statistics presented.	No
Savas, E.S.		1974	719	No relevant statistical data: information tables only.	No
SCAT–Services to Community Action and Trade Unions		1988	977	No statistical variance information presented.	No
Schneider, K.		1992	770	No statistical variance information presented.	No
Seear, R.		1994	808	No statistical data presented.	No
Seghers, F.		1986	54	No statistical data: information tables only.	No
Slater, R.B.		1992	155	Anecdotal evidence: no statistical details provided.	No
Stein, L.		1994	178	Raw results presented only.	No
Stevens, B.J.		1977	926	No statistical variance information presented.	No
Stevens, B.J.		1984	509	Reported in 510.	No
Szymankiewicz, J.		1994	512	No variance data presented.	No
Szymanski, S.	Wilkins, S.	1993	206		Yes
Szymanski, S.		1993	1,001		Yes
Thobe, D.		1992	207	Raw data only presented.	No
Tucker, W.		1992	151	Anecdotal evidence: no statistical details.	No
UK Audit Office		1987	898	Results reanalyzed by present author.	Yes
US General Accounting Office		1994a	988	No statistical variance information presented: mean cost savings only.	No
US General Accounting Office		1994b	990	Case studies: no statistical variance estimates provided.	No
US General Accounting Office		1991	989	Case studies: no statistical variance estimates provided.	No
Walsh, K.	Davis, H.	1993	632	Case studies: no statistical variance estimates provided, and no public/private division.	No
Ward, J.D.		1992	149	Raw opinion data presented only.	No
Weis, K.A.		1991	589	Different hypothesis tested.	No
West, M.L.		1993	148	No statistical information supplied.	No
Wheeler, J.R.	Zuckerman, H.S., and Aderholdt, J.	1982	821		Yes
Whitehead, B.	O'Sullivan, B.	1991	160	No statistical information presented.	No
Zwanziger, J.	Melnick, G.A.	1988	894	Different hypothesis tested.	No

TABLE 6.2 Studies Included in the Meta-analysis

Authors (Date)	Sample	Country Studied	Performance Measures	Analysis	Controls	Findings
Albin 1992	Waste management services at 58 local councils	Australia	Expenditure/head, rate revenue/head, and range of services	Regression analysis	Few	Contracting does not lead to a significant cost reduction. There is no expansion of services or reduction in rates.
Ascher 1987	A range of services in Wandsworth council	United Kingdom	Reported savings for contracts	Paired t test	Few	Both contracting out and competitive testing (in-house) resulted in savings.
Bails 1979	School transport costs in six states of the U.S.	United States	Cost per pupil	Regression analysis	Several	Contracting out lowers transport costs.
Berenyi and Stevens 1988	Eight services across 20 local cities in Los Angeles area	United States	Service cost	Regression analysis	Several	Contracting out saved 0% to 48% of costs.
Berglund 1992	Two public and two private manpower training centers	United States	Costs per student for programs, and quality ratings	t test	Few	Public centers were more cost effective.
Buck and Chaundy 1992	Refuse collection cost of 331 municipalities in the U.K. over 1983–86	United Kingdom	Refuse collection cost	Regression analysis	Many	Contracting out resulted in costs 33% lower.
Carver 1989	Property tax assessment services for 100 communities in Massachusetts	United States	Average expenditure on service	Regression analysis	Few	Public provision appeared appreciably less expensive than contract.
Domberger, Meadowcroft, and Thompson 1986	Refuse collection services across 60 municipalities in the U.K.	United Kingdom	Refuse collection cost	Regression analysis	Many	Both contracting out and contracting in-house resulted in cost reductions of around 20%.

(continues)

TABLE 6.2 *continued*

Authors (Date)	Sample	Country Studied	Performance Measures	Analysis	Controls	Findings
Domberger, Meadowcroft, and Thompson 1987	Review of domestic services costs for 1,500 hospitals	United Kingdom	Hospital domestic services cost	Regression analysis	Many	Competitive tendering reduces prices and raises the performance of contractors. The influence of ownership is negligible.
Domberger, Hall, and Li 1994	Analysis of 61 cleaning contracts in Sydney	Australia	Cleaning services	Regression analysis	Many	Cost savings from contracting out were 34% and contracting in-house were 22%.
Feldman 1987	68 bus transport firms	United States	Bus transport cost	Regression analysis	Many	Weak evidence only is found for greater private sector efficiency.
Ferris 1988	Multiple services in 500 U.S. cities	United States	Local government expenditures	Regression analysis	Many	City expenditures decrease with increased contracting out.
Folz 1985	14 local cities in U.S.	United States	Municipal service costs	Pearson product-moment correlations	Several	Cities that contract with others or with the private sector are more productive.
Greene 1994	Several services were compared across 12 matched U.S. cities	United States	Municipal service costs	ANOVA, and rank correlation coefficient	Few	Mixed findings provided little support to suggest higher efficiency with contracting out.
Harding 1990	School bussing at 363 schools in Indiana, U.S.	United States	Cost of bussing service	Regression analysis	Many	Mixed findings provided weak evidence of greater private sector efficiency.
Hensher 1989	15 public bus operators in Australia	Australia	Total factor productivity	t test	Few	Private operators were more cost efficient.
Holcombe 1991	Seven contracts for the provision of waste water treatment facilities	United States	Cost of treatment facility	Regression analysis	Several	Private provision is associated with higher costs.
Kemper and Quigley 1976	Refuse collection in 129 U.S municipalities	United States	Cost of collection	Regression analysis	Several	Private collection is 25–36% dearer than municipal, whilst collection contracted out is 13–30% cheaper than municipal

Kitchen 1976	Refuse collection in 48 Canadian municipalities	Canada	Average unit cost of refuse collection	Regression analysis	Many	Municipal collection is much more expensive.
Martin and Stein 1993	Per capita spending for seven services in 877 U.S. cities	United States	Per capita spending for service area	Regression analysis	Many	Contracting has no appreciable effect on overall expenditure for services.
Mehay and Gonzalez 1993	Police services in 53 Californian counties	United States	Sheriff expenditures in areas	Regression analysis	Many	Intergovernmental contracting lowers costs, and so does being adjacent to areas contracting.
Musgrove 1988	Bussing in 88 school districts in Missouri	United States	Per pupil costs, and quality satisfaction	F test and t test	Few	There is no difference in cost or quality of transport.
Pack 1992	Computer network reliability of 55 clients	United States	Various reliability measures	t tests	Few	Outsourcing results in around 30% improvement in network quality.
Pommerehne and Frey 1977	Refuse collection costs for 103 Swiss cities	Switzerland	Refuse collection cost per ton or per household	Regression analysis	Many	Private collection is less costly than public collection.
Szymanski and Wilkins 1993	Refuse collection costs for 1984 to 1988 in the U.K.	United Kingdom	Refuse collection cost	Regression analysis	Many	Contracting out and contracting in-house both reduce costs.
Szymanski 1993	Refuse collection costs before and after CCT in the U.K.	United Kingdom	Refuse collection cost	Regression analysis	Many	Both contracting out and in-house reduced costs.
UK Audit Office 1987	Domestic support services in the 22 NHS authorities	United Kingdom	Contract costs	Paired t test	Few	Contracting out or in-house reduced costs
Wheeler, Zuckerman, and Aderholdt 1982	10 hospitals under management contracts in seven states	United States	Return on assets	F test	Few	Improved profitability occurred under management contracts.

NOTES: Controls refers to the presence of controlling statistically for the impacts of possible mediating variables. Codes adopted were as follows:

"Few"   statistical controls for two or fewer variables present

"Several"   statistical controls for three to six variables present

"Many"   statistical controls for seven or more variables present

Summary details of effect size derivations are shown in Appendix C. Table 6.2 also indicates the range of typical key findings from these reports. Even with these more statistically explicit reports, a wide range is again found. In addition to the studies of Domberger, Meadowcroft, and Thompson (1986, 1987) and Berenyi and Stevens (1988), which showed that private provision resulted in substantial cost savings, further supporting studies also reported that cities that contracted out were more productive in terms of service unit costs, or that they spent less (Folz 1985, Ferris 1988). Meanwhile, others found only weak evidence of greater private sector efficiency from their empirical work (Harding 1990). Even others found that private service provision was statistically associated not with lower costs, but with higher costs (Holcombe 1991, Carver 1989). Before reviewing these findings in greater depth or undertaking the meta-analysis, though, we shall describe the literature itself.

CHARACTERISTICS OF THE LITERATURE

Reports on the effectiveness of privatization (as contracting out) were found between the years 1974 and 1995. The distribution of years of publication is shown in Figure 6.2. Distributions for all studies retrieved and for those studies included in the meta-analysis are presented.[8] It is evident that a wide distribution of publication dates was found, with the more recent few years having the most frequent reports. The two distributions for all studies and for those studies included in the meta-analysis were found to be statistically similar.[9]

FIGURE 6.2   Publication Year of Studies (Contracting Out)

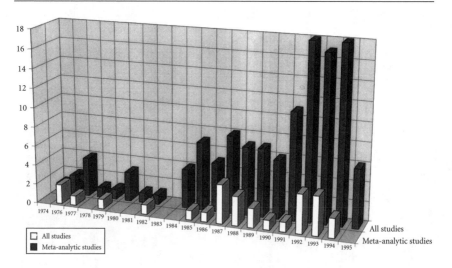

Research from a range of countries was found. These were grouped according to those found in the United States, Canada, Britain, Europe (other than the United Kingdom), Australia, and other. The distributions of countries actually studied in the various reports are shown in Figure 6.3. The dominance of studies undertaken on the United States is apparent, with 66 percent of all claimed empirical findings relating to the U.S.[10]

The studies also appeared to cover several levels of government. Figure 6.4 indicates the level of government covered. The majority of studies reported evidence relating to local government. As well as local government, state and federal, or a combination of these, was also apparent.[11]

A range of study types was found. Some reports were a basic before and after study design, where a case or series of cases were analyzed before and after the instigation of contracting. Some reports were cross-sectional. Such studies attempted to analyze the associations between variables such as the presence of contracting in a city over one particular time period. Therefore, instead of seeking the presence of performance changing over time, possible variations in performance over space were analyzed here. Few studies adopted an explicit control group in their analysis, with most studies attempting typically to control for the effects of other variables and background variation through statistical (regression) techniques. Other types of studies were also found, and extensive surveys were uncovered. Agencies surveyed were asked to reveal either their current practices, results from their own experiences of contracting, or else their own attitudes to the practice of contracting.

The studies that were found comprised several different types of publication. For all studies presenting empirical findings, research journals provided the largest proportion at 38 percent. Magazines/newspapers, published reports, and either books or book chapters followed this, representing 20 percent, 13 percent, and 12 percent respectively. The publication profile for those studies that were to be included in the meta-analysis was broadly similar.

One item of critical importance, noting the intense interest of some groups to the outcomes of contracting research, might be the funding source of any study. Unfortunately, the vast majority of studies did not report the source of funding. This may have been due to several factors, but the consequence of this is that without this information there is now no way of determining, as part of the later meta-analysis, whether the source of funding appears to have had any influence over the study results obtained.

In a similar vein, it is also interesting to review the disciplines of those presenting study findings. Figure 6.5 indicates that for all studies reporting empirical results, some 43 percent did not report their discipline. However, of those that did, by far the largest group presenting findings was Economics. Of the 57 percent of studies that reported disciplines, 20 percent were from Economics and 8 percent from Business/Commerce. The next largest disciplines reported were Finance/Accounting, Public Administration, and Politics/Law, with all three at 7 percent. The least repre-

FIGURE 6.3a   Countries Studied (All Studies)

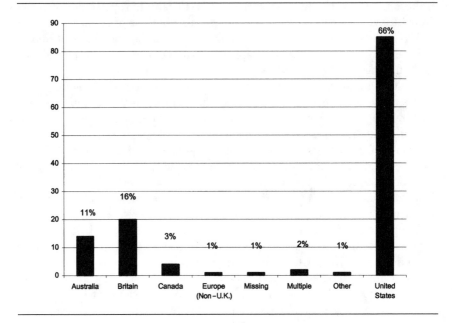

FIGURE 6.3b   Countries Studied (Meta-analysis Studies)

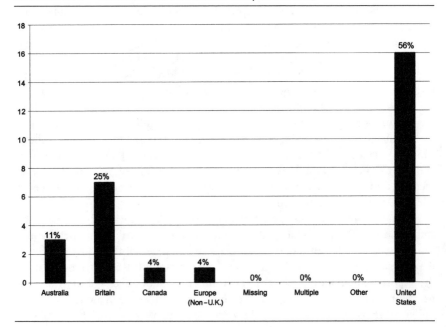

FIGURE 6.4a   Levels of Government Studied (All Studies)

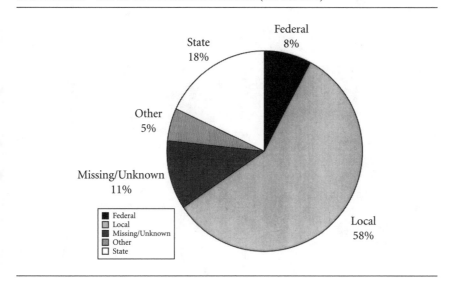

FIGURE 6.4b   Levels of Government Studied (Meta-analysis Studies)

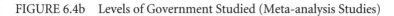

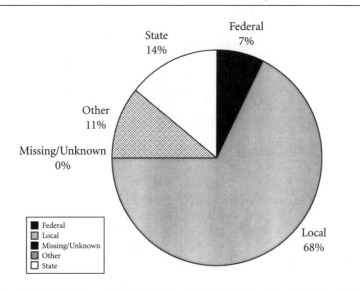

FIGURE 6.5a   Disciplines of Authors (All Studies)

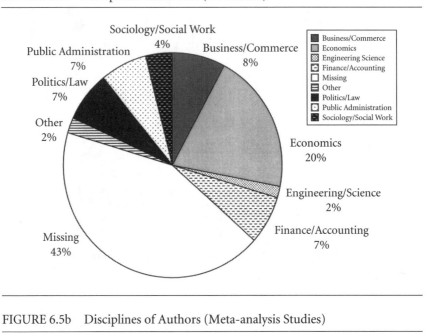

FIGURE 6.5b   Disciplines of Authors (Meta-analysis Studies)

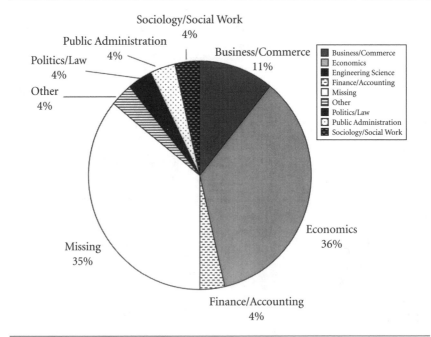

sented professions in reporting empirical findings were Sociology/Social Work and Engineering/Science, at 4 percent and 2 percent respectively. Other professions together made up less than 2 percent. Again, the distribution of disciplines behind those studies to be included in the meta-analysis appeared to be broadly similar.[12]

Comparing this information on disciplines behind the empirical research into contracting, a few tentative comments might be made. Firstly, the findings seem to be coming from a different mix of disciplines from the performance framework established in Table 4.5. Secondly, the disciplines presenting these empirical findings are also quite different from the local government people actually involved in delivering local services. Many of the local government services are engineering, production oriented, or in the human/health services area, and yet these groups appear to be the least well represented in empirical work.[13]

Next, the disciplines behind the contracting research are likely to follow very closely the established performance norms for each discipline. Thus, economists are likely to concentrate on economic/financial aspects of performance—whereas the sociologist's concerns are likely to be found in the more human dimensions of performance. With a preponderance of economists apparently presenting the empirical findings, it is little wonder that the dimensions of performance covered in the studies of contracting seem to be almost entirely economic. Figure 6.6 indicates the performance dimensions covered in these studies. Out of the 278 empirical results for all performance dimensions covered in the literature, clearly the economic dimension dominated.[14] While economists may view this as the only important dimension involved in this reform option for government, it is certainly not the only one. It operates alongside all others, not as a dominant perspective but as a contributory one.

Lastly, we should be aware that those making judgments tend to do so from their own training grounds. The economist may therefore concentrate on production economics and costs, and the engineer on infrastructure standards and long-term system integrity. Any decision on privatization as contracting out will require a balance of these perspectives.

As a point of interest, a note was made of the sector generally favored by each report as it was read. This required some personal judgment on my part, and is acknowledged. Figure 6.7 indicates the relative proportions of studies generally favoring one or another sector for production of services. My reading of the literature would place the edge with the private sector, but with an almost equally strong number indicating no particular favor toward one sector or another, or perhaps being ambiguous. A smaller proportion solely favored the public sector alone for the production of services.[15]

As noted previously, these privatization studies covered a wide range of sophistication in terms of the design and the statistical control of variables other than the ownership variable. The studies were coded in terms of the assessed degree of research sophistication for possible later analysis.

FIGURE 6.6a   Empirical Performance Dimensions Reported (All Studies)

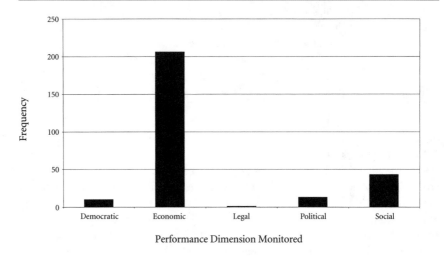

Performance Dimension Monitored

FIGURE 6.6b   Empirical Performance Dimensions Reported (Meta-analysis Studies)

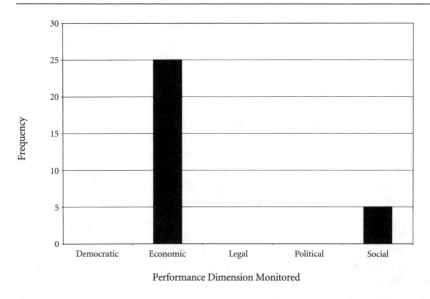

Performance Dimension Monitored

FIGURE 6.7a   Sector Generally Favored by Report (All Studies)

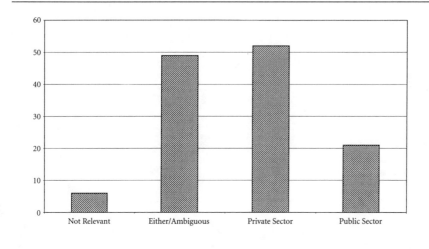

FIGURE 6.7b   Sector Generally Favored by Report (Meta-analysis Studies)

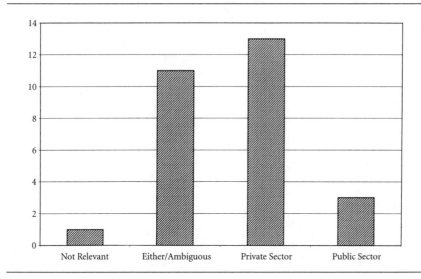

7

Reviewing the Effectiveness of Privatization as Contracting Out

I argued in the previous chapter that a meta-analysis can be utilized for combining and contrasting quantitative empirical findings from privatization. Dimensions of a more qualitative nature are less amenable to the techniques of meta-analysis. In this chapter, a review of privatization as contracting out is conducted for all dimensions of performance, firstly using the traditional narrative review method and then, where possible, adopting the meta-analytic perspective.

The framework that was established in Chapter 4 will be used as the foundation on which to assess the performance of privatization. This framework included the five performance dimensions of economic objectives, social objectives, impacts on democratic processes, legal aspects, and political performance. Each of these dimensions provide a contextual background of community expectations and values. Against this, the available empirical evidence, whether case study or statistical, will be analyzed. Where possible, both narrative and meta-analytic techniques will be adopted, so that robust conclusions on the performance of privatization can be developed.

A LOOK AT THE EMPIRICAL FINDINGS

We noted previously that one option in any review is to go systematically through all of the available literature. This philosophy enables the reviewer to summarize findings, review study design characteristics, comment on the veracity of the conclusions reached, and discuss potential applications to the reviewer's context. With 129 empirical studies found, however, this would produce a mind-numbing list!

An alternative approach might be to observe firstly that we have in these findings, not every possible finding ever made in this area—since that would be an impossibility, despite the care taken in the searching process—but a reasonable sample. However, I would not usually expect to try to obtain an overview of what's going on in a single study by reviewing in detail each single data point in the sample. Indeed, with a sample of empirical findings of this size, I should not expect to do so in this review! An alternative approach might therefore be to describe, say graphically, the overall range and distribution of findings that are in this sample. Although this type of overview has its own limitations, it at least enables an appreciation of the whole sample to be achieved. The review perspective being adopted here is that of level 1 in Figure 6.1 of Chapter 6.

Using this philosophy, my initial focus will concentrate on one particular dimension of the findings—the most commonly reported statistic—the claimed savings compared to the previous form of service provision. Other dimensions will be discussed more fully later. If all reported findings on cost savings in the full literature were taken at face value, a distribution of results would be evident. With an interest in a range of possible contracting options (i.e., contracting out/outsourcing/competitive tendering/compulsory contracting/in-house contracting, etc.) the face-value results were categorized in terms of which sector was contracting to which sector.

Figure 7.1 shows the distribution of reported findings for contracting from the public sector to the private sector. Some 135 instances were discovered of cost-savings estimates in this category. The average face value cost saving claimed was around 14 percent. The reported contracting savings varied from a low of +290 percent (i.e., an increased cost) in the case of some information costs, to a saving of 80 percent in the case of meter-reading services for a water supply utility.[1] Reported findings for contracting from the public sector to the public sector or from the private sector to the private sector were much fewer in number. Twenty-

FIGURE 7.1   Distribution of Reported Cost-savings Estimates

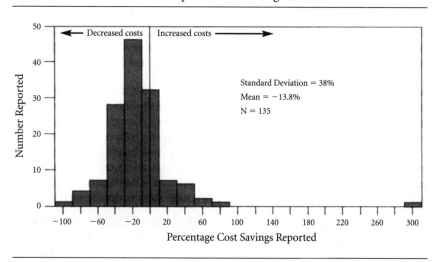

Standard Deviation = 38%
Mean = −13.8%
N = 135

four instances of "public to public" contracting were found, and nine instances of "private to private" contracting.[2] Table 7.1 shows the summary of these distributions of face-value findings.[3]

From this table, it is observed that cost savings appear to have been reported across all three options for contracting. In other words, the contracting of public services—whether being to the private sector or public sector—has led to savings claims. Likewise, when private sector services were contracted to other private organizations, savings were again reported.

Of some note is also the observation that fourteen studies reported cost savings from mechanisms other than direct contracting. Typical examples of these included the following:

- Direct competition (from, say, the threat to contract out services) which resulted in in-house teams reducing the cost of services
- Service-cost reductions due to the close proximity of other agencies who themselves engaged in competitive tendering
- The act of specifying the work to be done in the form of a contract

Apparently, reforms coming in many shapes and sizes may well result in cost savings.

Accompanying this initial impression of the cost savings estimates, some major limitations must be raised. Firstly, this type of review clearly does not differentiate those rigorous and carefully controlled studies undertaken from the back of the envelope guesstimates or those announcements designed more as a good news corporate press release. Indeed, all estimates of cost savings are treated as equally reliable. The good news press release is equal in reliability to the sophisticated study. Secondly, this type of review also does not take into account the fact that different studies had different sample sizes. Thus, the anecdote with a sample size of one is effectively treated the same as the study with one thousand observations. For these reasons, the characteristics of mean and standard deviation shown in Table 7.1 would not be regarded seriously. They have no real statistical veracity.

TABLE 7.1   Summary of Empirical Cost Savings Presented in the Contracting Literature

Sectors Contracting	*Number of Cost Savings Estimates*	*Average (%)*	*Standard Deviation (%)*
1 From public sector to private sector	135	14	38
2 From public sector to public sector	24	22	14
3 From private sector to private sector	9	18	14
4 Other mechanisms	14	13	10

These shortcomings can, however, be overcome by adopting a more formal (higher level) review approach.

Clearly, this book cannot look comprehensively at all performance dimensions for all services within all of the 129 recorded studies. In the next two sections, I will therefore focus on a narrative review of one specific service—refuse collection—as an illustration of some key methodological issues that need to be noted as part of a narrative approach. I will then attempt a broader narrative review of contracting out different types of public sector services. Following this, a meta-analysis will be undertaken of these services.

SOME KEY HISTORICAL AND METHODOLOGICAL HIGHLIGHTS: REFUSE COLLECTION

It is not my intention here to revisit all major studies on refuse collection. It is nonetheless instructive to focus on some of the work undertaken that would normally be regarded as omnibus work. Studying this enables us to gain an appreciation of some of the most widely known pieces of research in this area. It helps us to appreciate the requirements of research studies if findings are to be regarded as having reasonable integrity.

Early work from the United States on contracting clearly saw this mechanism as a central plank for the privatization movement. Indeed, the very close association of contracting with the word "privatization" in the U.S. is testament to the notion that the early motives behind contracting to the private sector were more likely to be of a political nature rather than economic.

By far the most famous work on the costs of production under contract conditions in either the public or private sectors has been in the area of refuse collection and disposal. An example of an early study produced in this area, and having impressive and appealing results, is that by Bennett and Johnson (1979). These two economists compared the costs of collection in the state of Virginia. In their words, "the contention that the private sector should be more efficient than the public sector is confirmed." In Fairfax County, where private firms compete for each customer's business, it was found that of the twenty-nine private firms operating, all but one charged less than the Solid Waste Division of the county. The difference was marked—at $127 per year for municipal collection versus an average of $87 per year for the private companies. Bennett and Johnson adopted an array of statistical tests to show that this difference was statistically significant, and could not have arisen simply by chance. As Donahue (1989, p. 60) points out, however, although this analysis is conceptually plausible and suffered from no calculation errors, it is a good deal less convincing than the authors assert.

The key problem is that they simply average all the private costs, average all the public costs, and compare the two numbers. This analysis does not control for distance from the dump, dispersal of households served, quality and frequency of service, and other factors aside from organisational form.

These concerns are not simply academic whining. Donahue notes that Hirsch (1965) had apparently earlier examined twenty-four communities in St. Louis, Missouri, and found that costs were affected by the frequency of pickups (costs increased by 25 percent for three weekly pickups rather than two), and the pickup location (where it was 33 percent more expensive for collection at the back of the house rather than at the curb). They were also surprised not to find population density a significant variable as well, since the shorter distance between pickup sites would, one assumes, have led to lower transport costs, other things being equal. Hirsch found that, contrary to Bennett and Johnson, the difference between public and private efficiency was not statistically significant.

Savas, who was to go on to become one of the most ardent promoters of privatization in the U.S., followed these studies with further analysis. Looking at 1,378 U.S. communities, and controlling for scale, organizational form, and pickup point, his results were as shown in Table 7.2.

Savas found that if the municipality contracted with private firms for refuse collection, it was 9 percent cheaper than their own provision. However, private competitive arrangements were a third more expensive than the local government service. The importance of ensuring collection route contiguity in refuse collection was evident here. In the context of this current review, these results demonstrate the importance of controlling for these types of variables, if possible, to ensure a rigorous research study. Savas has published extensively in this area, and much of his material is liberally spiced with political rhetoric.

Many other studies could be noted as having followed this work. Mention of only two will be made here. In the U.K., another team of economists (Domberger, Meadowcroft, and Thompson 1986) studied the possible influence of competitive tendering on the production cost of the local government refuse collection service. Their analysis of 610 authorities through 1983–84 revealed cost differentials of 22 percent when contracting was being undertaken with the private sector, and 17 percent when the service was tendered but retained in-house. Controls for a wide

TABLE 7.2   Service Provision Costs Under Public and Various Private
Arrangements

Organizational Form	Cost Per Ton
Public	$28.28
Private: Contract	$25.78
Private: Franchise	$28.23
Private: Competitive	$38.54

SOURCE: Savas 1977b

range of variables were present. Domberger's cost equations are outlined in Table 7.3, where a full listing of results is also indicated.

Of importance here is the fact that each t statistic indicates the relative strength of the association between the cost of collection and each variable. The bigger the t statistic, the stronger and more certain is the relationship. Also, the cost impact

TABLE 7.3   Cost Equations Illustrating the Statistical Controls Adopted and Detailed Results for the Analysis of Domberger, Meadowcroft, and Thompson 1986

| | | OLS Results | |
Variable	Description	Coefficient	t Statistic
CONSTANT		−2.76	−3.97
UNITS	Number of units	1.04	54.94
WAGE	Average earnings	0.90	7.51
FREQ1	More than once a week	0.0065	10.62
FREQ2	Less than once a week	−0.0036	−2.78
METH1	Curbside	−0.0026	−10.88
METH2	Other collect and return	−0.0012	−2.45
METH3	Skip or other normal method	−0.00071	−2.68
METH4	Special collections	0.00030	0.16
DEN	Density of units	−0.015	−1.88
DISP	Average distance to disposal	−0.028	1.87
HOUS	Percentage of units that are domestic households	−0.43	−5.28
RECLAIM1	Reclaimed paper	0.000073	4.27
RECLAIM2	Abandoned vehicles	0.000087	1.44
RECLAIM3	Bottlebanks	−0.00037	−0.31
CONTRACT	Privately contracted	−0.25	−7.66
TEND	Tendered but retained in-house	−0.19	−4.52
	Number in Sample	610	
	$\underline{R}^2$	0.927	
	R^2	0.925	

Through regression analysis, the economist team Domberger, Meadowcroft, and Thompson isolated the determinants of the cost of refuse collection. The "cost function" adopted for the analysis was as follows:

Log C = a_1 + $a_2$logUNITS + $a_3$logWAGE + a_4FREQ1 + a_5FREQ2 + a_6METH1 + a_7METH2 + a_8METH3 + a_9METH4 + a_{10}logDEN + a_{11}logDISP + a_{12}logHOUS + a_{13}RECLAIM1 + a_{14}RECLAIM2 + a_{15}RECLAIM3 + a_{16}CONTRACT + a_{17}TEND + e

This Cobb-Douglas formulation of the production function implies that the cost of production is a function of the level of output, the frequency of pickup, input wage costs, the method of collection, the density of housing, the distance to disposal, the proportion that is domestic, the extent of reclamation of paper and bottles, and whether after tendering, the collection is undertaken by in-house or external private companies. The regression results were as shown here.

of a variable, such as the cost savings from contracting in-house, for instance, can be gauged by calculating the impact of each individual coefficient on the collection cost.

Finding that the cost difference between the "contracted out" and "contracted in" arrangement was not statistically significant, Domberger, Meadowcroft, and Thompson concluded that both resulted in cost reductions "of around 20 percent." This is the origin of the now much quoted "20 percent cost reduction rule" used as a basis for contracting out and competitive tendering in public sector policy.

Work one year later by Domberger, Meadowcroft, and Thompson on hospital domestic, cleaning, and laundry services (1987) also lent support to their earlier work. Here, it was found that the cost of production was 34 percent less when services were contracted out after tendering, and 22 percent less if services were tendered and then retained in-house. The sample size was large, at some 2,947 contracts. Domberger, Meadowcroft, and Thompson saw these further results as consistent with their 20 percent rule for achieving cost reductions through competitive contracting.

Since these key studies, data on contracting in the United Kingdom have been analyzed on several other occasions, including, for example, Szymanski and Wilkins (1993) and Buck and Chaundy (1992). These authors have found results broadly consistent with the earlier findings. Some recent case studies, such as that of Jensen (1990), have also provided contrasting evidence by showing that the public sector under some circumstances can provide superior performance. Jensen's study yielded cost savings of 33.9 percent in Phoenix, Arizona, compared to alternative private sector bidders.

These key findings on refuse collection are significant in that they illustrate the largest body of findings for any service in the literature. They are typical of the types of discussions and debates, with much of the data originating in the U.S. or U.K. They are atypical, however, in that there is much more data available than there is for other services.

NARRATIVE REVIEW OF CONTRACTING OUT PUBLIC SECTOR SERVICES

Looking at studies of contracting out for all service types, the focus now is on only those studies with a reasonable research integrity. A listing of such studies is provided in Table 7.4. This table presents highlights from the findings of these studies along with other important study parameters.[4] Around three dozen studies are listed here and are broadly considered representative of all. The country studied, the level of government, and type of service contracted, along with the general conclusions reached, are all detailed.

It is clear that the body of empirical literature itself is large. As a consequence of the amount of evidence available and the presence of many interest groups on

TABLE 7.4 Summary of Key International Empirical Findings on Contracting Out

Study	Country/Activity	Change in costs (%)	Change in Quality	Comments
Kemper and Quigley 1976[b]	Over 100 U.S. cities, refuse collection	Contracting saved 20%		Private (individual) collection was 30% more expensive than municipal, but contracted collection was 20% cheaper than municipal collection.
Savas 1977a	315 U.S. cities in 1975, four functions	-15 to -29	improved	Random sample of cities, savings obtained when public and private sector won contract. Regression showed cost savings greatest for largest cities.
Edwards and Stevens 1978	77 U.S. cities in 1975, refuse collection	-10 to -41		Employed econometric and regression models, savings greater for largest cities.
Savas 1980[b]	206 U.S. cities, refuse collection	Contracting saved 20%		Price of private collection 22% less than municipal costs.
Berenyi 1981	10 U.S. local councils, 1971-77, refuse collection	-7 to -50	none	Cost reduction obtained when either private or public sector won contract.
Kramer and Terrell 1984	81 local councils, social and welfare services in San Francisco area, 1980-81	Usually reduced		Changes in costs not quantified.
Stevens 1984[b]	121 U.S. cities, and eight services in Los Angeles area in 1980	up to 49% cost reduction	quality maintained	Multiple regression analysis. Savings varied with payroll preparation at the lowest, and asphalt overlay construction at the highest.
Folz 1985[b]	Productivity is analyzed in 14 U.S. cities	not quantified		Costs reduced for one group of the two analyzed. The productivity of cities that contract out (to either government or private sectors) is higher than those that do not.
Mehay and Gonzalez 1985	53 local council and county governments in U.S., in the early 1980s, three functions	-9 to -20		Study of contracting between levels of government, based on multiple regression analysis.
McDavid 1985	126 local councils in Canada, refuse collection	-24 to -29 +28 to -68		Multiple regression, cost reductions usually larger when contract won by private sector rather than mix of private and public contractor.
Hartley and Huby 1986	213 U.K. local government councils and National Health Services	Averaged -26, +28 to -68	reduced in 25% of cases	Based on a 1985 survey with 57% response rate, data and methodology sound.
Domberger, Meadowcroft, and Thompson 1986	Refuse collection by 305 local councils in the U.K., in 1983-84	-20	no change	Multiple regression, change in cost per ton.
Millward 1986	103 local councils in Switzerland, 1970, refuse collection	-20		Employed multiple regression analysis.
Pirie 1986	55 local councils in U.K., several functions	-20 to -40		Based on survey, but unclear whether sample was representative.

Study	Description	Cost change (%)	Other findings	Notes
Domberger, Meadowcroft, and Thompson 1987	Domestic services in a sample of over 2,000 U.K. hospitals functions	−20 to −30		Multiple regression analysis employed.
Feldman 1987[b]	Costs for 68 bus transit firms in the U.S.	"weak evidence"		Weak evidence only is found for greater private efficiency. Contracting is unlikely to result in signficant cost savings.
Moore 1987	U.S. federal government defense and air traffic control, early to mid-1980s	−30 to −50		Review by U.S. Administration of Defense contracts and air traffic control operations.
Confederation of British Industry 1988	Range of U.K. central government, National Health Service and local governments in mid-1980s	−17 to −28		Cost reductions 23% for central government, 17% National Health Service and 28% local government.
Hensher 1987	London buses in the mid-1980s	Averaged −20		Change in costs compared to public monopoly levels prior to competitive tendering.
Carver 1989[b]	Property tax assessment service for 100 local communities in Massachusetts, in 1976–85	+24% more expensive		Multiple regression analysis, controlling for population.
Mennenmeyer and Olinger 1989[b]	Hospital care for Medicaid patients, 267 hospitals in California in early 1980s	−10 to −23		11% to 23% price concessions were achieved by contracting.
Pack 1989	15 U.S. councils, several functions from early to mid-1980s	−5 to −60	33% of councils dissatisfied	Initial cost reductions of −5 to −60% declined over a five-year period.
Evatt Research Centre 1990	460 local councils in Australia, 1989, large number of functions	Usually increased	Usually reduced	Based on observations of survey respondents.
Harding 1990[b]	Bus transport in U.S. schools	+18 to −35	none	Two statistical models produced mixed findings.
Rimmer and Webb 1990	127 local councils in Australia, 1986, three functions	−10 to −24		Difference in average costs between councils using CTC and those using in-house provision.
Holcombe 1991[b]	Seven privatization agreements for wastewater treatment operations reviewed, 1980s	Contracts more expensive		After controlling for other factors, theoretical benefits of contracting are not passed onto clients.
Rehfuss 1991[b]	Several case studies in U.S. during 1980s	−19 to −65		Competition, not contracting, is seen as the driver of efficiencies.
Walsh 1991	Survey of 40 U.K. local councils, in 1989–90, several functions	Averaged −6 to −7, +6 to −17		Government-supported study, high-quality data, change in costs after one year of compulsory CTC.
Albin 1992	58 cities in Australia in 1990–91, functions not specified	Usually reduced	none	Bivariate regression analysis, cost reductions not quantified.

(continues)

TABLE 7.4 *continued*

Study	Country/Activity	Change in costs (%)	Change in Quality	Comments
Domberger et al. 1993	65 state government agencies in Australia in 1993, several functions	−4 to −51		Cost reductions vary according to function, with building and vehicle maintenance yielding the highest savings, whilst transport and catering produced less savings.
Martin and Stein 1993[b]	Total spending on seven functions over 877 cities in U.S.	−44% to +28%		Although contracting reduces employment, reductions in total spending for the same functions were not found.
Paddon 1993a[b]	Review of U.K. and Europe experience	Mixed findings		Savings are not guaranteed, and quality and accountability are problems.
Rimmer 1993	327 local councils in Australia, several functions	Commonly no change		Multiple regression, some cost reductions in city councils but not in rural.
Savas 1993[b]	Many U.S. and international studies reviewed	−28 to −50, and −37%		Savings quoted were between 28 and 50% (before and after studies), 33% (time series studies), and 37% from the threat of contracting out.
Farago and Domberger 1994	Survey of government business enterprises, 1993	−8 to −46		Enterprises providing gas, water, electricity, and sewerage services.
Greene 1994[b]	Productivity ratios for 70 U.S. cities in late 1980s, six functions	Mixed findings		Mixed findings provided little support to suggest that efficiency was higher in cities that used private firms to provide public services.
Centre for Public Services 1995a[b]	General review of U.K. experience in contracting.	n.a.		Contracted services resulted in corruption and secret business influence in government.
Domberger, Hall, and Li 1994	61 contracts for cleaning services in Australia.	A 13% increase to a 54% cost decrease	7% decrease to 36% improvement	Competitive tendering reduces prices and raises the performance of contractors. The influence of ownership is negligible.

NOTES: [a]Adapted from Domberger and Rimmer (1994)
[b]Additional key studies from current review

the topic, it is quite possible for selective reading of the literature to produce an impressive array of evidence favoring one side or the other.

ECONOMIC PERFORMANCE

Most of the evidence presented by contracting out and competitive tendering studies relates to economic efficiency in one form or another. There is little doubt the weight of evidence appears to support the notion that on average the unit costs of services are reduced through competitive tendering of public services. Many of the empirical studies having strong research design integrity also support the notion that contracting saves costs, including, for example: Domberger, Meadowcroft, and Thompson (1986, 1987), Domberger et al. (1993), Savas (1977a), McDavid (1985), and Millward (1986). It is therefore no real surprise that the major international review of Domberger and Rimmer (1994) concluded after reviewing two decades of contracting experience that competitive tendering and contracting "usually leads to substantial reductions in service costs." They went further and concluded that such gains appeared to be consistent over this period of time, throughout all of the countries reviewed, and over all levels of government.

Mind you, the commonly reported conclusion of service-cost reductions with competitive contracting is in one way not surprising at all. Since we are presumably accepting those contract bids that are lower than the alternatives, we would expect, all other things being equal, that those contracts for which the best price was achieved from external bidders would indeed deliver lower prices (by definition) than the internal costs that had not been subject to competitive bidding or else had lost the bidding process. Thus, the United States General Accounting Office (USGAO) (1994a) reports that the private sector bid "winners" had 39 percent lower costs than the alternative in-house bids, whilst at the same time the private sector bid "losers" had costs 33 percent more than the alternative winning in-house bids! If the sample was based simply on the contracts in which the private sector won contracts, it would not be surprising to find that "contracting out saved 39 percent." Such a finding would need careful interpretation, however, since it would not reflect any inherent lower public sector productivity, but rather would be more a reflection of the value of competition through a contract tendering or bidding process. Alternatively, if the research was based only on the in-house winners, it would not be surprising to find that "contracting out, if pursued would have resulted in 33 percent higher costs"! The point here is that careful statistical control is necessary in order to ascertain the behavior of production costs in a systematic way. Costs may vary systematically with, first, the action of contracting per se (and in the main, the introduction of competition), and, second, with the sector undertaking the work.

The existence of savings on contracting appears to occur for both contracting of services direct to the customer, such as with the common case of either cleaning or refuse collection, and in those instances where contracts are taken on by an agency, for example to provide hospital services on behalf of, say, the Federal

Government (Mennemeyer and Olinger 1989). Again, savings across most types of services seem to occur on the face of it, though a remarkable range of cost impacts also appear to have been documented for individual services. Cost savings for services appear to vary from a general +28 percent cost increase (Hartley and Huby 1986), to a large −49 percent cost decrease for the case of asphalt road construction services (Berenyi and Stevens 1988), where public sector provision was found to be an incredible 96 percent more expensive. Much of the evidence and careful study appears to relate to services such as refuse collection and cleaning, however, and although most studies find that cost savings are possible on average through contracting, the extent to which these savings accord with Domberger, Meadowcroft, and Thompson's 20 percent rule has been unclear. Recent work led by Domberger has broadened the applicability of the cost savings notion. These studies (Domberger et al. 1993, Domberger, Hall, and Li 1995) have been undertaken across several levels of government, but have again pointed to cost savings of around 20 percent, for a whole range of different services.

Having made this general observation of the literature, it also has to be said that the empirical evidence on cost savings from contracting out is by no means unanimous. Several studies such as Rimmer (1993), Feldman (1987), Greene (1994), and McEntee (1985) argue that there is no difference in costs with contracting. Others point to cost increases (Holcombe 1991, Evatt Research Centre 1990, Milne 1987), or issues such as corruption (Gewirtz 1987, Folz 1985, Finder 1993, Centre for Public Services 1995a, and Kobrak 1995). I will return to these issues later.

An interesting point is the result that savings occur through competitive contracting across a wide range of possible arrangements. Savings appear to have been found for contracting irrespective of whether the contract arrangement is from the public to private sector, from the private to private sector, from the public to other public sector bodies, or from the public sector to in-house production teams.

Cost savings noted for private sector companies outsourcing to other private sector companies are quoted in references such as Ambrioso (1992), Slater (1992), and Pack (1992), to name three. Cost savings obtained were quoted as being between 10 and 60 percent, but Pack's statistical study suggested a range of between 15 and 45 percent, and is likely to be more reliable. Furthermore, cost savings from in-house production teams appears to vary from the 17 to 22 percent found by Domberger, Meadowcroft, and Thompson (1986, 1987), but can be as high as 38 percent based on several years of competitive contracting experience in Phoenix, as noted by Jensen (1990). Finally, contracting from one public sector agency to another is not a well known practice. Nevertheless, where it has been studied it appears to have resulted in benefits in terms of cost savings. Savings of 9 percent have been suggested from intergovernmental contracting (Mehay and Gonzalez 1993).

Hence, it appears to be possible to achieve savings through competition and through the careful construction of specifications to form a contract for future work. The mechanisms of both outsourcing and insourcing can be used for this. The role of competition here cannot be overstated. Even the threat of competition from external contractors is reported by Savas (1993, p. 45) in the case of the U.S. Department of Defense to have saved 37 percent of costs compared to the original (in-house) cost of performing the work. McDavid and Schick (1987) also argue this same point—that the threat of contracting out stimulated the same level of savings as actually adopting contracting out. The ability to benchmark internal performance against nearby contractors also appears to be a powerful driver. Domberger, Meadowcroft, and Thompson (1987) indicate that when hospitals in the U.K. did not tender, but were merely adjacent to those that did, costs were 7 percent lower (and statistically significant at the .005 level) than they would otherwise have been. Likewise, Mehay and Gonzalez (1993) similarly point to cost savings of 12 percent for areas not directly subject to the threat of competition but adjacent to areas in which competition is occurring. These savings were again assessed as statistically significant at the .005 level.

The extent to which costs are saved through each one of these particular mechanisms is not certain, but it appears that savings are greatest through contracting outside the organization. How have such efficiencies been achieved? The better-designed studies, such as Domberger, Meadowcroft, and Thompson (1986), appear to indicate that the largest influence on greater efficiency is enhanced flexibility of the workforce—not reductions in working conditions and salaries as has sometimes been advanced by unions. Anecdotal evidence such as that presented by the Centre for Public Services (1995a) indicates that instances where savings are made at the expense of salaries and working conditions do occur; however, this does not appear to have been borne out as a widespread practice in the larger survey work.

Past this, though, several cost-savings issues remain uncertain. For example, do the cost savings measured on individual contracts actually result in lower overall costs to government, and in turn lower overall costs through rate reductions to the community? The first point here is that there may well be greater monitoring and supervision costs associated with contracting out. Rarely are such costs measured. Reported estimates of the costs of monitoring contract specifications and contract completion vary from around 2 or 3 percent (from Department of Treasury and Finance 1997 and Savas 1977a) up to as high as 20 percent from Osborne and Gaebler's classic 1993 book *Reinventing Government*. The reliability of these estimates is also unknown, but is assumed to be low. Typical estimates documented in the literature would be at the lower end of this range. We might posit that the cost of developing specifications, contract preparation, and organizing for contracting processes would be in the vicinity of, say, at least 2 percent of the total contract amount (LGIU 1994). Some proportion of the costs of developing and monitoring contracts is likely to be needed even if the provision of services is not subject to tendering, of course, but this amount has not been specified in general. The lack of this type of information puts in doubt the accuracy of service delivery cost savings under contracting.

The second issue here is that, although the logic of reduced direct costs through contracts should, all other things being equal, mean reduced costs overall to the government, there is a worrying lack of evidence supporting this. Indeed, the recent U.S. review of Martin and Stein (1993) and the Australian review of Albin (1992) actually found evidence of the opposite. Both of these reports found that the cost savings through contracts were not passed on to the community but were apparently absorbed through greater numbers of management positions and other rewards to the organization.

On a broader scale, the Centre for Public Services (1995b) also addresses the question of whether reduced direct costs through councils results in lower overall costs to government as a whole. It estimated that local contracting-out cost savings in the U.K. of £16.4 million were also accompanied by greater national unemployment costs of £24.4 million, resulting in a negative net benefit. This is in direct contradiction to Moore (1986, p. 68), who asserts, without supporting details, that the U.S. Department of Defense experience points to "fewer than 5 percent" of workers being left without jobs after contracting out, and that their "public assistance payments" of US$0.2 million would have little effect on this department's estimated savings of US$65.5 million. These two conclusions using this broad-scale economic perspective are wildly different. Few other reports on this issue were found.

A further issue associated with increased economic efficiency is the concern that any cost savings initially measured under contracting may evaporate over time. As far as this has been measured in studies, the effect has been found to exist—but not to the extent of fully evaporating the savings (Pack 1989).

The last issue on economic efficiency concerns competition. The need to ensure competition as contracts are being managed is paramount. I shall return to this issue later. Having reviewed in a narrative way the key findings relating to the economic performance of contracting out, I will now move on to conduct a meta-analytic review of this dimension of privatization.

EFFECT SIZES: ECONOMIC PERFORMANCE BY SERVICE

Effect Size Analysis

The foundation of the meta-analytic approach to reviewing past studies is the determination of effect sizes. Effect sizes were calculated for all studies. Table 7.5 shows the overall results for all effect sizes relating to economic performance. Included in this category were both "cost" measures, one measure of financial improvement (return on assets), and several "productivity" estimates. This table also indicates the weighted mean effect size for all economic performance measurements, and for each service category. To obtain the weighted mean effect size, all effect sizes were weighted by their respective sample sizes, thus placing a relatively greater weight on larger sample sizes.[5] Figure 7.2 presents a histogram of all economic performance effect-size estimates. The negative effect sizes on the left

TABLE 7.3   Economic Effect Sizes and Confidence Limits for Studies of Contracting Out

Study	N	Est. r	Zc	Wtd Av Z	p (wtd)	Min CI	Max CI	Min CI Tot	Max CI Tot	Chi Sqr	Chi Square tot	Sig Level:	Unwtd Av Z	p(unwtd)
All Economic Measures	20131			−0.11	0.0000	−0.12	−0.09	−0.12	−0.09		394.21	<0.005	−0.24	0.0000
Cost	20030			−0.11	0.0000	−0.12	−0.09	−0.12	−0.09		378.30	<0.005	−0.26	0.0000
Cleaning	6067			−0.11	0.0000			−0.14	−0.09		62.57	<0.005	−0.49	0.0000
Berenyi and Stevens (1988)	20	−0.47	−0.51			−0.99	−0.04			2.72				
Berenyi and Stevens (1988)	20	−0.68	−0.82			−1.30	−0.35			8.50				
Domberger, Meadowcroft, and Thompson (1987)	2947	−0.16	−0.16			−0.19	−0.12			5.50				
Domberger, Hall & Li (1994)	61	−0.26	−0.27			−0.52	−0.01			1.35				
UK Audit Office (1987)	18	−0.68	−0.83			−1.33	−0.32			7.66				
Domberger, Meadowcroft, and Thompson (1987)	2947	−0.05	−0.05			−0.08	−0.01			13.60				
UK Audit Office (1987)	54	−0.66	−0.79			−1.06	−0.51			23.23				
Corporate	120			0.19	0.0416			0.01	0.37		0.29	>0.50	0.14	0.0996
Berenyi and Stevens (1988)	20	0.07	0.07			−0.41	0.55			0.25				
Carver (1989)	100	0.21	0.21			0.01	0.41			0.04				
Engineering Works	889			−0.09	0.0088			−0.15	−0.02		0.02	<0.75	−0.06	0.0526
Greene (1994)	12	−0.04	−0.04			−0.69	0.61			0.02				
Martin and Stein (1993)	877	−0.09	−0.09			−0.15	−0.02			0.00				
Fire	12			−0.26	0.4361			−0.91	0.39				−0.26	0.3922
Greene (1994)	12	−0.25	−0.26			−0.91	0.39			0.00				
Health	877			0.03	0.3988			−0.04	0.09				0.03	0.4016
Martin and Stein (1993)	877	0.03	0.03			−0.04	0.09			0.00				
Maintenance	60			−0.56	0.0001			−0.83	−0.28		0.23	>0.75	−0.56	0.0000
Berenyi and Stevens (1988)	20	−0.57	−0.65			−1.12	−0.17			0.14				
Berenyi and Stevens (1988)	20	−0.49	−0.53			−1.01	−0.06			0.01				
Berenyi and Stevens (1988)	20	−0.45	−0.49			−0.96	−0.01			0.08				
Multiple	523			−0.17	0.0001			−0.26	−0.08		5.27	<0.10	−0.55	0.0000
Ascher (1987)	15	−0.57	−0.65			−1.22	−0.09			2.80				
Ascher (1987)	8	−0.69	−0.85			−1.73	0.03			2.30				
Ferris (1988)	500	−0.15	−0.15			−0.24	−0.06			0.17				
Other	909			−0.01	0.7330			−0.08	0.05		17.94	<0.005	−0.25	0.2623
Berenyi and Stevens (1988)	20	−0.77	−1.01			−1.49	−0.54			17.00				
Greene (1994)	12	0.26	0.27			−0.39	0.92			0.70				
Martin and Stein (1993)	877	0.01	0.01			−0.06	0.07			0.24				
Parks/Recreation	889			0.06	0.0567			0.00	0.13		4.94	<0.05	−0.30	0.9896
Greene (1994)	12	−0.59	−0.67			−1.33	−0.02			4.89				
Martin and Stein (1993)	877	0.07	0.07			0.01	0.14			0.05				
Police/Security	889			−0.03	0.4423			−0.09	0.04		0.49	<.25	−0.14	0.2768
Greene (1994)	12	−0.25	−0.26			−0.91	0.40			0.48				
Martin and Stein (1993)	877	−0.02	−0.02			−0.09	0.04			0.00				
Refuse	6045			−0.22	0.0000			−0.25	−0.20		74.21	<0.005	−0.33	0.0000
Albin (1992)	58	−0.19	−0.19			−0.46	0.07			0.04				
Berenyi and Stevens (1988)	20	−0.72	−0.91			−1.38	−0.43			7.97				
Buck and Chaundy (1992)	329	−0.39	−0.41			−0.52	−0.30			11.11				

(*continues*)

TABLE 7.5   continued

Study	N	Est. r	Zc	Wtd Av Z	p (wtd)	Min CI	Max CI	Min CI Tot	Max CI Tot	Chi Sqr	Chi Square tot	Sig Level:	Unwtd Av Z	p(unwtd)
Domberger, Meadowcroft, and Thompson (1986)	610	−0.30	−0.31			−0.39	−0.23			4.59				
Domberger, Meadowcroft, and Thompson (1986)	610	−0.18	−0.18			−0.26	−0.11			0.88				
Greene (1994)	12	−0.09	−0.09			−0.75	0.56			0.15				
Kemper & Quigley (1976)	129	−0.25	−0.26			−0.43	−0.08			0.14				
Kitchen (1976)	48	−0.80	−1.09			−1.38	−0.80			33.88				
Pommerehne and Frey (1977)	103	−0.41	−0.44			−0.63	−0.24			4.54				
Szymanski and Wilkins (1993)	1460	−0.21	−0.21			−0.26	−0.16			0.25				
Szymanski (1993)	386	−0.21	−0.22			−0.32	−0.12			0.02				
Szymanski (1993)	217	−0.12	−0.12			−0.26	0.01			2.19				
Szymanski and Wilkins (1993)	1460	−0.16	−0.16			−0.21	−0.11			6.14				
Szymanski (1993)	386	−0.21	−0.21			−0.31	−0.11			0.03				
Szymanski (1993)	217	−0.12	−0.12			−0.25	0.01			2.27				
Training	913			−0.04	0.2827			−0.10	0.03		0.10	<.75	−0.01	0.4816
Berglund (1992)	36	0.02	0.02			−0.32	0.36			0.10				
Martin and Stein (1993)	877	−0.04	−0.04			−0.1	0.03			0.00				
Transport	1745			0.03	0.2031			−0.02	0.08		5.31	<.25	0.07	0.1863
Bails (1979)	437	−0.02	−0.02			−0.12	0.07			1.28				
Feldman (1987)	68	0.24	0.24			0.00	0.49			2.91				
Harding (1990)	363	−0.01	−0.01			−0.11	0.10			0.50				
Martin and Stein (1993)	877	0.06	0.06			−0.01	0.12			0.62				
Water Treatment														
Holcombe (1991)	32	0.40	0.43	0.43	0.0221	0.06	0.79	0.06	0.79	0.00			0.43	0.0371
Health														
Wheeler and Zuckerman, Aberholdt (1982)	60	−0.28	−0.29	−0.29	0.0242	−0.55	−0.03	−0.55	−0.03	0.00	15.79	<0.05	−0.29	0.0277
	101			−0.15	0.1976			−0.37	0.08				−0.10	0.4938
Productivity														
Engineering Greene (1994)	12	0.18	0.18	0.18		−0.47	0.83	−0.47	0.83	0.00			0.18	
Fire Greene (1994)	12	0.13	0.13	0.13		−0.53	0.78	−0.53	0.78	0.00			0.13	
Multiple Folz (1985)	14	−0.24	−0.24	−0.24		−0.83	0.35	−0.83	0.35	0.00			−0.24	
Other Greene (1994)	12	0.28	0.28	0.28		−0.37	0.94	−0.37	0.94	0.00			0.28	
Parks/Recreation Greene (1994)	12	0.11	0.11	0.11		−0.54	0.77	−0.54	0.77	0.00			0.11	
Police/Security Greene (1994)	12	−0.30	−0.31	−0.31		−0.97	0.34	−0.97	0.34	0.00			−0.31	
Refuse Greene (1994)	12	0.11	0.11	0.11		−0.54	0.77	−0.54	0.77	0.00			0.11	
Transport Hensher (1989)	15	−0.80	−1.10	−1.10		−1.67	−0.53	−1.67	−0.53	0.00			−1.10	

FIGURE 7.2   Histogram of Effect Sizes for Economic Performance

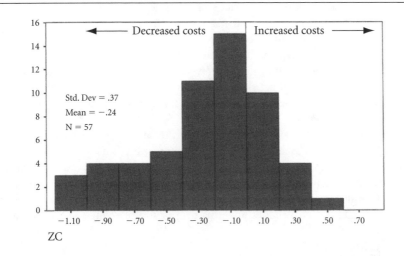

side of the graph represent improved performance (reductions in cost under contracting), whilst those on the right represent worse performance (cost increases under contracting).

Several points are evident. First, the mean effect size for all economic estimates was −0.11. This mean was derived from the 57 economic effect estimates available from the 28 studies, with a combined total sample size of N = 20,131. This mean effect size has confidence limits of (−0.09, −0.12)[6] and is different from zero with a significance level of p < .0001 (Z = 15.187).[7] Hence, overall, global contracting measurements report an average cost reduction.

In Chapter 5, I introduced the concept of "file drawer" studies. This was the number of unreported nonsignificant studies that would be needed to reduce the current meta-analytic results to a significance level of p = .05 or higher. Such a "file-drawer" analysis in this case indicates that a total of some 3,918 unretrieved positive effect sizes (studies showing cost increases) would be needed to reduce the conclusion of an overall cost saving to nonsignificance. Knowing that the appeal for unreported study results in the South Australian local government sector failed to bring out any new result whatsoever, the existence of almost 4,000 studies in file drawers around the world with positive effect sizes is considered unlikely.

A distribution of effect sizes is present nonetheless, albeit that the bulk of the effect sizes are clearly negative. Not all effect sizes were negative, though. Of the 57 effect sizes measuring economic performance—all cost and productivity measures together—42 were negative and 15 positive. A binomial sign test reveals that at better than a p < .0001 level of confidence, this number of negative signs of effect estimates could not have arisen by chance.[8] This further supports the overall contention that contracting usually results in lower costs.

Applying the sign test to different service categories also provides some insight. For cleaning, all seven identified effect sizes were negative. This proportion (7/7) was significant at the .01 level.[9] In the case of refuse collection, all but one of the 16 signs were negative. This proportion (15/16) is again significant, at the .01 level.[10] No other service type had a significant proportion of signs one way or the other at the .05 level, though this is hardly surprising, because most groups had only a small number of effect sizes in the sample.[11] For all other service types taken as a group, the proportion of negative signs found (i.e., 20/34) was likewise not significant at even the .10 level.[12]

These initial results tend to show that in the case of refuse collection and cleaning, contracting has almost certainly resulted in cost savings. The statistical results for these services (even from a robust test like the sign test) are very strong. For other services, however, the sign test has suggested that the effect of contracting has been less certain. Although around two-thirds of results for these other services have found cost reductions, this proportion of reductions could have arisen by chance.

Results from Table 7.5 also deserve comment. We noted that the overall effect of contracting on economic performance was negative—that is, cost savings were reported overall. All economic effect sizes can also be tested to see the extent to which they are homogeneous. To do this, a 2 test is adopted (Rosenthal 1991, p. 74).[13] The chi square result for all economic measures was highly significant ($x^2 = 394.2$, and $p < .005$), and suggests that there are indeed systematic differences between these effect sizes. This is not really surprising since many different studies have been cumulated, these having been sourced internationally, and these also having included different service types. Additionally, these economic effect sizes have also related to two different sets of performance measures, first cost and financial performance, and second productivity.[14]

Looking at the individual effect sizes, the "worst" estimate is an effect size of +0.42 from Holcombe (1991) for the case of providing facilities for waste water treatment. At the other extreme, Kitchen's early work (1976) on refuse collection and Hensher's estimates for public transport productivity in 1989 had (Fisher-corrected) effect sizes of −1.09 and −1.10 respectively.

The mean (weighted) effect size for cleaning was −0.11, with relatively narrow confidence limits −0.09 to −0.14. This was based on a combined sample size of 6,067. All effect sizes were negative, and all were also significantly less than zero. It is therefore not at all surprising that a high level of significance was associated with the cleaning weighted average effect size. Significant heterogeneity was also present in this sample.[15] Thus, overall, cleaning services showed strong cost savings with contracting.

For corporate services, the mean effect size was +0.19 with confidence limits +0.01 to +0.37. Hence, based on this small sample of two (and N = 120), a significant increase in the cost of corporate services under contracting was found. The significance level associated with this average weighted effect size was less than .05, but not .01. This sample was also not heterogeneous.[16] Services defined as corporate here included payroll services from Berenyi and Stevens (1988), and tax assessment services analyzed in Carver (1989).[17]

Engineering works showed a weighted mean effect size of −0.09, and confidence limits of −0.02 to −0.15. This mean effect size was significantly different from zero at a level of .01. The sample included only two studies (N = 889), and did not exhibit significant heterogeneity.[18]

The one single sample (N = 12) of fire services from the United States showed an effect size of −0.26, but with a wide confidence interval (−0.91 to +0.39). This size was therefore not significantly different from zero at .05, indicating no significant cost-savings measurements reported.

Likewise, the one single cost-based health services sample effect size of +0.03 (N = 877) was also not significantly different from zero at a level of .05. Confidence intervals for this cost-based effect size were −0.04 to +0.09.

Maintenance services provided the largest effect size of any one single group, with a weighted mean effect size of −0.56, and confidence limits of −0.28 to −0.83. All three maintenance samples were obtained from the Berenyi and Stevens study. The weighted average effect size was significantly different from zero at the level of .01. These three samples (N = 60), were not heterogeneous.[19]

Two parks and recreation samples (N = 889) yielded a mean effect size of +0.06, but had wide confidence limits (−0.00 to +0.13). This weighted average increase in costs with contracting was therefore borderline as to its statistical significance at the .05 level. This sample was heterogeneous.[20]

The two police/security samples (N = 889) from the United States showed a mean effect size of −0.03, with confidence limits −0.092 to +0.040. This measured cost reduction was therefore not significantly different from zero. No heterogeneity was present in this sample.[21]

For refuse collection, the fifteen cost-based estimates available and the large cumulative sample size (N = 6,045) resulted in a mean effect size of −0.22. Narrow confidence limits on this weighted average of −0.20 to −0.25 were found, it being highly significant at the .0001 level. This sample did, however, show significant heterogeneity.[22] A file drawer analysis revealed that 1,324 unretrieved effect sizes (or studies) would be needed to reduce this conclusion to nonsignificance. The existence of this many unpublished studies is doubted.

For the two training services samples (N = 913), the mean effect size was −0.04. Wide confidence limits (−0.10 to +0.03) were present, however, indicating that this sample mean was not different from zero. This sample was not significantly heterogeneous.[23]

Transport services showed a mean effect size of +0.03, and confidence limits of −0.02 to +0.08. Hence, this average increase in costs was not statistically different from zero. The sample of four effect sizes (N = 1,745) was not heterogeneous.[24]

Holcombe's single effect size for water treatment ($z_r = +0.42$) was mentioned previously, and had confidence limits of +0.06 to +0.79. It was therefore significantly different from zero at the .05 level.[25] Thus, in his single sample, the resulting cost increase with contracting could not have arisen by chance.

The single financial performance effect size found for health gave an effect size of −0.29, with confidence limits of −0.03 to −0.55. It was therefore significantly different from zero at the .05 level.[26]

A group of eight productivity-based effect size estimates is also shown in the table. In this group, only one productivity effect size estimate was significantly different from zero, with most studies having small sample sizes. Overall, the average (weighted) effect size for productivity was −0.15 (N = 101), but with confidence limits −0.37 to +0.08, the average effect size for this group as a whole was not significantly different from zero at the .05 level.[27] Thus, it may be concluded that although these eight studies showed an overall improvement in productivity (as shown by the negative effect sign), this was not different from zero, statistically. This group of productivity effect sizes was also found to be significantly heterogeneous. Hence, it should not be regarded as a random sample of effect sizes from one distribution.[28] The apparent inconsistency of this finding with the significant overall cost reduction finding over all services may be due to the low number of productivity-based studies available, or the smaller available total sample size.

Figure 7.3 presents a plot of weighted average effect sizes and confidence limits for all service types. The weighted means for both the cost-based and productivity-based effect size groups are evident in this plot. Negative effect sizes (showing cost decreases with contracting) for services including cleaning, engineering works, maintenance, and refuse collection are evidently different from zero.

FIGURE 7.3   Effect Sizes and Confidence Limits for Service Types

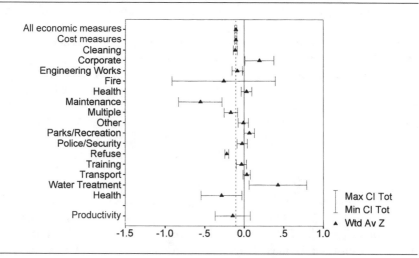

Some positive effect sizes (showing a cost increase) are also evident, with corporate services and the single water treatment effects both being significantly greater than zero.

Several groups of effect sizes are also evidently not different from zero, including fire, health, police/security, training, and transport, as well as the entire group of "productivity" effect sizes. For these, no change in costs was evident.

I shall now review the estimates of average effect size for each service type. For each service type, a difference may exist between the average effect size depending on whether estimates were weighted by study sample sizes, as they have been so far in the analysis, or whether averages were unweighted. For some services differences are marked. Table 7.6 presents a summary of average effect size estimates (both weighted and unweighted), and the levels of significance of each average compared to zero.

Table 7.6 indicates the general conclusions that could be drawn on the significance levels of average effect sizes for each service. Where both averaging methods produced significance levels less than .05, the highest agreed significance level is shown. Where both averaging methods did not produce consistent significance levels , .05, the level is indicated as not significant ("ns"). This is a conservative presentation of significance levels for these averages, since in the several cases where inconsistent significance levels were found, the more conservative of the two levels dominates the conclusion shown in the table. [29]

CONTRACTING OUT AND CONTRACTING IN

How do the effect sizes for those services contracted with the private sector differ from those services that have been contracted in-house? This simple-sounding question is one that turns out to be quite difficult to solve. Indeed, it is not possible to wholly resolve this in a meta-analysis. Because of the heterogeneity of the data, the usual multiple regression approaches to isolating the probable individual effects of each of the various study characteristics cannot be used (Hedges and Olkin 1985, p. 148). This is because the assumptions of the standard analysis of variance (ANOVA) technique are not met for effect size data. In short, effect size estimates probably do not have the same distribution within cells since the variance is inversely proportional to the sample size, and furthermore, studies within any one class may well not share one common underlying effect size.

Nonetheless, some observations can be made. The possible influence of a moderator variable, such as the sector providing the service, can be gauged through a one degree of freedom contrast test (Rosenthal 1991, p. 80, and Johnson, Mullen, and Salas 1995). This test essentially indicates whether or not two distributions of effect sizes (not weighted by sample sizes) are apparently different or not.[30] This finding must be treated with caution, however, and variables which test as "significant" should not, strictly speaking, be interpreted as giving strong evidence for any causal relationships (Rosenthal 1991).

TABLE 7.6 Summary of Conclusions on Average Effect Sizes for Services, and Significance Levels

Average Effect Size Service Summary	No. of Studies/ Effect Size Estimates	Weighted:			Unweighted:			Sig. Level Conclusion
		r_{ave}	Z	p	r_{ave}	Z	p	
All Economic Effects								
Cost:								
Cleaning	7	−0.11	−8.870	<.0001	−0.49	−9.683	<.0001	<.0001
Corporate	2	+0.19	+2.037	0.042	+0.14	+1.661	0.097	ns
Engineering Works	2	−0.09	−2.621	0.009	−0.06	−1.938	0.053	ns
Fire	1	−0.26	−0.779	0.44	−0.26	−0.856	0.39	ns
Health	1	+0.03	+0.844	0.40	+0.03	+0.839	0.40	ns
Maintenance	3	−0.56	−3.974	<.0001	−0.56	−6.070	<.0001	<.0001
Multiple	3	−0.17	−3.845	<.0001	−0.55	−4.366	<.0001	<.0001
Other	3	−0.01	−0.341	0.73	−0.25	−1.121	0.26	ns
Parks & Recreation	2	+0.06	+1.906	0.057	−0.30	+0.013	0.99	ns
Police & Security	2	−0.03	−0.768	0.44	−0.14	−1.088	0.28	ns
Refuse	15	−0.22	−17.244	<.0001	−0.33	−15.54	<.0001	<.0001
Training	2	−0.04	−1.074	0.28	−0.01	−0.704	0.48	ns
Transport	4	+0.03	1.273	0.20	+0.07	1.321	0.19	ns
Water Treatment	1	+0.42	2.289	0.022	+0.42	2.085	0.037	0.037
Financial								
Health	1	−0.29	−2.181	0.029	−0.29	−2.201	0.028	0.029
Total Cost (& Fin.)	49	−0.11	15.304	<.0001	−0.26	−14.539	<.0001	<.0001
Productivity								
Various	8	−0.15	−1.289	0.20	−0.10	−0.684	0.49	ns
Total Economic	57	−0.11	15.187	<.0001	−0.24	−13.737	<.0001	<.0001

Calculations on the effect sizes for public and private provision were undertaken to test for a possible difference in means for this moderator. Analysis of the fifty-seven effect size estimates by sector revealed that contracting with the public sector had a mean (unweighted) effect size that was not statistically different from that for the private sector at the .01 level. In other words, contracting with either sector resulted in cost savings of the same size, from a statistical perspective.[31]

Likewise, looking only at the cleaning and refuse collection services data as a group, no difference in the average effect sizes for savings from private sector and public sector provision were found at the .01 level, although a difference in favor of private provision was present at the .05 level.[32]

Overall, therefore, these calculations suggested that contracting with either sector results in cost savings. This confirms one of the key conclusions of the major international review by Domberger and Rimmer (1994) in that cost reductions are attained whether public or private sector organizations win contracts. This finding, that there was no general tendency for private provision to be any more cost-effective than public provision of services under contract, is a significant one for this book.

OTHER POSSIBLE MODERATOR VARIABLES

Additional statistical tests were also undertaken to ascertain the possible presence of other moderator variables. Amongst these variables were the author's discipline, the study publication date, the sophistication of the analysis, the publication type, the level of government, the type of contracting, the type of performance measure adopted, and the country studied. Contrasts were also undertaken to compare effect sizes by the type of service as well.

For the first of these variables, a strong association was found between the author's discipline and effect sizes of studies. Studies from the disciplines of Finance/Accounting and Business provided the highest effect sizes ($r_{ave} = -0.81$ and -0.46 respectively). These were significantly greater than both Economics ($r_{ave} = -0.16$) and Politics/Law ($r_{ave} = -0.05$), at a level of significance of .01. Hence, the discipline of the researcher does indeed appear to be a moderator of the effect size reported.[33] The implication here is therefore that researchers from politics/law would be seeing quite different effectiveness results coming out from their discipline compared to those being published by friends in finance or accounting. The perception of contracting effectiveness, and indeed from our measurements, the reality of contracting effectiveness, differs by over an order of magnitude.

For the second of these variables, a strong association was also detected between the date of publication and effect size. Later studies produced significantly smaller effect sizes ($p < .01$). Indeed, those published on or after 1990 ($r_{ave} = -0.07$) averaged only a fraction of those published before this time ($r_{ave} = -0.45$). This finding tended to confirm the often voiced concern in narrative reviews on the usefulness and relevance of older reported results. Older results did tend to present much larger effect sizes in contracting and were therefore quantitatively different from more recent findings. Importantly, this result disagrees with the conclusion of major international reviews such as Domberger and Rimmer (1994, p. 448). In reviewing the cost reductions reported since 1977, they concluded that "the levels of cost reductions resulting from the use of CTC does not appear to have changed over this period of time." The analysis above indicates a strong reduction in reported effect sizes in statistical terms. Although the precise cause of this reduction cannot be determined, there is no doubt as to its existence from the meta-analytical perspective.

A further test was undertaken to ascertain the extent to which the sophistication of a study—in terms of the number of statistical controls applied—might influence effect sizes. Studies with a larger number of controls produced effect sizes averaging around one-half of those for studies with fewer controls.[34] These were significantly different at p < .01. Hence, the more careful a study, the lower the effect size for contracting found. This broadly confirms the suspicion that studies with more controls tend to present quantitatively different results than simpler studies.[35]

Looking at the type of publication as a potential moderator variable, it was found that the average effect size for theses (r_{ave} = 0.00) was significantly lower than published effect sizes (at r_{ave} = −0.27) at the .01 level. This was consistent with previously noted meta-analytic work.[36]

Likewise, the possible influence of the level of government as a moderator variable was analyzed. Here, it was found that observations at the local government level (r_{ave} 5 20.23) were significantly different from (lower than) the effect sizes for state and federal governments (r_{ave} 5 20.40 and 20.53) at the .05 level. Thus, higher levels of government, although only few in number, have published higher effect sizes than lower levels of government. Again, we should reflect on what this means. What is certain is that professionals are seeing different results arising from state and federal government compared to those from local government.[37] This result again disagrees with the conclusion of the international review of Domberger and Rimmer (1994). On this issue they concluded that "the level of cost reductions is similar for each level of government." The analysis above detected a tendency for higher levels of government to have published higher effect sizes. Although the actual variable that causes this moderation in effect size is open to debate, there is a statistically significant tendency for different levels of government to report different effect sizes. From the meta-analytical perspective, this observation has probably not arisen by chance.

Turning now to the type of contracting being reported, it was apparent that studies reporting on competitive tendering (r_{ave} = −0.45) had significantly higher effect sizes than those reporting simply "contracting out" (r_{ave} = −0.21) or else "compulsory competitive tendering" (r_{ave} = −0.17). This finding is of course complicated by the fact that all compulsory competitive tendering (CCT) studies were from the U.K. and that this finding is likely to be influenced by the difference in countries studied.

No association was found between the type of performance measure adopted and average effect size, up to a significance level of .05. Cost-based measures ($r_{ave} = -0.26$) were no different from productivity-based measures ($r_{ave} = -0.10$), from a statistical perspective.

Comparing countries studied, it was evident that the average for effect sizes from the United States ($r_{ave} = -0.15$) was significantly lower than the averages for both Australia ($r_{ave} = -0.52$) and Britain ($r_{ave} = -0.35$) at the .01 level. Hence, it could be concluded that findings for the United States are likely to be different from those for other countries, as far as the economic impacts of contracting go. Possible reasons for this difference may be the length of time that agencies in a country have been contracting in or out, the types of contracts employed, different legislative environments, cultural effects, or any one of many other differences that exist between countries. Importantly, this result again differs with the conclusion of the international review of Domberger and Rimmer (1994). Reviewing findings predominantly from Australia, the United Kingdom, and the United States, they concluded that "the level of cost reductions is similar . . . for each of the countries reviewed." The analysis above detected a tendency for the U.S. effect size levels to be significantly smaller than the results from both Australia and Britain. Although the causes of this moderation in effect size are open to debate, there is again little doubt of the existence of this phenomenon, and little doubt that it could have arisen purely by chance.

Looking once more at the type of service as a potential moderator, it was found that maintenance, cleaning, and refuse collection had the largest average (unweighted) effect sizes ($r_{ave} = -0.56$, -0.49, and -0.30 respectively). The smallest effect sizes were associated with corporate services ($r_{ave} = +0.14$), engineering ($r_{ave} = +0.02$), and training ($r_{ave} = -0.01$). Other services had effect sizes between these two extreme groups. Contrasting these effect sizes, maintenance and cleaning services had a significantly higher average effect size than all others at a level of .05. At a level of .01, the second observation of these findings is that nine of the twelve services listed (i.e., from "police" to "corporate" services) were found to be not significantly different from each other. Statistically, therefore, these services appeared to be effectively only one category. Hence, from the statistical perspective, it appears that one can only be confident of differences between the average effect sizes for service types for only a small proportion of the twelve services analyzed.

MEANING OF EFFECT SIZE FINDINGS

Meta-analysis may well be a conceptually sophisticated way of gaining a picture of many research findings, but exactly what is the meaning of an effect size? What does an average weighted effect size of $r_{ave} = -0.11$ (20,131 observations), or an unweighted average effect size of $r_{ave} = -0.24$ for the fifty-seven effect sizes actually mean? To what extent are these findings either practically meaningful or trivial? Unfortunately, neither experienced behavioral researchers nor experienced statisticians appear to have a good intuitive feel for the practical meaning of effect sizes, according to Rosenthal (1991, p. 133).

One suggestion to help interpret the practical meaning of effect sizes is to get a comparative feel by looking at other studies in a similar field. For example, Boyd (1991) looked at the relationship between firms undertaking strategic planning and their financial performance. Looking at some 2,496 organizations, he found an average weighted effect size of $r_{ave} = 0.15$, and saw this as "modest." He suggested that extensive measurement problems had led to this correlation underestimating the true relationship between planning and financial performance. In the field of law, the meta-analytic investigation by Narby, Cutler, and Moran (1993) into the relationship between authoritarianism and a juror's perception of defendant culpability also found a similar average effect size. Here, the overall average effect size found was $r_{ave} = +0.16$. They described this effect size as "not trivial in magnitude," and argued that these findings had important implications on the selection of jurors for trials. In the medical field, Rosenthal (1991, p. 136) also makes some relevant observations. He comments that small r's have been produced in the past in several areas of research despite these results subsequently being well known and being widely regarded as "results of major medical, behavioural, and/or economic importance." He then lists the effect sizes found in areas such as the taking of aspirin and the incidence of heart attack (r = 0.03), being a veteran of the Vietnam War and the onset of subsequent alcohol problems (r = 0.07), and the influence of psychotherapy and improving one's situation (r = 0.32). With these effect sizes as background, the average effect sizes of $r_{ave} = -0.11$ (weighted) for contracting government services could be regarded as a result of some importance, and not trivial.

The second suggestion for interpreting this effect size was to determine the practical significance of this finding in terms of, say, the relative percentage savings in costs. Information for average data characteristics was available for forty-five of the fifty-seven economic effect sizes. These percentage savings estimates could therefore be adopted as a guide for the likely practical implication of the effect sizes found. Table 7.7 indicates the percentage estimates that could be computed from the data available in each of the studies, along with the corresponding statistical effect sizes. On this basis, the overall (unweighted) average economic percentage gain from contracting was found to be −15.6 percent (n = 45). On a service by service basis, percentage gains ranged from −30.5 percent for the case of maintenance savings (n = 3) and −30.2 percent for cleaning (n = 7) to an estimated cost increase for corporate services of 24.1 percent (n = 1). Several services reported single figure percentage improvements. Interestingly, the average cost-saving estimate for refuse services was found to be 19.3 percent, surprisingly close to Domberger's oft quoted 20 percent rule.

TABLE 7.7 Percentage Cost Savings for Services with Information Available

Service Type	Number of % estimates available	Average cost saving for category (%)
Economic Measures		−15.6
Cost:		−15.7
Cleaning	7	−30.2
Corporate	1	+24.1
Engineering Works	2	−24.2
Fire	1	−17.6
Health	1	+3.5
Maintenance	3	−30.5
Mutiple	1	−19.9
Other	3	−5.9
Parks & Recreation	2	−7.5
Police & Security	2	−8.5
Refuse	13	−19.3
Training	2	+0.9
Transport	2	+16.1
Productivity	1	−10.6

A little caution is needed when translating these findings to practice. Firstly, it is clear that the gains reported for services vary. One savings rule for all is clearly not appropriate. Secondly, although the overall average saving (unweighted) was found to be 15.6 percent, this cannot necessarily be adopted as the savings potentially available to an agency. Again, different methods of calculating the average produce different results. For instance, if the means for each service type are averaged (unweighted by either the number of data points or the number of studies in each service category) the overall mean percentage cost saving found is 9.8 percent. Leaving aside questions of statistical confidence levels, this mean is lower than the mean for all cost saving estimates because although cleaning and refuse services are only two of the thirteen service categories, they make up almost one-half of the available cost-saving estimates (i.e., twenty of the forty-five available percentage estimates).[38] A further issue to be considered is the fact that the forty-five service measurements that yielded sufficient information to calculate percentage cost savings themselves yielded effect sizes that averaged −0.28. This is a little different from the overall (unweighted) average effect size for all cost- and productivity-based effect sizes of −0.24, or only 87 percent of this value. With the knowledge that there is a general trend for greater effect sizes to be associated with greater percentage reductions and that a zero effect corresponds to a zero cost reduction, the expected cost-savings estimates above should therefore be further reduced. Making these adjustments, the previously calculated average cost savings estimates of 15.6 percent (for all estimates) and 9.6 percent (for all service categories) reduce to 13.6 percent and 8.5 percent respectively.[39]

Thus, depending on whether all estimates or all service categories are equally weighted when calculating the average, contracting probably leads to an average overall cost reduction of around 8 to 14 percent over all services.[40]

Additionally, the potential of several different moderator variables to alter the cost impacts of contracting is also likely to be substantial. A further set of issues complicates any interpretation of contracting with the private and public sectors. These concern our lack of knowledge on the size of costs involved in contract preparation and contract performance monitoring, and also the fact that several inconsistencies exist in financial practices between the two sectors. Such inconsistencies include, for example, the need to provide for a profit margin in the private sector, and the existence of differential tax rates between the two. These issues will be discussed in the next section. Strictly speaking, as well, the overall cost savings potentially available to a government agency is the sum of each of the separate dollar savings available from each specific service. Consequently, the overall cost savings available to an agency is dependent on the relative proportion of each of the various services being provided.

The last suggestion to help us better understand the meaning of an effect size is to use the binomial effect size display concept put forward by Rosenthal (1991). The average (weighted) effect size of -0.11 (or -0.24 unweighted) could be interpreted using this concept. We would first note that with an average effect size of -0.11, this accounts for only 1 percent of the variance observed in the studies, since $r^2 = 0.11^2 = 0.01$, or 1 percent. On first glance, this appears to be a rather trivial level of "success." However, Rosenthal and Rubin (1982) argued that the average effect size of -0.11 can be converted to show the increase in success rate between an experimental group and a control group, in order to help make clearer the importance of the finding. From Rosenthal (1991, p. 134) the experimental group success rate is computed as 55.5 percent, compared to a control group success rate of 44.5 percent.[41] This represents an increase in "success" of 11 percent. In the medical context, treating patients with a particular new drug found to have an average effect size of 0.11 would result in some 11 percent more people being alive after the administration of the new drug. Extending this medical analogy to our case, 11 percent more agencies would be found to have significantly improved financial health (i.e., cost savings) through the application of contracting. In the case of the unweighted average effect size of -0.24, this accounts for 6 percent of the variance observed in the studies, since $r^2 = 0.24^2 = 0.0587$ or 6 percent. The equivalent experimental group success rate is computed as 62 percent, compared to a control group success rate of 38 percent. This represents an increase in "success" of 24 percent. Again, this interpretation of the average effect size for contracting suggests that such improvements are far from trivial.

OTHER ISSUES IN COST COMPARISONS

As alluded to above, the desire to achieve a simple straightforward cost comparison between service costs in-house and providing services through private or public sector contracts is not wholly fulfilled. It is complicated by several other issues.

Firstly, a recurring theme through the contracting literature is the attention, at least in the debate, to the question of additional costs involved in preparing for competitive tendering or contracting, the preparation of the contract itself, and contract performance monitoring costs.

Few of the studies included in the meta-analysis shed much light on this area. Indeed, few actual empirical measurements of the size of any of these types of costs appear to have been made. Buck and Chaundy (1992, p. 20) quote from earlier work in the U.K. in which a small data set of seventeen local authorities was analyzed. They quote the average costs of organizing the tendering process as 3.6 percent of the contract value, and thereby reduce the cost savings available commensurately. They also quote the average costs of monitoring as varying from 4.3 to 5.8 percent of total refuse collection costs, and importantly note that "there was no evidence that monitoring costs were higher for private contractors than for in-house providers." The U.K. Audit Office (1987) also presents an estimate for the costs of tendering of around 4.1 percent,[42] this being around one-fifth of its estimated 20 percent cost-savings figure. These estimates aside, Berenyi and Stevens (1988) was the only study in which the data subjected to meta-analysis explicitly included contract administration and support costs. They quote municipal contract management costs as comprising 6.6 percent of the total contract price. Thus, it is observed that, although these costs have been recognized conceptually as having major potential implications on the possible cost savings available from contracting, none of the twenty-eight studies adopted in this meta-analysis (with one exception) explicitly estimated such costs.

We earlier noted some other estimates relevant to this discussion. Although these estimates are from reports which were not included in the meta-analysis, their inclusion in this discussion is timely for completeness. Typical of the estimates for the cost of developing specifications, contract preparation, and organizing for contracting processes is that from LGIU (1994) in the United Kingdom. They quote around 2 percent of the total contract amount for these tasks. In a similar vein, the Department of Treasury and Finance (1997) quotes an average cost of managing outsourced contracts at 1.9 percent for Australian data collected from managers of over 9,000 contracts. Interestingly, it notes that contract management costs varied from a low of around 1.6 percent (for contracts over $10 million) to about 11.3 percent (for contracts below $0.1 million). Estimates for the cost of monitoring contract specifications and contract completion were noted as varying from these 2 percent estimates, or 3 percent from Savas (1977a) in the United States, up to as high as 20 percent from Osborne and Gaebler (1993). As was noted previously, the reliability of these estimates is uncertain—but is assumed in most cases to be low. Emphasizing this unreliability, it is indeed amazing that Osborne and Gaebler, for instance, can be so positive on the virtues of contracting on the one hand, and, whilst being aware of Domberger's widely quoted 20 percent cost saving rule, calmly concede that "to do it right, cities often spend 20 percent of the cost of the service on contract management"!

Nonetheless, it is clear that some costs are necessary for an organization to undertake contracting, albeit that the level of such costs is uncertain at present. Of course, some proportion of the costs of developing and monitoring contracts is likely to be needed even if the provision of services is not subject to contracting. This amount, concerned with simply reviewing service requirements, monitoring service performance, and assessing the need for improvements or change has not been specified, however. We are therefore left concluding that in order to allow for the one-off costs of the contracting/tendering process as a whole, as well as the costs of contract administration and monitoring, cost savings are likely to be further revised downwards below the 8 to 14 percent estimates made in the previous section.[43] If the estimates of contract process preparation and contract document development are reviewed, most are generally in the vicinity of 4 to 6 percent.[44] We might then assume for the sake of practicality that, say, one-half of this cost is related to the contracting process and one-half to service review costs that would occur in any event. On this basis, our estimate of cost savings achieved through contracting would be around 6 to 12 percent—around, say, 2 percent lower than noted in the previous section. In the absence of such assumptions, we are left concluding that the jury is still out on the precise magnitude of costs associated with contract preparation and processes. In addition, it is also concluded that to the extent that different costs may exist in monitoring contracts carried out in the private and public sectors, this factor should also be included in the assessment of cost savings. Unfortunately, little reliable information is available on the relative costs of monitoring contract performance of either sector, let alone differences between the two.

Furthermore, it should be recognized that with the growth of the contracting movement a much greater interest appears to have been taken in the need for service review, the measurement of service delivery performance, and contract development and monitoring costs. Indeed, one could seriously question whether it is now possible to properly assess the "before" and "after" levels of contract-monitoring costs, for example, owing simply to the increase in the interest of contract performance, and hence contract-performance measurement, during the "after" period. In other words, even if increased contract-monitoring costs were detected in a performance review of, say, an external contractor, one could not be certain whether such increased costs were due simply to the act of contracting externally, or our increased interest and expectations in this area. The lack of this type of information puts in doubt the extent to which we can be prescriptive and certain about service delivery cost savings under contracting.

Blatant inconsistencies that exist in the financial practices between the two sectors also cloud the cost-savings assessment issue. When comparing contract costs, the first inconsistency concerns the common practice of comparing the price of contracts tendered by the private sector (which by definition would be expected to include a profit margin for shareholder return) against the cost of work undertaken in providing a service through the public sector. Strictly, costs should not be compared to prices. Such a comparison logically results in an underestimate of the likely cost savings under contracting. Likewise, the absence of taxes paid for inputs to production in the public sector differs with the presence of such taxes in the private sector. Again, very few studies explicitly adjusted the comparative data to account for this difference. If the profit margin included in private sector contract bids was taken out as part of a meta-analysis of financial performance and an adjustment was made for differential tax payments, these would presumably result in an upwards revision to the average cost-savings estimate. Both of these adjustments would compensate in the opposite direction to any upwards adjustment that may be required to account for contract administration and monitoring costs.

If a slightly different perspective of costs is taken, then a different conclusion may also result. For example, rather than looking at the costs to the public agency or the total spending by the agency, Albin (1992) took the perspective of the individual taxpayer. He asked the question, Do those councils that have a greater level of contracting out also have a lower level of rates? His regression analysis of data from fifty-eight local councils in Australia did not support this. Indeed his analysis indicated that rates were highest amongst councils that contracted out, not lowest. This finding was significant at the .05 level. Albin's interpretation of his results was that any cost savings that might occur through contracting services may well be captured by senior managers to maximize their own utility (rather than the taxpayer's utility)—the very behavior that contracting is supposed to restrain. No other analyses corroborating Albin's conclusions were found. Additional analyses on this issue are clearly desirable.

Rather than using the agency's perspective of costs or that of the individual, one could also take the overall view of costs from the community perspective. Again, the conclusions using this broader view may well be quite a different matter altogether. The only analysis found of costs adopting this broader viewpoint was that of Escott and Whitfield (1995). This work was also published by the Centre for Public Services (1995b). Here, in line with much of the earlier work from Whitfield presenting the downside of privatization, it was argued strongly that contracting out is not in the community interest for the United Kingdom as a whole. Using a figure for cost savings of 6.5 percent, from previous U.K. work looking at forty local government case studies, the estimated national savings from contracting were estimated to total £124 million. This covered the areas of building, cleaning, education, catering, refuse collection, and sports and leisure management. Against this, the national cost of job losses due to contracting out (some 74,010 jobs) was estimated at £250 million. By this analysis, the costs of contracting clearly exceeded the savings gained. Thus, this report concluded that "the government is, in effect, subsidizing CCT. Local Authorities make £124 'savings' whilst central government is responsible for 97 percent of the £250.1m costs" (Centre for Public Services (1995b, p. 22). Again, no corroborating evidence could be found in the literature search supporting the conclusions of this analysis, albeit that other comparable analyses are clearly desirable. The need for other analyses taking this perspective is particularly strong in view of what could be seen as the predictability of the Centre's research findings. It is likely that those favoring the contracting-out mechanism would criticize the 6.5 percent savings estimate adopted in this analysis as too low. Such critics could then point out that by increasing this estimate and assuming a reasonable proportion of people losing jobs are reabsorbed back into the workforce, then there may be no net losses to the community overall. But there may also be no net community gain. Such a criticism would probably have some veracity, and is therefore important to the debate. Most importantly, however, the criticism from the Centre for Public Services illustrates the fact that, even putting aside the human, psychological, and emotional dimensions of unemployment, any financial savings achieved at the level of the local public agency may well evaporate when additional costs of unemployment are also included in the analysis. The irony here is that if indeed there was in reality no overall net community benefit in contracting out (or even worse, a net disbenefit as is claimed in the above mentioned analysis), intergovernmental arrangements in the United Kingdom and Australia, at least, are such that contracting out would continue to be implemented. A rational decision in the broader community's interests overall is unlikely to be taken by a local government public agency adopting a strictly commercial approach to the issue, and under a narrow managerialist philosophy, simply pursuing cost savings.

CONCLUSIONS ON COST SAVINGS

This analysis has shown that contracting studies have typically reported real cost savings. Adopting the meta-analytic concept of "effect size," effect sizes of -1.10 (a cost decrease) to $+0.42$ (a cost increase) were found. The average effect sizes estimated were -0.11 (weighted) or -0.24 (unweighted). These effect sizes were found to be highly significant and were interpreted as being equivalent to an average cost saving of 8 to 14 percent. Overall, the reliability of this average saving was beyond doubt. Cost savings differed between services and a general rule could not be applied to all. Services such as maintenance, cleaning, and refuse collection showed highest effect sizes, and were equivalent to cost savings of around -30.5 percent, -30.2 percent, and -19.3 percent respectively. Other services such as corporate services, training services, and engineering services yielded little or no savings or cost increases depending on the exact statistical tests employed.[45] The estimated cost savings for these services were +24.1 percent, +0.9 percent (i.e., cost increases), and −24.2 percent (cost savings) respectively.

There was very little statistical difference between the sector actually undertaking the contracted services—effect sizes for contracted private provision and in-house provision were not generally different. Privatization, per se, was therefore found to offer only marginal benefits, if any, whilst contracting offered significant benefits.

Several other moderator variables tested were detected as significant. Reported effect sizes (and hence, cost savings) were found to vary by country, the author's background, the date the study was published, the study sophistication, the level of government undertaking the contracting, source of funding, publication type, and the type of service.

Overall, therefore, savings of around 8 to 14 percent were found. Such estimates, however, would need to be revised downward to account for the existence of contract development and monitoring costs, and revised upwards to account for the other inconsistencies in public and private financial arrangements such as differential tax rates. Adjustments would also be needed in recognition of the likely effects of moderator variables.

SOCIAL PERFORMANCE

Narrative Review of Social Performance

So far, I have assessed privatization (viewed as contracting out, or outsourcing) as it relates to economic efficiency—or more specifically, saving money. But have cost savings under contracts been accompanied by reductions in service quality or other changes in service levels? What have been the social impacts, if any? After all, contracting out has been introduced as a major part of the privatization ideology, against a backdrop of social privatization promises. Recall the table of objectives in Chapter 2. These broad promises have included, as well as simply improved efficiency, a series of benefits to the consumer: better services with improved quality, lower prices, and greater choice. These three possible "social" benefits have all been nurtured through the general belief that economic growth also provides wide-ranging benefits to the community as a whole. In this section, I will look at the evidence on such social benefits, and aim to determine the extent to which privatization benefits have been delivered to date. As well, I will also consider the possibility of undesirable social impacts such as employment effects and equity impacts. Initially, I will adopt the traditional narrative review approach, but this will be supplemented by meta-analytic findings where research measurements are available.

Let us turn to the first social performance issue—the question of better quality services.

In reviewing the costs of service provision, most studies included in the meta-analysis adopted statistical controls to ensure that when measuring any changes in costs, overall levels of production or service levels were controlled for. The question of possible changes in service "quality," however, is more vexed. Quality is a multidimensional concept, and many parameters have relevance. Consider for a moment the well-documented case of refuse collection and disposal services. Quality in this instance could be seen to include two separate lists of items. Firstly, the number of times per week refuse is collected, the location of bin pickup, the type of wastes collected, and the collection of recyclable material might all be construed as having some relevance to quality. Indeed, they could logically be part of a broad definition of quality. These variables, "production" oriented variables, have typically been controlled for in the better refuse studies included in the previous meta-analysis. Many of the remaining quality dimensions have not, however. This second group of items might include aspects of collection such as spillages, noise levels, presence of unpleasant odors, interactions with customers/citizens, the number of complaints received, etc. We might call these quality variables. So, what do we know of contracting in terms of these quality variables?

An array of findings is evident in the literature. Claims and counterclaims are found. On the one hand, numerous examples of contracting-out failures are presented in reports such as SCAT (1988) from the U.K. The words in the report titles accurately reflect the tenor. "Taken to the Cleaners—The Lincolnshire Experience," or "Dirty Schools: Exploited Cleaners: Contract Failures" present a powerful mental picture and a strong judgment. Dozens of case studies of incomplete and poor quality cleaning are given—stories outlining scant regard by companies for their employees, for service levels, and for their clients. As an example, a 1985 U.K. survey by the National Union of Teachers of fifty-four schools reveals "a noticeable deterioration of cleanliness" at 74 percent of schools surveyed, for instance. Other case study examples also outline poor quality contracting. Hirsch (1991) cites another case, this time in the U.S., of the Los Angeles County fleet maintenance contract awarded in 1988. The contract price was $12 million—promising a $2 million (or 8 percent) reduction on the previous year's actual expenditure. Nine months into the first year of the contract, however, the contractor requested another $3.2 million, making the first year's fee $15.2 million, and soaking up all projected savings. More importantly though, Hirsch concludes that "altogether the contract for maintenance and repair of county vehicles resulted in numerous complaints from various county departments about massive service backlogs, shoddy repair service, and delays in providing information so that the county could properly bill its Departments."

Countervailing case studies are also presented in the literature. Donahue's (1989) review of privatization experience includes the anecdote of the Wollman Memorial Skating Rink in Central Park, New York City. This is a classic. After several years of preparing and project planning, the city closed down the rink in

1980 for a rebuilding project scheduled to take two years and costing just under $5 million. The rebuilding work went badly. Mid-project delays, poor quality workmanship, and various other technical flaws in the project led, after an amazing six years and some $12 million, to an essentially worthless piece of work. It would need to be rebuilt from the ground up. Expressing his amazement to the New York mayor, the developer Donald Trump offered to build the rink at no profit to himself. Trump completed the project in three months, and at a total cost of $2.3 million.

These anecdotes are typical of the literature. For every good case study anecdote supporting one side of the quality argument, a contrasting story can usually be found supporting the other. Repeating anecdotes is unlikely to assist in properly resolving the quality debate, however. As Donahue (1989, p. 133) stresses, "argument by anecdote . . . is doomed to inconclusiveness."

Other studies have attempted to be a little more systematic in their approach and have quoted higher private sector contract failure rates in support of public sector provision. Carnaghan and Bracewell-Milnes (1993, p. 8) cite an analysis of more than 5,000 contracts published by Public Service Action showing failure rates for contracts held by private contractors at four and one-half times higher than for in-house held contracts, and in the health sector, some eighteen times higher.[46]

A review of this quality question by Domberger and Rimmer (1994) has argued that "whilst there is broad consensus that CTC leads to reductions in costs, there is less consensus about its impact on service quality." Indeed, Domberger and Rimmer's international review of service quality included ten studies, but showed no consensus about its impact on quality of service. Two of these ten studies concluded that quality usually reduced on contracting, whilst two more found that between 25 and 33 percent of councils were dissatisfied, with contract specifications not being met. The largest single group—four of these ten studies—concluded that no change in quality occurs under contracting. One study found that quality usually improves, and one found that quality either does not change or else improves. Adding to this lack of consensus on quality is the comment made by Domberger and Rimmer that it is difficult to determine whether reductions in service quality were due to the contractor not adhering to the contract specification or else to a policy decision to use contracting as a mechanism to reduce service quality. Nonetheless, the point is made. The findings and conclusions on quality are diverse.

Of the studies included in the meta-analysis, only a few specifically controlled for quality as a variable in determining the cost of contracting. Berenyi and Stevens (1988) is one such example. Their study controlled for quality and found that despite major cost savings being gained through contracting out, no loss in quality was measured. This finding was statistically significant at the .05 level. Likewise, Holcombe (1991) also failed to detect any relationship between the cost of a contract and quality at the .05 significance level. Most other studies that referred to the issue of quality at all cited only casual evidence to support their general belief. Kemper and Quigley (1976), for instance, noted after they found that private refuse costs were higher, "there is no casual evidence that private quality is better; indeed, town regulations give the impression that the quality of service may be a problem of private service. . . . Our conversations with town officials revealed some dissatisfaction with the dependability and littering of private collectors." Likewise, Domberger, Meadowcroft, and Thompson (1986) recognized that although their analysis of refuse collection did account for the two most important aspects of service quality in the broad sense—method and frequency of collection—no information was available on other dimensions of service. They then quoted a small-scale recent study of five authorities in which it was cited that "those authorities which have (awarded private contracts) have considered that they have continued to receive the same standard of service required at a lower cost than they were paying before."

Rather than controlling for the quality variable in the analysis of contract costs, some studies looked more specifically at the question of whether a relationship might exist between the sector providing the services and the service quality itself. Three such studies were found. Berglund (1992) firstly looked at two public and two privately contracted manpower training centers in the United States. He looked at a series of quality ratings and concluded that there was little difference between the quality offered by the private provider as compared to the public provider. The conclusion was that both had their strengths and weaknesses, but that these strengths and weaknesses did not neatly align with ownership of the provider. Secondly, Musgrove (1988) reviewed the quality of busing in eighty-eight school districts in Missouri, again in the United States. He also found no difference in the quality of transport in either case, at the .05 level of significance. The most comprehensive and carefully designed study to be undertaken so far on this question is undoubtedly that of Domberger, Hall, and Li (1994). The team in this third study looked at the experience of sixty-one cleaning contracts in Australia. Through an analysis using econometric models, the relationship of price and quality to assorted variables including the sector providing the contracted service was studied. Privately tendered cleaning services in "special schools" were found to have 35.6 percent higher quality than in-house work, this being statistically significant at the .05 level. For other schools and commercial contracts, quality differences measured under contracting out were a 19.2 percent improvement and a 6.7 percent decrease in quality—neither of which were statistically significant. Their analysis of hospital cleaning contracts showed no difference (i.e., 0.0 percent) in quality between services tendered to the public sector and services tendered to the private sectors. In both the price equations and the quality equations, the effects of competition swamped the effects of ownership in their analysis. These studies will be discussed further as part of the meta-analytic perspective in the following section.

The second and third issues noted above, those of lower prices and a better choice of services, were rarely mentioned in the studies included in the meta-analysis. To some extent, the concept of lower service prices to purchasers has been covered in the previous analysis if we view the government in the role of purchaser of services from contract providers. A lower price to government for services means a reduced cost. But for consumers or citizens it is different. The single report that might rate as an exception to this was Albin (1992), which was noted previously. Recalling this, his analysis of fifty-eight local councils in Australia found a significant increase, rather than reduction, in rates for those councils where greater levels of contracting out were occurring. Thus, to the extent that the rates for a citizen could be regarded as a client "price," these were found not to decrease. He looked also at the range of services provided by councils to ascertain whether or not councils that had higher levels of contracting out also provided a wider range of services. The presumption here was that savings achieved through contracting might fund these additional services. On this issue, no significant relationship was found. It appears that the promise of lower prices and greater choice in services has not been delivered.[47]

Another performance issue worthy of consideration and within the social dimension is employment impacts. Contracting out certainly appears to lead to fewer people employed from the vast majority of studies. The employment analysis of Martin and Stein (1993) looked at 877 U.S. cities and estimated that between 0 and 93 percent fewer full-time equivalent staff were employed in cities that use contracting out, as compared to those that do not. In nearly all of the seven service types analyzed, this reduction is significant at the .05 level. Likewise, Ferris (1988) found that, as expected, increased use of contracting out reduces public employment levels. Milne (1987) notes also that in his six U.K. case studies, the introduction of compulsory tendering was associated with one-half of those experiencing compulsory redundancies. Escott and Whitfield (1995) also found a 21 percent decrease in employment in four key services following the implementation of CCT in the U.K. They cite several other studies in which reductions in employment had been estimated for the United Kingdom: A 1993 Department of Environment study of sixty-two contracts is quoted in which job losses were found to be between 5 and 16 percent; a Public Service Privatization Unit Study of 652 contracts is also cited where employment was found to be reduced by 23 percent for refuse collection and street cleaning when public sector organizations had won contracts, and by 31 percent when contracts had been won by the private sector. For the case of building cleaning contracts, these reductions were found to be 5 percent and 9 percent respectively. A further study of refuse collection employment losses argued that a 21 percent reduction overall had been experienced, based on an analysis of 39 contracts in Manchester (Escott and Whitfield 1995, p. 148).

Few reports were detected claiming that contracting out or contracting in does not lead to any loss of jobs. The study of Albin (1992) noted that councils that contracted out tended to have lower overall employment levels, but that this tendency was not statistically significant at the .05 level. Another exception was the Industry Commission (1995, p. 17) of Australia. Looking at the effect of contracting on employment, it came to the conclusion "public sector employees may be particularly affected . . . but there are likely to be overall increases in employment." This conclusion was nothing short of staggering in view of the employment figures presented in the Commission's own report. For the 17 Australian contracting-out cases presented with full employment statistics, some 9,969 staff were involved, of which 59 percent joined the private contractors, 8 percent were redeployed, and 29 percent were made redundant.[48] When bids were won in-house, 1,454 staff were involved, of which 58 percent were retained for the contracted work, 24 percent were redeployed, and 17 percent were made redundant.[49]

Throughout many of these research reports, it is not always clear whether total job losses overall were being presented—thus including both the job losses within the public agency authority that did not win the contract as well as any employment gains for the new contractor. Nonetheless, where total employment effects were presented, such as was the case for the Industry Commission (1995) of Australia and for Escott and Whitfield (1995), reductions in overall employment levels appear to be beyond doubt. What is less clear is the number of job losses or redundancies that remain long-term unemployed and the number of job-losers or redundancy-takers who subsequently take on other relevant employment. Our knowledge of labor reabsorption into the economic system appears seriously deficient. It is surprising that there is such a scarcity of studies on the relationship between employment and privatization as contracting out. Perhaps it is an example of where an effect is considered so self-evident that it does not receive the serious attention by scholars it deserves.

Even if one is prepared to adopt the general conclusion that contracting usually leads to fewer people in employment in the short term, and leave unresolved questions of labor reabsorption, further consideration is needed in order to establish whether or not any differential impacts may occur here through such changes. As far as employment goes, who are the winners and losers? How is our sense of equity affected? Albin's analysis in Australia identifies that in terms of full-time jobs, contracting favors professional groups of employees. Albin's data shows that with greater contracting, the number of senior professionals (such as engineers) is increased, whilst simultaneously leading to a decline in the size of the blue collar workforce. These findings were statistically significant at the .05 level. Differential employment impacts have also been researched for the greater use of part-time workers under contracting. The flexibility which part-timers bring has been reported as one of the key underpinnings for cost savings according to the U.K. Audit Office (1987, p. 2). They note that savings under contracting have arisen from the following factors:

- the need to draw up specifications (including the rationalization of existing operations);
- less favorable working conditions;
- greater use of part-time staff;

- changes in working practices, and
- increased productivity.

Escott and Whitfield (1995) comprehensively reviewed the employment impact and the gender impact of CCT in the United Kingdom. They looked at the experience of five U.K. local government services following the introduction of compulsory competitive tendering through the Local Government Act (1988). It was concluded firstly that the introduction of CCT had resulted in a loss of jobs and of hours of pay for manual workers, and that, secondly, the impact has been greater on women than on men. The analysis was based primarily on 123 contracts in 39 authorities. Total employment levels were reduced by 21 percent following the first round of CCT, with full-time jobs down 12 percent and part-time jobs reduced by 22 percent. Since 91 percent of the employment prior to CCT was part time, part-time workers accounted for most of the overall job losses.[50] Looking at the changes in employment by gender, they found that the reduction in the number of women employed was 22 percent, whilst the reduction in men employed was 12 percent. Escott and Whitfield also importantly noted that "women accounted for 93 percent of employment in these services in 1988–89 (the pre-contract period) and for 96 percent of the net job loss." The hours of work, pay, and conditions in terms of holidays, sick pay, maternity leave, and training were also argued as being reduced. Overall, it was concluded that "the differential between male, usually full time, and female, usually part time, manual workers has been exacerbated under CCT" and that "many of the 'savings' made under CCT of manual services have been achieved through the flexible use of lowest paid, part time manual workers."[51] Differential employment impacts appear to have occurred with contracting here.

Dunleavy (1986) goes even further in his criticism than simply describing changes with contracting as differential. He argues that privatization is simply "a continuation of strategies already well developed by senior policy-level bureaucrats for advancing their class (and frequently their gender) interests against those of rank and file state workers and service consumers." He continues, saying that these class interests are advanced at the expense of job losses and worsened conditions for rank and file state workers, producing "a qualitative and quantitative reduction of services to recipients, especially the poor and the working class."

In the context of the United States experience, Stein (1994) also reveals that whilst privatization in the form of contracting out has led to a reduced staffing numbers overall, black people (African-Americans) have been disproportionately affected. The 1979 Saint Louis workforce totaled 8,523 people, of which 55.5 percent were black (African-American). Just over a decade later, the 1990 workforce totaled 3,618 people, of which 44.0 percent were black. Thus, the African-American representation in the workforce had been reduced both in raw numbers and as a proportion. Stein argued that much of this was due to black people losing jobs in greater numbers than whites, St. Louis having closed hospitals and privatized health-care delivery. A differential employment impact again appears to have occurred.

The relative weighting of these social impacts in our pursuit of economic efficiency is a central consideration in the decision to contract. Unfortunately, neither the social impacts associated with overall employment reductions nor those caused by differential employment impacts appear to have been subject to any extensive empirical analysis to date. In considering the social aspects of contracting out services, therefore, we are left wallowing in an emotional debate with little strong empirical support behind arguments from either side.

A META-ANALYSIS OF NONECONOMIC
PERFORMANCE MEASUREMENTS

It is instructive to turn to measurements of noneconomic performance where these have been taken, to assist our narrative review of social performance. In this section I review these noneconomic measurements and investigate what can be learned from the meta-analytic perspective.

Table 7.8 lists the limited number of noneconomic performance measures from the literature that could be subjected to an analysis of effect sizes. The first observation is clear. There is a lack of statistical study in the whole area of noneconomic impacts, including the quality performance dimension, compared to the relatively large amount of research having been undertaken into economic performance. The few noneconomic measures found in these studies related to disparate interests. These measures included dimensions such the quality of training (Berglund 1992), quality of transport services (Musgrove 1988), and the quality of cleaning undertaken through various contracts in Sydney, Australia (Domberger, Hall, and Li 1994). Also included are noneconomic measures of both the range of municipal services offered and the level of rate benefits to ratepayers (Albin 1992).

Also evident in this table are some effect sizes that did not strictly measure the contracting-out relationship, but have significant policy implications in the area. These will be discussed shortly. For all noneconomic measurements available, effect sizes were calculated in the manner already described.

What can be learned through this meta-analytic perspective? We might firstly wish to comment on the signs of the results, but the proportions of one sign or another were not significantly different from those proportions expected by chance, at the level of .05. This is hardly surprising given so few studies.

The previous section noted that three studies had looked directly at the question of whether a relationship existed between the sector providing the services and the service quality itself. As indicated in Table 7.8, Berglund's (1992) study of manpower training centers in the U.S. yielded an effect size of $z_r = +0.05$ (with confidence limits -0.40 to $+0.50$). Consistent with effect size signs in the case of economic effects, the positive sign in front of the effect size indicated a worsening of quality (albeit slight) under contracting out to the private sector. The sample

TABLE 7.8 Noneconomic Effect Sizes and Confidence Limits for Studies of Contracting Out

Study	N	Estimated r	Zc	Wtd Av Z	p (wtd)=	Min CI	Max CI	Min CI Tot	Max CI Tot	Chi Sqr	Total Chi Square	Signif. Level
Noneconomic Measures	590			0.03		-0.05	0.11	-0.05	0.11		7.36	>0.10
Quality				-0.01	0.8623			-0.10	0.08		1.03	>0.90
Berglund (1992)	22	0.05	0.05			-0.40	0.50			0.06		
Musgrove (1988)	88	0.09	0.09			-0.13	0.30			0.74		
Domberger, Hall, and Li (1994)	364	-0.03	-0.03			-0.14	0.07			0.23		
Other				0.20	0.0372	0.01	0.39					
Albin (1992)	58	0.05	0.05			-0.22	0.31					
Albin (1992)	58	0.34	0.35			0.09	0.61					
Other Relationship Effects	3193			-0.10				-0.13	-0.06		11.32	<0.01
Public sector relationships	3138			-0.09	0.0000			-0.13	-0.06		5.21	<0.10
Domberger, Meadowcroft, and Thompson (1987)	2947	-0.08	-0.08			-0.12	-0.05			0.29		
Mehay and Gonzalez (1993)	138	-0.22	-0.23			-0.39	-0.06			2.38		
Mehay and Gonzalez (1993)	53	-0.31	-0.32			-0.60	-0.04			2.54		
Private sector relationships												
Pack (1992)	55	-0.41	-0.44	-0.44	0.0015	-0.71	-0.17					

size for this case was 22. Musgrove's (1988) review of quality of busing in Missouri yielded an effect size of $z_r = +0.09$ (with confidence limits -0.13 to $+0.30$). This effect size was again positive (and hence indicated a slightly worse quality under contracting) based on N = 88. The third and most comprehensive study, from Domberger, Hall, and Li (1994), yielded an effect size of $z_r = -0.03$ (with confidence limits -0.14 to $+0.07$.) Thus, a slight increase in quality under contracting of cleaning services was found, based on N = 364. None of the individual effect sizes were significantly different from zero. The effect sizes for these three quality studies along with their respective confidence limits are shown in Figure 7.4.

For all three studies combined, the weighted mean effect size was r_{ave} 5 20.01 (with confidence limits 20.10 to 10.08). Hence, based on this small sample of three studies (and N 5 474), no significant increase or decrease in the quality of services under contracting was found. [52]

The group did not show significant heterogeneity at the .05 level, and the variation in effect sizes for quality is likely to have been simply due to sampling error.[53]

The finding that quality-related effect sizes have a magnitude not significantly different from zero again extends the recent review of Domberger and Rimmer (1994). They argued that the effect of contracting on service quality was still an unknown quantity. The above statistical findings confirm that average quality effects are not negative or positive, but as best we can tell at present, do not differ

FIGURE 7.4   Effect Sizes and Confidence Limits for Studies on the Relationship Between Contracting and Service Quality

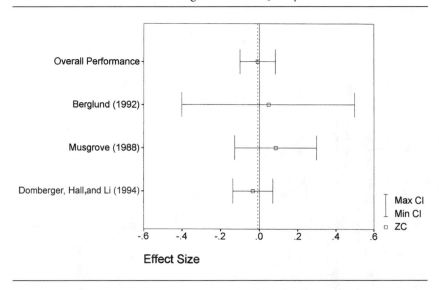

Effect Size

significantly from zero. Furthermore, the work of Domberger, Hall, and Li (1994) not only looked at the possible relationship between the sector providing services and quality levels, but also the extent to which quality levels themselves might depend on contract price. This was the only study found examining this relationship. They found "a weak price-quality trade off" statistically significant at the .10 level only. Combining these two conclusions, we could infer that there is no consistent relationship between the sector providing services under contract and service quality. This finding, along with those so far in this chapter, leads one to conclude that it is possible, on average, to provide services more cheaply whilst also maintaining service quality.[54]

Quality aside, the study by Albin (1992), which was noted previously, is also worthy of review. His analysis was of the possible existence of lower municipal rate payments by citizens with greater contracting out, and the possibility of a wider range of services being provided to citizens with more contracting. The fifty-eight Australian local councils analyzed pointed to an increase, rather than a reduction, in rates with more contracting, and failed to show a wider range of available services.

Albin's finding on the relationship between the extent of contracting out and the existence of lower rates to citizens represented an effect size of some +0.35, as shown in Table 7.8, with confidence limits of +0.09 to +0.61. In other words, significantly higher rate payments were found. This is the only analysis found that had looked at this question in a statistical manner. This lack of statistical support for the notion of reduced rates is worrying. Reports from management seminars (such as Proust 1995 speaking of the City of Melbourne, for instance) have asserted that rates have been reduced by 25 percent over the previous five years through a number of reforms such as council amalgamations and competitive contracting. Others, such as Doherty (1989, p. 27) have claimed that contracting out initiatives have themselves directly resulted in major tax reductions for the city of Rochester, New York. "Conservatively estimated," according to Doherty, "recent privatization applications are directly responsible for a $3.4m reduction in the city's 1987–1988 operating budget. The Municipal property tax levy would have been 8.9% higher had these savings not been realised." The contrast between the bold management claims and the lack of formal statistical support is stark.

The relationship between contracting out and the range of services, on the other hand, gave an effect size of only +0.05, with confidence limits of −0.22 to +0.31. To make anything other than a passing comment on these single data point observations would be inappropriate.

The last part of Table 7.8 presents the effect sizes calculated for various "other relationships." These data points were available as a spin-off from the data collection process for this research project. The findings of Domberger, Meadowcroft, and Thompson (1987), and Mehay and Gonzalez (1993) suggest, for instance, that other reform mechanisms may also be effective as well as the reform of contracting services. Both of these studies indicated that agencies in areas adjacent to those actually contracting services improved their own economic performance without contracting their own services. The Domberger, Meadowcroft, and Thompson (1987) study provided an effect size of -0.08 in studying the position of hospitals that had not tendered, but were in the same area as others who had. This effect size was not of the same magnitude as others in Domberger's work, but was nonetheless highly significant. Mehay and Gonzalez (1993) also provided two effect sizes for the position of cities in the United States where, although they did not contract out their sheriff services, they were next to a city that did. Here, an effect size of -0.23 was found for this relationship. For those cities that actually supply law enforcement services, an effect size of -0.32 was determined. In other words, expenditures for policing services were reduced where the city supplied services on contract itself, or was next to a city that was contracting out its services. All three effects represent a "secondary" impact of contracting rather than the direct effect.

The weighted mean effect size for this group of three effect sizes was $r_{ave} = -0.09$ (with confidence limits of -0.06 to -0.13). This weighted average was highly significant at the .01 level. Likewise, the unweighted mean, at $r_{ave} = -0.21$ was again highly significant.[55] The size of these estimates of average effect sizes is interesting. They are around 92 percent (in the case of the weighted mean) and 86 percent (for the unweighted mean) of the levels of the effect sizes for directly contracting. This seems unexpectedly high.

The last listed effect size is that of Pack (1992). He studied the effect on the quality of private computer network operations of outsourcing network management. Extensive data collection of various network measurements for fifty-five AT&T clients provided several effect size estimates. These were then averaged. The resultant effect size estimated was -0.44, and was highly significant at .01.[56] Because this measurement was taken of contracting between a private sector company and other private sector firms, it was separated out from the rest of the work. Its size nonetheless suggests that contracting out between private sector companies may also provide major improvements—in this case in computer network quality.

Overall, then, what is our judgment on the social dimension of performance for contracting out government services? What can be concluded about the promised consumer benefits such as improved quality, price, and choice, as well as potential social impacts such as employment impacts and equity issues? Several things. First, recall that noneconomic effect sizes of some importance have been detected in the international literature to supplement our narrative literature reviews. On the question of quality impacts of contracting out services, for instance, the average effect size for all available quality information was found to be not significantly different from zero. This implied that there is no statistically significant relationship between the sector providing services under a contract and the level of quality delivered, thus taking further the less definite conclusion of previous international reviews that saw no consensus on the quality issue and contracting. My reading of both the literature and the available meta-analytic findings has been a little more optimistic. It appears that lower costs are not, as a general rule, accompanied by detrimental changes to service quality levels. In other words, it seems that it is possible to provide services more cheaply whilst also maintaining service quality.

On the separate question of service price and greater choice, it has been concluded that, despite the measured reduction in local production costs for services, there is surprisingly little evidence around confirming that such lower production costs are passed through to citizens or consumers. The lack of statistical support here may simply be due to insufficient studies having been undertaken, but what little evidence that does exist suggests that under contracting, much of the savings made in theory are soaked up elsewhere in the organization or its high-level staffing. Perhaps the lesson here is to be careful not to assume that once contracting services, an organization automatically spends less as a matter of course. From the evidence, we know it doesn't.

Finally, the meta-analysis also enabled us to get a new perspective on various other spin-offs that appear to accompany contracting reforms. Agencies in areas adjacent to those actually contracting services, or else other service groups elsewhere in the contracting organization appear to improve their own economic performance without contracting services. From the measurements, the gains were significant and around four-fifths the size of gains made directly through contracting. The lesson here appears to be that a little bit of contracting goes a long way. The benefits and changes that apparently occur when organizations contract services appear to flow on smoothly to adjacent groups and agencies.

After considering the issue of employment, I concluded that contracting does lead to fewer people employed in the short term. Unfortunately, groups such as women working part time, and minorities such as blacks were affected more than others here. The contracting game therefore appears to have differential effects, with winners and losers. The biggest winners in the organization appear to be executives and contract managers who attract higher salaries, whilst the losers are women and part-timers, who are now employed on a more "flexible" basis. Of course, to the extent that cost savings for contracted services are passed through to citizens and consumers, they would be regarded as winners as well. The lesson here is that contracting out government services does indeed have social implications, and that these ought to be part of the decision to contract services for public agencies. Perhaps contracting many government services is inevitable. At a minimum, though, decisions on the speed at which contracting reforms are pursued should recognize these social impacts. They should also recognize our lack of knowledge about labor reabsorption rates, and further, should recognize that government has a role in balancing the pursuit of greater economic efficiency with social responsibilities.

DEMOCRATIC PERFORMANCE

There were no specific promises made about democratic performance in the same way as promises of cost savings were made when implementing contracting. Nonetheless, it might be assumed in the absence of any explicit discussion or promises that traditional aspects of the democratic process will be left unaffected by contracting.

One major concern about contracting is the possibility of corruption. This is evident through several major cases cited in the measured international review of Donahue (1989), and later in Kobrak (1995). Both argue that corruption is almost inevitable with contracting. A string of corruption cases within the contracting process in the U.S. Defense Department demonstrate that even with processes having been streamlined over several decades, and despite close media scrutiny and increased professional attention, the risk of corruption is ever present. The presence of this issue does not appear to have visibly affected private companies to their detriment in the financial sense. Indeed, many private companies apparently deal with the problem of significant corruption, but the resulting financial shortfalls are rarely spoken of. In most cases, such corruption does not usually impede the company from providing good returns to its shareholders. Corruption, although it may exist, is typically therefore not an overwhelming financial (or economic) issue in countries such as Australia, the United Kingdom, or the United States.

Undue Influence

The risk of corruption is more a risk to the democratic fabric itself through influence in political processes. Although stealing from the till of a private company might have some minor economic effect, it is unlikely to have any political consequence. Corruptly paying off government officials or donating large amounts to party election funds on the basis of having some influence over policy or being granted a contract at a later date, however, could quite rightly be seen as a threat to the democratic process. Instances of this occurring in the U.K. have been documented by Centre for Public Services (1995a, p. 23), and in the U.S. by Donahue (1989), Finder (1993), Schneider (1992), Van Horn (1991, p. 276), and Kobrak (1995). All share a common concern that this part of the privatization movement is not being given appropriate recognition and prominence.

This aspect of the contracting out phenomena should not be understated. After reviewing the extensive work of U.S. federal auditors, Schneider (1992), for instance, concluded that "the fraud problem is now endemic to all agencies." In the same vein, Kobrak repeats the old but in his view wise adage that "there are only two types of donors to political parties in the U.S.—those who currently have government contracts—and those who would like to have government contracts!"

A clear and direct connection between political party campaign contributions and subsequent contracting out decisions has often come to light in the U.S. Van Horn (1991, p. 276), for example, cites an instance where the accounting firm Price Waterhouse was awarded a contract despite not submitting the lowest bid, but after having "regularly and generously contributed to the governor's campaign coffers." According to Van Horn, this came to light only after the failure of Price Waterhouse to deliver vehicle registration and driver licensing services. Van Horn (1991, p. 276) also notes that dozens of county and municipal officials have been indicted and convicted of taking kickbacks in return for contracts. A U.S. attorney is quoted as remarking that "bribery for business" deals in New Jersey municipal public works departments are "systemic" in some parts of the state.

Almost identical accusations have been made on the other side of the Atlantic. The Centre for Public Services (1995a, p. 23) charges that the "contract culture brings with it the corruption culture." They note that many of the companies that have benefited from the contracting regime have made substantial donations to the Conservative party in the United Kingdom. The extent to which these donors properly won contracts on the basis of their own performance and tender bids is unknown. This reinforces the need for public sector contracting processes to be clear and open to scrutiny if elected leaders are to be accountable for decisions.

Evidence supporting the other side of this argument is sparse, and is limited to argument or anecdotes by authors such as Savas (1987). In arguing that privatization "is the key to both limited and better government" (p. 288), he sees corruption in contracts as an isolated phenomenon, so that in the words of Gormley's 1989 book review, "we need not fret a great deal about it." Indeed, Gormley notes that Savas "even goes so far as to equate kickbacks by government contractors with campaign contributions by union members." As Gormley rightly points out, "this disturbing analogy suggests a true believer whose zeal has gotten the better of him"!

The extent to which corruption in the form of kickbacks is worse under private contracting than it is under public provision is unclear but assumed to be higher. Such behavior is the undesirable underbelly of "homo economicus." Observe that, although the profit motive has figured as a central motivating force of managers in the writings of privatization supporters, the other side of the coin—the cash kickback for a favorable decision—has not. It has nonetheless obviously been an underlying motivational force for those convicted of corrupt behavior, and features in the writings of those opposing privatization. The concept of homo economicus can support both sides of the argument.

The existence of corruption in these cases covers two types of concern melded together. Firstly, a particular donor may have undue influence over policy matters at the political level. This conflicts with one of the fundamental values of the traditional public sector nominated in Chapter 4—that of collective choice through the political process. Secondly, corruption in the awarding of contracts to mates or party loyalists conflicts with the values of fairness and openness in the public sector. These values differ markedly from the practice of winning by any legal means in the market, and secret tactical decisions pursued in the private sector. The extent to which the public is willing to change from traditionally oriented values towards a mixture of traditional and more private business values will be tested over the coming decades. Different countries clearly have differing cultures regarding the acceptability of private business involvement in public policy processes. The extent to which the private business sector is or is not considered to have "undue" influence over government policy and decision processes is therefore likely to vary from culture to culture. For countries with a Westminster tradition, new mixtures of private and public provision will at a minimum emphasize the need for "open" government and for accountability mechanisms to be strengthened rather than weakened. The place of whistleblowers in the public sector will be a litmus test. Whistleblower legislation permits open disclosure of acts of fraud or maladministration that would otherwise remain secret. Such potential disclosure well exemplifies the differences between the two value systems.

In terms of frequency, one would also have to conclude that empirical evidence on fraud and corruption in contracting has been sparse. Nonetheless, the potential for serious conflict here exists, and its mere existence—even if this occurs in a small proportion of cases—tends to cast significant doubts on the integrity of both service production systems and public decisionmaking processes.

Accountability

The glue holding a democratic system of government together is the notion of accountability. The concept is broad, and in some ways, elusive. At its heart, the idea of accountability is that when we are requested by others to achieve something, we report back to them on how we have performed.[57] It is central to each of the five evaluation framework dimensions—economic, social, democratic, legal, and political. Accountability is also a strong thread running throughout our evaluation of privatization actions. Indeed, in the case of contracting government services, one of the major claims of the proponents of outsourcing is that accountability is improved through the adoption of this process. Claims are made on both sides. Most reviews or discussions on contracting simply assert that contracting should improve accountability in theory. The Industry Commission (1996, p. 5), for instance, argues that "if implemented well, CTC can enhance accountability . . . primarily by clearer specification of objectives and allocation of responsibility . . . and by improving information on standards and outcomes." Many simply consider it "obvious" that accountability will be increased compared to in-house service provision. Others, such as Mulgan (1997) or Donahue (1989), caution against such simplicity, with the latter arguing that "there is no reason to believe that private organisations will always, or usually improve accountability."

To the extent that information on the unit costs of services becomes explicit through the contracting process, moves to improve the specification of services and units costs should be regarded as an improvement in accountability, at least in the sense of establishing a better understanding of financial parameters. As we learn about unit costs through these reforms, there is little doubt that this aspect of accountability can improve. Contracts, of course, can be made with either in-house or external teams, however, and need not imply outsourcing. The contracting process is the lever for improvements, rather than the sector providing the services.

But the concept of accountability is broader than simply unit costs for deliverables. What frameworks can we adopt to assist us in considering accountability issues when contracting services?

Corbett (1992) provides one. He warns that, as well as upward accountability up the line to the minister, parliament, and the people, two other forms of accountability also exist: accountability inwards, to a personal or moral public code, and accountability outwards, to the community. It is likely that accountability to the community (through mechanisms such as freedom of information legislation, the ombudsman, and the law courts) will become increasingly important in the future.

Stone (1995) provides a more sophisticated framework for considering accountability. But what can we learn from a theoretical perspective on accountability? A lot. Stone sees accountability in terms of five dimensions:

- accountability as parliamentary control;
- the managerialist conception of accountability;
- accountability as judicial and quasi-judicial review;
- accountability as constituency relations, and
- market accountability.

These five perspectives of accountability are outlined in Table 7.9.

Each of these five conceptions of accountability implies a different relationship with individual citizens. Each also serves to remind us that accountability is a multifaceted concept in a democracy. Some accountability systems are top-down, and some are bottom-up. The simple question, Does accountability improve with contracting? requires consideration of all dimensions. Of course, the relationship between government and citizens is an interesting one, too. Citizens allow government to have ultimate power, but the price is a suitable system of accountability. As citizens relate to government, whether as users, clients subject to regulation, participants, litigants, or interested citizens, they expect such accountability to exist.[58]

Several authors have pointed to the inadequacies of contractual arrangements in maintaining full accountability. Gilmour and Jensen (1998) argue that whilst

TABLE 7.9   Five Perspectives of Accountability

Accountability as parliamentary control	Here, administrators and agencies are responsive to the concerns of members of Parliament in the context of particular policies or actions in legislating, supporting ministers, providing prompt answers to ministers as issues arise so that legal obligations and administrative requirements are complied with. Traditionally, this has been termed ministerial responsibility.
The managerialist conception of accountability	This accountability has three features. It involves strategic rather than detailed control, it emphasizes agency self-evaluation, and it incorporates periodic external evaluation and a rationalization of agency responsiveness. The agency is required to meet certain objective tests and meet specified performance measures, along with audits.
Accountability as judicial and quasi-judicial review	Accountability here is understood to be process-oriented, with the application of strict formal standards for decisionmaking. For example, administrative or statutory rules to prevent conflict of interest in decisionmaking and avenues for the application of legal processes to test the degree of accountability. Examples include the review of administrative decisions in the courts through state or federal administrative appeals tribunals.
Accountability as constituency relations	Accountability here is viewed in terms of institutionalizing the concerns of individuals. These can include governing boards, the requirement that certain authorities hold an annual meeting of constituents, the use of public hearings by advisory bodies or regulatory agencies, or the existence of consumer councils or ombudsmen to take up individual grievances and monitor performance.
Market accountability	Accountability under this dimension includes the responsiveness of service providers to a body of "sovereign" consumers. This requires a choice of suppliers as well as a choice of quality and quantity of service with the ability for the consumer to opt out of the purchase.

SOURCE: Stone 1995.

contracting may offer efficiencies, it may also simultaneously enable government and its officials to escape legal responsibility for actions of the state. This amounts, in their view, to "a wholesale loss of government accountability." They argue that, irrespective of political accountabilities, private companies may not be held legally accountable under contracting. To them, "when public functions are delegated to private actors and are allowed to be transformed into 'private' actions, public accountability is inevitably lost." Mulgan (1997) also argues that contracting out at best involves a trade-off between efficiency and accountability, and at worst, involves a reduction in both. "Denials of such a trade-off are fallacious rhetoric," in his mind. He further points out that accountability is "limited to the terms of the contract," and that in contracting out services, public organizations surrender a degree of day-to-day responsibility and accountability.

Everyday examples of the accountability inadequacies have recently also been provided by the Australian Commonwealth Ombudsman.[59] After noting that accountability and probity are particularly important given the strong statutory and discretionary powers of government agencies, she then notes:

> contracting out is one mechanism by which governments can deliver their services. However, the rules associated with contracting are muddy, contradictory, or not yet written, and when it comes to issues of accountability and redress there is a new twilight zone. It is this blurring between public accountability and commercial remedies (through for example, contracts and/or common law) that needs to be carefully considered in the contracting context because current redress mechanisms cannot cover all the situations and questions being raised. . . . The department and contract supplier are party to the contract—the service recipient is excluded. . . . Service standards cannot be enforced if contract specifications are not clear. . . . The Ombudsman Act, the FOI Act and the Privacy Act may not be available unless the jurisdiction of these institutions is extended to cover this new form of service delivery. . . . I believe that a range of hybrid strategies will be necessary.

These comments relate very much to the expectations of people as citizens as well as consumers, and are central to assessing the accountability question. The ombudsman lists a multitude of issues relating to accountability and public interest matters, statutory powers relating to freedoms or entitlements, service provision, enforcement and oversight, and community standards. Each deserves full consideration. She notes also that the New Zealand experience provides a useful reference point on the need for an extension of some administrative law, freedom of information, and privacy legislation in order to cover the activities of privatized enterprises. "Experience has shown this to be important in the maintenance of public confidence in, and the probity of, these activities," she notes. Interestingly, Mulgan (1997) also draws on the New Zealand experience, arguing that where contractual arrangements preclude the intervention by the minister in remedying a deficiency in the provision of a public service, "members of the public may consider, with some justice, that their rights of public accountability have been seriously compromised."

Overall, then, we might reflect that assertions suggesting accountability has improved or has reduced with contracting out ought to be seen as too vague. Which specific part of these accountability mechanisms have been affected, in what way, and with what empirical results might be more enlightened questions to pursue in order to add to our knowledge base. We may conclude that under the managerialist conception of accountability and with our experience of market accountability, accountability may well have improved on average. Other aspects of accountability, however, are not seen in such terms. Concerns raised from empirical experience suggest that other dimensions of accountability may well have declined.

One major factor when the question of accountability and contracting services is being considered is the reality that our expectations have also risen compared to the past. As the public administration era has been superseded by new public management practices, we have expected the old culture of administering orders with political actors being responsible to be replaced with a new one.[60] The traditional notion of accountability, despite its theoretical attractions, did not appear to work well. The new culture is managing for results, with managers now encouraged to be accountable for meeting specific deliverables and service levels. The move has been from a concept of accountability where political leaders were expected to be responsible for everything, to one where managers were responsible for the implementation of political decisions and policies.

We might at this stage also ponder the fundamental question—assuming for a moment that accountability is increased by outsourcing services: To the extent that the manager and the contractor are more accountable for clearer service specifications, does this also mean that the political leadership is less accountable? I suspect the answer to this conundrum, to a large degree, is yes.

What are the implications here? Under any move to outsource government services, critical decisions will be needed to determine just what institutional arrangements should be formulated in the future to ensure adequate accountability, especially to ensure that there is no overlap without generating major costs or frustrations. Private companies wishing to provide public services may have to accept a higher degree of public intrusion than is common in normal commercial dealings.[61] Importantly, the accountability requirements deemed appropriate for a particular service to the public should be specified as part of the initial contract, rather than as an afterthought following the decision to contract out.

Also central to these concerns on accountability are issues of commercial-in-confidence and the extent to which commercial contracts can lessen the openness expected traditionally from public agencies. Openness of government decisions and processes deserves further discussion. It is a key foundation of democratic processes, and is fundamentally at odds with the "closed" requirements of commerciality, competition, and private sector contracts. Reviewers have reached differing conclusions on the extent to which openness in government is compromised by the granting of private sector contracts. Some reviewers have argued that contracting out, by definition, encourages closed and secretive deals. Buck and Chaundy (1992), for instance, note that since the 1988 Local Government Act in the U.K. many authorities have refused to submit information about their services because it is now seen as being commercially sensitive. They note that recent data from the Chartered Institute for Public Finance is not publicly available. In this same vein, Szymanski (1993, p. 14) points to the figure of around one-quarter of the 403 local Authorities in England and Wales as having refused to reveal the value of contracts although they are required to do so by law. This lack of information supply may have major implications on accountability. Through their refusal, these councils not only appear to have given scant regard to their own accountability, but importantly, they have also broken the law.[62] Others such as Savas sit at the opposite end of this argument. They insist that this issue is simply overstated.[63]

Recent experience in Australia has highlighted the closure of avenues traditionally available to the community for inquiry into areas central to government accountability. The unavailability of information on the costs associated with Melbourne's World Congress Centre development in 1990, and more recently in respect to the Grand Prix Corporation and Intergraph Company, has been justified by both sides of politics on the grounds of this information being commercial-in-confidence. Closing off these avenues of information under this veil does indeed reduce accountability—at least as it has been practiced in the past. As Ernst (1995) warns, an accountability vacuum is evident in the recurring problems being experienced in Victoria in getting even the most basic information about the awarding of state contracts. As he puts it, "the conventional machinery of public accountability can seize up in the 'Contract State.'" Lessons from the 1980s and 1990s are also instructive here. Commercial confidentiality was used as the reason for the suppression by the private sector Westpac Bank of information relating to the mismanagement of foreign currency loans, secret commissions, and illegal behaviors resulting in client losses of $33 million. In Western Australia, commercial confidentiality was the reason given for secrecy from both the public and from Parliament in relation to the Western Australian government's deals supporting private interests through Rothwells Bank and the Bond Corporation in the Kwinana petrochemical project. Both of these scandals, subsequently known as the "Westpac Letters Affair" and "WA Inc.," centered around the inappropriate use of the commercial-in-confidence shield. No doubt other governments around the globe could also provide examples of such inappropriate secrecy.

A loss of accountability for reasons of commercial-in-confidence need not necessarily follow the granting of contracts, since summaries of such contracts could be provided to the public for information.[64] However, the fact that privatization has in general been accompanied by a loss of access to contractual and performance information could be seen as marking a different priority of government in balancing both the need to conduct its business, and the right of the public to continue to have access to performance information relating to government accountability. The extent to which communities are sensitive to reduced access to such information is ultimately tested at the ballot box.

Overall, then, arguments for the likelihood of improved accountability need to be weighed up alongside the empirical findings from the above mentioned case study examples. These criticized the closure of processes to public scrutiny, and emphasized the need to consider accountability in the broader sense, as well as the part that relates to financial measures. In terms of the empirical statistical evidence included in the meta-analysis, the only study of relevance was that of Carver (1989). He looked at accountability as an issue in his study of tax assessments in Massachusetts, and concluded that from the statistical perspective "no change in accountability was discernible." It is therefore concluded that whether or not accountability generally increases or decreases with contracting is an important component of performance. Although accountability was often discussed in the literature as a central concept, it was rarely evaluated with any rigor. Empirically, then, the question of accountability remains open. Nonetheless, there are some lingering concerns that some dimensions of public accountability are in fact reduced with contracting, not improved, despite the greater accountability promised.

Absence of Competition

One further aspect of note is the potential influence of corruption on competition. The case of New York's garbage collection service well illustrates this point. Here, the reputed involvement of some 475 companies in the refuse collection and disposal market has not led to good competition. The contracting cartels for refuse disposal are reputed to operate so effectively that the existence of this number of companies does not lead to true competition. Interestingly, the absence of competition and the presence of corruption in this sector also cannot be regarded as a temporary phenomenon. Several years after the observations and analysis of Donahue (1989), attempts to clean up the $1.5 billion trash hauling industry in New York were again in the daily New York press. Simmons (1995) reported that the current mayor was "planning his most ambitious assault ever on the mob by zeroing in on its waste carting industry." Proposed actions included legislation to install certified monitors to oversee garbage carting. According to his report, since first allowing private haulers to pick up commercial garbage in 1957, a cartel had been formed that had eliminated competitors and had forced up prices to the highest in the nation. Simmons quoted New York City's rates as some 63 percent higher than those for Los Angeles, 194 percent higher than those for Chicago, and 246 percent higher than those for Philadelphia. The mayor's actions are said to have been initiated after his attention had been drawn to the fact that the Manhatten District Attorney had indicted twenty-

TABLE 7.10   Examples of the Evasion of Fair Competition in Australia

Companies	Example of Competition Evasion	Date	Outcome
Thomas Nationwide Transport (TNT) Ansett Australia	Price-fixing and regulating market shares in the express freight market	Aug. 1994	$5m fine
Mayne Nickless	As above	Dec. 1994	$6m fine
AMP	Misleading and deceptive misrepresentations on its 80/20 investment scheme	Jan. 1995	Repayment of $50m to 260,000 customers
Multiplex Constructions Leighton Contractors	Collusive tendering on a Commonwealth Offices project (Sydney)	Sept. 1995	Repayment of $0.75m each as unsuccessful tenderers
Pioneer Concrete (Qld) Boral Resources (Qld) CSR (Qld)	Rigging prices for concrete in South East Queensland	Dec. 1995	$6.6m fine $6.6m fine $6.6m fine

SOURCE: Adapted from Field (1995) and Bice and Salmons (1995).

three companies the previous June for price-fixing. Thus, corruption remains an endemic and systemic problem in this particular industry, following the introduction of the private sector forty years ago.

In other industries, too, recent court decisions have highlighted the insidious nature of companies systematically avoiding competitive markets. Dubbed "Vitamin Inc.," "the U.S. Justice Department fined Swiss pharmaceutical and chemical giant F. Hoffmann-La Roche $US500 million and its German counterpart, BASF Aktiengesellschaft, $US225 million for their roles in a decade-long conspiracy to set prices and carve up the world market for vitamins," according to Schmidt (1999).

Of course, examples of the absence of real competition in the commercial world are not limited to the United States. Parallels to this have been documented around the globe. Field (1995) reports, for instance, that throughout 1994–95 several prominent Australian companies were involved and convicted of attempting to evade fair competition. Table 7.10 illustrates some examples.

The commercial incentives for avoiding fair competition are presumably large, and ever present. In support of this, Bice and Salmons (1995) comment after the conviction in Australia of the Pioneer, Boral Resources, and CSR companies, that massive fines had failed to deter collusion in the U.S. and Canada. Here, it was reported that jail terms had been implemented for those involved.

LEGAL PERFORMANCE

Few cases were found of court verdicts, appeals, or ombudsman criticisms following the contracting out of services aside from those already mentioned. Recall the concerns of Gilmour and Jensen (1998) mentioned in the discussion on accountability: They noted that it is often not a simple matter to determine whether services being delivered under a contract are subject to public law or private law. This is no mean admission! They pointed out that in the United States, actions by the state are subject to rules including the Bill of Rights, the Fourteenth Amendment, a host of general management laws, the requirements of executive orders, budget circulars, and for the state and municipal levels of government, Section 1983 of the Civil Rights Act of 1871. Private behavior is not so constrained, being subject only to common law such as contract, tort, or property actions. This potentially leaves a dilemma for those with an interest in assessing the performance of contracting on a legal basis. It is a dilemma on which I will spend little time, however, as I am more interested in actual empirical evidence, rather than conceptual or theoretical legal concerns.

Legal arrangements documented within contracts obviously form an important thread to contracting. As noted by Domberger (1994), most contracts include financial penalties of one sort or another to support specifications being met. Also, in his review of Australian experience with contracting, Domberger notes the likely existence of collusive tendering. He suggests that in considering the integrity of contracting, we need to balance this concern against the real possibility of potential bias in favor of in-house bidders. This balance is essential.

It is also important explicitly to include within the contract aspects of price control if relevant to the service. This is particularly so in view of the research of Holcombe (1991). He reviewed the philosophy of contracts for a series of water treatment plants in the U.S., and then contrasted these ideas against the actual contracts for seven case studies, along with the operational experience of each. Holcombe's work had two major findings.

His evaluation of privatization agreements found firstly that "although there are standard wills, standard leases, and standard loan agreements . . . there are no standardized privatization agreements; each of the agreements examined in this study differed significantly in provisions and in the wording of similar provisions." He commented that a possible reason for the lack of standardization is the newness of water treatment contracts in the U.S. Furthermore, he argued that contracts for municipalities might often be less than favorable. In drawing up the agreement, privatizing firms have an informational advantage, since they already know a great deal about the task and probably about other agreements. Also, the private firm has an incentive to strike a profitable bargain, irrespective of unforeseen costs or circumstances.

Secondly, he found that privatizing firms were allowed to pass on most of their costs to the municipality. In five of the seven cases, most costs were "passed through" to the customer. In theory, there are significant advantages of having a profit-making firm rather than a nonprofit organization engage in production. In practice, though, the full costs of production inefficiencies were borne by the private firms in only two of these seven cases. Thus, in nearly all cases, although contracts should in theory have resulted in lower costs to the service recipients, they did not. In five of the seven cases, the actual contracts themselves were structured in such a way that any cost increases to the contractor (such as raw materials or labor costs) were passed through. The customer paid for any cost inefficiencies. Thus, no incentive actually existed to ensure efficiency once the contract had been awarded. This illustration emphasizes the requirement to assess not the theory of contracts but the practice. Contracts may well need to ensure more accountability for economic as well as other dimensions of performance.

POLITICAL PERFORMANCE

A major goal of contracting out in many areas has been the reduction in trade union power. Through contracting, greater flexibility in workforce numbers and working practices has been encouraged. Power has shifted from unions and the workforce over to employers and the funders of services. In modern parlance, power has shifted away from the providers, over to the purchasers. The extent to which contracting has also rewarded loyal party supporters by opening up desirable new markets is unclear, but anecdotes from the United Kingdom remind us that it remains a possibility (Centre for Public Services 1995a).

Indeed, Kobrak (1995) refers to the relationship between private business and government in the United States as "cosy politics." This reference reminds us that the advent of contracting may well result in a shift in the balance of power away from the traditional power base of the unionized workforce towards private businesses intent on gaining contracts. This cannot be dismissed, as it has been by advocates such as Savas, as an unimportant and minor issue. When, as Kobrak states, business had an undue influence on around two-thirds of the Housing and Urban Development Capital Works funds in the U.S. throughout the 1980s, this influence is no small matter. Donahue (1989) again points to the "chronic troublesomeness" of the relationship between government and business in the contracting of U.S. military projects. In support of his concern, he notes that all defense contractors have political action committees for channeling contributions to legislators, and direct links into the armed services themselves. Importantly, Donahue notes that between 1964 and 1986, some eleven major Pentagon and congressional reports looking to improve military procurement pointed to more competition as a key. Such calls, in Donahue's mind, spring from the powerful intellectual aesthetics of economic theory, our sometimes blind faith in the benign effects of competition, and repeated instances of discovering sole source suppliers in the military. Surprisingly, it is simply assumed that competition is easy to arrange and somehow self-enforcing. This repeated call for competition appears to forget that, although competition does tend to boost efficiency, it is also costly. Donahue quotes the case of the Nike Ajax missile system, which in the late 1950s saved $5 million, whilst the cost of circulating technical information to prospective bidders was estimated at $23 million. More importantly, in order to ensure competition in some markets, a government supplier may well need to make a decision to stay in the market—to continue to row as well as steer. The action of staying in the market certainly demonstrates the priority for better market competition above the narrower perspective of assessing the costs of an individual contract to an organization.

Politically, contracting out can represent an opportunity to reduce the level of services offered to the community. If this is done, much of the flack can then be taken by the contractor, or at a minimum, the contractor can act as a buffer between the organization and those directly affected by the service reduction. Such service reductions would rarely be an explicit political goal, and would most likely be part and parcel of the "small government is good government" philosophy. It is also a logical extension of the practice of new public management to separate policy from implementation—to separate political decisions from service provision. Notwithstanding any productive efficiencies that may arise in this separation, it does have a political advantage. Education standards and operations become a matter not for government but for the contracted schools, whether public or private. Health becomes not a matter for government, but for hospital networks contracted to meet specifications. Even emergency services become a matter not for government, but for contracted suppliers. Supporters of this policy/ service-provision divide argue that accountabilities are being more appropriately distributed between the responsible parties, whilst opponents claim governments are simply trying to pass the buck and avoid responsibility altogether. In any event, to avoid the possibility of such reductions occurring with contracting, a statement of intent that services will not be reduced would be sensible for governments implementing contracting arrangements. The extent to which this has actually occurred in practice is unclear.

A further issue of relevance to the political arena is the existence of risks. Contracting inevitably involves a range of commercial risks. Traditionally, neither the community nor government have welcomed the taking of commercial risks, however, and the attendant probability, even though small, of failures. It is possible for commercial risks to become significant political capital and hence even small commercial failures can become large political risks for elected leaders.

The extent to which the community wishes to encourage or discourage stronger links between business and government will be tested over the coming decades. As businesses become more dominated by fewer major players, these linkages are likely to be the subject of more debate. Likewise the extent to which the community is prepared to view privatization as simply an economic issue will depend on changing community values, on the importance of other dimensions, and on community awareness. The question of how employment losses are handled politically is one aspect of this. In Australia, conservative political leaders currently follow the belief that employment changes are not the responsibility of a minister, but simply a matter for the markets. In Canada, anecdotes from defense provide a very different picture. Howard (1998) paints the Alternative Service Delivery Program as a hot public policy issue, and one which ranked high on the political scale of interest once employment implications of efficiencies were made explicit.

Lastly, and at the risk of repeating the point, it cannot be stressed too much that much of the rhetoric accompanying calls to contract out or subject public sector services to competitive tendering have at their root the privatization ideology. The call to outsource "in line with world best practice of the private sector" is one strand of the privatization belief structure. To the believers, the call to compete with superior private sector efficiency is self-evident. To opponents, the simplicity of this mantra and the underlying assumption that economic efficiency is the only important element of the decision amounts to simplemindedness.

CONCLUSIONS

After this review of privatization as contracting out, what do we now know? Where are we left after a brief narrative review of the literature and a meta-analysis of two decades of studies measuring contracting performance?

A massive distribution of findings is available from the literature. Literally, we can find what we wish to find and quote from dozens of studies justifying our own predetermined beliefs about contracting. Focusing in on those research studies that had reported the statistical characteristics of measurements taken, I came to more definitive conclusions. Looking at the measurements themselves, it was observed that they were mostly from local government, mostly U.S. in origin, and mostly from refuse collection, cleaning, and maintenance services. A significant association between cost savings and contracting was found corresponding to a level of around 6 to 12 percent, depending on how the average was taken, and assuming a few percent for the cost of contracting process. Overall, therefore, it was found that contracting resulted in cost savings, although the precise figures were subject to some important qualifications.

The largest cost savings found were in cleaning, maintenance, and refuse collection (19 to 30 percent), and each of these was highly significant. No significant reductions were found for other services (which varied from average savings of 8 percent to a 24 percent cost increase). Statistically, services were also found to be heterogeneous—meaning that we must treat services as if they are all quite different, statistically speaking. The meta-analysis indicated that both contracting out services and contracting services in-house produced cost savings. Focusing on the picture of how effect sizes appeared to differ, several moderator variables were examined. It was found that the sector providing the service (i.e., the "privatization" of service provision itself) had only a weak impact, if any. Other variables moderated reported results far more strongly. For instance, the author's discipline strongly influenced reported results, with the Finance/Accounting and Business disciplines reporting the highest effect sizes. Studies published after 1990 reported effects sizes only 14 percent the size of those before this date, on average. More sophisticated studies also appeared to show smaller effect sizes, as did those from the United States and measurements from research theses. The largest effect sizes also seemed to have been reported in studies of federal government, compared to state and local government, and compulsory competitive tendering also showed smaller effect sizes than noncompulsory contracting.

On the question of the quality impact of contracting government services, a meta-analysis of the literature found that from the few sets of measurements existing, there is no discernable relationship one way or the other. In other words, as best we know at present, contracting does not reduce or increase quality, as a general rule. It was also determined that there were some real flow-on effects from contracting services, both inside the organization to those groups not contracting, and outside the organization to organizations not contracting. This has the important implication that a little bit of contracting discipline seems to go a long way in terms of changing culture and encouraging efficiencies.

In terms of other social dimensions of performance, contracting did appear to lead to fewer people employed. It also led to some serious differential impacts, at least in the short term, with women part-time workers and minority groups bearing the brunt of efficiencies. Under the democratic performance dimension, some risks were seen to occur with contracting in terms of the potential for players in the business sector to have undue influence on political processes. The effect of contracting on accountability was concluded to be an open question from the empirical evidence. However, it was noted that government accountability has several relevant aspects to its character, and whilst service operations and management accountability may have improved, other aspects such as openness to scrutiny and accessibility to government information have not. Some significant legal differences were found in the literature between the general assumptions made about contracts, and the actual wording and implications for costs in practice. In terms of political performance, the practice of contracting was seen as being associated with risks, which although they were the usual commercial risks, could become powerful capital for opposing political parties.

8

Performance Data for Privatization as Enterprise Sales

Having undertaken a review of privatization in the form of contracting out, I will now turn to privatization viewed as the sale of an enterprise. In these next two chapters, I review the international performance measurements made for such sales. In this chapter, I will discuss the selection process, and will also describe what this data looks like—where it is from, who produced it, and how it was reported. In Chapter 9, I then undertake a brief narrative review and a meta-analysis of this data. Through this, I seek to gain a better picture of the evidence on the performance of government enterprises when they are sold to the private sector. As the discussion progresses, my aim is not only to get a better definition of the issues at stake in these privatizations, but also to get an improved understanding of how enterprise performance itself changes when privatized, and, importantly, to achieve better clarity as to the winners and losers of privatization processes.

SEARCHING FOR DATA

As was the case for contracting out, the literature is again voluminous. A large body of reports appears to claim empirical evidence on the performance of selling enterprises. Recall that the search undertaken to ensure maximum coverage of findings on this topic covered the three major databases ABI/INFORM, PAIS, and DAO. Additionally, the bibliographies of all major reviews and the majority of other references were covered, as well as thesis listings and some suggestions from colleagues.

Some 292 references directly relating to the performance of privatization as the sale of enterprises were identified, along with a further 266 relevant general reviews and discussions of the effectiveness of relationships between public and private sector business. Abstracts of all references were read, and the retrieval of all articles was followed up. A closer look was then made at these 292 references, all of which were listed as potential sources of empirical evidence on the effectiveness of enterprise sales. Eleven of these studies presented the same findings in multiple publications. Of the remainder, success was achieved in retrieving some 230 of these. After scrutiny, a total of 162 reports presented some form of empirical result on the effectiveness of selling one or more enterprises.

All of these reports, however, could not be included in the meta-analysis. For inclusion in this quantitative meta-analysis, the acceptance criteria were again twofold. Firstly, the study obtained needed to research performance impact(s) of an enterprise sale or sales using empirical evidence. Secondly, the study either had to report sufficient statistical information on these performance measures, or had to present sufficient empirical performance information to enable statistical estimates of variance to be developed through a reanalysis by this author. In other words, the quantitative relationship between the sale of an enterprise to the private sector and its performance (or associated impacts) had to be explicit, with the statistic used to test significance being reported or else some other estimate of variability.

Those studies considered as potentially having relevant empirical findings are listed in Table 8.1. This table indicates whether the results from each report retrieved could be included in the meta-analysis. Again, clearly, most could not. Most commonly, insufficient statistical information was reported. In several cases, raw data was presented, and it was possible to analyze these data from first principles to provide statistical information for inclusion.[1] As was the case for the previous analysis of the effectiveness of contracting out, results of any one research study were included only once.[2]

The actual criteria for inclusion in the meta-analysis deserve some discussion. Strictly speaking, only studies that formally include statistical controls for background variations in the performance measure being assessed should be included in a meta-analysis. For example, in meta-analyzing the effectiveness of drug treatments on depression, Anderson and Tomenson (1994, p. 239) included in their analysis only results from "double blind randomized controlled trials in depressed patients." The importance of ensuring the existence of the double-blind experimental design, where a statistically optimal set of measurements can be ensured, is clear for the case of medical research. A clear and unequivocal association between the drug treatment and the level of depression is being sought. Yet, the importance of careful statistical controls in other research, such as that presently being undertaken, is also high.

In the drug treatment meta-analysis of Anderson and Tomenson, the exclusion of studies from the analysis was determined on the basis of insufficient information being reported. As well, though, criteria for exclusion also included low drug dosages, patients suffering from other illnesses as well as depression, and any other condition that resulted in the likelihood of treatment groups not strictly being comparable. If such strict criteria had been applied to this research work on the relationship between enterprise sales and performance, only one single study

TABLE 8.1 Enterprise Sales Empirical Studies

Result?	Author (Primary)	Other Authors	Year of Publication	Reference Number	Comments re Inclusion in Meta-Analysis	Included in Meta-Analysis?
Yes	Abdala, M. A.		1992	569	Insufficient statistical results presented.	No
Yes	Adam, C.	Cavendish, W., and Mistry, P.	1992	332	Insufficient statistical results presented.	No
Yes	Aggarwal, R.	Leal, R., and Hernandez, L.	1993	186		Yes
Yes	Anonymous		1992	12	See 521.	No
Yes	Anonymous		1988	36	No statistical results presented.	No
Yes	Anonymous		1994	177	No statistical privatization results presented.	No
Yes	Anonymous		1985	251		No
Yes	Anonymous		1994	430	No statistical results presented.	No
No	Anonymous		1995	1034	No statistical privatization results presented.	No
No	Anonymous		1995	1035	No statistical privatization results presented.	No
On Order	Anonymous		1995	1036	No statistical privatization results presented.	No
On Order	Anonymous		1995	1052	No statistical privatization results presented.	No
Yes	Arbey, B.M.		1994	1057	No statistical privatization results presented.	No
Yes	Avishur, A.		1993	548		Yes
Yes	Bhaskar, V.	Khan, M.	1994	1071		Yes
Yes	Bishop, M.	Thompson, D.	1995	1027		Yes
Yes	Bishop, M.	Thompson, D.	1992	33	Regulatory reforms analyzed.	No
Yes	Bishop, M. (Eds).	Kay, J., and Mayer, C.	1994	943		No
Yes	Bishop, M.R.	Kay, J.	1994	327	See 944.	No
Yes	Bishop, M.R.	Kay, J.A.	1992	532	No statistical results presented.	No
Yes	Boardman, A.	Freedman, R., and Eckel, C.	1989	865	Insufficient statistical results presented.	No
OOM			1986	866	Insufficient statistical results presented.	No
On Order	Bourn, J.		1995	1043	No statistical privatization results presented.	No
Yes	Bunn, D.	Vlahos, K.	1989	270	No statistical privatization results presented.	No
No?	Burawoy, M.	Hendley, K.	1992	452	No statistical results presented.	No
Yes	Centre for Public Services		1995	979	Insufficient statistical results presented.	No
Yes?	Chernoff, J.		1994	179	No statistical privatization results presented.	No
Yes	Chi, K.S.		1989	68	No statistical privatization results presented.	No
Yes	Chwee-Huat Ta		1992	15	No sale, thus no results.	No
On Order	Conyon, M. J.		1995	1048	Insufficient statistical results presented.	No
458	Cook, C.	Kirkpatrick, C.	1995	1064	Insufficient statistical results presented.	No
Yes	Cowan, G.L.		1983	955	See 458.	No
Yes	Crespo, M.		1994	183	No statistical privatization results presented.	No
Yes	Davies, J.R.	McInnes, W.	1982	70	No statistical privatization results presented.	No

(continues)

TABLE 8.1 *continued*

Result?	Author (Primary)	Other Authors	Year of Publication	Reference Number	Comments re Inclusion in Meta-Analysis	Included in Meta-Analysis?
On Order	Dinavo, J.V.		1995	1065	No statistical privatization results presented.	No
Yes	Domberger, S.		1993	773	Reanalyzed the data.	Yes
No	Duncan, I.	Bollard, A.	1992	337	No statistical privatization results presented.	No
Yes	Dunleavy, P.		1986	1008	No statistical privatization results presented.	No
	Dunsire, A.	Hartley, K., and Parker, D.	1991	20	Insufficient statistical results presented.	No
Yes	Dunsire, A.		1991	523	Insufficient statistical results presented.	No
Yes	Dunsire, A.	Hartley, K., Parker, D., and Dimitriou, B.	1988	650	Insufficient statistical results presented.	No
Yes	Edlin, B.		1994	361	Insufficient statistical results presented.	No
Yes	Engen, J.R.		1994	362	Insufficient statistical results presented.	No
Yes	Ernst, J.		1993	17	No statistical results presented.	No
Yes	Ernst, J.		1993	147	No statistical privatization results presented.	No
Yes	Ernst, J.		1991	519	Insufficient statistical results presented.	No
Yes	Ernst, J.		1994	957	Insufficient statistical results presented.	No
Yes	Fernyhough, C.J.		1990	18	No statistical privatization results presented.	No
Yes	Foreman-Peck, J.	Manning, D.	1988	688	Insufficient statistical results presented.	No
No?	Foster, C.D.		1992	331	No statistical results presented.	No
Yes	Franks, S.		1993	43	No statistical results presented.	No
Yes	Galal, A.	Shirley, M. (eds)	1994	329	No statistical privatization results presented.	No
Yes	Galal, A.	Jones, L., Tandon, P., and Vogelsang, I.	1994	521	Predictive analysis, empirical measurements.	No
Yes?	Gerchunoff, P.		1993	622	Insufficient statistical results presented.	No
Yes	Giday, A.	Coloma, G.	1994	366	Incomplete statistical analysis of performance of privatized companies.	No
Yes	Gray, G.		1987	418	No statistical results presented.	No
Yes	Green, R.	Vogelsang, I.	1994	946	Insufficient statistical results presented.	No
Yes?	Hachette, D.	Luders, R., and Tagle, G.	1993	619	Insufficient statistical results presented.	No
No	Hall, T.		1994	356	No statistical results presented.	No
Yes	Hammond, C.J.		1992	32	No statistical results presented.	No
Yes	Hartley, K.	Parker, D.	1990	266	Insufficient statistical results presented.	No
Yes	Haskel, J.	Szymanski, S.	1992	944		Yes
Yes	Hayashi, P.M.	Sevier, M., and Trapani, J.M.	1987	960	No before/after privatization presented.	No

	Author	Co-author(s)	Year	No.	Notes	
Yes	Heald, D.		1989	34	No statistical privatization results presented.	No
Yes?	Heilman, J.G.	Johnson, G.W.	1992	485	Insufficient statistical results presented.	No
Yes?	Hendley, K.		1992	484	No statistical results presented.	No
Yes	Hofheinze, P.		1994	182	No statistical privatization results presented.	No
Yes	Hume, A.M.	Pinto, B.	1993	26	No statistical results presented.	No
On Order	Hunt, L.C.	Lynk, E. L.	1995	1045	No before/after privatization presented.	No
Yes	Hunt, L.C.	Lynk, E.L.	1990	63	No statistical privatization results presented.	No
Yes	Hutchinson, B.		1994	1054	No statistical privatization results presented.	No
Yes	Hutchinson, G.A.		1991	522		Yes
Yes	Hutchinson, G.A.		1990	577	See 522.	No
Yes	Hyman, H.J.		1980	966	Insufficient statistical results presented.	No
Yes	Ilokwu, J.E.		1991	571	No before/after privatization presented.	No
Yes	Jenkinson, T.	Mayer, C.	1988	40	No statistical results presented.	No
Yes	Jenkinson, T.	Mayer, C.	1994	945	Insufficient statistical results presented.	No
Yes	Johnson, M.		1994	262	Insufficient statistical results presented.	No
No	Kaplan, S.N.		1991	1074	No before/after privatization results presented.	No
Yes	Kay, J.A.	Bishop, M.R.	1989	1014	Insufficient statistical results presented.	No
Yes	Keller, A.Z.	Dogan, C., and Eroglu, O.	1994	365	No statistical results presented.	No
Yes	Kelsey, J.		1993	336	No statistical privatization results presented.	No
Yes	Kikeri, S.	Nellis, J., and Shirley, M.	1992	19	No statistical results presented.	No
On Order	Kikeri, S.	Nellis, J., and Shirley, M.	1994	1059	Insufficient statistical results presented.	No
No?	Kramer, R.M.	Lorentzen, H., Melief, W.B., and Pasquinelli, S.	1993	441	No statistical results presented.	No
On Order	Kunda, A.		1994	1056	Insufficient statistical results presented.	No
953	Leeds, R.S.		1988	657	Insufficient statistical results presented.	No
953	Leeds, R.S.		1987	658	Insufficient statistical results presented.	No
953	Leeds, R.S.		1987	659	Insufficient statistical results presented.	No
Yes	Leeds, R.S.		1991	660	Insufficient statistical results presented.	No
Yes	Leeds, R.S.		1994	953	No statistical results presented.	No
No?	Lensing, W.C.		1988	546	Insufficient statistical results presented.	No
Yes	Letwin, O.		1993	477	No statistical results presented.	No
Yes	Lieberman, I.W.		1988	41	No statistical privatization results presented.	No
No	Likierman, A.		1994	287	No statistical privatization results presented.	No
954	Linz, S.J.		1990	1031	Insufficient statistical results presented.	No
Yes	Lorch, K.		1991	655	Insufficient statistical results presented.	No
Yes?	Lorch, K.		1993	954	Insufficient statistical results presented.	No
408	Luders, R.J.		1990	44	Reanalyzed the data.	Yes
	Luders, R.J.			880	See 408.	No

(continues)

TABLE 8.1   *continued*

Result?	Author (Primary)	Other Authors	Year of Publication	Reference Number	Comments re Inclusion in Meta-Analysis	Included in Meta-Analysis?
No	Mack, J.		1995	1013	No statistical privatization results presented.	No
Yes	Marsh, D.		1991	1018	Insufficient statistical results presented.	No
861	Mayer, C.	Meadowcroft, S.	1986	876	See 861.	No
	Mayer, C.P.	Meadowcroft, S.A.	1985	861	No statistical privatization results presented.	No
Yes	McGowan, F.		1988	38	No statistical results presented.	No
No	Megginson, W.L.	Nash, R., and Van Randenborgh. M.	1994	298	No statistical results presented.	Yes
298	Megginson, W.L.	Nash, R.C., and Van Randenborgh, M.	1992	654	See 298.	No
Yes	Meller, P.		1993	373	Reanalyzed the data.	Yes
Yes	Menyah, K.	Paudyal, K., and Inyang, C.	1990	61		Yes
Yes	Miller, A. N,		1994	1038	No statistical privatization results presented.	No
No	Miller, P.		1995	1046	No statistical privatization results presented.	No
Yes	Moussios, A.		1994	545	Effect sizes derived from ARIMA results.	Yes
Yes	Nelson, L.	Kuzes, I.Y.	1994	181	No statistical privatization results presented.	No
Yes	Nunnencamp, P.		1986	695	No statistical privatization results presented.	No
Yes	Nuruzzman, S.A.M.		1989	578	No statistical privatization results presented.	Yes
On Order	Ogden, S. G.		1995	1053	No statistical privatization results presented.	No
Yes	Okumura, H.		1994	364	No statistical results presented.	No
236	Ott, A.F.	Hartley, K. (Eds)	1991	664	See 236.	No
Yes	Parker, D.		1992	14	See 480 / 263.	No
Yes	Parker, D.	Martin, S.	1993	185	Reanalyzed the data.	Yes
Yes	Parker, D.	Hartley, K.	1991	263		Yes
Yes	Parker, D.	Hartley, K.	1991	480		Yes
Yes	Parker, D.	Martin, S.	1995	1032		Yes
Yes	Parker, D.		1994	1066	No statistical privatization results presented.	No
Yes	Parker, D.		1994	1075	Reanalyzed the data.	Yes
Yes	Perera, M.H.K.		1991	570	No before/after privatization presented.	No
Yes	Pilarski, A.		1994	176	No statistical privatization results presented.	No
Yes	Quiggen, J.		1994	1000	Insufficient statistical results presented.	No
No	Quiggen, J.		1994	1006	No statistical privatization results presented.	No
On Order	Ramanadham, V.V. (Ed)		1995	1067	Insufficient statistical results presented.	No
965	Ramanadham, V.V. (Ed)		1988	666	Insufficient statistical results presented.	No
Yes	Rees, R.		1994	324	No statistical privatization results presented.	No
Yes	Robson, P.		1993	372	Insufficient statistical results presented.	No
No?	Rodriguez, F.		1992	478	Insufficient statistical results presented.	No
No?	Roth, G.		1986	611	No statistical results presented.	No

	Author	Co-author(s)	Year	N	Comment	
Yes?	Sakita, M.		1989	498	No statistical results presented.	No
No	Samson, C.		1994	1016	No statistical privatization results presented.	No
Yes?	Sanchez, M.	Corona, R., Herrera, L. F., and Ochoa, O.	1993	437	Insufficient statistical results presented.	No
Yes?	Sanchez, M.	Corona, R., Ochoa, O., Herrera, L.F., and Olvera, A.	1993	620	Insufficient statistical results presented.	No
Yes	Santamara, M.	Harris, C.	1992	453	Insufficient statistical results presented.	No
?	Saunders, P.		1994	323	No statistical privatization results presented.	No
Yes	Scarpaci, J.L.		1987	229	No statistical privatization results presented.	No
Yes	Schwartz, G.	Lopes, P.L.	1993	25	No statistical results presented.	No
Yes?	Sergent, K.	Forde, P.	1992	505	Insufficient statistical results presented.	No
Yes	Seth, R.		1989	24	No statistical performance results presented.	No
Yes	Sheill, A.		1991	335	No statistical privatization results presented.	No
Yes	Shirley, M.	Galal, A., and Keefer, P.	1995	1072	No before/after privatization presented.	No
No	Sigmund, P.E.		1990	1030	No statistical privatization results presented.	No
Yes	Sinha, P.K.		1993	547	Reanalyzed the data.	Yes
Yes	Smith, P.		1994	359	No statistical nationalization results presented.	Yes
Yes	Stover, W.A.		1985	69	Insufficient statistical results presented.	No
No	Suleiman, E. N.		1990	1029	No statistical privatization results presented.	No
Yes	Taggart, M.		1990	282	No statistical privatization results presented.	No
Yes	Taggart, M.		1992	322	No before & after results (property rights analysis)	No
Yes?	Tallant, D.J.		1993	568	Insufficient statistical results presented.	No
No?	Thomas, C.W.		1991	492	Reanalyzed the data.	Yes
Yes	Thomson, L.		1993	27	No statistical privatization results presented.	No
No	Veljanovski, C.		1989	35	No statistical privatization results presented.	No
?	Veljanovski, C.		1987	328	No statistical privatization results presented.	No
No	Vickers, J.	Yarrow, G.	1988	325	Insufficient statistical results presented.	No
No	Walker, R.G.		1994	991	Insufficient statistical results presented.	No
Yes?	Whitfield, D.		1983	333	Insufficient statistical results presented.	No
Yes	Wilcox, S.		1994	363	Insufficient statistical results presented.	No
Yes	Wilson, G.		1993	42	No statistical results presented.	No
Yes	Wright, M.	Thompson, S.	1993	30	No statistical results presented.	No
Yes	Yamamoto, K.		1993	28	No statistical results presented.	No
Yes	Yarrow, G.		1986	853	Reanalyzed the data.	Yes
Yes	Yarrow, G.		1989	271	Reanalyzed the data.	Yes
Yes	Yoder, R. A.	Borkholder, P.	1991	55		Yes
Yes?	Zuleta, L.A.	Jaramillo, L., Ballen, C.E., and Gomez, A.M.	1993	621	Insufficient statistical results presented.	No

(which itself studied only one enterprise sale) would probably have been included in the database. Moussios (1994) appears to be the only piece of research that both has a strong statistical design and specifically controls for the impacts of privatization (as ownership change) as well as variables such as regulation. This study looked at the performance of British Telecom. Several other studies did have a statistical control for general background trends in performance over time, but did not relate changes in performance directly to changes in regulation, competition, and other variables as well as the sale of the enterprise. From a strictly scientific perspective, therefore, the available data on enterprise performance could be regarded as somewhat "dirty." Indeed, for those more used to the rigor of research in fields such as psychology or medicine, this privatization performance data could be regarded as filthy! The implications of this dirty-data issue will be discussed further at a later stage. For the present, however, it was decided to include those results from studies that did not have the desired strict controls as well as those that did, and test for possible differences in effect sizes found. At a minimum, this at least allows us to gain a better picture of the international evidence as far as the performance measurements that have been taken. At a maximum, it may also help push our learnings on the effectiveness of enterprise sales a little further, whilst encouraging stronger future research designs.

After exclusions, twenty-four studies were available for the meta-analysis. Some of the major characteristics of these twenty-four studies are indicated in Table 8.2. Also shown are some typical key findings from each. A wide range of conclusions is found. Evidently, several studies support the finding that the sale of enterprises leads to improved performance from the company's perspective (Megginson, Nash, and Van Randenborgh 1994, Meller 1993, and Parker 1994a). Selling public enterprises also leads to improvements from the perspective of shareholders (Sinha 1993, Menyah, Paudyal, and Inyang 1990, and Aggarwal, Leal, and Hernandez 1993).

Others pointed to a finding of no performance increase (Domberger 1993, Hutchinson 1991, Moussios 1994, Parker and Hartley 1991b, and Yarrow 1989). These results clearly deserve further discussion, from both a narrative and a meta-analytic perspective, and will be examined further in Chapter 9. Before doing this, however, let me describe the literature itself.

CHARACTERISTICS OF THE LITERATURE

Reports on the effectiveness of privatization as the sale of enterprises were found over the period 1980 to 1995, and covered a range of industry sectors. The actual distribution of publication dates is shown in Figure 8.1. Distributions for all studies retrieved and for those studies included in the meta-analysis are presented.[3] Most of these studies reviewed privatizations from the United Kingdom. Some 50 of the 106 studies with empirical results (46 percent) were from the U.K., with the next largest group being studies of less developed countries such as Chile, Mexico, or Bangladesh at 20 percent. Results for multiple countries comprised 10

TABLE 8.2 Studies Included in the Meta-analysis

Authors (Date)	Sample	Country Studied	Performance Measures	Analysis	Controls	Findings
Aggarwal et al. (1993)	Three sets of initial public share offerings are studied in three Latin American countries, between 1980 and 1990	142 offerings in Brazil (62), Chile (36), and Mexico (44)	Share market financial returns in short term and long run	t statistic	Average share market returns	Initial one day returns are between +2.8% and +78.5%, but long run market adjusted returns are between −19.6% and −47.0%, showing long run under-performance.
Arbey (1993)	Growth in private expenditure data from 49 countries is analyzed	49 low, middle, and high income countries	Average annual growth rate in GNP (per capita)	t statistic calculated from standard errors	Few	A bigger private sector is associated with greater GNP growth for middle income countries, but less growth for low income countries. No relationship was found for high income countries.
Avishur (1994)	Productivity analysis of British Telecom, 1959–90	United Kingdom	Total factor productivity	t statistic	Few	Privatization of British Telecom improves efficiency by 2% to 3%, depending on the analysis method adopted.
Bhaskar and Khan (1995)	62 jute mills in Bangladesh	Bangladesh	Employment	t statistic calculated from standard errors	Continued operation of state mills adopted as control	Before and after study conducted, using continued operation of state mills as the control.
Domberger (1993)	Pre-1988 privatizations in the U.K. are studied	United Kingdom	Changes in employment, total factor productivity and profitability	t statistic calculated from data	Few	Productivity growth appears wholly unrelated to privatization. Profitability growth in privatized companies was weaker than for straight public companies.

(continues)

TABLE 8.2 *continued*

Authors (Date)	Sample	Country Studied	Performance Measures	Analysis	Controls	Findings
Haskel and Szymanski (1992)	Seven privatized companies in the U.K.	United Kingdom	Top executive remuneration	Paired t test calculated from data	Public sector and average private sector changes	Privatization has a large negative impact on employment.
Hutchinson (1991)	17 U.K. firms were studied, in five categories, each with control data	United Kingdom	Labor productivity, and profitability	t statistic	Industry type, industry time trends	Privatization had a positive influence on profitability, but a negative influence on labor productivity.
Luders (1993)	Performance of 12 selected firms reviewed	Chile	Rate of return on equity, and employment	Reanalysis of data, t statistic	None	Large capital losses did occur with divestiture, but privatized firms seem to show higher rates of return and higher employment levels.
Megginson, Nash, and Van Randenborgh (1994)	61 companies from 32 industries worldwide	18 countries	Various profitability, efficiency, and employment measures	Wilcoxen rank sum test for medians	None	Privatization led to profitability increases of between −0.2% and +2.5%, efficiency increases of 10.6% to 25.1%, and an employment increase of 5.7%.
Meller (1993)	12 firms in Chile, 1989–90	Chile	Return on owner's equity	Reanalysis of data, t-test	None	Privatized firms have in general been much more efficient than public firms.
Menyah, Paudyal, and Inyang (1990)	13 initial privatization share issues on the International Stock Exchange, 1981–87	United Kingdom	Market adjusted financial rate of return	t-test	Average market returns	On the first day, privatization returns were 33.1% greater than private sector issue returns, and overall were 31.6% greater.
Moussios (1994)	Privatization of British Telecom, 1982–93	United Kingdom	Service quality, investment, and profitability	ARIMA transfer function model	National productivity, regulatory intensity	Privatization failed to generate a significant and lasting stimulus for improved performance.

Author (year)	Sample	Country	Performance measure	Method	Control variable	Findings
Nuruzzman (1989)	59 textile mills, 1983–86	Bangladesh	Efficiency	Regression analysis	Several	Privatization was associated with higher efficiency increases than observed elsewhere.
Parker and Hartley (1991a)	Five privatized organizations, between 1971–87	United Kingdom	Labor productivity and employment	Outputs, and Time	Productivity in public corporations and manufacturing	Comparative productivity growth observed for 4 of 5 cases.
Parker and Hartley (1991b)	Three privatized and nationalized firms between 1971–81	United Kingdom	Profitability and value added	t-test	Time	Privatization does not appear to guarantee improved performance, nor nationalization worsen performance.
Parker and Martin (1995)	11 privatized firms in the 1980s	United Kingdom	Annual % changes in labor and total factor productivity	Paired t-test	Whole economy, and manufacturing performance	Privatization was associated with improved labor productivity in a slight majority of cases, but for TFP mixed results were found.
Parker and Martin (1993)	11 privatized firms in the period 1983 to 1992	United Kingdom	Annual average percentage change in value added per employee	t statistic calculated from reanalysis	Inflation	Privatization has been associated with improved performance in six cases, mixed performance in one case, and with worsened performance in three cases.
Parker (1994a)	British Telecom performance reviewed, 1984–93	United Kingdom	Profitability, employment, labor, and total factor productivity, R&D investment	t statistic calculated from reanalysis	None	Privatization has led to improved profitability, labor productivity, and service quality. Prices have reduced, but so has employment, R and D spending, and total factor productivity.
Sinha (1993)	40 privatizations, 1981–91	United Kingdom	Financial returns to investors	t statistic	Average market performance	Governments underprice offerings to secure the sale of the whole issue. Large institutional investors make the most handsome profits.

(continues)

TABLE 8.2 *continued*

Authors (Date)	Sample	Country Studied	Performance Measures	Analysis	Controls	Findings
Smith (1994)	49 U.K. share offerings 1977–93	United Kingdom	Percentage share price yield	t statistic calculated from reanalysis	None	Anyone prescient enough to buy and hold every privatization issue would be a superinvestor.
Thomson (1993)	12 electricity generating companies, 1988–92	United Kingdom	Extent of disclosure of information	Data reanalyzed, t-test	None	Privatization resulted in a general loss of information, both required financial detail and voluntary disclosures.
Yarrow (1986)	5 privatized companies, 1981–85	United Kingdom	Profit margins	t statistic calculated from reanalysis	Control group of comparative firms	Limited evidence shows profit margins improved for privatized firms in a similar way to margins for public companies.
Yarrow (1989)	7 companies privatized between 1981–87	United Kingdom	Profitability as a proportion of assets	t statistic calculated from reanalysis	None	The idea that privatization will quickly lead to substantial performance improvements is not well supported by the data. Profitability and labor productivity have improved in both the public and private sectors alike.
Yoder and Borkholder (1991)	Expenditures in 45 countries analyzed, 1980–86	International	Private sector spending as a proportion of GNP	Pearson correlation coefficient	None	GNP growth is not related simply to the size of either the private or the public sectors.

NOTES: "Controls" refers to the presence of controlling statistically for the impacts of possible mediating variables.

FIGURE 8.1　Publication Year of Studies (Enterprise Sales)

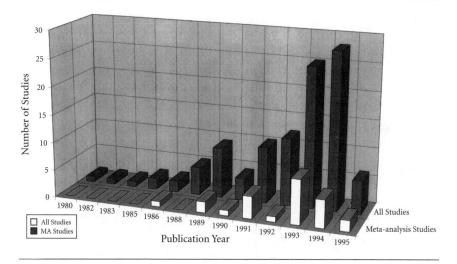

percent of studies, whilst countries that were studied less often included Europe (non-U.K.) at 6 percent, the United States (4 percent), and Canada (1 percent). The profile of studies used in the meta-analysis was similar to this. The distribution of countries studied is shown in Figure 8.2.[4]

Overall, therefore, studies of the U.K. dominated this review, along with less developed countries next.

Looking at the types of publications providing general empirical results, about one-half were from the research journals (48.1 percent), with book chapters (20.7 percent), magazines (16.0 percent), and theses (8.5 percent) providing the next largest categories. For those studies adopted in the meta-analysis, a higher proportion were from both research journals (66.7 percent) and theses (20.8 percent). Formally, these two distributions were significantly different. They are shown in Figure 8.3.

The professional backgrounds of the authors were also analyzed and are shown in Figure 8.4. For the 71 percent of cases where this was evident, the largest contributing disciplines were Economics at 33 percent, Business/Commerce at 14 percent, and Finance/Accounting at 8 percent. The professions least represented were Engineering/Science at 2 percent, Public Administration at 3 percent, and Sociology/Social Work and Politics/Law each at 4 percent. Those studies included in the meta-analysis had a higher proportion of economics, business/commerce, and finance/accounting authors. Formally, the two distributions were different.[5]

The most common measures of performance were economic in nature. Of these measures, the largest group of results related to efficiency of one type or another. A surprisingly wide range of methods was also adopted to measure performance in these studies of enterprise sales.

FIGURE 8.2a   Countries Studied (All Studies)

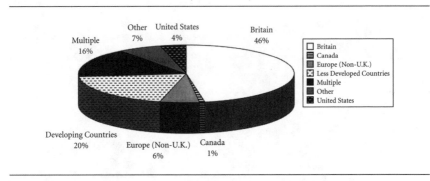

FIGURE 8.2b   Countries Studied (Meta-analysis Studies)

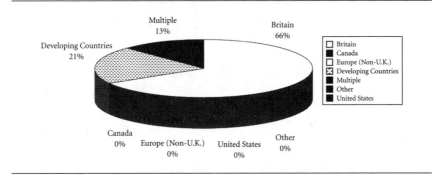

FIGURE 8.3   Publication Types

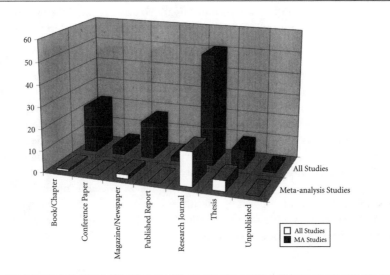

FIGURE 8.4a   Disciplines of Authors (All Studies)

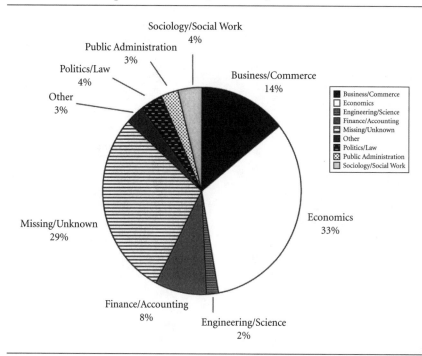

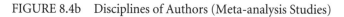

FIGURE 8.4b   Disciplines of Authors (Meta-analysis Studies)

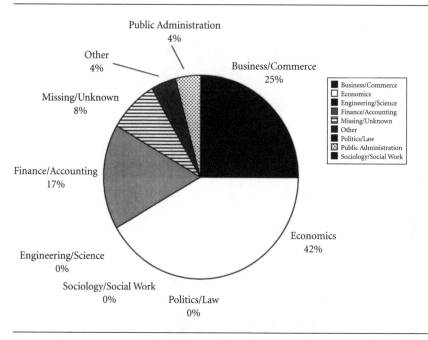

9

Reviewing the Effectiveness of Privatization as Enterprise Sales

One of the central questions for investigation in this book was simply, What is the general relationship between performance and privatization when we view privatization as the sale of a government enterprise? Does a change in ownership of service production lead to improved performance? Through contracting out, a temporary change in ownership was achieved. The full sale of an enterprise offers a permanent change in ownership. To the extent that performance is improved with private ownership, the sale of an enterprise may offer a permanent change for the better.

But in what ways, from a methodological perspective, would we expect an assessment of the effectiveness of contracting out to differ from an assessment of the sale of an enterprise? One would think that they would be quite different. Indeed, the ways in which these two types of privatization evaluation would differ are worth covering in some detail, because they are likely to have real implications for the remainder of this research.

Firstly, both the number and degree of specification of services is different. Contracting out evaluations typically involved the accurate specification of a single service delivered over a time period—in concept, at least, a relatively simple arrangement. An enterprise sale, on the other hand, would typically involve a much higher degree of complexity all round. Rather than one single service, dozens or even hundreds of services may be transferred through the sale of an enterprise. Rather than the accurate specification of one service, a broad requirement to deliver a range of services, with general overall controls for characteristics such as price increases for only a small basket of services, is typically put in place. This is likely to leave the newly privatized agency with more flexibility to alter service delivery conditions, and indeed the very existence of some services, to enable the firm to move towards a more favorable financial position.[1] The possibility of major changes in service levels occurring or the potential not to provide some services at all both have significant implications for assessing the performance of privatized firms. In Chapter 7, I discussed the implications of making coarse and unsophisticated comparisons between the delivery of private and public refuse services. The service of refuse collection, which on first sight might have been considered a relatively simple and straightforward service to analyze, was found to be quite complex when it came to the question of evaluation. This book investigates the hypothesis that the sector providing a service matters. In the case of refuse collection, for instance, assessing the costs of providing the service through the private or public sector required strict statistical controls to be established for over a dozen variables such as route contiguity, the frequency of pickup, the place where the bin is collected, and so on, as well as the object of our interest—the sector providing the service.[2] The difficulty—in fact impossibility—of ensuring such careful statistical control for every service being provided in a newly privatized firm is clear. In practice, such statistical control in an assessment is highly unlikely to occur. This may have important implications in view of our previous finding that the simpler studies of contracting out performance produced effect sizes that were larger than those from more sophisticated studies. It may well be extremely difficult to measure with any accuracy at all levels of service and quality outcomes after a sale.

The second way in which an assessment of contracting out may differ from an enterprise sale concerns the sale transaction. Rather than being a single point in time, the sale transaction itself may take years, and be undertaken in several stages. The end point of the transaction may involve 100 percent private ownership or any other proportion. A classic example here was the case of British Aerospace. A 51.6 percent stake of British Aerospace was sold in February 1981. The remainder of this company was sold in May 1985.[3] The privatization of British Airways is a further example. The privatization of this company "some time in the future" was announced initially in July 1979, and a timetable for the sale was first proposed in May 1980.[4] British Airways was actually sold in January 1987. This followed a recession in air transport and legal difficulties after the collapse of Laker Airways.[5] Thus a large period of anticipation preceded the actual sale.

Thirdly, there are usually major differences between the objectives sought in contracting out services and those sought when selling an enterprise. Such differences have implications for this evaluation. The objectives of contracting almost wholly related to cost savings. Most performance measurements were therefore concentrated in the general area of costs in our assessment of contracting performance. In contrast, a much broader array of performance measurements, and hence evidence, is logically necessary for the case of enterprise sales, where objectives sought are far broader. Moreover, both the regulatory and the competitive environments in which the newly privatized firm produces its services are likely to be highly influential. Enterprises may be privatized with or without major changes to the competitive environment. The effects of competition in service efficiency or effectiveness may also be differential across services. Likewise, massive systemic regulatory arrangements—as distinct from the legal arrangements made as part of the privatization transaction itself—may or may not occur along with the sale of an enterprise. Again, the effects of regulation may differ across services, too. Thus, although competition, deregulation, and privatization are commonly thrown together in political phraseology, a strict scientific assessment seeking to isolate the effects of ownership changes on performance would require separate measurement and statistical control of each of these variables.

These assessment difficulties[6] are likely to be significant in this section, where the empirical evidence on actual enterprise sales is to be assessed. Again, this reinforces the judgment made earlier that on a strict assessment, much of the performance data on the sale of enterprises is dirty. This inevitably taints any analysis of the data.[7]

Having outlined these methodological issues, let us embark on a review of each of the performance dimensions for the sale of public enterprises. Consistent with the previous review of contracting out government services, the narrative review of enterprise sales will again analyze findings considered to be broadly representative of the empirical literature. The aim will not be to review all findings comprehensively, since this would be impossible. I will seek simply to discover, in as unbiased a way as possible, both the range of empirical findings and the extent to which each of the findings contrast with others or are corroborated by others. Where I can, I will also employ meta-analysis techniques to help explore the possibility of learning more from the statistical evidence.[8]

ECONOMIC PERFORMANCE

A Narrative Overview

This review will not wade laboriously through each of the available 162 reports in the traditional narrative manner, summarizing, reviewing, commenting on, and discussing findings and analysis methods. Rather, I will adopt the overview approach used earlier when looking at the performance of contracting out. To begin, let us firstly be reminded that despite the care taken in the searching process, the review is unlikely to cover all findings in existence. Rather, it will be looking at a reasonable sample of empirical findings. An overview of these findings should enable us to gain a strong appreciation of the whole range of empirical evidence. Also remember that in doing a narrative review care must be taken to differentiate between less sophisticated analyses and more strongly controlled studies, and between analyses having different sample sizes. Remember, too, the warning that narrative reviews can lead to an emphasis on parts of the available evidence or those findings that are more palatable to the reviewer.

Three groups probably rank as the most well known researchers looking at the effectiveness of enterprise sales. These three groups include Galal et al. (1994), who produced a major document—commonly referred to as "the World Bank Study"; Megginson, Nash, and Van Randenborgh (1994) from the United States;

and any of a number of research teams from the United Kingdom, including authors such as Bishop, Parker, Martin, Hartley, Thompson, Dunsire, or Yarrow (see Parker and Hartley 1991a, for example). Table 9.1 presents highlights from the findings of these studies as well as others. Around thirty studies are listed. Also presented is the country and industry sector studied, the number of firms analyzed, and results on performance changes measured, along with some of the key conclusions made in each analysis.

The table is structured broadly in line with the performance framework developed in Chapter 4. Thus, for the dimension of economic performance, empirical findings are presented in terms of efficiency, labor productivity, total factor productivity, profitability, financial returns to shareholders, welfare, investment levels, and economic development. The body of empirical international literature is clearly large. Consequently, as was the case for the performance review of contracting out, it is again possible for an impressive display of evidence favoring one side or the other to be amassed.

Productivity

A major foundation underpinning privatization is the belief that enterprise efficiency will improve. A wide spread of productivity evaluation results is evident in Table 9.1. Look at the performance of enterprise sales in the United Kingdom, for instance. At the one end, the sale of enterprises was confirmed as generally being associated with improvements in total factor productivity by Green and Vogelsang (1994). At the other end, Hutchinson's 1991 analysis concluded that privatization had had a negative influence on labor productivity. Some analyses found a growth in labor productivity (Parker and Hartley 1991a, Parker and Martin 1995). The bulk of other reports analyzing the U.K. experience was not at either of these two extreme positions, however. Perhaps our focus should more properly be on these—they found rather more mixed results. Indeed, when analysts controlled for the general changes in productivity[9] that occurred throughout the 1970s and 1980s, they appear to have mostly found results that did not directly link the sale of enterprises with productivity increases. Thus, Domberger (1993) concluded that "changes in total factor productivity appear to be wholly unrelated to privatization." Likewise, Parker and Martin (1995) reported that privatization was associated with mixed results for total factor productivity (TFP) after recognizing productivity changes over the whole economy. Yarrow (1989) additionally observed that the notion of substantial improvements following privatization "is not well supported by the data."

In 1987 Veljanovski understandably reported "little hard evidence" of improved performance, mostly because of scarcity of data. More surprising, however, was a subsequent conclusion from Bishop, Kay, and Mayer (1994, p. 13) several years later. They also produced a similar end result—that from the perspective of productivity, "privatization had little effect." Their overall reasoning

TABLE 9.1 Summary of Key International Empirical Findings and Conclusions on the Effectiveness of Enterprise Sales

Study	Ref	Country/Industry Sectors Analyzed	Findings	Comments/Conclusions
Productivity/Efficiency				
Bishop, Kay, and Mayer (1994)	327	Overall review of all U.K. privatizations through the 1980s	Privatization had "little effect"	Both efficiency and productivity of firms has increased, however, many of the significant improvements in TFP took place before privatization. Privatization has had only modest effects.
Lorch (1991)	954	59 textile mills in Bangladesh, 1983–1986	Static efficiency improved, dynamic efficiency did not	Static efficiency (improve current outputs) improved, whilst dynamic efficiency (longer term improvements in efficiency) did not.
Nuruzzman (1989)	578	59 textile mills in Bangladesh, 1983–1986	Privatization increased efficiency	Privatization was associated with increased efficiency in both privatized and public sector mills. Privatized mills had higher efficiency increases.
Veljanovski (1987)	328	Overall review of U.K. privatizations through the 1980s	Little hard evidence of improved performance	Little hard evidence of improved performance exists, in most cases because of insufficient time since the sale.
Yarrow (1989)	271	7 U.K. companies privatized, 1981–1987	Improved labor productivity and profitability, but probably not caused by sale	The existence of quick and substantial performance improvements is not well supported by the data. In many cases there has been improved labor productivity after the sale, but the same is true over time in both the public and private sectors generally.
Labor Productivity				
Duncan and Bollard (1992)	337	Coal Corporation of New Zealand, 1987–1992	Corporatization improved labor productivity by around 100%	Major improvements in labor productivity occurred with corporatization, without privatization.
Hutchinson (1991)	522	17 firms in five sectors, in the U.K.	Labor productivity worsened	Privatization had a negative influence on labor productivity.
Parker and Hartley (1991a)	480	5 privatized organizations in the U.K., 1971–1987	Labor productivity grew	Comparative labor productivity growth observed for 4 of 5 cases.
Parker and Martin (1995)	1032	11 privatized firms in the U.K. throughout the 1980s	Labor productivity improved	Privatization was associated with improved labor productivity in a slight majority of cases after recognizing productivity changes over the whole economy.

(continues)

TABLE 9.1 Continued

Study	Ref	Country/Industry Sectors Analyzed	Findings	Comments/Conclusions
Total Factor Productivity				
Avishur (1994)	1071	British Telecom, 1951–1990	Privatization improved TFP	TFP improvements after privatization were about 2% to 3%.
Bishop and Thompson (1992)	33	9 U.K. public enterprises, 1970–1990	Regulatory reforms have improved TFP before sale	Regulatory reforms in the U.K. have resulted in major improvements in TFP, and particularly through the 1980s. This is distinct from any changes associated with privatization.
Domberger (1993)	773	Selected U.K. companies, 1979–1988	TFP changes unrelated to privatization	Changes in TFP appear wholly unrelated to privatization.
Green and Vogelsang (1994)	946	British Airways, U.K., 1979–1991	Generally increased after announcement and sale	Productivity clearly higher than it used to be. Timing of improvement not necessarily related to sale or announcement, though this probably provided credibility to reduce labor without industrial action in 1981.
Parker and Martin (1995)	1032	11 privatized firms in the U.K. throughout the 1980s	Mixed results	Privatization was associated with mixed results for TFP productivity after recognizing productivity changes over the whole economy.
Financial Performance				
Anonymous (1995)	1034	General review of the U.K. privatization program	Profits in real terms have increased	Most privatized companies were more profitable in real terms in 1994 than in the year before they were sold.
Bishop and Kay (1989)	865	12 privatized firms in the U.K.	Profitability has improved	Profits have grown, but it seems that the causality runs from growth and profitability to privatization rather than the other way around.
Duncan and Bollard (1992)	337	Coal Corporation of New Zealand, 1987–1992	Corporatization improved returns on equity by over 10%	Returns on assets improved by 18.3% after corporatization, without privatization.
Domberger (1993)	773	Selected U.K. companies, 1979–1988	Profitability changes are unrelated to privatization	Improved profitability appears to be wholly unrelated to privatization.
Green and Vogelsang (1994)	946	British Airways, U.K., 1979–1991	Generally increased after announcement and sale	Profitability clearly higher than it used to be. Timing of improvement not necessarily related to sale or announcement.
Hutchinson (1991)	522	17 firms in five sectors in the U.K.	Profitability improved	Privatization has had a positive influence on profitability.
Leeds (1991)	953	One firm in Jamaica: the Caribbean Cement Company	Probably improved	Profitability in this company began improving some three years prior to the privatization, and continued through it.

Luders (1993)	44	Performance of 12 selected firms reviewed in Chile	Privatized firms showed higher profitability and employment	Large capital losses did occur to the community with the divestiture of public assets. Privatized firms seem to show higher rates of return and higher employment levels.
Meller (1993)	373	12 firms in Chile 1970–1990	Privatized firms show higher financial rates of return	Two years after privatization, privatized firms show higher rates of return than they had when they were public firms. Many privatized firms show very high returns.
Miller (1994)	1038	General experience of U.K.	Profits generally increased	Profits of 10 of the 13 firms analyzed increased regularly.
Megginson, Nash, and Van Randenborgh (1994)	298	61 firms from 18 countries worldwide	Privatization increased profits	Privatization led to profitability increases of between −0.2% and +2.5%, efficiency increases of 10.6% to 25.1%, and an employment increase of 5.7%.
Moussios (1994)	545	Privatization of British Telecom, 1982–1993.	Privatization itself did not increase profits	Privatization failed to generate a significant and lasting stimulus for improved performance.
Parker and Hartley (1991b)	263	Three privatized and nationalized firms in U.K., 1971–1981	No guarantee of improvement	Privatization does not appear to guarantee improved performance, nor nationalization worsen performance.
Parker and Martin (1993)	185	11 privatized firms in the U.K., 1973–1992.	Value added has generally improved, but not always	Value added has improved at six firms, has been mixed or has declined at the remainder. Privatization may be associated with one-off productivity gains.
Yarrow (1989)	271	7 U.K. companies privatized, 1981–1987	Improved profitability, but probably not caused by sale	The existence of quick and substantial performance improvements is not well supported by the data. In many cases there has been improved profitability after the sale, but the same is true over time in both the public and private sectors generally.
Shareholder Returns				
Sinha (1993)	547	40 U.K. privatizations, 1981–1991	Extent of underpricing of sales, and returns to investors	Governments underprice offerings to secure the sale of the whole issue. Large institutional investors make the most handsome profits.
Smith (1994)	359	49 U.K. share offerings 1977–1993	Returns to sharebuying investors	People who bought and held every privatization issue in the U.K. would be superinvestors.

(continues)

TABLE 9.1 *Continued*

Study	Ref	Country/Industry Sectors Analyzed	Findings	Comments/Conclusions
Total Welfare				
Galal et al. (1994)	521	12 sectors from U.K., Chile, Malaysia, and Mexico were analyzed	Changes in total "welfare"	World welfare increases in 11 of the 12 cases.
Abdala (1992)	569	Case study of ENTel, Argentina projected over the period 1990–2000	Changes in "welfare" of various groups such as consumers, owners, employees, etc.	World society better off by \$1.4 billion, but Chile worse off by \$2.2 billion. Consumers worse off by \$4.1 billion.
Investment Levels				
Parker (1994a)	1075	British Telecom, 1984–1993	Research and development investment	Privatization led to reduced levels of R&D investment.
Lorch (1991)	954	59 textile mills in Bangladesh, 1983–1986	Investment in new capacity not improved after sale	Privatized mills were no more likely to promote investments in new capacity or technological upgrading.
Economic Development				
Yoder and Borkholder (1991)	55	45 countries were analyzed 1980–1986	Various development indicators	GNP growth is not related simply to the size of the private sector.
Arbey (1993)	548	49 countries analyzed, 1965–1989	Annual average GNP growth rate	Private sector spending and GNP growth rate were found to be linked only for middle income countries. No link was found for high income countries, and the link for low income countries seemed to be in the opposite direction.
Lorch (1991)	954	59 textile mills in Bangladesh, 1983–1986	Trade balance	Privatization did not improve the country's trade balance.

was that, although both efficiency and productivity of firms had generally increased, many of the significant improvements in TFP had actually taken place *before* privatization. Their logic is persuasive. They firstly observed that "there is little doubt that the efficiency of firms that began the 1980s in public ownership has improved considerably. Profits generally rose in the years following privatization and investors have earned substantial returns over and above those on the stock market as a whole."

This observation was then heavily qualified, however. Under monopoly power, Bishop, Kay, and Mayer remind us that profits are a poor guide to efficiency, and that productivity measures such as TFP need to be scrutinized. After observing that productivity within the U.K. as a whole had increased, they then added the bite:

> On the face of it, this is an impressive performance. However, many of the most significant improvements in total factor productivity in the monopoly utilities took place before privatization. They resulted from the imposition of hard budget constraints by the government, clear commercial goals, performance pay, and decentralized and accountable management. Privatization had little effect. Indeed, in some cases, notably British Steel and British Airways, it was these improvements that actually made privatization possible.

Yarrow (1989) also points to the productivity improvements simultaneously observed in privatized firms, and throughout both the private and public sectors generally. Green and Vogelsang (1994) argued from a slightly different perspective, but again concurred that the timing of productivity improvements was not necessarily related to the sale of the enterprise or the announcement. They nonetheless comment that the existence of the impending sale probably provided credibility to reduce labor without industrial action. A similar thrust was also put forward by Bishop and Thompson (1992, p. 1,189). Analyzing the major regulatory changes that occurred in the United Kingdom through the 1970s and 1980s, they conclude that regulatory reforms in the U.K. have resulted in major improvements in TFP, particularly through the 1980s. In discussing the cause of such productivity improvements, they note that scale effects might account for up to a maximum of one-half of this productivity growth. They also add the pointed comment that "the changes in the regulation of enterprises in public ownership has had an impact upon performance which is distinct from that resulting from, or anticipating changes in ownership."

Outside of the United Kingdom, little specific analysis on productivity appears to have occurred. Both Lorch (1991) and Nuruzzman (1989) analyzed the privatization of textile mills in Bangladesh that occurred around 1983. From the sample of fifty-nine mills, Nuruzzman concluded that privatization increased efficiency, and that this increase was indeed greater than the increase in efficiency also found in the public mills. Lorch's analysis confirmed that an increase in static efficiency had occurred. This was not the case for dynamic efficiency, which looked at investment in new capacity, technological upgrading, and the development of human capital. Luders (1993) studied the performance of twelve selected privatized firms in Chile. Whilst the extent of any potential bias that might have resulted from his selection rules is unclear, his findings were striking for their frankness. He notes that, on the one hand, large capital losses did occur with divestiture. These losses amounted to between some 50 and 64 percent of the value of assets, depending on the valuation method. On the other hand, Luders also finds that privatized firms seemed to show higher rates of return and higher employment levels than previously. Another example of a productivity analysis from outside the U.K. was that from Duncan and Bollard (1992). They studied reforms to the New Zealand public sector, looking at before and after employment as well as financial data. Some productivity conclusions are possible from this analysis. Their analysis of reforms to the State Coal Mines Department pointed to improved labor productivity of around 100 percent over the period 1987–92. These improvements were measured, however, before and after *corporatization*—not privatization. This of course serves to raise the central question of whether productivity improvements are possible through a number of mechanisms, one of which may be the privatization option. It also supports the notion that in observing the effectiveness of reforms to a government department, performance measures such as labor productivity may well improve from a relatively low base—the above example showing an extraordinary gain in a period of five years.

Thus, the weight of narrative evidence overall appears to favor the following conclusions:

- The evidence supporting the existence of productivity improvements following the sale of an enterprise appears to outweigh that suggesting a worsening of productivity, but much of the findings seem to present a mixed picture. There is certainly no clear and unequivocal general link between the sale of enterprises and subsequent productivity improvements.
- Although productivity has generally appeared to improve after privatizations, it has also improved throughout the economy as a whole. Much of the improvement observed, therefore, is apparently unrelated to the sale of enterprises per se.
- The strength of the link between the sale of enterprises and improved productivity appears at best to be weak, and at worst, to be nonexistent.

Profitability

Again, a wide range of findings appears to have been made on profitability. The range is strangely reminiscent of the previous discussion on productivity! Several studies concluded that privatization was clearly followed by higher profitability.[10] Of these, the study of Megginson, Nash, and Van Randenborgh (1994) analyzed some sixty-one firms globally, and deserves further discussion, which will be undertaken at a later point. For the present it is observed that their analysis detected profitability increases of between −0.2 and +2.5 percent. Leeds (1991) concluded that profitability was higher, but argued that it rose some three years prior to the sale itself. What of the other extreme? Although no studies claimed that privatization had led to a worsening of profitability, one study with strong statistical controls, Moussios (1994), concluded that privatization had indeed failed to generate a significant and lasting stimulus for improved performance. Parker and Hartley (1991b) likewise pointed to a weak relationship between privatization and improved profitability. They further warned that privatization does not appear to guarantee improved performance, nor nationalization worsen performance. None of the findings at these two extremes were the most common, however.

The most frequently made conclusion was that, although profitability rose in the period after the sale of an enterprise, the privatization per se was not the cause of this improvement. Thus, Domberger (1993), for instance, concluded that improved profitability appeared to be wholly unrelated to privatization. Likewise, Green and Vogelsang (1994) commented that, although profitability was clearly higher than it used to be, the timing of improvements was not necessarily related to either the announcement of the sale or the sale itself. In the last section, I noted Yarrow's (1989, p. 341) comment that a quick and substantial performance improvement was "not well supported by the data." Yarrow added pointedly that "in many cases, there has been a history of improving profitability and labor productivity since privatization, but, over the relevant period, the same is also true of both the private and public sectors more generally."

Perhaps we should investigate this line of causality further, as did Bishop and Kay (1989b). They concluded that profits have grown, but added that "it seems that the causality runs from growth and profitability to privatization rather than the other way around." Overall, therefore, there appears to be considerable doubt as to whether privatization per se has led to improved profitability levels.[11]

One further analysis is worthy of observation here. Duncan and Bollard (1992) studied changes to the New Zealand public sector, and presented before and after profitability data for the case of corporatization. This data showed an improvement of 18.3 percent for returns on assets, and an improvement of over 10 percent in the case of returns on shareholders' equity. We might again ponder the effect of the corporatization, as distinct from privatization. Findings such as these put into doubt the notion that the sale of public enterprises is required to drive financial performance improvements.

As with all of the above studies, much could be made in discussion of matters such as the integrity of study designs, statistical controls employed or not employed, and a host of other methodological issues. Clearly, study sophistication is a critical issue. To what extent has each of the various studies controlled for improvements that may have been occurring throughout the economy generally and may not have actually been related to the sale of enterprises? For the moment, it is observed that, even isolating the more sophisticated studies as a group, they still do not appear to present one single consistent picture. A range of findings on the level of profitability improvements again exists.[12]

Shareholder Returns

How have the shareholders fared with the sale of enterprises? This depends on our definition of shareholder. Philosophically, the former shareholders (i.e., the community), or the new shareholders (who bought shares through the stock market) are both shareholders in a sense.

Looking first at the latter, that is, the buyers of shares in a privatization float, investment returns to this group are straightforward to ascertain. A relatively consistent finding emerges here. Both Sinha (1993) and Smith (1994) looked at returns to the new owners of shares in the United Kingdom and commented that those who bought shares saw excellent financial returns on their outlays. Smith even goes as far as to say that those who bought and held every privatization issue in the U.K. would be "superinvestors." Sinha then goes a little further and analyzes the different returns received by the various investor groups, observing that large institutional investors made the most handsome returns. Nonetheless, the conclusion remains firm—investors did well during the U.K. privatizations. Although excellent returns to new share buyers appears to be a relatively consistent finding in the literature, such gains are not always guaranteed, and losses to shareholders following privatization floats have been reported for Chile and Japan.[13]

On the second type of shareholder—the community, as former owners of the public enterprise—Sinha (1993) presents more sinister findings. His analysis suggests that more often than not, governments do tend to consistently underprice offerings to secure the sale of the whole share issue. In other words, shares are purposely underpriced to ensure that the float is a politically successful event. Consequently, the former shareholders consistently lose at least some of the value of the enterprise from this practice. This issue will be discussed later.

Total Welfare

The tradition of welfare economics enables projected welfare changes for all groups in the community to be made explicit. Adding these welfare changes together provides an estimate, at least conceptually, of the change in total welfare for all stakeholders. Using this philosophy, Galal et al. (1994) reviewed the projected performance of twelve privatizations throughout four countries. Their overall results appear to be a glowing endorsement of the sale of enterprises. Some eleven of the twelve cases reviewed showed an increase in total welfare. Gains in overall welfare varied between 1.6 and 12.0 percent in the case of the United Kingdom, and up to between 2.1 percent and an amazing 155.0 percent in the case of Chile. In only one case (for Mexico's Mexicana de Aviacion) was there a negative total welfare gain of −7.0 percent. As one of the most widely known privatization evaluations, this World Bank analysis is worthy of further consideration.

Observe first that the analysis of Galal et al. is, strictly speaking, not an analysis of "before and after" data. It is an analysis based on a few years of actual data on the one side, and expected future efficiency gains, assumed improvements, and projected prices on the other. As Galal et al. (1994, p. 21) explain, greater private sector efficiency is *assumed,* along with an expectation that "the gap will widen at an increasing rate for five years and remain stable thereafter." These estimates are then subject to the actual regulatory and political constraints being applied in each case-study country. One could logically question whether this analysis should rate on the same level as others that use *actual* performance data, or whether, as was the case adopted in this research, one should view this analysis differently. Relying on this work to provide actual empirical evidence was judged to be dubious, despite the advanced analytical framework developed. Secondly, looking at the distribution of gains and losses in welfare across all groups gives another picture to that reached on first impression. The insights, as they relate to winners and losers in the privatization debate, will be outlined later in this chapter.

The analysis of Abdala (1992) also used this welfare philosophy for the case of Argentina's ENTel. His analysis showed an overall worldwide gain in welfare of $1.4 billion. Clearly however, massive winners and losers appeared to occur as part of this overall gain. Abdala's analysis is interesting because estimates made for Argentina as a whole were presented. His analysis suggests that, despite the overall worldwide welfare gain, Argentina as a country lost by more than this worldwide gain—indeed by an amount of some −$2.2 billion. Other aspects of his analysis from the perspective of consumers will be discussed later.

Investment Levels

Here, the few studies investigating this aspect suggested that privatization was accompanied by reduced research and development (R&D) funding. Parker's 1994 analysis of British Telecom found that "there has been an almost continuous decline since privatization." Furthermore, he added that despite the reduction in long-term speculative R&D investment, "it is perhaps surprising that a smaller share of BT income is being spent on R&D, and that investment is now declining, in what is a high-tech business."

Lorch's analysis of textile mills in Bangladesh also came to much the same conclusion, noting that there was no greater likelihood of investments in new capacity or technological upgrading at the privatized mills than at the public mills.

Economic Development

The dimension of national economic performance was understandably the most difficult to tie directly back to the sale of enterprises. No studies were found that directly attempted to do this. Those few analyses that looked at the issue of economic development investigated the strength of linkages between economic development and privatization as proxied by the level of private sector spending in a country. If, as it is asserted, a linkage exists between increased privatization and economic growth, a positive correlation should be found. Yoder and Borkholder (1991), for example, analyzed forty-five countries using various indicators of development such as income levels, income distributions, GNP growth rate, life expectancy, and literacy. In the case of GNP growth rate, for instance, they found an average correlation coefficient of only r = +0.03. For low income, lower-middle income, and upper-middle income countries separately, the correlation coefficients were r = +0.47, r = −0.22, and r = +0.13 respectively. Only the first of these was significant statistically at the 0.10 level. When they reviewed all development indicators as a whole, around one-half of the correlations (thirteen out of twenty-four) had positive coefficients, whilst the remainder had negative coefficients. They therefore concluded that "apparently, the size of neither the private nor the public sector makes a significant difference in and of itself," and that "it appears that the claims of privatization have been overstated and unsubstantiated" (p. 432).

Arbey's analysis over a period of two and a half decades found similarly confused results. Private sector spending and GNP growth rates were reported to be positively linked only for middle-income nations in his analysis of forty-nine countries (Arbey 1993, p. 54). No significant link was found for high-income countries, and the link for low-income countries was found to be in the opposite direction, at a significance level of 0.05.

In the absence of a direct causal analysis of the economic outcomes of privatization, these analyses could be criticized on a number of methodological grounds. Nonetheless, if these analyses are accepted as a sample, and as one part of the evidence, then a tentative conclusion is possible. From this narrative review of the effect, we could tentatively conclude that if a simple linkage between privatization and economic development exists, it appears at best to be weak. Alternatively, the linkage may be complex, or even nonexistent.

META-ANALYTIC REVIEW OF ECONOMIC PERFORMANCE

Effect Size Analysis

Effect sizes were calculated for all of the twenty-four studies identified as having presented measurements or statistical details of research measurements. Source details for these calculations are presented in Appendix D.

Table 9.2 shows the overall results for seventy effect sizes estimated for the economic performance of privatized enterprises. Included in this category were all of the available economic performance dimensions listed previously: profitability, efficiency, productivity, financial, shareholder return, welfare, investment, and

TABLE 9.2 Economic and Social Effect Sizes and Confidence Limits for Studies of Enterprise Sales

Author (Primary)	N	Est r	Zc	Wtd Av Z	p (wtd)=	Min CI	Max CI	Min CI Tot	Max CI Tot	Unwtd Av Z	p (unwtd)=	Chi Sqr	Total Chi Square	Signif. Level:	Z (wtd)	p (wtd)=
All Economic Measures																
Productivity	2272			0.01	0.6189			-0.03	0.05	0.19	0.2262		71.09	<.005	0.4974	0.6189
Labor Productivity				0.09	0.0051			0.03	0.15	0.58	0.0002		34.33	<.005	2.8029	0.0051
Luders (1993)	8	0.78	1.05			0.17	1.92					4.58				
Luders (1993)	14	0.87	1.34			0.75	1.94					17.31				
Luders (1993)	9	0.82	1.14			0.34	1.94					6.65				
Hutchinson (1991)	306	0.05	0.05			-0.07	0.16					0.55				
Hutchinson (1991)	306	0.06	0.06			-0.05	0.17					0.30				
Hutchinson (1991)	306	0.04	0.04			-0.07	0.15					0.82				
Moussios (1994)	46	0.38	0.40			0.10	0.70					4.11				
Labor Prod Growth Rate				-0.10	0.0018			-0.16	-0.04	-0.04	0.0228		7.93	<.25	-3.1250	0.0018
Hutchinson (1991)	306	-0.19	-0.19			-0.31	-0.08					2.58				
Hutchinson (1991)	306	-0.08	-0.08			-0.20	0.03					0.10				
Hutchinson (1991)	306	-0.04	-0.04			-0.15	0.08					1.29				
Parker & Martin (1995)	22	-0.15	-0.15			-0.60	0.30					1.11				
Parker & Martin (1995)	22	-0.13	-0.13			-0.58	0.32					0.94				
Parker (1994)	13	0.32	0.33			-0.29	0.95					1.90				
Total Factor Productivity				0.04	0.6752			-0.17	0.26	0.04	0.6823		0.00		0.4191	0.6752
Avishur (1994)	90	0.04	0.04			-0.17	0.26					0.00				
Total Factor Productivity Growth Rate				-0.23	0.1057			-0.52	0.05	-0.22	0.1139		3.75	<.25	-1.6178	0.1057
Parker & Martin (1995)	22	-0.25	-0.25			-0.70	0.20					1.70				
Parker & Martin (1995)	22	-0.27	-0.27			-0.72	0.18					1.92				
Parker (1994)	13	-0.12	-0.12			-0.74	0.50					0.13				
Technical Efficiency				0.26	0.0012			0.10	0.42	0.26	0.0015		0.00		3.2380	0.0012
Nuruzzman (1989)	155	0.26	0.26			0.10	0.42					0.00				
Financial	2278			0.06	0.0065			0.02	0.10	0.30	0.0013		106.14	<.005	2.7205	0.0065
Return on Assets				0.26	0.0673			-0.02	0.55	0.26	0.0663		0.00		1.8295	0.0673
Megginson, Nash & Van Randenborgh (1994)	51	0.26	0.26			-0.02	0.55					0.00				

(continues)

TABLE 9.2 continued

Author (Primary)	N	Est r	Zc	Wtd Av Z	p (wtd) =	Min CI	Max CI	Min CI Tot	Max CI Tot	Unwtd Av Z	p (unwtd) =	Chi Sqr	Total Chi Square	Signif. Level:	Z (wtd)	p (wtd) =
Return on Equity																
Hutchinson (1991)	306	0.06	0.06	0.08	0.0154	-0.05	0.17	0.01	0.14	0.39	0.0054	0.09	41.83	<.005	2.4226	0.0154
Hutchinson (1991)	306	0.10	0.10			-0.01	0.21					0.19				
Hutchinson (1991)	306	0.01	0.01			-0.10	0.12					1.38				
Megginson, Nash & Van Randenborgh (1994)	55	-0.08	-0.08			-0.35	0.19					1.29				
Parker (1994)	14	0.40	0.43			-0.16	1.02					0.29				
Parker & Hartley (1991)	8	-0.58	-0.66			-1.54	0.22					4.28				
Parker & Hartley (1991)	8	0.74	0.96			0.08	1.83					2.40				
Parker & Hartley (1991)	8	0.87	1.35			0.47	2.23					5.89				
Yarrow (1989)	9	-0.76	-1.00			-1.80	-0.20					9.58				
Yarrow (1989)	10	0.45	0.48			-0.26	1.22					0.32				
Yarrow (1989)	9	0.26	0.26			-0.54	1.06					0.00				
Yarrow (1989)	6	0.00	0.00			-1.13	1.13					0.21				
Meller (1993)	7	0.44	0.47			-0.51	1.45					0.61				
Meller (1993)	6	0.68	0.82			-0.31	1.95					1.67				
Meller (1993)	6	0.61	0.72			-0.42	1.85					1.23				
Meller (1993)	7	0.62	0.72			-0.26	1.70					1.69				
Meller (1993)	7	0.90	1.49			0.51	2.47					7.98				
Meller (1993)	7	0.33	0.35			-0.63	1.33					0.30				
Meller (1993)	7	0.69	0.86			-0.12	1.84					2.43				
Return on Equity Growth Rate																
Hutchinson (1991)	306	0.08	0.08	-0.02	0.4779	-0.03	0.19	-0.09	0.04	-0.02	0.4794	3.33	5.48	<.10	-0.7097	0.4779
Hutchinson (1991)	306	-0.10	-0.10			-0.22	0.01					1.98				
Hutchinson (1991)	306	-0.05	-0.05			-0.16	0.06					0.18				
Return on Sales																
Domberger (1993)	10	0.30	0.31	0.36	0.0000	-0.43	1.05	0.20	0.51	0.29	0.0444	0.02	28.70	<.005	4.4585	0.0000
Megginson, Nash & Van Randenborgh (1994)	55	0.40	0.42			0.15	0.69					0.20				
Moussios (1994)	48	0.39	0.41			0.11	0.70					0.11				
Yarrow (1986)	25	0.23	0.24			-0.18	-0.18					0.32				
Yarrow (1989)	9	-0.30	-0.31			-1.11	0.49					2.68				
Yarrow (1989)	10	0.92	1.60			0.86	2.34					10.78				
Yarrow (1989)	9	-0.81	-1.12			-1.92	-0.32					13.08				
Yarrow (1989)	9	0.19	0.20			-0.60	1.00					0.15				
Yarrow (1989)	8	0.71	0.88			0.00	1.75					1.35				

Category / Study	N															
Value Added Growth Rate				0.08	0.6968			-0.33	0.50	0.13	0.8005		6.38		0.3896	0.6968
Parker & Hartley (1991)	8	-0.32	-0.33			-1.21	0.54					0.87				
Parker & Hartley (1991)	8	0.23	0.24			-0.64	1.12					0.12				
Parker & Hartley (1991)	8	0.75	0.97			0.10	1.85					3.97				
Parker & Martin (1993)	10	-0.35	-0.37			-1.11	0.37					1.42				
Investor Returns	132			0.50	0.0000			0.32	0.67	0.07	0.0000		27.30	<.005	5.4293	0.0000
Aggarwal, Leal & Hernandez (1993)	9	-0.89	-1.40			-2.20	-0.60					21.57				
Menyah, Paudyal, and Inyang (1990)	34	0.30	0.31			-0.04	0.66					1.05				
Sinha (1993)	40	0.52	0.57			0.25	0.89					0.20				
Smith (1994)	49	0.67	0.81			0.52	1.10					4.47				
Investment	113			0.94	0.0000			0.74	1.13	-0.02	0.0050		301.22	<.005	9.4364	0.0000
Capital Investment				1.35	0.0000			1.14	1.55	0.78	0.0000		162.98	<.005	12.7879	0.0000
Parker (1994)	99	-0.50	-0.55			-1.14	0.04					39.67				
Megginson, Nash & Van Randenborgh (1994)	14 / 37	0.20	0.21			-0.13	0.54					44.22				
Moussios (1994)	48	0.99	2.67			2.38	2.97					79.10				
R&D				-2.41	0.0000			-3.00	-1.82	-2.41	0.0000		0.00		-7.9847	0.0000
Parker (1994)	14	-0.98	-2.41			-3.00	-1.82					0.00				
Economic GNP Growth	192			-0.10	0.1916			-0.25	0.05	-0.02	0.4576		10.43	<.05	-1.3058	0.1916
Arbey (1993)	49	-0.16	-0.17			-0.45	0.12					0.21				
Arbey (1993)	49	-0.36	-0.37			-0.66	-0.08					3.46				
Arbey (1993)	49	0.08	0.08			-0.20	0.37					1.53				
Yoder, Borkholder & Friesen (1991)	17	0.47	0.51			-0.01	1.03					5.18				
Yoder, Borkholder & Friesen (1991)	28	-0.15	-0.15			-0.54	0.25					0.06				
Other																
Productivity				-0.01	0.7899			-0.05	0.04	-0.01	0.7907		2.18	<.90	-0.2664	0.7899
Labor Productivity				0.01	0.7200			-0.05	0.08	0.01	0.7202		0.68	<.75	0.3585	0.7200
Hutchinson (1991)	306	-0.02	-0.02			-0.13	0.10					0.23				
Hutchinson (1991)	306	0.00	0.00			-0.11	0.11					0.03				
Hutchinson (1991)	306	0.05	0.05			-0.06	0.16					0.42				

(continues)

TABLE 9.2 continued

Author (Primary)	N	Est r	Zc	Wtd Av Z	p (wtd)=	Min CI	Max CI	Min CI Tot	Max CI Tot	Unwtd Av Z	p (unwtd)=	Chi Sqr	Total Chi Square	Signif. Level	Z (wtd)	p (wtd)=
Labor Prod Growth Rate				-0.02	0.4622			-0.09	0.04	-0.02	0.4632		0.90	<.75	-0.7353	0.4622
Hutchinson (1991)	306	0.01	0.01			-0.11	0.12					0.27				
Hutchinson (1991)	306	-0.01	-0.01			-0.12	0.10					0.05				
Hutchinson (1991)	306	-0.07	-0.07			-0.18	0.04					0.57				
Firms Financial Performance				0.01	0.7421			-0.04	0.05	0.12	0.3549		9.84	<.50	0.3291	0.7421
Return on Equity				0.02	0.5590			-0.05	0.08	0.25	0.0830		4.25	<.50	0.5844	0.5590
Hutchinson (1991)	306	0.00	0.00			-0.11	0.11					0.11				
Hutchinson (1991)	306	0.03	0.03			-0.09	0.14					0.01				
Hutchinson (1991)	306	0.01	0.01			-0.10	0.13					0.01				
Parker & Hartley (1991)	8	0.32	0.33			-0.54	1.21					0.49				
Parker & Hartley (1991)	8	0.70	0.87			-0.01	1.75					3.62				
Return on Equity Growth Rate				0.00	0.9107			-0.07	0.06	0.00	0.9108		0.07	<.975	-0.1122	0.9107
Hutchinson (1991)	306	0.01	0.01			-0.10	0.12					0.04				
Hutchinson (1991)	306	-0.01	-0.01			-0.12	0.10					0.01				
Hutchinson (1991)	306	-0.01	-0.01			-0.12	0.10					0.02				
Value Added Growth				-0.01	0.9641			-0.63	0.61	-0.01	0.9342		5.27	<.025	-0.0450	0.9641
Parker & Hartley (1991)	8	-0.63	-0.74			-1.62	0.14					2.64				
Parker & Hartley (1991)	8	0.61	0.71			-0.16	1.59					2.64				
No Reform (Control Group)																
Return on Sales				0.22	0.3330			-0.23	0.67	0.38	0.1857		0.29	<.75	0.9680	0.3330
Domberger (1993)	5	0.52	0.58			-0.81	1.97					0.26				
Yarrow (1986)	20	0.18	0.18			-0.30	-0.30					0.03				
Social																
Service Quality				0.08	0.0254			0.01	0.15	0.09	0.0471		64.04	<.005	2.2357	0.0254
Moussios (1994)	144	-0.02	-0.02			-0.19	0.14					1.59				
Moussios (1994)	131	0.61	0.71			0.53	0.88					49.82				
Moussios (1994)	144	-0.16	-0.16			-0.33	0.00					8.62				
Moussios (1994)	144	-0.08	-0.08			-0.24	0.09					3.63				
Moussios (1994)	96	0.02	0.02			-0.18	0.22					0.35				
Moussios (1994)	96	0.06	0.06			-0.14	0.27					0.03				

	N															
Disclosures																
Thomson (1993)	622	-0.32	-0.33	-0.33	0.0000	-0.41	-0.25	-0.41	-0.25	-0.33	0.0000	0.00	0.00		-8.1649	0.0000
Employment				-0.18	0.0592			-0.36	0.01	-0.23	0.0360		23.14	<.005	-1.8870	0.0592
Bhaskar & Khan (1995)	93	-0.49	-0.54			-0.91	-0.17					3.65				
Parker & Hartley (1991)	31	0.64	0.76			0.24	1.29					12.37				
Parker & Hartley (1991)	17	-0.52	-0.58			-1.11	-0.06					2.30				
Parker & Hartley (1991)	17	-0.63	-0.74			-1.33	-0.15					3.48				
Parker (1994)	14	-0.44	-0.47			-1.06	0.12					0.92				
Megginson, Nash & Van Randenborgh (1994)	39	0.16	0.16			-0.17	0.48					0.42				
Executive Remuneration																
Haskel & Szymanski (1992)	12	0.55	0.62	0.62	0.0634	-0.03	1.27	-0.03	1.27	0.62	0.0632	0.00	0.00		1.8563	0.0634
Other																
Nationalization																
Employment				-0.51	0.0034			-0.85	-0.17	-0.37	0.9268	11.85	27.94	<.005	-2.9280	0.0034
Parker & Hartley (1991)	22	-0.86	-1.30			-1.75	-0.85									
Parker & Hartley (1991)	17	0.51	0.56			0.04	1.09									

economic development measures. A further fourteen effect sizes relating to the social performance dimension were also included, covering service quality, employment, executive remuneration, and the extent of disclosure of information. In addition, another twenty effect sizes are presented for measures of economic and social performance following nationalization, or other reforms.

Overall, the twenty-four studies included in this meta-analysis provided effect sizes covering eighteen different areas of performance with privatization. With eighteen areas of performance, it is sensible to ask whether it is logical to combine all types of performance areas together in order to determine one overall "grand average" effect size. The answer to this question is probably no, but this answer is somewhat arbitrary.[14] With fewer effect sizes in any one single category of performance, we will also emphasize the combining (or summarizing) function of meta-analysis rather than determining the possible role of moderator variables. Table 9.2 indicates the weighted mean effect size[15] for all performance categories.

Productivity

A summary of the average weighted effect sizes for each of the areas of performance within the productivity performance category is shown in Figure 9.1. The average effect size for the productivity category as a whole is also shown, although we might interpret this only with extreme caution. So, what can we learn from this analysis?

Several observations are possible. Firstly, mindful of the economic objectives of privatization, successful privatizations should see indicators for labor productivity

FIGURE 9.1   Productivity Effect Sizes for the Sale of Enterprises

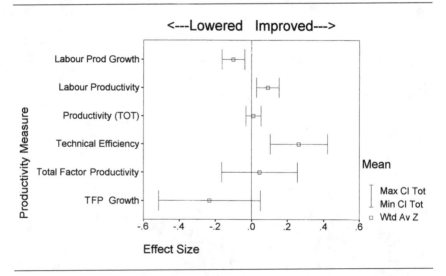

and total factor productivity increasing. This analysis revealed that a significant ($p < .01$) increase in labor productivity was reported on average ($r_{ave} = +0.09$, with 95 percent confidence limits $+0.03$, $+0.15$).[16] Likewise, the single technical efficiency effect size reported was different from zero ($p < .001$) at $r_{ave} = +0.26$ and with limits of $+0.10$ to $+0.42$. No significant increase in total factor productivity was observed, however, with the single TFP effect estimate being positive (indicating an improvement) at $r_{ave} = +0.04$, but with 95 percent confidence limits of -0.17 to $+0.26$. Secondly, we can also come to a useful conclusion looking at all of the absolute productivity performance changes together as a group. All of the nine effect sizes for labor productivity, total factor productivity, and technical efficiency were positive. This observation could not have arisen by chance and was significant[17] at the .01 level. Thirdly, more mixed conclusions were drawn from the analyses of growth rates in labor productivity and growth rates in total factor productivity. Both were negative, and significantly so at the .01 level.[18] The eighteen effect size estimates measuring all aspects of productivity were, not surprisingly, strongly heterogeneous.[19]

Calculations for the possible influence of several moderator variables were undertaken.[20] They revealed that studies of the sale of enterprises had reported significantly larger labor productivity gains than other types of productivity gain. This finding was consistent with the notion that privatization reduces overmanning, and reduces union influence in such work practices. Looking at the impact that the presence of one or more controls in the analysis may have had, it was found that the average effect size for studies that used controls ($r_{ave} = +0.11$) was only 12.4 percent of the size of the average for studies that did not ($r_{ave} = +0.95$). This finding was highly significant (with $p < .01$).[21] Tested as a separate group, these more sophisticated studies still yielded a significant average effect size (i.e., a productivity gain) at the .05 level.

The search for privatization results also yielded one study (Hutchinson 1991) that reported on the productivity impact of nationalizations. His study reviewed the performance of British Aerospace, Ferranti, and Rover after these were nationalized in the mid-1970s. As a part of the productivity analysis, the absolute labor productivity gains from privatization were contrasted against labor gains measured from these nationalizations. If privatization studies report productivity gains, then perhaps nationalization studies show productivity losses? This was not the case. The analysis did confirm, though, that whereas meager labor productivity gains were measured for nationalizations in the United Kingdom, the average effect sizes reported for U.K. privatizations were significantly greater, at a level of .01.

Firm Financial Performance

A range of financial performance results were found for the firm itself. If we consider the entire category of thirty-six financial performance measures as a whole, the average weighted effect size was $r_{ave} = +0.06$ with confidence limits ($+0.02$ to

+0.10). This was based on the 2,278 measurements taken, and was significant at the level of $p < .01$. Thus, a statistically significant improvement was reported on average across all financial performance measures as a group. The performance measures in this group each measure something different, however. Looking now at these performance measures individually, a significant improvement was observed in average return on sales. These nine effect size estimates had the largest average weighted effect size at $r_{ave} = +0.36$ ($p < .0000$), and with confidence limits ($+0.20$ to $+0.51$). Likewise, the single return on assets estimate was not significant at $r_{ave} = +0.26$ ($p < .07$) with limits (-0.02 to $+0.55$), whilst the average return on equity for the nineteen estimates available was also significant at $r_{ave} = +0.08$ ($p < .02$), with limits ($+0.01$ to $+0.14$). These are shown in Figure 9.2.

In terms of the growth rate for return on equity, an average effect size of $r_{ave} = -0.02$ was found from Hutchinson's three estimates. This average had wide confidence limits (-0.09 to $+0.04$), and was not significant at the .10 level. The growth in value added performance measure showed a positive average effect size at $r_{ave} = +0.08$, but again was not significant at the .10 level for the four available studies.

How many unreported analyses lying at the bottom of file drawers would be needed to reduce the reported measurements down below statistical significance? A "file-drawer" analysis reveals that for the financial performance category as a whole, a total of 101 unretrieved negative effect sizes (or studies) would be needed. This number of studies around the world may be possible, but is unlikely.

FIGURE 9.2   Effect Sizes for Firm Financial Performance

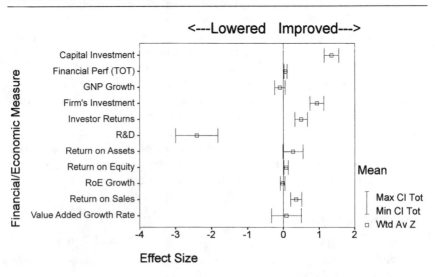

Effect Size

This financial performance category of effect sizes was also strongly heterogeneous for the thirty-six estimates.[22] Again, such heterogeneity was not surprising.

A degree of consistency was also found between the weighted and unweighted average effect sizes, when all were calculated. What was less clear, however, was the possible extent to which these improvements may have also been observed in nonprivatized firms. This requires further analysis.

Moderating Factors

To what extent have improvements in financial performance been found in nonprivatized firms as well as those that were privatized? Have more sophisticated studies revealed findings that are different from the simpler studies? These and other questions require the use of contrast tests.

Looking at the type of financial performance measure reported, it was concluded that from a statistical perspective, unweighted average performance gains for each of these areas were not distinguishable from each other.[23] Interestingly, there was also no association found between the presence of one or more controls in the analysis of financial performance and the effect size. Studies adopting controls showed an average of $r_{ave} = +0.32$, some 87 percent of the size of the average for studies that did not adopt controls ($r_{ave} = +0.36$).[24] Looking at the country studied, changes in financial performance for privatizations in Chile provided significantly greater effect sizes than those reported for both the United Kingdom and those studies where multiple countries had been analyzed. These differences were significant at the .01 level. The average effect size for the United Kingdom ($r_{ave} = +0.22$) was less than a third that for Chile ($r_{ave} = +0.77$). Large improvements in the use of human resources, and a lessening of corruption in the latter country may have contributed to such large gains. Results reported after 1990 were also found to be greater than those reported before at a significance level of .05. This was not the case at a level of .01, however. It was noted that effect sizes for Chile were reported in the after-1990 period. Lastly, several studies provided information on the financial impact of nationalizations as well as privatizations. With the availability of these measurements, the opportunity was taken to contrast the financial performance gains from privatization against those gains measured from nationalization. For this contrast test, twenty-nine absolute financial performance effect sizes for privatization were used—that is, return on equity (RoE) and return on sales (RoS) effect sizes. These were contrasted against the available five nationalization absolute effect sizes—that is the RoE effect sizes. It was evident in this comparison that the privatized firms had larger average effect sizes ($r_{ave} = +0.35$) than nationalized firms ($r_{ave} = +0.25$), but not significantly so at .10.[25] Also telling was a contrast of financial performance improvements in a control group that saw no ownership reforms ($r_{ave} = +0.38$) against that for privatization performance ($r_{ave} = +0.29$). Here, no significant difference was found at the .10 level.[26]

The finding that when all absolute financial performance data are combined, no significant difference is detected between the performance improvements measured after nationalizations and those measured after privatizations is interesting. This may be due to large variability being shown in both, the relatively small sample sizes available to date, or else may have a more fundamental interpretation. For example, since both nationalization and privatization reforms appear to have resulted in performance gains, albeit with privatization gains being larger, perhaps both were right for their time? In other words, it is not the type of ownership that is behind the performance improvement, but the package of urgent internal reforms instituted at the time, that lead to improvements. Perhaps many of the reforms required at a particular time could be initiated under either private or public ownership?

Likewise, it is also an interesting finding that average performance improvements after privatization were not statistically different from those few measurement sets available for a control group where no reforms had occurred. This may have been due to the low sample size currently available, poor control group characteristics, or again, a more fundamental cause. On the issue of statistical control group employed, the five public enterprises used as a control group by Domberger (1993) and the five used by Yarrow (1986) were not a truly random sample of public sector agencies. The inclusion, by Yarrow for example, of British Airways, which was privatized in 1987, is a case in point and could be the subject of considerable discussion. Although British Airways was, strictly speaking, still government-owned throughout Yarrow's 1981–84 analysis period, its privatization had already been announced. Any performance improvements at BA could thus logically be attributed to this announcement, rather than any general improvement occurring in the public sector as a whole. This was acknowledged by Yarrow in his work. Reanalysis excluding the British Airways performance data in the Yarrow control group did not change the statistical conclusions, however.

These findings on the financial performance of privatization each adds something to the privatization debate. Firstly, we can say that reported financial improvements have been no different from those reported following nationalizations. Secondly, average reported improvements following privatization were no different from those reported from control groups where no ownership change had occurred. Again, privatization by itself appears to have a weak association with improved profitability based on the measurements to date. These conclusions, however, were also unfortunately necessarily weak, having been made on the basis of one degree of freedom contrast tests and using data recognized as far from optimum.

Firm's Investment Behavior

One issue of concern that arose in the narrative review was that of a potential downturn in long-term investment within the firm after privatization. The investment behavior of a firm is unlikely to be reflected in short-term financial results or productivity measures. Indeed, budget cuts in longer term research and development activities are likely to improve financial figures[27] in the short term. What do the effect size estimates say on this issue?

Two main groups of effect sizes occur in this category. For the three measures relating to capital investment (n = 99), a strongly positive average of $r_{ave} = +1.35$ (p < .0000) and limits of +1.14 to +1.55 was found. Quite the opposite finding was revealed for the single measure relating specifically to research and development. Here, a strong negative effect size (p < .0000) of r = −2.41 was found for the fourteen measurements available. If we were bold enough to combine all of these measures of long-term investment into one we would find that the average weighted effect size for all four estimates in this category (n = 113) was a strong $r_{ave} = +0.94$ (p < .0000), with confidence limits +0.74 to +1.13.[28] In other words, despite the existence of measurements in opposite directions, there appears to be a generally positive association between privatization and long-term expenditures on capital investment and research and development, as best we know at present. The location benefiting from this expenditure—whether overseas or local—was an issue not tackled in the analysis, albeit that it is a real policy area of importance. The investment behavior category of effect sizes was also strongly heterogeneous at the .01 level.[29]

Financial Return to Shareholders

What can we now learn from a meta-analysis in terms of financial returns to shareholders? Four effect size estimates were available. These averaged $r_{ave} = +0.50$ (p < .0000), with limits of +0.32 to +0.67. This average was significantly positive, with narrow confidence limits on the basis of both weighted and unweighted estimates. This indicates the strong confidence with which we can say that privatizations are associated with large returns to shareholders, at least based on past evidence.

More fundamentally, however, this association is important for a second reason. High shareholder returns were achieved primarily by underpricing the initial share offerings, rather than necessarily through any increase in productivity of the firm. This therefore represents a considerable wealth transfer from the community, as the former owners, to the new shareholders. The concept that the gains by shareholders have come primarily at the expense of the community as former owners is rarely made explicit in the political debate, although sometimes noted in the literature (Menyah, Paudyal, and Inyang 1990). This sample of four effect sizes was also significantly heterogeneous.[30]

With so few studies available here, only one contrast test was possible to investigate moderator variables. Here, it was found that returns reported for investors in Chile were significantly less, at a level of .01, than those reported in the United Kingdom.

National economic growth

Growth in the national economy was clearly an objective of privatization. On this basis, meta-analytic evidence of success was sought. However, this topic is one of some size, and could command a research project in its own right. My comments here relate only to those references that arose in the search for privatization results, rather than those possible from a more comprehensive search on this topic alone.

Two studies presented associations between privatization and economic growth, yielding five effect size estimates. As a group, these estimates had a negative weighted average effect size of $r_{ave} = -0.10$, with 95 percent confidence limits from -0.25 to $+0.05$. This average was not significant at the .10 level.[31] Hence, no significant association between the size of the private sector and economic growth was found for this international data. The simple notion that privatization leads inexorably to greater economic growth was not supported in this case. Perhaps the mechanisms for economic growth are more complex. This sample was also heterogeneous.[32]

THE MEANING OF EFFECT SIZES

How should we interpret the particular effect size estimates discussed so far? I noted earlier that there are several possible suggestions for the interpretation of effect sizes. The first suggestion was to compare this effect size with other effects in the same field or involving the same variables. Secondly, it was suggested that the relative practical performance gains could be determined for these average effect sizes. Also suggested was the concept of using the binomial effect size display. I will adopt each of these.

Looking firstly at other activities in the field, I previously noted the meta-analytic study of Boyd (1991). He looked at the impact of strategic planning on a firm's financial performance and found a "modest" average weighted effect size of $r_{ave} = 0.15$. The analysis of Narby, Cutler, and Moran (1993) on a juror's perception of defendant culpability was also noted previously, with the overall average effect size of $r_{ave} = +0.16$. Rosenthal's effect sizes for aspirin and incidence of heart attack ($r = 0.03$), and the influence of psychotherapy and improving one's situation ($r = 0.32$) were also presented as being critical findings in the fields of medicine and psychology. How do our findings on the sale of enterprises compare?

The average effect sizes for enterprise sales have a wide range, but generally appear to be on a par. Labor productivity average effect sizes ($r_{ave\,(weighted)} = +0.09$, and $r_{ave\,(unweighted)} = +0.58$) look healthy compared to those found in Boyd's strategic planning work. Those for total factor productivity ($r_{ave\,(weighted\,or\,unweighted)} = +0.04$) appear smaller. Effect sizes for returns on sales ($r_{ave\,(weighted)} = +0.36$, and $r_{ave\,(unweighted)} = +0.29$), returns on assets ($r_{ave\,(weighted\,or\,unweighted)} = +0.26$), and returns on equity ($r_{ave\ (weighted)}$ = +0.08, and $r_{ave\ (unweighted)}$ = +0.39) again appear to be healthy in comparison. Likewise, the financial returns to shareholders ($r_{ave\ (weighted)}$ = +0.50, and $r_{ave\ (unweighted)}$ = +0.07) were also healthy.

What is the practical significance here? Only a limited amount of information on average data characteristics was available for the measurements in this analysis. Consequently, the number of percentage improvement estimates that could be calculated was small, and the data sparse. For labor productivity, the (unweighted) average absolute percentage gain from the sale of enterprises was estimated at 29.6 percent from the four estimates available. Although an impressive figure, it should nonetheless be interpreted carefully, comprising three large percentage estimates from Chile and one small estimate from the U.K. A 2.1 percent improvement for total factor productivity was evident from the single available estimate, and a return on assets estimate from Megginson, Nash, and Van Randenborgh (1994) was an improvement of 0.92 percent. On the other hand, return on equity improvements averaged 8.4 percent (eleven available estimates), and the average return on sales improvement was +2.7 percent (eight estimates available). Investor returns produced the highest estimated average financial improvement at 17.0 percent above usual market returns.

As was the case previously, some caution is needed here when translating these findings to practice. Firstly, improvements clearly varied, and one improvement rule for performance changes is inappropriate. Secondly, percentage improvement estimates were only available for a proportion of all effect sizes obtained from the literature, and resulting percentages could not simply be adopted as the likely improvement figure. For instance, four percentage estimates were available for the seven labor productivity effect sizes. The average for the four effect sizes for which percentage estimates were available was +0.98, which is much higher than the (unweighted) average for this category of +0.58, or a little over one half of this value. Knowing that greater effect sizes will usually be associated with greater percentage improvements and that a zero effect size corresponds to a zero performance change, the expected percentage improvement estimates above should be adjusted. Making these adjustments resulted in the following percentage improvement estimates.

Labor productivity	+17.5%
Return on equity	+7.6%
Return on sales	+2.8%
Economic growth	−0.0%

These improvement estimates should also be interpreted in conjunction with the statistical-significance work undertaken previously. Labor productivity gains and financial returns on equity and sales were all detected as statistically significant. Thus, we could conclude that, in essence, global enterprise sales have generally been associated with a reported average overall financial performance improvement of around 3 to 8 percent, and a productivity improvement of 17 percent. The potential effects of moderator variables was also noted.

One further major issue arises here. How were financial performance improvements achieved? Labor productivity has increased significantly, but what other things have contributed towards improved financial returns? Have prices risen, or decreased? Have service levels decreased or has quality reduced? What are the impacts of any changed financial accounting practices or adjustments? What has been the role of market competition? Each of these questions deserves consideration. The issue of service quality and prices will be discussed in the following section.

On the issue of changed accounting practices, there is some information available, though it is not statistical in nature. Heald (1989, p. 347) notes that "the weakness of enforcement mechanisms . . . should alert decision makers to the scope which privatized electricity companies will have to manipulate their accounts unless a coherent framework for accounting is established ahead of privatization." Likewise, Thomson (1993, p. 152) also argued strongly in his analysis of information disclosure following privatization that "managers might have had an incentive to get rid of the 'bad news' immediately before privatization to ensure higher future profits, and growth from a low profit base."

Other than these warnings, we must rely on anecdotal evidence, and as such, this may be unreliable. It is certainly possible to make accounting "adjustments" to profitability through one-off provisions in the before period that could artificially deflate this profit figure and correspondingly inflate the after-period profit. One recent example from Victoria, Australia, clearly illustrates this (Davidson 1996b). The state's Auditor General qualified the accounts of the first electricity distribution company privatized by the Kennett government. A reported loss of $36 million for the 1994–95 financial year was, in the view of the Auditor General, actually understated by some $70.9 million, and should have been a profit of $44.9 million. These "provisions" of $70.9 million included one provision for $23 million for tax liabilities on income that would be earned in the following year, 1995–96. Notwithstanding the accounting procedures and regulations governing such provisions, there does indeed appear to be some flexibility in the development of the company's income statement to paint a different picture of profitability, and as a consequence, be subject to some manipulation by parties. If such adjustments did occur in the data used for this meta-analysis, these would presumably have had a biasing effect. The actual extent of practices such as this occurring is unknown.

The last suggestion for better understanding the meaning of effect sizes was Rosenthal's binomial effect size display concept. We might consider that the (weighted) average effect size for labor productivity of +0.09, accounting for only 1 percent of the variance observed in the studies, since $r^2 = 0.09^2 = 0.0081$ or around 1 percent. As was the case for contracting in Chapter 7, this effect size can be converted to show the increase in success rate between an experimental group and a control group in order to help make the importance of the finding clearer. From Rosenthal (1991, p. 134) the experimental group success rate is computed as 55.5 percent, compared to a control group success rate of 44.5 percent. This represents an increase in success of 9 percent. For the case of effect size estimates for returns on equity, assets, and sales (which showed weighted average effect sizes of between +0.08 and +0.36), these would represent increases in success of between 8 and 36 percent. These are not insubstantial.

Conclusions on Economic Effect Sizes

These meta-analytic results increase our knowledge of the performance of companies following privatization. Many of the performance changes were in the directions argued in the bulk of narrative reviews, but our meta-analytic conclusions were not always so.

First, it is concluded that reported labor productivity improvements have been significant following privatization. This was not the case for total factor productivity improvements that were not statistically significant. This is consistent with the notion that privatization reduces overmanning. Second, it was also concluded that the presence of controls in productivity evaluation studies resulted in effect sizes that were very much smaller than those studies that did not use controls. This implies that the productivity gains themselves are likely to be due mainly to the changing external environment, with only a small part of this gain being associated with the enterprise sale itself. Next, the labor productivity gains found for privatizations were significantly greater than those meager gains measured from nationalizations in the United Kingdom.

In terms of the firm's financial performance, several more conclusions are possible. The fourth conclusion is that significant improvements in financial performance were found to be reported with privatizations. Effect sizes for returns on sales and returns on equity were both significantly positive, with the returns on assets being positive but not significant. Again, those evaluation studies that used controls in the analysis produced smaller effect sizes, though the impact of controls in this case was only slight. Improvements in financial performance over different countries varied significantly, with effect sizes for Chile at over three times those produced for the United Kingdom. Looking also at some limited effect size data for privatization as a reform compared to nationalization, it was found that privatization financial performance improvements were not significantly different from financial performance improvements measured during nationalizations. Likewise, the financial improvements that accompanied privatization tested as not significantly different from those measured in control groups that were not privatized.

Clearly, these performance signals confirm that with privatizations, reported firm financial performance does indeed improve significantly. However, since the gains do not appear to be different from those made in control groups of companies, there is some doubt as to whether privatization per se caused them.

The firm's investment behavior was analyzed and it was concluded that, on average, a positive association was present after privatizations. In other words, reported capital investment increased following privatization. Returns to shareholders were also on average significantly positive, with returns to the United Kingdom shareholders being much greater than those in Chile.

On the question of national economic performance, no simple direct link between the size of the private sector and economic growth was supported by the data.

SOCIAL PERFORMANCE

The sale of enterprises potentially has major social consequences. Indeed, social impacts of enterprise sales have often been at the forefront of privatization reports. As well as unforeseen social impacts, political promises of better services, reduced prices, and employment generation deserve careful scrutiny. Performance in these areas clearly cannot be judged simply through business financial reports. In this section, I will aim to provide an overview of performance in meeting a broad range of social promises made to communities. I will give an idea of the breadth of conclusions reached on social issues, as well as the degree to which these judgments form a coherent picture, or else conflict. The review will not be comprehensive, by definition, but will aim to establish some bounds on the question of social impacts and performance.

Many areas of this social dimension are emotionally charged, and the issues have at times been at the center of a history of social change. For example, the formation of single government organizations for the supply of water and electricity in Australian states was commonly viewed as being an advantage for the community good. Compared to the fragmented and uneven coverage of private services at the time, these were greeted with considerable praise by all sides of politics, and seen as delivering an equitable access to essential modern services of high quality. The possibility, indeed some might even argue the probability, that such historical advances could be reversed in this age of economic rationalism would be incomprehensible to past advocates of universal vertically integrated public utilities. But what does the evidence say?

A NARRATIVE REVIEW OF SOCIAL PERFORMANCE

A broad range of performance areas is relevant here. In this section I will firstly look at service prices, service quality, and other consumer benefits. I will then discuss the availability of services, employment impacts, equity issues, and other relevant social impacts. Table 9.3 presents key conclusions from nineteen studies representative of the international literature. Details of the country and industry sector studied in each case are shown.

TABLE 9.3   Summary of Key Conclusions Reached on Social Impacts

Study	Ref	Country/Industry Sectors Analyzed	Findings/Conclusions
Service Prices			
Ernst (1993a)	17	U.K. utilities	Privatization did not result in more competition, or in general lower prices.
Johnson (1994)	262	U.K. water sector	Prices rose by 55% over four years.
Engen (1994)	362	Venezuela's telephone company CANTV	Prices rose by 400% over two years.
Abdala (1992)	569	Privatization of ENTEL, Argentina's telecommunications company	Consumers are expected to be $4.07 billion worse off, mainly due to substantially increased telephone charges. One example is the 500% increase in connection charges.
Saunders and Harris (1994)	323	U.K. privatization program	Prices have fallen sharply in some areas and risen in others. Overall, the consumer has gained from privatization.
Service Quality/Value			
Ernst (1993a)	117	U.K. utilities	Privatization did not result in more choice or improved quality.
Yarrow (1989)	271	U.K. privatization program	Service quality reduced at British Telecom.
Engen (1994)	362	Venezuela's telephone company CANTV	Call completion rates have risen from 30% to 70%, and most pay phones now work.
Sakita (1989)	498	Privatization of Japanese National Railways	Services were "cut down."
Miller (1994)	1038	U.K. privatization program	Consumer responsiveness has, for the most part, been positive.
Moussios (1994)	545	British Telecom	Of the six service quality measurements analyzed, half improved and half worsened.

(continues)

TABLE 9.3 *continued*

Study	Ref	Country/Industry Sectors Analyzed	Findings/Conclusions
Galal et al. (1994)	521	12 privatizations around the world	Consumer welfare was projected to increase in 4 of the 12 cases analyzed, and "total" global welfare increase in 11 of the 12.
Service Accessibility			
Johnson (1994)	262	U.K. water sector	Water disconnections doubled after privatization.
Robson (1993)	372	U.K. water sector	An unprecedented doubling of water disconnections has occurred.
Lensing (1994)	546	Case study of a hospital privatization in the United States	Privatization has led to "prestige medicine," and overmedicalization, and to some in the community now living in "no-care zones."
Ernst (1993a)	17	U.K. utilities	Privatization resulted in a deepening of "fuel poverty" and "water poverty" in the U.K.
Employment			
Meller (1993)	373	Chile privatization program	Employment increased throughout the program, with 9 of the 11 firms in his sample showing higher employment levels.
Sakita (1989)	498	Privatization of Japanese National Railways	Employment was reduced by 22.1% (though this figure could have been half as high again if employment had not been seen as a "social good").
Domberger (1993)	773	U.K. privatization program	Non privatized firms shed substantially more labor than their privatized counterparts during the 1980s.
Haskel & Szymanski (1992)	944	U.K. privatizations	Privatizations reduced employment by 25%.
Douglas (1994)	1076	New Zealand privatization program	Employment was reduced in NZ Telecom from 27,000 to 12,000 in three years, and in Forestry, from 7,000 to 2,700.

Equity			
Rodriguez (1992)	478	Mexican privatization program	Privatization worsened income distribution in Mexico.
Abdala (1992)	569	Privatization of ENTEL, Argentina's telecommunications company	Major discrepancies between the winners (foreign buyers) and the losers (consumers) occurred in this privatization. Argentina as a country is expected to be $2.2 billion worse off.
Ernst (1993a)	17	U.K. utilities	Low income consumers have been affected more adversely than the generality of consumers, thus deepening the social contours of inequality. Prices increased whilst executive salaries skyrocketed.
Lorch (1991)	954	Bangladesh textile industry	Privatization changed income distribution in favor of the new owners at the expense of managers and owners.
Menyah, Paudyal, and Inyang (1990)	61	U.K. privatization program	Wealth was transferred from citizens to those who acquired shares in privatized issues.
Other Issues			
Kelsey (1993)	336	New Zealand privatization program	Consumer watchdogs were progressively weakened.
Kelsey (1993)	336	New Zealand privatization program	Transparency decreased.

Many other benefits were promised with privatization as well as economic and financial improvements. Reduced prices, greater choice, increased service quality, and better customer focus were all part of this.

Prices

Most studies reviewed that assessed service prices concluded that this promise had not been delivered. Several examples of marked price increases after the sale of public enterprises were evident. Johnson (1994) quoted price increases of 55 percent over four years for the United Kingdom water industry, Engen (1994) found a 400 percent increase over two years for the case of Venezuela's telephone system, and Abdala (1992) noted substantially increased telephone charges in Argentina. Ernst (1993a) stated simply that privatization did not generally result in lower prices. He quoted George Yarrow in citing that "electricity prices are now 25 percent higher for domestic consumers than they would have been had the industry remained in public ownership." Yarrow (1994) further argued that the price effects of privatization were different for different user groups. For large power consumers, the U.K. privatizations generally resulted in beneficial price changes. For domestic consumers, though, it appeared likely that privatization had had the effect of leading to higher domestic electricity prices than would otherwise have been obtained. The projections of Galal et al. (1994) are also informative from the perspective of benefits to consumers. Of the twelve cases analyzed from the United Kingdom, Malaysia, Chile, and Mexico, no benefits were projected for domestic consumers in three cases, and losses to the consumers were projected in five. In other words, despite the earlier-mentioned aggregate finding from this report projecting overall worldwide improvements in social welfare in eleven of twelve cases, domestic consumers either did not gain anything or else lost in eight of the twelve cases analyzed. Clearly, in this analysis, consumers were not expected to be major winners as part of the privatization process.[33]

Some authors did not agree with these sentiments and argued that on the question of prices, consumers have gained. Saunders and Harris (1994, p. 75), for instance, note that the fate of the consumer depends very much on the effectiveness of the regulator. They note that because the regulator is independent of government and generally aims to keep prices down in order to force efficiency savings, prices for companies such as British Gas and British Telecom have fallen by 5 to 7.5 percent per year in real terms. In the case of water, real prices rose, but were being used to finance massive new investment programs. Overall, they stated: "On prices, therefore, our conclusion is that the consumer has gained from privatization." The importance of regulation as an issue is discussed later in this chapter. Notwithstanding these conclusions, little information was found in reports that could assist with a more rigorous statistical analysis of the price question. The information typically available simply presented "after" data alone.

Competition

Has privatization typically produced benefits through greater competition? Several authors agreed that in the case of privatizations in the United Kingdom, they were, on the whole, undertaken without sufficient attention to increasing competition.[34] Thus, in the words of Yarrow (1989, p. 343), a "pre-occupation with ensuring a rapid transfer of ownership has led to relatively little effort being applied to finding ways of opening up markets to greater actual and potential competition: state monopoly has been replaced by private monopoly."

This lack of focus on ensuring greater market competition is a factor that privatization advocates bemoan as a major lesson from the U.K. It appears to have had the effect that no wider choice was available to consumers than before.[35] From an academic perspective, however, the U.K. program provides an interesting and unique set of data. For these enterprise sales, analysis can be undertaken looking primarily at the effect of ownership change with minimal changes in competition, albeit with some changes in regulation for most of the enterprises.

Service Quality

In terms of service quality, little research information is again available. This is unfortunate. Those studies that reviewed service quality resulted in mixed findings. Thus, the 1994 review of British Telecom by Moussios (1994) concluded that for the six service quality measures analyzed, half improved and half worsened. Yarrow (1989), again looking at British Telecom, concluded that service quality generally reduced following its privatization. Ernst (1993a) concluded that privatization did not result in improved service quality. A review of the privatization of the Japanese National Railways by Sakita (1989) also reported that services were reduced by being "cut down" following its sale. Furthermore, Lensing (1994) concluded that service quality following privatization of a U.S. hospital led to prestige high-tech medicine increasingly being used to solve day-to-day problems, and the overmedicalization of women's care, childbirth, and geriatric care. Simultaneously, Lensing observed that the uninsured working poor, chronically ill, and disabled were now situated in "no-care zones" following privatization because of inaccessible and unavailable services.

Opposing these critical conclusions were those of Miller (1994), who believed that the consumer response had generally been positive in the U.K. privatizations, and the conclusions of Engen (1994) in the case of Venezuela. Engen reported that with telephone call completion rates having risen from 30 percent to 70 percent, and with most pay phones actually working after privatization, these represented real service improvements—albeit at the 400 percent price increase noted previously.

It is curious that with promised citizen benefits having achieved such a high political profile, so little formal measurement appears to have been done. Perhaps the same beliefs that encouraged policymakers to largely overlook the need for stronger competition in the U.K. also led them to largely overlook questions of real service improvements. Once privatized, superior private sector performance and the market would presumably ensure that service quality improvements occurred.

Service accessibility was also a major issue for Ernst (1993a), who argued that the rise in electricity charges in the U.K. deepened the level of fuel poverty and gave rise to a new phenomenon of water poverty. He quotes an increase of over 300 percent in the number of income support recipients who are in debt for water charges, and a 177 percent explosion in water disconnections. Robson (1993) supported the concern of "an unprecedented doubling of water disconnections," as did Johnson (1994) also.

Employment

On employment impacts, there is a curious diversity of findings. Based on the significantly higher labor productivity reported for privatized companies, one would expect a decrease in employment levels, ceteris paribus. Meller (1993) reports that nine of the eleven Chilean firms analyzed showed higher employment after the sale than before, whilst Megginson, Nash, and Van Randenborgh (1994) also reported an employment increase of 5.7 percent. The reason for higher employment levels in Chile is uncertain, but discussion of the data used in the Megginson, Nash, and Van Randenborgh global analysis is warranted. It appears that this analysis simply adopted employment figures taken from annual reports before and after. Thus, for the case, for instance, of British Airways, employment of between 36,000 and 39,000 people was recorded in the three years before, whilst between 43,000 and 52,000 was recorded after. How could this have arisen in the competitive international air industry? British Airways' acquisition of its largest British competitor, British Caledonian, with around 7,500 employees[36] is no doubt a large part of the answer. The number of similar acquisitions by other privatized companies is unknown, but Yarrow (1989) argues that growth by acquisition was "a fairly general characteristic of newly privatized firms." To the extent that privatized firms were acquisitive, the reported employment data is likely to be clearly flawed. Any rational analysis of employment numbers would sensibly require "before" employment figures for both the publicly owned company and those target companies later to be acquired, as well as "after" data for the acquisitive privatized firm. On these grounds, the employment findings for reports such as Meller (1993) and Megginson, Nash, and Van Randenborgh (1994) should be treated with extreme caution.

These two analyses aside, most other studies assessing employment figures concluded that privatization results in employment reductions. Douglas (1994) reports that whilst he was a minister in the New Zealand government, employment was reduced in N.Z. Telecom from 27,000 to 12,000 in three years, and in forestry from 7,000 to 2,700. He goes further, stating that the New Zealand government reduced staff numbers at a rate four times faster than in the U.K. The overwhelming impression from these quotes is the air of pride—almost boasting of the achievements that he had delivered! This aside, other reports support this notion of reduced employment. These included that of Haskel and Szymanski (1992), who found a 25 percent employment reduction with privatization, and Sakita (1989). In the latter case, employment following privatization was reduced by 22.1 percent, with Sakita noting that this figure could have been around 50 percent higher, as 11.1 percent of people were taken on by the new private rail company in Japan as a "social good." Adding to the debate, the analysis by Domberger (1993) found that, although employment reductions did occur with privatizations, nonprivatized firms actually shed more labor than their privatized counterparts during the 1980s.

Several other impacts of privatization are worthy of discussion, albeit that they were not included in the initial listing of benefits or outcomes that were to be achieved through the sale. The first of these relates to the issue of equity. Others to be discussed at a later point include effects on transparency, and population attitudes.

Equity Considerations

Some authors argued that privatization programs worsened the country's income distribution. Rodriguez (1992) argued just this point in the case of Mexico, whilst Ernst (1993a) argued the same for the United Kingdom. Ernst further added that the social contours of inequality had been deepened by privatizations, since low-income consumers had been affected more than other consumers. He also commented that the existence of such inequalities had been accentuated by the fact that whilst prices had been increasing, executive salaries inside the privatized companies had skyrocketed.[37]

Similar major issues of equity arose in the analysis by Abdala (1992) looking at Argentina's telecommunications company ENTel. His analysis, using a similar "welfare" philosophy to that adopted by Galal et al., showed an overall worldwide gain in welfare of $1.4 billion. Massive winners (e.g., foreign investors) and losers (e.g., domestic consumers) appeared to occur as part of this overall gain. Consumers were identified as a major loser. Abdala stated without reservation that "as a group they are expected to be worse off by US$4,071 million. Failure to properly regulate the industry, combined with the government's yearning objectives of divestiture, has left the consumer exposed to a private monopoly that managed to substantially increase the price of telephone services" (Abdala 1992, p. 89).

What separates Abdala's analysis out, however, is not so much these observations of consumer losses—these have been suggested by many other authors as well. It is interesting because estimates made for Argentina as a whole were also presented. On this score, his analysis suggested that despite the overall "worldwide welfare gain," "when excluding foreigners in welfare calculations the net change in social welfare within the industry turns out to be negative by US$2,227 million" (p. 90). Thus, Argentina as a country is expected to be a major loser—indeed, by an amount of some −$2.2 billion. The clarity of this finding and the ease with which such figures can be bandied about with minimal comment or concern is astounding.

This theme of winners and losers is also central to the work of Dinavo (1995, p. 135). He reviews privatization in developing countries and asks the simple question, Who is to gain from privatization in developing countries? Admitting that it is a complex question, he nonetheless offers a qualified answer. Both developed and developing countries gain in his view. He cautions, however, that in developing countries, the ruling elites and government officials are likely to benefit before the population as a whole benefits. He notes also that "the group that will gain the most from privatization in the developing countries is the developed industrialized nations, specifically, the multi-national corporations and the private investors."

The wealth transfers implied above are massive. Ralston Saul (1997, p. 12) remarks that the revolutionary privatization of 80 percent of Mexico's state firms created thirty billionaires, all friends of the president or the party in power, whilst real wages plunged 52 percent. Of course, not all wealth transfers are as spectacular. But neither are wealth transfers limited to developing countries. Menyah, Paudyal, and Inyang (1990) report that U.K. privatization issues on the International Stock Exchange (London) provided excess returns above those of private sector flotations by 31 percent over a thirty-two week period. This implies a massive wealth transfer to those who acquired the U.K. shares. The size of this transfer has been put at around £2.5 billion by Jenkinson and Mayer (1994, p. 296) in comparison to usual private sector share floats. Menyah, Paudyal, and Inyang also comment that other government transactions such as the nationalization of some private companies in France at the beginning of the 1980s likewise resulted in similar wealth transfers. Thus, wealth transfers are clearly an impact when ownership is changed towards either the private or public sectors. As such, they deserve more careful consideration in the future than they have had in the past.

META-ANALYTIC REVIEW OF SOCIAL PERFORMANCE

Some thirteen effect sizes were estimated for the noneconomic measurement sets available relating to the sale of enterprises. These covered six sets of measurements for service quality, six measurement sets for employment, and one single set of measurements for executive remuneration.

Service Quality

On the promise of better services with privatization, six service quality effect size estimates were found. All were from the study by Moussios (1994) into the privatization of British Telecom. Several sets of measurements for the impacts of privatization on the quality of different services were made. These varied from slight quality improvements for pay phone services and call failures, through to more significant deteriorations in network reliability and directory and operator services. The weighted average effect size for all services from this study was positive, at r_{ave} = +0.08, and with confidence limits of +0.01 to +0.15, was significant at the .05 level.[38] This average effect size for service quality measurements is shown in Figure 9.3.

These six service quality effect sizes were also heterogeneous.[39]

We might again ponder the availability of so few sets of service quality measurements—and all from the one single author. Despite much fanfare and loud assertions on the quality of services after privatization, little formal statistical research appears to have been undertaken on this important issue.

From the little meta-analytic knowledge we have on service quality, it would still be relevant to question the extent to which these changes in quality performance appear to be directly related to the sale of the enterprise, as distinct from any changes in regulation, changes in accountability mechanisms, or changes in the degree of competition. In the analysis by Moussios, the use of sophisticated auto regressive integrated moving average (ARIMA) transfer function modeling techniques enabled the first two of these three additional variables to be modeled. As well as including a variable that accounted for the degree of state or private ownership in each month between 1982 and 1993, he also included a variable for the status of public accountability and the degree of regulatory intensity. Public accountability measurements reflected an initial period of monthly service quality indicators, the cessation of these on the grounds of commercial sensitivity for

FIGURE 9.3   Effect Sizes for Social and Other Performance Dimensions

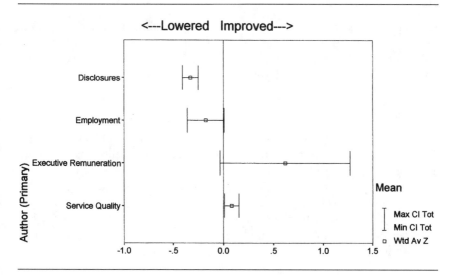

more than four years, and the resumption of earlier service quality indicators at the request of the telecommunications regulator.[40] Regulatory intensity measurements also reflected the price controls experienced under four different regimes from 1982 to 1993.[41] In order to determine the relative impact of the two additional influences compared to that of changed ownership, regulatory and accountability effect sizes were calculated for all six of the quality indicators published by Moussios. Average effect sizes were then compared through a standard one degree of freedom contrast test.

It was found that the effect size for regulatory intensity ($r_{ave} = +0.30$) was 3.4 times that for ownership change ($r_{ave} = +0.09$). In the case of public accountability status, where BT had to provide systematic information on service quality, the effect size ($r_{ave} = +0.98$) was some 11.2 times that for ownership change. In other words, for British Telecom, the impacts of regulatory intensity and public accountability requirements were several times more important in effecting improved performance than a change in ownership. In each of these cases, differences were statistically significant at the .01 level.

Employment

Six effect size estimates (n = 93) were available for employment. This category as a whole averaged $r_{ave} = -0.18$, and with limits of -0.36 to $+0.01$, was just outside the range of significance at .05. Hence, statistically, privatization reduced employment, on average, in this sample only at a significance level of .059. This sample was also found to be heterogeneous.[42]

Executive Remuneration

The single effect size estimate for executive remuneration yielded a positive effect size (i.e., an increase in remuneration after privatization) of r = $+0.62$. This had wide confidence limits, from -0.03 to $+1.27$, however, and hence was just outside significance, at the .05 level, compared to zero.

Conclusions on Social Effects

Most assessments of service prices reviewed were narrative, and concluded that the promise of lower prices after privatization had not been delivered. Curiously, no statistical analyses of the effect of privatization on prices were found, and hence, no meta-analytic conclusions on this issue were possible. Likewise, the promise of greater competition in countries such as the United Kingdom had fallen by the wayside. Rather, the community simply witnessed a preoccupation with speed in order to ensure a rapid and hence politically successful transfer of ownership.

On the promise of service quality, another strange imbalance existed between the high profile of benefits promised to citizens, and the low profile few measurements that appear to have been undertaken. A traditional narrative review revealed service quality findings on both sides. Examples of both better services and worsened services were evident. Only one study, providing only six sets of measurements, was available for meta-analytic review. This analysis of British Telecom also suggested that service quality improvements had been variable—some had improved and some had worsened, but on average, a positive improvement had been achieved. The impacts of regulatory intensity and public accountability requirements for this case were also revealing. Based on our meta-analytic measurements, the size of the performance improvement effects from stronger regulatory and public accountability requirements were several times that associated with the change in ownership.

Unfortunately, the social contours of inequality appear to have been deepened by privatizations. Low-income consumers appear to have generally been affected more than others based on the narrative review. In terms of employment, the significant reduction suggested in the narrative review of this issue was only weakly confirmed in the meta-analysis of the few available effect sizes. Rocketing executive remuneration was also one issue in the minds of communities where privatizations had occurred, and was the subject of major political tension. From the meta-analytic perspective, it was found that although the levels of pay for new executives did rise markedly, the rise was only weak in the statistical sense.

More broadly, it was nonetheless clear that privatization was accompanied by major winners and losers. The spread of individual incomes appears to have widened. Globally, cases of some countries were presented where, although the entire country had a negative welfare change estimated with privatization, the large gains made by international investors were sufficient to offset this and result in an overall world welfare gain. This raised to center stage the question of wealth transfer. The review suggested that a major impact of privatization has been the transfer of wealth that typically occurs between different groups in the community or between countries. For both emerging economies and Western countries, massive wealth transfers have occurred when governments have floated public companies at bargain basement prices to ensure a politically successful sale. Due consideration of winners and losers in the privatization process deserves much more attention in the future than it has received in the past.

DEMOCRATIC PERFORMANCE

A Narrative Review of Democratic Performance

Clearly, a wide range of issues is relevant when discussing the democratic dimension of performance. The very definition of democracy is a sizable topic on its own, and an area where a review such as this can only hope to touch on some of the threads of the argument rather than cover it comprehensively. The definition of democracy is something that is also culture dependent, rather than absolute. In countries such as the United States of America, the United Kingdom, and Australia, for example, the community has come to expect a political process characterized, at least ideally, by the public sector values noted in Table 4.3, Chapter 4. That is, collective choice occurring through the political process, recognizing the need for resources and the equity of such need, the role of citizenship, and the central importance of fairness. Overall, such democracies aim to pursue justice through open processes. In New Zealand, Taggert (1992, p. 371) also saw the fundamental values of public law in terms of openness, fairness, participation, impartiality, and rationality. Importantly, he saw these values, together, as an important "yardstick against which to measure the activities of privatized enterprises with market power" within a democracy.

The existence of these values over time has led to a whole raft of mechanisms as checks and balances on the decisions and processes of government. A few examples are sufficient to show this: the ombudsman (for citizen redress), the office of merit protection (to ensure fairness in job promotions), the Administrative Appeals Tribunal (for due process and fairness in decisions by public bodies), the auditor general (for objectivity on public sector financial issues), and the existence of legislation in areas such as freedom of information (for openness in government). These examples illustrate just part of the machinery of government developed over time in the pursuit of equity and accountability within our democracy. Each of these is a part of the democratic process. As such, this "holistic" democratic process needs to be differentiated from a less sophisticated notion of democracy as simply an election that is conducted every three or so years, from which an "elected dictatorship" arises (Spindler 1996). Indeed, one might argue that the activities of community groups demonstrating opposition to the privatization of a government agency are as much a part of the democratic process as is the election of a political party favoring such a policy.

The issue to which I now turn briefly is the extent to which privatization appears to have affected the mechanisms of democracy. At the outset, it must be recognized that quantitative assessments of these areas of performance are generally inappropriate. Measurements made are likely to be supplemental in nature, rather than central. By definition, judgments are also made very much from an individual perspective, and are based on one's expectations of government, one's fundamental personal values, and on an individual sense of the right balance between competing public and private values.

A number of impacts relating to democratic processes and democratic values have been reported from past sales of public enterprises. Such issues cover accountability, the disclosure of information, transparency of processes, the influence of groups such as businesses on democratic decisionmaking processes, and privatization as a transfer of power. I will now touch on each of these.

Accountability

A central and pervasive dimension of democracy is that of accountability. Whether simply through the polls, or else through a longer and more complex chain of responsibility for decisions and actions, accountability is at the heart of modern democratic processes. To what extent does the sale of a public enterprise affect accountability?

Authors such as Bishop, Kay, and Mayer (1994) argue that accountability is clearly increased through a sale. They argue that:

> one of the more striking consequences of privatization is the extent to which it has made the behavior and performance of privatized companies more transparent. Previously, public sector enterprises were submerged in the depths of government ministries and accountability for performance was almost impossible to establish. After privatization, distinct enterprises have been created with clearly defined lines of responsibility.

Hence, to the extent that privatization has separated out performance of any one particular area of a larger (public sector) organization, and to the extent that more clearly defined lines of responsibility have been created, better accountability mechanisms may have been established—at least potentially. Although no empirical data is presented supporting this argument, it is appealing in its simplicity. Indeed, it is difficult to argue with privatization proponents when they stress that the very financial reporting requirements of the newly privatized firms promote improved accountability—at least in the narrow managerialist or financial sense.[43]

Others, such as Ernst (1994a), and Saunders and Harris (1994) argue exactly the opposite—that privatization has resulted in reduced accountability. Saunders and Harris note, for instance, that from the perspective of customers "on accountability, the case of the water industry at least suggests that customers have gained little if anything from privatization, and that some may have lost" (p. 75).

Survey data for the United Kingdom seeking public perceptions on accountability to customers in the water industry were also presented, but this was not unequivocal. After the completion of enterprise sales, users were asked whether it had increased accountability to customers. A mere 28 percent of respondents agreed that it had, whilst 39 percent disagreed. Some 19 percent neither agreed nor disagreed, and 15 percent did not know, out of the sample of 828 respondents. Apparently, performance on the second dimension of Stone's accountability framework noted in Chapter 7, that of market accountability, has been equivocal.

Taggert (1992, p. 371) was even more scathing of claims of improved accountability. He argued from the New Zealand perspective that the legal process of privatization itself strips away most of the broader accountability mechanisms that operate in the public sector—ombudsman review, freedom of information, scrutiny by the auditor general, and ministerial responsibility. He was explicit in his concern for this reduction in accountability, noting that "there is an account-ability vacuum which the courts may be drawn into." On this basis, he saw per-formance on some of Stone's other accountability dimensions—those relating to public accountability—as being poor.

The various threads to this debate on accountability are complex, and at this stage largely unresolved. In total, it might be concluded that although managerial accountability may have increased, this is likely to have been at the cost of a de-crease in the broader public accountability mechanisms, and with at most ques-tionable accountability impacts on customers. Within this debate it may also be important to make the distinction between the deliverables required of the for-mer or newly privatized companies (that is, the service and quality levels as well as the risk profiles expected of each), the accountability processes themselves, and the group to whom the accountability is being directed—the community in gen-eral or specific consumer groups. It is probable that quite different judgments will be made on each of these aspects.

Transparency and Disclosure of Information

One central dimension of accountability is openness and the extent to which dis-closure of information is affected. In the first instance, the actual sale of the enter-prise needs to be "open." As Kikeri, Nellis, and Shirley (1992, p. 70) put it,

> one of the principal lessons of experience is that every privatization transaction must be transparent. Transparency can be assured through clear and simple selection cri-teria for evaluating bids, clearly defined competitive procedures, disclosure of pur-chase price and buyer, well defined institutional responsibilities, and adequate moni-toring and supervision of the program.

They cite several examples of lack of transparency in the initial programs of Mexico, Pakistan, and Guinea. We could add to these a myriad of other examples from countries as diverse as the United Kingdom and Australia. In Guinea, the World Bank reports that the SANOYA textile complex was sold for ECU 1 mil-lion after undergoing an ECU 42 million rehabilitation. Likewise, Huilerie de Kasa, a coconut oil producer, was sold for GNF 6 million when two generators in the plant alone were worth GNF 30 million.[44] In the United Kingdom, Wiltshire (1990) notes that subsequent to the sale of the Rover organization, the U.K. Pub-lic Accounts Committee revealed that the Thatcher government deliberately un-dervalued Rover to allow a takeover by British Aerospace, deceiving the European Commission and the U.K. taxpayers and voters. In Australia, a similar example of deliberate undervaluation has been the subject of accusations directed at the re-formist government of Victoria in its sale of the state's Electricity Research Labo-ratory to a high profile businessman.[45] Again, the need for independent watch-dogs to monitor the politically motivated actions of an overzealous reforming government is evident.

More importantly, however, the extent to which the openness of ongoing operations is affected following privatization also deserves discussion. On this score, U.K. research by Thomson (1993, p. 154) and Heald (1989, p. 346) concludes that the disclosure of information declined following privatization of the electricity supply industry. Thomson provides evidence on the extent of voluntary disclosure of performance, cost, and financial information. He concludes that the period of privatization saw "a general loss of information, both of the previously required financial and cost detail, and of the voluntary disclosure of performance indicators encouraged by industry consensus working through the Electricity Council."

He comments that this reduction in disclosure may simply be due to the sensitivity of the new competition culture, or may also be related to the stakeholding power of the small shareholder/customer group.

Privatization as the sale of enterprises certainly brings into focus the sharp differences between the traditional values expected of the public sector, with a degree of openness accompanied by formal checks and balances, and competitive private sector practices where speedy commercial decisions are made behind closed doors. The adoption of closed decisionmaking practices along with contempt for proper parliamentary procedures throughout the New Zealand privatization process even led Kelsey (1993) to conclude that the privatization reform was itself "anti-democratic." It transferred power from the sovereign state to the international marketplace, she explained. Indeed, during the New Zealand corporatization and privatization program, the roles of the traditional watchdogs such as the auditor general and ombudsman became increasingly contentious, and less powerful. In support, she cites examples of ministers before select committees refusing, in the House, to answer questions on state-owned enterprises that still retained partial state ownership. Such refusals were done on the grounds of commercial confidentiality. She also notes numerous clashes between the reforming government and these independent watchdogs.[46] The treasured democratic notions of openness and due process were under attack in New Zealand, in Kelsey's view. This occurred under the increasingly central influence of groups such as the N.Z. Business Roundtable—a group of forty-three chief executives from the country's largest companies. When a series of allegations surfaced revealing that the government had accepted large political donations, mainly from roundtable members, New Zealanders began realizing that a power transfer had occurred. The community, as Kelsey puts it, asked the question whether government was now effectively in the pockets of big business. In Kelsey's eyes, this was not simply an allegation of corruption:

> The issue was not whether individual politicians were doing favors for their mates. It was the systemic transfer of power over the country's economic, social and political future to individuals and institutions of private capital, driven by profit and market forces, backed by the institutions and agencies of international capital who remained shadowy figures in the background.

Clearly, in Kelsey's view, a massive transfer of power had taken place away from the sovereign state, with privatization playing a key role. Such concerns, even if only partly true, raise the arguments of then New Zealand Auditor General Brian Tyler to prominence. Tyler insisted that the radical changes being introduced through the 1980s demanded more, not less, accountability to Parliament. Such a stand continues today, as it did then, however such sentiments do not win favor with reformist governments seeking to deal with more compliant and obedient public servants on short-term contracts. Neither does such as stand win favor from the directors of newly privatized enterprises.

What of the objective of reducing corruption? Whilst case studies on this issue exist, no statistical work could be found in the literature. Case studies such as those evident in Kunda (1994) well illustrate that, in any event, the reforms needed to reduce corruption appear to be different depending on the existing conditions under which corruption is currently flourishing. Thus, Kunda (1994, p. 23) reports that in Zambia, the attempted privatization of the number one state asset, the Zambian Consolidated Copper Mines, sparked off a divisive controversy in government resulting in the dismissal of two deputy ministers. One of these, Dr. Mathias Mpande, charged that a group of prominent politicians and an unnamed business cartel were working towards taking control of the Zambian economy. Mpande argued that "the nation should be allowed to debate its privatization to protect democracy." The smell of corruption here was putrid! On the other hand, Russell (1994) argues that privatization itself is often deemed necessary in reducing corruption within government. Whether the privatization reform has reduced or increased corruption may well be related to the extent to which free disclosure of information is genuinely occurring within a country in the first instance, prior to any consideration of privatization policies.

Effect Sizes for Information Disclosure

Can a meta-analytic review of evidence assist here? Yes, a little. One study provided information on the extent of information disclosure before and after privatization. Information presented by Thomson (1993) was reanalyzed, enabling an association to be determined between the extent of information disclosed (as the dependent variable) and ownership status (as the independent variable). This yielded a significantly negative effect size indicating less information forthcoming after the sale ($r = -0.33$), and with limits of -0.41 to -0.25, was significant at the .01 level.

Interpreting this, we can be very sure that less information was available following this privatization case compared to that available before.

In the previously mentioned study of Moussios (1994), the associations between changes in public accountability and service quality were also mentioned. The fact that legislation and other mechanisms were implemented to ensure that British Telecom's services improved strongly suggests that privatization led to a reduction in accountability here as well.

Conclusions on Democratic Performance

So, what can we now conclude as to the effects of privatization on openness, fairness, due process, and participative aspects of democracy? On the question of accountability, the narrative review raised a major concern. It was concluded that privatization has in some international cases stripped away many of the broader accountability mechanisms that traditionally operate in the public sector—ombudsman review, freedom of information, scrutiny by the auditor general, and ministerial responsibility. As such, it could be concluded that whilst managerial accountability may have itself been increased for the firm, this may have occurred at the cost of a decrease in traditional public sector accountability mechanisms. Privatization as the sale of enterprises has certainly brought into focus the sharp differences between the traditional values expected of the public sector, with a degree of openness accompanied by formal checks and balances, and private sector practices where quick commercial decisions are made behind closed doors. From the little meta-analytic information internationally available on information disclosure, we can be certain that significantly less information was available following the privatization of the electricity industry in the United Kingdom.

The increasing use by reformist governments of the commercial-in-confidence veil was also noted with concern. The issue here was not solely that individual politicians may be doing favors for their mates. It was as much a concern over the possibility that power over a country's economic, social, and political future was being transferred systematically away from the sovereign state towards private individuals and institutions of international capital driven by profit and market forces. In the context of this concern, it was concluded that radical changes being introduced by reformist governments ought to demand more accountability rather than less to Parliament. At a minimum, the continuation of existing scrutiny checks should be encouraged. Desirably, though, strengthened accountability mechanisms to the public, to citizens, and to Parliament are required. Such a stand does not win favor with reformist governments, bureaucrats, or executives of these enterprises. Stronger independent accountability mechanisms are also needed to address the undue influence that various business and private groups may potentially have on political decisions and public policymaking. Lastly, the review discussed the issue of corruption. Here, it was concluded that both privatization and nationalization had been used as reform mechanisms to combat its spread.

POLITICAL PERFORMANCE

Again, it will clearly not be possible to discuss in any depth many political facets of privatization. I will therefore attempt to highlight just some of the major relevant political threads to the sale of enterprises. The line separating those issues that logically ought to be discussed under the heading of democratic performance from those that more rightly belong to the political sphere is arbitrary. I will therefore continue some of the themes begun in the previous section. These will include the inherently political nature of privatization, the perspective of privatization as a transfer of power and wealth, and the apparent success of privatization as an election winner.

The Political Nature of Privatization

It has been recognized previously that privatization as a strategy is inherently political. In Western countries, it is symbolic of a clash of values, and the relative weight that any one party places on notions of equity and need, as against markets and individualism. A reformist government with leanings towards the markets has a strong desire to provide evidence to voters of political initiatives moving the country towards these ends. The need for such symbols indeed might be considered the reason for the observation by Vickers and Yarrow (1988a, p. 429) that "the razzmatazz associated with stock market flotations is the most visible immediate aspect of privatization."

In the case of attempted privatizations in non-Western countries such as the former Soviet Union, it is even clearer that political change is at the heart of the program. Hence, Nelson and Kuzes (1994) state that "in nearly every important detail, the Yeltsin government's privatization program is intended to promote the realization of political more than economic goals. . . . This is not an economic program; it is a political program. It is 5 percent economics and 95 percent politics."

The centrality of politics to privatization is hardly surprising. Parsons (1995) reminds us that the very definition of "public," and hence within the political realm, is itself a contestable issue. Distinctions between what is considered public or private have undergone considerable changes over centuries and will continue to be open to debate and renewal.

Consider the following scenario: A union strike has occurred inside a monopoly (private) gas supplier and is apparently preventing the construction of new capital facilities to supply next winter's peak gas needs. This single issue (where workers have prevented a corporation from constructing a planned capital facility) can have multiple interpretations as to the underlying problem. At one extreme, this issue may be interpreted as a "public" problem using phrases such as "the public should not be held to ransom by union power." Such an interpretation is totally defensible. As a public issue, it demands government intervention and policies for solutions. At the other extreme, another interpretation, and just as defensible, is that there is actually no problem at all. "This is simply a private matter between a private company and its staff," we might say. As such, it would demand no government intervention. Either of these two extreme interpretations or any one of many possibilities in between is valid. The judicious use of language brings to the fore our own definition of the problem, as either in the public or private domain. Perhaps in the end analysis, we may see this issue as having an element of the public interest at its heart. However we framed the issue, an array of policy responses would be possible. The solution may be seen as greater competition, greater regulatory strength or even government using its coercive powers to uphold particular courses of action deemed expedient to solve the problem as perceived.

The point is that many such issues are inherently political, throughout the processes of framing issues, of defining problems and of developing policy responses. Problems involve perceptions, and our perceptions of reality are shaped by our values, beliefs, ideologies, and interests, as well as our own bias (Parsons 1995, p. 88). Furthermore, on the grander scale, the extent to which government needs to intervene in such issues is of course simply part of the ongoing debate of the role of government. This question itself is centuries old. As Hughes (1994, p. 97) puts it, "'What should governments do?' forms perhaps part of the oldest continuous debate in political philosophy."

Privatization as a Shift in Power

Assessments made of the relative success of privatization in altering the balance of political power are interesting. The review by Marsh (1991, p. 472) in the United Kingdom noted that "there is little doubt that one of the chief initial concerns of the Conservative government was to curb union power. . . . The Thatcher government also believed that the Heath government had been brought down by the trade unions, or more specifically the NUM [National Union of Miners]."

The unions, according to Marsh, were affected by both aspects of privatization—contracting out and enterprise sales. On contracting, there has undoubtedly been a loss of jobs, and pressure on working conditions and pay levels as discussed in the previous chapter. On the sale of enterprises, Marsh argues that "there seems little doubt that the situation for unions has worsened in many of these companies" (p. 473). This conclusion is tempered a little, however, observing that there is no clear pattern in these declines as they relate to privatization. But overall, the message is clear: Privatization has resulted in a general loss of union power.

The use of reform techniques by the state to shift power between groups is of course not unique to privatization. The same can be said of all aspects of political life, including changes to all of the three major areas relevant in considering government utility reform—those of ownership (whether public or private), regulation (whether light or strong), and competition (whether monopoly or market-based). Thus, policies promoting greater competition, for example, policies promoting private ownership, or policies promoting lighter regulation can all be said to shift power away from or towards those areas considered targets by the current governing party.

Political Success

Politically, most authors agree that privatization has generally been a success in Western liberal democracies. In reviewing the work of others, Marsh, for example, notes that Conservatives in the United Kingdom gained 10 percent more of the vote among new shareholders compared to those who had never owned shares, while Labor lost 9 percent of the vote. Others concur, with Rees (1994) noting that privatization was not electorally unpopular, in part because of the public perception of the poor performance of the public enterprises throughout the 1970s. Further, we might reflect on the concept of the share-owning population. This is smart politics, since along with the greater chance of share-owners voting Conservative, there is also a strong likelihood of a windfall gain on the share market. As well, there is likely to be greater political unpopularity with any possible future policy to ever renationalize these utilities. Electorally, most people see British privatization as a resounding success through the majority of the Thatcher years. The continuity of the multiple term Conservative government in the United Kingdom from 1979 up until the mid-1990s also attests to this.

As was previously noted, there is no doubt a massive wealth transfer occurred in the United Kingdom. Underpricing of initial floats was the largest component of this transfer of wealth, according to Vickers and Yarrow (1988a, p. 181). In their view, the techniques used by the U.K. government in privatizing were seriously flawed. The setting of prices, the desire to sell large portions rather than to stage smaller tranches for sale, and the expenses associated with each of the sales were all mentioned in this regard. Huge transaction costs both within and away from the U.K. economy were incurred. How then might we assess the stated political objectives of maximum sale proceeds and widened share ownership? Based on these concerns, we might heed the judgment of Vickers and Yarrow (1988a, p. 192) that the first aim has not been achieved successfully, and on the second, it has only been done in a highly expensive and distorted way. Furthermore, not all commentators regard the U.K. privatization program as politically successful, at least more recently. By the beginning of 1995, even the bastion of economic news—the *Economist*—was carrying admissions such as "most Britons see privatization as a rip-off," and that "to say that privatization is unpopular is an understatement." Despite the *Economist*'s own judgment that "privatization has worked superbly," it also had to admit that "politically, it is beginning to look like a disaster."[47]

In New Zealand, the program had also slowed by 1994 because the government feared a social and electoral backlash. In the words of Hall (1994), "there is little doubt that one reason for Labor's landslide defeat four years ago was the state assets sale program." Foreign ownership of privatized SOEs had finally surfaced to become a serious political concern for the public. More importantly, though, an antiprivatization backlash is thought to have contributed to the support and drive for a completely new "mixed member Parliament" system put to a referendum in 1993. In spite of opposition from both major parties, the New Zealand political system has now itself been transformed. Parties now need to form European-style ruling coalitions in order to govern, mitigating against the type of radical policies adopted through the 1980s and 1990s. Most recently, the government of New

Zealand has essentially been stalled over the proposed sale of its Wellington Airport. In total, we would have to conclude that New Zealand has seen a surprisingly strong citizen reaction to the privatization policy reform tool. This has represented a belated but significant rebuff for both sides of politics that had been strong supporters for two decades (De Vries, O'Reilly, and Scoular 1998).

Privatization programs have highlighted the clash of values. Governments have been criticized for being responsible for a situation where executive salaries have risen markedly (by around 110 percent compared to corresponding public sector salaries) at the same time as privatized companies have been announcing staff layoffs. Again, legal, financial, and banking advisers receiving substantial fees have also been increasingly viewed by the public as at odds with the call for greater economic efficiency espoused by governments. Such actions are being viewed as inherently inequitable.

Having made these political observations, however, one point is perfectly clear: In one sense, even if the promised economic and social benefits of privatization fail to materialize, or are met only to a marginal degree, this is irrelevant. Provided there are no overwhelming or catastrophic economic or social dis-benefits of changing ownership, the sale of public enterprises and assets is likely to be far easier than cutting public expenditure, or announcing tax rises, at least in the short term.[48] The sale of enterprises does demonstrate policy delivery as well, particularly when tied to debt reductions, and governments can be seen as leaders of action. Such obvious political advantages are likely to continue to be recognized across a wide political and cultural spectrum.

Interestingly, little appears to have been written in the rigorous sense about other key goals such as reducing public sector debt, though it would be surprising if these types of fiscal objectives had not been largely achieved. One of the exceptions here includes the analysis of the Reserve Bank of Australia, where it is reported that proceeds from Australian enterprise sales have been used largely to reduce debt.[49] Observations of New Zealand are also relevant, where between 1987 and 1993 all but a small part of the NZ$11.6 billion raised through privatizations was used to retire debt.[50]

And what of the suggestion that privatization enables governments to reward political loyalists? Such colorful accusations have received much attention, and this remains an area of considerable concern, at least potentially. Some examples of payoffs have indeed occurred, as documented by authors such as Hutchinson (1994) and Whitfield (1992). In Hutchinson's case, he notes that in 1987 Alberta Premier Don Getty "handed a number of coveted private wine boutique licenses to well placed Tories" and that, not surprisingly, this move continues to haunt subsequent administrations. The extent to which such cases represent systemic risks, however, or just "one-off" instances is uncertain. Many of the references in this area are suggestive rather than definitive, and actual cases of demonstrated corruption are rare. Chittenden (1996), for instance, outlines how the Tory government's recent rail privatization plans in the United Kingdom were suspended just hours before new franchising arrangements were to take effect in the U.K., and is a case in point. The allegations of fraud halted the plan, and provided good copy for the *Times*, but neither the veracity of the allegations nor the extent to which such practices exist (if proven) were clear. What is certain, however, is that even if only a few cases of paybacks occur, doubts over corruption and allegations of cronyism will linger when reformist governments create an atmosphere of less openness in the availability of information. Silence, in this instance, seems to amount to guilt in the public's eyes, whether the case is proven or not.

LEGAL PERFORMANCE

Most legal issues again do not lend themselves to quantitative judgments, but a brief discussion of some of the legal threads arising in the sale of an enterprise is appropriate here. Looking more at the ongoing operations of the enterprise rather than the sale transaction itself, the most critical legal questions relate to issues of regulation and arrangements that encourage competition. Ernst (1993a) as well as several other authors all argue that regulation following privatization of most U.K. enterprises was too light. He goes as far as to say that:

> in my view, the major lesson to be learnt from the British experience is this: that a strong legislative framework of regulation, in tandem with the existence of independent, vigorous and consumer-oriented regulatory bodies, is an essential precondition for the protection of ordinary consumers. Even the British Government belatedly recognized this, and in 1992 additional legislation was introduced to strengthen the powers of the water, gas, electricity (and telecommunications) regulatory bodies.

Veljanovski (1987), in assessing the United Kingdom experience, also reminds us of the criticisms that occurred about monopoly abuses in the case of British Gas and about price and service quality in the case of British Telecom. He then comments that, although privatization is supposed to free up utilities from government, such companies are still restricted. It could even be argued that such companies were under stronger regulation than was previously the case. As Marsh (1991) points out:

> The lack of competition facing the privatized companies has ensured that the question of regulation is very important. Indeed, it is one of the paradoxes of privatization that it has involved greater regulation. . . . The government is at the center of this regulation despite the Conservative's stated desire to reduce intervention.

Saunders and Harris (1994) even went so far as to argue that ownership changes in privatization forced stronger regulation, and that from this consumers then benefited. The central role of regulation in producing benefits as part of privatization is apparent. Thus, legal issues are not simply an aside, but are critical to the debate. Some respected commentators even turn the privatization argument on its head, arguing that in some circumstances "regulation is so acute that public ownership is preferred" (Vickers and Yarrow 1988a).

On the question of encouraging competition, it should be said that more recent privatizations have essentially learned from the failings of earlier high-profile reform programs. Indeed, having placed a far greater emphasis on competition and formal regulation, privatization reformers in Victoria, Australia, have effectively passed their own judgment on the importance of shortcomings in privatization programs from the United Kingdom and New Zealand.[51] To encourage competition, the privatization process of the electricity sector in Victoria thus first saw a single vertically integrated government monopoly transformed into a total of some twelve corporate entities. Five of these distribution companies, five generators, and a transmission company were then all privatized.[52] Likewise, the desire for stronger regulation saw an independent Victorian Office of the Regulator General established.[53]

Internationally, as well, we might make the observation that privatization as a reform technique must be placed firmly within the context of legal structures for property ownership, market structures for business, and within the broader context of attitudes towards government policies. In the former Soviet Union it is apparent that attempts to privatize have been thwarted. Not only has this been due to massive changes necessary in community attitudes, but also by the almost complete absence of the legal structure to underpin new property rights arrangements.[54]

In reviewing legal issues there is lastly the need to discuss the actual legal conditions relevant to the operation of a privatized firm, rather than simply covering issues in concept. The analysis of Thomas (1991) is an exemplary case in point here. His legal analysis suggests that far from an accountability vacuum existing in the area of a prisoner's recourse to legal appeal in U.S. private prisons, these inmates have in fact greater legal recourse to appeals than do current inmates of public sector prisons. Despite the implied conflict with the earlier arguments of Gilmour and Jensen (1998), the message is still clear. There is a continued need for strong and independent analysis of the legal fabric of privatization in each jurisdiction to inform and guide debate.

CONCLUSIONS

What can now be said about the sale of public enterprises? The combination of narrative and meta-analytic reviews increases our knowledge of the empirical performance of privatizations. Firstly, it is reasonable to conclude that reported labor productivity improvements have been significant following privatizations. This is consistent with reductions in overmanning having occurred. Second, the presence of controls in productivity evaluation studies resulted in effect sizes that were very much smaller than studies that did not use these. This implies that the productivity gains themselves are likely to be due mainly to the changing external environment, with only a small (but nonetheless statistically reliable) part of this gain being associated with the enterprise sale itself. Next, the labor productivity gains found for privatizations were significantly greater than those meager gains measured from nationalizations in the United Kingdom.

In terms of the firm's financial performance, I observed that significant improvements in financial performance were reported with privatizations. Effect sizes for returns on sales and returns on equity were both significantly positive. Again, those evaluation studies that used controls in the analysis produced smaller effect sizes, though only slightly. Improvements in financial performance over different countries varied significantly, with effect sizes for Chile over three times those produced for the United Kingdom. Looking also at some limited effect size data for privatization as a reform compared to nationalization as a reform revealed that financial performance improvements were not different, from a statistical perspective. Likewise, the financial improvements that accompanied privatization tested as not significantly different from those measured in control groups that were not privatized. The conclusion is that although reported firm financial performance does improve significantly, gains do not appear to be different from those made in control groups of companies and that, consequently, there is some doubt as to whether privatization per se caused them.

Next, the firm's investment behavior was analyzed. I concluded here that on average, a positive association was present after privatizations. In other words, reported capital investment increased following privatization. Returns to shareholders were also on average significantly positive, with returns to the United Kingdom shareholders being much greater than those in Chile. On the broader question of national economic performance, the data did not support a simple direct link between the size of the private sector and economic growth.

On the social performance dimension, most narrative assessments of service prices concluded that the promise of price reductions had not been delivered. Likewise, the promise of greater competition in countries such as the United Kingdom had not been met. This was due to a preoccupation with ensuring a rapid and hence politically successful transfer of ownership. The high profile of benefits promised to citizens was found to be quite different from the profile and sparse measurements that appear to have occurred to date. The narrative review revealed service quality findings on both sides, with some services better and some worse. One study, providing only six sets of measurements, was available for meta-analytic review. On average, a positive service quality improvement was found for this analysis of British Telecom. The impacts of regulatory intensity and public accountability requirements for this case were also revealing. Based on the meta-analytic measurements, the size of the performance improvement effects from stronger regulatory and public accountability requirements were several times that associated with the change in ownership.

I concluded that the social contours of inequality appear unfortunately to have been deepened by privatizations. Low-income consumers have generally been affected more than others based on this review. In terms of employment, significant reductions were likely, whilst executive remuneration rose markedly. More broadly, major winners and losers have typically been evident with privatization. The spread of individual incomes appears to have widened. On a national scale, cases were reviewed where a country as a whole was expected to lose, but with international investors gaining handsomely, an overall world welfare gain was calculated.

Privatization as a strategy was also recognized as inherently political. Indeed, the sale of government enterprises has highlighted a clash of values. Nonetheless, I noted that even if the presumed economic and social benefits of privatization evaporate, or are only marginal, the sale of public enterprises and assets is likely to be far easier for governments than cutting public expenditure, or announcing tax rises in the short term. In other words, privatization will continue, barring catastrophic results, because it is politically attractive. A common risk with all privatization programs is the allegation of corruption. Irrespective of whether such allegations are proven, doubts over corruption and cronyism are likely to linger when reformist governments create an atmosphere of less openness in the availability of information. Citizens are likely to interpret silence as guilt.

Lastly, legal issues were seen not simply as an aside, but as central to the privatization debate. Almost all commentators insist that regulatory or competitive arrangements following the U.K. privatizations were too light. Paradoxically, far from freeing up firms from the influence of governments, privatizations in the U.K. as well as elsewhere have involved greater regulation for firms.

10

Learning to Get the Balance in Privatization

Pressures for greater privatization within public sector activities have occurred as part of a much broader context. This context has been international in scope, and has been part of a wider move of government organizations away from the traditional practices of administration, towards a style of managing for results. Processes of contracting and competitive testing are now becoming well developed in many areas—at least by the look of the guidelines appearing.[1] Likewise, the processes of selling enterprises have also been further developed.

My focus in this closing chapter is on the learnings from the international evidence on privatization and on the policy implications of these. Human services, information technology outsourcing, refuse collection, history, and politics each have something to teach us if we seek to get the best value balance from privatizing public sector services. In striving to deliver better services, whether through the sale of enterprises or through contracting out, a learning approach is desirable. The task is to observe, to analyze, and to question as we move forward, using the frameworks I have introduced through this book.

I will firstly look at the question of a learning philosophy, and contrast this against other philosophies operating inside reforming public agencies. Some comments on theories introduced earlier in this book will then be made. These theories underpin the thrust towards privatization, and it would be a sensible part of our learning to discuss the extent to which the predictions of these theories appear to have been met, in retrospect. Next, I will look at the broad meta-analytic findings from my work on contracting out services and the policy implications of these to public sector services as a whole. As a part of this, I will explore the practices of private companies as well. Finally, I will look at the meta-analytic findings of enterprise sales. Based on these, I will investigate some of the policy implications and suggest tentative directions for future privatization reforms.

THE LEARNING PHILOSOPHY

The first thing that might be said about many government reforms—whether they be privatization or the strengthening of competition—is that within the dimension of economics, the aims of reforms are nearly always laudable. In theory, for instance, privatization should encourage more efficient market behavior, and competition should drive down prices through greater innovation and intelligent production. It is not so much the aims of reforms on which we ought to base our discussions, however, but the reality of achievements in reform as well as the reality of the extent to which existing circumstances are changed for the better or worse. In a sense, privatization, competition or other public sector reforms can become like motherhood. No one would argue against them in principle. Nonetheless, political leaders continue to argue that such reforms are urgently needed, and that they must proceed without being slowed by messy debate. The more ardently the suggestion is made that we "take this reform pill because it's good for you," the more we might want to look at the extent to which the community as the patient benefits from the medicine.

Of course, in asking questions in today's managerial climate, individuals run the risk of being labeled as someone who is "against us": There appears to have been an increasing tendency to be either with privatization reformers or against them these days—a kind of "us and them" syndrome. It is as if government reform was just a military operation requiring complete compliance from all cogs within the machine rather than reform implementation being the output of an evolutionary and adaptive process as suggested two decades ago (Majone and Wildavsky 1978, Browne and Wildavsky 1984), or a learning process as authors such as Senge (1992) suggest more recently.

Using an evolutionary learning approach to policy implementation, we assume that broad directions are set and that these directions are implemented in highest priority areas initially. The effectiveness of this implementation is then evaluated and through careful study and reflection we learn which changes are optimal. This then allows us to review the set directions and, where necessary, adjust the steering wheel to better achieve desired community outcomes. Such an approach could be contrasted against the military or bureaucratic style, in which blind obedience and compliance to orders is required from all cogs. It can also be contrasted against the religious approach in which the reform minister delivers his manifesto to the hundreds of gathered managers, allowing no time for questions and discussion, and continues to preach even when the congregation has walked out to look into the church next door![2]

But learning requires a commitment to open evaluation and careful assessment. Which evaluations of, say, competition policy ought we believe? Do we take the political evaluation in which selective results are advertised and through which we are told yet again that contracting and competition reforms are good for us—just trust me . . . benefits will trickle through! On the other hand, should we believe the concerns from rural citizens who saw a wave of increased bank fees and reduced postal services following the deregulation of banking and post-office services in Australia and heed the assessment made by the *Good News Week* television comedy program? To quote them: "In proposing to deregulate the oil industry, Australia's Treasurer Peter Costello claims that petrol prices will fall . . . you know the same way that banks lowered their fees!" Do we take one side or the other here, or do we, on reflection, assume that the truth lies somewhere in the middle? This book favors the latter.

There is no doubt that all nations need to be more cognizant of finite resources and competitiveness in the face of globalization. The question, however, is not whether this need exists, but the real extent of the problem, its priority against other competing public policy issues, and how best we might simultaneously improve our use of resources and our competitiveness whilst being equitable. It is an inherently political question and is thus one of balance. Focusing simply on getting the best value for our limited resources, it would seem to make healthy sense if we were to base our proposed strategies on our learnings to date from empirical implementation. So, in the area of competitive tendering and contracting, what does the theory say? What does the evidence say? Likewise, for the sale of enterprises, what are the lessons?

THEORY

In Chapter 3, I commented that there was a large amount of theoretical and conceptual information providing a framework for the privatization of government services. These conceptual bases have included theories of public choice, transaction cost economics, and managerialism, to name three. These three areas have in common a philosophy that people are inherently selfish, and that economic interests provide the primary motivation and lubricant of human behavior. For contracting out government services, they also suggested that firms ought to minimize the costs of transacting their business by being careful about whether services are provided using in-house staff or through external parties. These academic theories have been exceedingly influential in providing supporting frameworks to underpin political reforms, but understandably, have also been the subject of much ideological and academic debate.

Those supporting moves towards a greater use of the private sector argue that, in line with the predictions of public choice theoretical ideas, government organizations are often captured by those who traditionally supply the services of the organization, and that in the absence of the profit motive, bureaucrats in government maximize the size of their own bureau rather than maximizing benefits to customers or citizens. In other words, bureaucrats look after their own interest, not the public interest. Proponents point out that organizations need to more carefully analyze decisions on whether to provide services using in-house resources or else buy services from external sources through a contract. In an age where corporate planning objectives, targets, and activity-based costing are becoming the norm, they argue that the role of government nowadays should be viewed as establishing high-level objectives and developing policies, rather than actually delivering the services per se. As Osborne and Gaebler (1993) put it, government ought to "steer not row." Those not supporting greater use of the private sector in the provision of public services point out that public choice ideas are used selectively. Thus, for example, the potential for self-interest to lead to service cost reductions is emphasized, rather than the potential for self-interest to lead to higher management salaries, or to underpin a greater willingness by managers to be more obedient to a specific political direction for the sake of bonus payments. Again, the pressure of self-interest leading to greater innovation and entrepreneurship is emphasized rather than self-interest leading to increased fraud and corruption, the reality that cozy relationships between businesses and ministers from political parties do occur, and the propensity for more information to be deemed commercial-in-confidence to ensure secrecy. Furthermore, they also argue that this theory is interesting, but it is just that: only a theory. Policy choices for public organizations ought to be based not on a set of theories, but on the basis of our past experience of what has worked well and what has not. Ideologically charged perfect theory always wins in a comparison with an imperfect current reality.

Notions of managerialism also underpin current reforms. The phrase "managing for results" encapsulates this philosophy in which objectives are established, strategies developed, programs are organized and resourced, and then performance is measured in terms of the efficiency and effectiveness of achieving objectives. Its central tenets extend these principles, emphasizing management skills, quantified performance targets, and devolution. Further, it encompasses the separation of policy from implementation, commercial from noncommercial functions, and the use of private sector practices such as corporate plans, short term contracts, monetary incentives, and cost-cutting. Benefits of this approach have included stronger partnerships with the private sector, greater cost consciousness in the knowledge of actual costs of delivering activities and products, and economic savings. This set of ideas has also, however, been criticized as an ideology that assumes that better management will prove an effective solvent for a wide range of economic and social ills (Pollitt 1993). Improvements to the productivity of public services have encouraged the view that management improvements can solve problems and make decisions previously conceived of as political in nature. The unquestioning application of techniques may well amount to simplistic ideology, but whether we agree with this or not, a narrowed emphasis on quantified targets and measures has often occurred at the expense of more fundamental areas such as relationships and community.

THE EFFECTIVENESS OF CONTRACTING OUT SERVICES

How should we interpret the research conclusions on the effectiveness of contracting out government services? How did the benefits compare to the theoretical predictions? What are the policy implications here?

Focusing not on newspaper reports, anecdotes, or government ideology, my study looked at the available international empirical measurements that have been made of service quality and costs under contracting. In essence, my research revealed several learnings. These were generally far more measured than much of the current policy discourse on the subject of contracting and outsourcing. I observed firstly that a significant average saving of around 6 percent (12 percent)[3] is probably experienced in contracting public sector services overall. This modest average cost saving was in contrast to the 20 to 30 percent often quoted by proponents of contracting, by some management consultants, or as seen in press and advertising statements. That said, the bulk of the documented evidence on contracting related to strong savings in the areas of garbage collection, cleaning, and maintenance services (i.e., between 19 and 30 percent). These findings supported the idea that large cost savings can be made for these specific areas.

For many other services however, particularly those more difficult to define and measure, little or no savings were found from the empirical evidence (which varied between an 8 percent saving and a 24 percent increase). Although this finding could have been influenced by the availability of only a few research measurements, even when combined as a group, little significant cost savings were evident. Statistically, cost savings available from different services were found to be quite different (i.e., heterogeneous). These findings were enlightening, and contrasted the claims of privatization proponents who espouse contracting out all government services as a cure-all solution to public sector ills.

In terms of service quality, the little empirical evidence available indicated that, on average, service quality was unaffected by contracting. Sometimes it was better, sometimes not. This implied that the claims of both sides were extreme. Service quality was not as a rule generally improved, as claimed by one side, or reduced, as claimed by the other.

Of more importance was the finding that contracting either in-house or outside the organization both led to cost savings. Thus, service specification and competition appeared to be the drivers of efficiency, not the sector doing the work. This finding is an important one in view of the privatization theme of this book. The question of gains achievable by enabling private provision in preference to public provision seemed to be resolved through the learning that gains were possible by contracting with either sector. Such an assessment of private sector versus public sector efficiency has major implications for policy reforms to the extent that competition and contracting policy is seen as an agenda to transfer service provision to the private or market sector rather than simply to improve value for money.

A significant flow-on also seemed to operate in that agencies not contracting services, but in areas adjacent to those doing so, showed cost reductions of around four-fifths that for areas contracting out. The presence of beneficial flow-on effects from areas subject to contracting to those adjacent to these reforms was interesting. Evidently, although these areas were not themselves actually contracting out services, the threat of competition and the acquisition of new financial performance knowledge itself also led to real performance improvements. Again, such a finding has implications for the use of contracting as a public sector re-form. It is not necessary to contract all services comprehensively in order to achieve extensive cost savings. A little bit of contracting reform appears to go a long way.

The review of contracting research findings also indicated that some unfortu-nate social impacts occurred with contracting reforms. Women and minority groups appeared to bear the brunt of contracting efficiencies consistently from the international studies. To the extent that governments continue to see them-selves as having a role in matters of equity as well as economic reform, this trade-off will need to be recognized explicitly in policymaking. Likewise, the potential for businesses to exert undue influence over political decisions, as well as the lack of transparency due to arrangements now being deemed "commercial-in-confidence," were also both seen to be real risks in the review.[4] Again, reform policies espousing cost savings through contracting need to be aligned with ac-tions to protect and strengthen checks and balances on government. The review concluded that contracting-out decisions for governments were clearly more than simply commercial in nature. The inclusion of social impacts, the recogni-tion of business influence in political decisionmaking, and issues such as conflicts of interest and commercial-in-confidence need to be given more attention than has been evident to date.

Several of these areas deserve some further exploration under our learning phi-losophy, particularly where there may be implications for future contracting reforms.

Cost Savings

The first point is that large differences still appear to arise as new evidence on contracting cost savings comes to light. We might recall that the early economic studies of Domberger, Meadowcroft, and Thompson (1986, 1987) were instru-mental in the field and suggested that contracting either in-house or externally was likely to result in cost savings of around 20 percent for garbage collection and cleaning services. This work was the source of the now popular "20 percent rule." Interestingly, more recent surveys of public sector managers have also consis-tently reported sizeable savings of around 20 percent or more from the use of competitive contracting over a range of service types. Examples here include:

- average reported cost savings from Domberger's CTC Consulting Group of 20 percent, 20 percent, and 26 percent for surveys of man-agers in the Australian states of New South Wales, Western Australia, and Victoria,[5] and
- reported average savings of between 26 percent and "one-third" for defense-related services in Canada, United Kingdom, and Australia (Howard 1998, Badelow 1998).[6]

Against these reports are the more modest average cost savings of around 6 percent found in the research in this book, as well as in other recent international surveys. These have included two further major survey reports from high-profile management consulting companies—the PA Consulting Group (1997) and Deloitte and Touche Consulting Group (1997)—both of which have similarly reported more modest cost-savings estimates for outsourcing. These international surveys suggest that average cost savings were likely to be very modest, at around 2 to 10 percent, to the extent that they exist at all. PA Consulting, for instance, reported an average cost reduction for outsourcing contracts outside the area of information technology (IT) at 10 percent for private firms. For IT, the PA Consulting report put the average cost reduction reported in Australia at just 2 percent, whilst Deloitte and Touche, looking at both private and public organizations, were even more circumspect. They noted that for their recent survey as well as earlier surveys, "then, as now, significant savings are rarely realized" for IT outsourcing. Recent support for more modest cost-savings estimates has also come from further international research into information technology outsourcing. Willcocks (1998) looked at 116 companies in the U.S. and Britain that pursued large-scale, single-vendor outsourcing contracts. His study reported that some 53 percent of these companies were not making savings from outsourcing, and that a total of some 64 percent of companies either regarded outsourcing as a failure (37 percent) or had mixed results (27 percent). Most organizations were reported to have underestimated the cost of outsourcing and the number of people and capabilities needed to oversee the project.

The contrast between these two sets of findings is striking. Reasons for this difference are largely unknown, though we might surmise several. The veracity of cost-savings reports from managers may well be questionable on the grounds that those answering the questionnaires have a dubious personal incentive for accuracy in reporting. Are managers always more optimistic than accurate when a manager's salary depends on implementing reforms to the system? To what extent might it have been possible for managers to simply report the more successful contracts rather than all contracts undertaken? This would presumably apply to both public sector and private sector surveys, although the gap between optimism and accuracy may be greater in the public sector, where reform may be seen as a political rather than a solely commercial issue. The other reason for doubting the veracity of cost-savings reports from public sector managers is that more formal evidence of savings such as reduced departmental budget levels has not been consistently observed. The cost-savings claims seem to have little or no correlation with real budget reductions. It may be that such differences are due to the use of different survey or research methods or else the study of quite different services. It may also be a reflection of the degree to which such estimates continue to vary wildly or continue to be based on differing assumptions.[7] Differences may also have arisen due to the differing savings that might be expected from outsourcing activities from the public and private sectors, particularly if one assumes, for instance, that private sector activities are always inherently more efficient, and hence smaller cost savings could be expected when private firms outsource.

An alternative interpretation of this discrepancy between more modest cost-savings results and others is that higher levels of savings are indeed accurate, and show that contracting is simply a strong lever for changed workloads, service levels, and production arrangements. It is useful to recall that the strongest correlation in the research was the simple relationship always found in studies between the amount of work done and the cost of that work. In other words, all other things being equal, a company will, on average, get what it pays for. Thus, when we hear of, say, a 40 percent cost saving through contracting out services, the strongest probability in my mind is that we are not doing in future what we did in the past. In all likelihood, we have carefully reviewed what work is really required, along with the levels of service, and it has been restructured. Desirable reform to our services and practices is at issue here, not necessarily the use of contracting out the service per se. Having said this, of course, it must also be added that contracting is indeed a powerful lever for such change to service levels, quality levels, and staffing levels and structures. There is no doubt that most workplaces have the potential for reviewing work outputs, as well as improving practices and procedures. This may be particularly so in cases such as defense services, which may have tended to be more insulated from budget-cutting pressures that have driven efficiencies in other areas of the public sector over the past decade or so.

There is a further alternative interpretation. Perhaps the two statements "contracting is accompanied by large cost savings" and "contracting alone results only in modest cost savings" are both partly true. In other words, contracting many services may well result in cost-savings gains on average, partly through the contracting process and partly through the thorough review of outputs and levels of service, as well as the restructuring activities that almost inevitably accompany contracts. The truth of contracting may well be in the middle, rather than at either extreme.

DO CONTRACTING BENEFITS OUTWEIGH COSTS IN PUBLIC SECTOR SERVICES?

A central observation made in this research based on the international empirical evidence suggested that cost savings for contracting out different public sector services were likely to be varied rather than simply being identical. Our findings were that nontraditional services experienced lower real cost savings on outsourcing. Cautionary advice relating to problems with applying competitive contracting in areas such as human services has also arisen in Victoria through the social sector (People Together Project 1998, Rance 1999). With this knowledge, we might proceed with the guiding philosophy of caution. But why, on a theoretical basis, might we expect differing effectiveness for contracting reforms for different services?

Importantly, what is left undiscussed by many outsourcing proponents is the difficult to measure cost of transactions, the ongoing costs associated with managing contracts (or governance costs), and the overall costs to the organization of organizing market competition and undertaking the transition to the new arrangements. This is an increasingly important area of the debate—particularly for complex services that can be difficult to define and tricky to measure. In general, none of these costs are well researched, let alone openly debated.[8]

Some of the theoretical ideas of Williamson (1975) as well as others are useful here, however. His transaction cost analysis theory adopted five main building blocks as a basis for explaining the development of large vertically integrated firms in capitalist economies. Paradoxically, this theory, which explains why private companies produce the majority of their services in-house, is one of the most useful foundations for exploring the effectiveness of outsourcing public sector services. Williamson's argument is that firms aim to minimize the costs of transacting their business. He suggests that this aim can often be achieved by vertical integration, that is, by taking over either the firms to whom they sell or else their suppliers. He sees large hierarchical firms in capitalist economies as being the result of these firms aiming to minimize transaction costs. Governance structures is a branch of transaction cost theory, and this theoretical area deals with alternative forms of organization structure, the contracting processes employed to undertake services, and the resulting transaction costs (Spicer et al. 1991). This area of theory dates back to the work of Ronald Coase over half a century ago (Coase 1937). The conceptual building blocks to the theory of transaction cost economics include uncertainty, frequency, asset specificity, measurability of attributes, bounded rationality, and opportunism (Ashton 1998). These may have potential relevance in the application of outsourcing to many public sector services. Uncertainty refers to the inability to foresee or control changes in the contractual environment. Contracts are unavoidably incomplete in the face of uncertainty and the limits to human rationality. The concept of frequency simply says that when few transactions occur between two parties, more general (and cheaper) governance structures will be adopted even though this will be less than ideal. The notion of asset specificity refers to the extent to which resources required to complete the transaction can be productively used elsewhere. Measurability is necessary to reduce the scope for opportunism. The greater the complexity of measurement, the greater the cost of writing, negotiating, and monitoring contracts.

What are the implications of this theory for contracting public sector services? Ashton (1998), for instance, notes that if transactions are infrequent, asset-specific, difficult to measure, or involve uncertainty, then the splitting of purchasers and providers inside an organization is likely to involve larger transaction costs. Ashton's work looked particularly at the area of health services, but parallels are still likely to exist with many other public sector services. After all, characteristics such as uncertainty, asset specificity, measurability of attributes, bounded rationality, and opportunism have been central to some public sector services for centuries. The suggestion is therefore that contracting for some services may not enhance, and may even reduce, the efficiency of public sector services because the additional transaction costs are likely to outweigh any gains in technical efficiency.

Aspects of this theory have of course been contested,[9] whilst acknowledging the contribution to our understanding of alternative governance structures. Of significance here is the work of authors such as De Hoog (1990) and Ring and Van De Ven (1992) who both investigate the notion of contracting using the competitive market-based contracting model. Ring and Van De Ven see transaction cost economics as "suffering from not adequately exploring other available governance structures, repeated transactions, the dynamic evolution of governance and transactions, and the key roles of trust and equity in any inter-organizational relationship." In particular, they argue that the elements of *trust* and *risk* are both central to understanding bargaining transactions. Importantly, they suggest that "the greater the risk in a transaction, the more complex the governance structure, ceteris paribus." This leads them to argue that governance structures based on markets are applicable only for low risk, low reliance on trust transactions. More risky transactions are seen as being best handled through a hierarchy, perhaps involving an organizational structure such as a joint venture, or through a high-trust relationship, termed a "relational contract," as employees typically have with their employer.

De Hoog (1990) looks at the notion of the competitive market as the basis for producing business outputs, and assesses the belief that the competition paradigm is the optimum when employing contracts. She argues that the competition model for contracting is but one of three, as shown in Figure 10.1.

She stresses that "there is no one best way to contract for services." Each model for contracting has its advantages and its weaknesses. Competition, for instance, stresses the complete specification of services, wide solicitation, and objective award decision and monitoring procedures. It can give financial benefits under certain assumptions, and certainly requires the use of powerful service-definition tools. However, its disadvantages in some public sector service areas include the fact that multiple suppliers may not exist, transaction costs can be high, and a complete specification of services may simply not be practical or even possible.

FIGURE 10.1   Models for Contracting Services

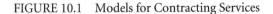

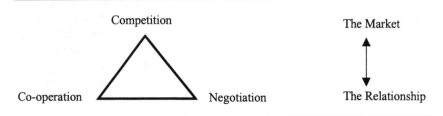

Relational contracting through either the negotiation or cooperation models, on the other hand, involves contracting with one or a few suppliers of your choice, partly specifying services, and then negotiating on the services to be delivered. The contractor chosen may well have had a long-term relationship with the client. The advantages of these types of contracts are that a limited number of suppliers are usually involved, transaction costs are low, and that uncertainty and complexity can be well accommodated. The disadvantages of such contracts are that the contracting process is more susceptible to decisions being made though "cozy" relationships or political allies, processes are typically closed with fewer systemic control mechanisms, and that, overall, familiarity risks breeding complacency. Thus, it is not surprising that the use of partnering or cooperative models may be seen by proponents of outsourcing as desirable, whilst to others such arrangements are criticized as being too cozy. Drawing on De Hoog's work, some truth exists in both claims.

Looking to the future, it could be questioned whether we now have some re-learning to do. To the extent that we continue applying contracting to every-thing that moves, we are bound to rediscover what the private sector found out decades ago. For the majority of business production transactions, relationship contracts (using cooperation with a limited number of external parties, or else using negotiation with in-house staff) are likely to be far more cost effective than full market testing.

PRIVATE SECTOR FIRMS AND MARKETS

Another learning from this research was that savings and reform gains were pos-sible through contracting with either the public or the private sectors, rather than solely through one or the other. What do the ideas of transaction cost eco-nomics and, for that matter, notions of the market and the popular purchaser/provider split model contribute to our understanding of how con-tracting may help to provide better public sector services? These notions do have direct application in contemplating the range of future delivery mechanisms. For instance, the use of both the negotiation and cooperation models in prefer-ence to the competition model may offer an alternative framework enabling the use of in-house teams, or the coproduction of services with another public or not-for-profit agency, under appropriately specified service contracts. Indeed, it may well be that the future direction taken in contracting out government ser-vices—as we rediscover the real cost of transactions—is to repackage contracting in terms of public-private partnerships or strategic alliances in the fashionable consulting jargon. To the extent that this becomes the case, we will of course run the risk of cozy relationships and undue influence from organizational or corpo-rate interests.

On the issue of relying more on private sector energies and market forces, it is often difficult to separate out the rhetoric from the reality—the politics from the practice. We all recognize that a large part of the political process is concerned with the rhetorical and the symbolic. But at least some attempt to try to separate the two is desirable if we are to determine the cost advantages possible through reengineering, restructuring, or reduction of services, as well as through the policy of outsourcing. Indeed, it is a prerequisite if we are to learn how to get the best value for our resources through the notion of the competitive market or, alternatively, the use of cooperation or negotiation. We might reflect on the practices of private sector companies and ask why, in the information technology area, for example, do Australian private companies currently outsource only 29 percent of their activities?[10] Again, why are only 15 percent of business support functions outsourced internationally?[11] Looking at all company expenditures, why would almost four out of five dollars spent stay in-house?[12] Transaction costs most likely have a lot to do with it. Relying on previously formed personal relationships that have worked out in the past is much more efficient than repeatedly going through a process of competitive tenders for the sake of fairness. It may well be that government agencies ought to go through competitive tendering processes to get business out to the private sector market, but to the extent that such processes are likely to increase transaction costs, and reduce resources available for other activities, this needs to be recognized explicitly. If business functions such as information technology, which are now seen as not belonging in government, result in negligible cost gains or cost increases when outsourced, the role of government has simply been remixed rather than reformed or reinvented. Rather than using contracting as a sensible business tool, and recognizing the beneficial flow-ons likely from judicious use of such reforms, it has been used as an element of a command structure driven by an ideology.

PROBITY, ACCOUNTABILITY, AND GOVERNANCE

Another learning from this research recognized the existence of social impacts and the possibility of undue business influence in political decisionmaking. Focusing on the latter of these two issues, it was suggested that a more contractual state led to issues such as conflict of interest and commercial-in-confidence rising in prominence. At the present time, when we are applying the contracting philosophy in a wholesale manner across all public sector services, I have no doubt we will be rediscovering some of the lessons of the past. Many of these lessons are likely to relate to issues of commercial-in-confidence, probity, conflicts of interest, tender processes, and the range of other different expectations that the community holds for the public sector compared to private companies. Even in our recent past, we can easily forget some of the major lessons of applying solely business values inside government. We noted that the phrase commercial-in-confidence was used by the private Westpac bank organization to suppress its $33 million loss from customers, and that the Western Australian state government itself quietly bankrolled the failed Rothwells Bank recovery attempt and Bond Corp's doomed Kwinana project behind the same shield. Let us be clear: It is not one political leaning or other that is at issue here. It is the need to be continually vigilant to balance our personal and political behavior with our desire for better organizational productivity and growth. It is the need to understand why the rigidity of public sector tender and procurement processes may well prevent the public sector from always achieving the benefits that the private sector can gain from outsourcing.[13]

The issue of accountability also seems to be a significant sleeper. It is typically oversimplified into terms of basic financial or customer interests alone, rather than the interests of citizens, of democratic process, or of advocacy roles for industry or local communities. Are some public sector services complex and not necessarily amenable to the simple-linear-sequential business model? I suspect so. Establishing the community's expectations on the potential roles of nongovernment or private companies across a breadth of services from justice through to human services or defense may be sensible here. Applying a cautious "learn as we progress" approach may therefore be the most sensible option in redefining our organizational arrangements, although I suspect we will continue to learn about the real impacts of changes from telephone calls to ministers, from adverse newspaper reports, and through political dynamics.

We certainly now know that it is physically possible to outsource just about anything. Although possible, whether it is sensible or desirable for good governance is another question. We would be well advised to stay in tune with international lessons in contracting and watch for developments. The rise to power of the Blair government in the U.K. saw the phrase "best value" come to the fore, along with the rediscovery of experimentation in deciding the most appropriate modes of public sector service delivery. Unfortunately though, this occurred only after U.K. observers such as Rhodes (1997) had already coined the phrase the "hollowing-out" of government due to the existence of organizations simply consisting of a multitude of contracts managed by a hollowed-out organization too often suffering from a large staff turnover and corporate amnesia. Are terms such as "hollowed-out government" or the American counterpart of "dumbed-down" government too strong?[14] Maybe. But simply asking the question points us in different directions than not asking. As a minimum, caution would seem to be preferable in service areas in which risks are higher and where payoffs are less likely.

The future for governance and accountability is likely to be somewhat predictable in some senses. Simply watch the incentives. If we learn anything from public choice ideas, it is that incentives to individuals are a strong determinant. So, what are the incentives relating to outsourcing? Wilson (1989) suggests, in his book *Bureaucracy: What Government Agencies Do and Why They Do It*, that when the military purchases new systems of any sort it puts in train a procurement bureaucracy designed not for efficiency but to avoid making a bad or unfair decision. This reputedly amounts to more than 1,200 pages of Federal Acquisition Regulation and Defence Regulation Acquisition as well as other DOD directives, Congressional authorization, and unwritten guidance! Incentives are designed to avoid waste, fraud, and abuse. As a consequence, almost everyone in the U.S. Defense "system" has an incentive, according to Wilson, "to overstate the benefits and understate the costs of new systems." We are not purchasing new defense systems here, but the point is still worthy of consideration. New service delivery systems are indeed being purchased by managers whose personal incentives are intimately bound up within the need for the reform itself to be seen as successful. What *are* the behavioral incentives at work here, and for whom are they working?

Looking forward again, the future environment is also likely to continue to involve a balance of both sectors—rather than one dominating the other. The history of many nations reminds us that contracting out services is not new at all for the public sector. One hundred years ago, Australia witnessed the well-developed practice of competitive contracting and tendering, honed over several decades, being interrupted by a Royal Commission which, in 1896, found widespread malpractice in the contracting-out system, including schedule rigging and inferior work. This led to the use of direct (in-house) labor forces. Subsequent decades saw periodic swings towards and away from the average in-house and external labor mix. In terms of history, therefore, perhaps we ought to regard ourselves as simply being further along a path of "well-rehearsed argument" on the effectiveness, efficiency, and probity of these two types of service production systems (McIntosh, Shauness, and Wettenhall 1997).

THE EFFECTIVENESS OF SELLING ENTERPRISES

Looking now at the sale of enterprises, how should we interpret the research conclusions here? Were the benefits promised in theory realized, and what are consequential policy implications?

Again, this research essentially revealed several learnings. These generally followed the flavor of previous narrative reviews, but with some additional nuances as well. We found firstly that reported labor productivity improvements had been significant following privatizations—consistent with reductions in overmanning. Importantly, though, these productivity gains were interpreted as having been due mainly to the changing external environment, with only a small part of this gain being associated with the enterprise sale itself. Having said this, we observed that the labor-productivity gains reported for privatizations were significantly greater than those meager gains measured from nationalizations in the United Kingdom. Thus, although we might conclude that productivity gains from enterprise sales have not been as large as we had hoped, reported gains have certainly outstripped those for nationalizations. These changes are broadly in line with our expectations that privately owned firms should generally have higher labor productivity.

We also observed that significant improvements in enterprise financial performance were reported with privatizations. In particular, we saw better returns on sales and returns on equity being reported. Improvements in financial performance reported for different countries varied markedly, with effect sizes for Chile over three times those produced for the United Kingdom. Looking also at some limited effect-size data for privatization as a reform compared to nationalization as a reform, we found that financial performance improvements were not different from a statistical perspective. This was a surprise. Likewise, the reported financial improvements that accompanied privatization tested as not significantly different from those measured in control groups that were not privatized. I concluded here that, although reported firm financial performance did improve significantly, there is real doubt as to whether privatization per se caused them. These findings were unexpected, and did not conform to my prior expectations.

Next, the firm's investment behavior was analyzed. We concluded here that, on average, a positive association was present after privatizations. In other words, reported capital investment increased following privatization. Returns to shareholders were also on average significantly positive, with returns to the United Kingdom shareholders being much greater than those in Chile. Evidently, firms invested more after privatization, and people who invested in the initial float did well.

The last of our economic interests concerned the broader question of national economic performance. Here, the data did not support a simple direct link between the size of the private sector and economic growth. In all likelihood, the connection, assuming there is one, is probably more sophisticated and subtle.

On the social-performance dimension, most narrative assessments of service prices concluded that promises of price reductions and greater competition had not generally been delivered. This was due to a preoccupation with ensuring a rapid and politically successful transfer of ownership. The high profile of benefits promised to citizens in this area contrasted the low profile and few measurements made to date. The narrative review revealed service-quality findings on both sides, with some services better and some worse. For the one available study, British Telecom, a positive service-quality improvement was found on average. Of great interest was the analysis of the impacts of regulatory intensity and public accountability requirements for this case. Here, the meta-analysis suggested that the performance-improvement effects from enhanced regulatory and public accountability requirements were several times that associated with the change in ownership. In other words, these measurements suggested that the best payoffs for improved performance from the customer's perspective were most likely to come from strengthening regulatory conditions and enhancing accountability requirements for firms rather than from the transfer of ownership. Although these findings must be regarded as preliminary, they are also fundamentally important, and deserve more research attention in the future.

Referring to the concepts introduced in Chapter 2, it is also apparent that the dimensions of enterprise ownership, regulation, and the degree of competition are each mutually exclusive. In our thinking about privatization, we need to separate out the ownership dimension from others as shown in Figure 10.2. In the hurly-burly of politics, they are intimately bound up in policy-speak and ten second media grabs. More freedom for utilities is promised, with light regulatory

FIGURE 10.2   Ownership, Competition, and Regulation

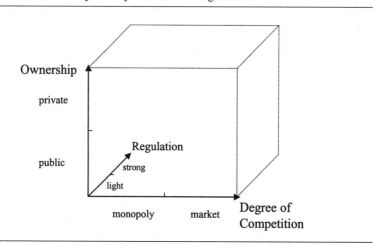

SOURCE: Adapted from Hartley and Parker 1991.

arrangements. Paradoxically, far from freeing firms up from the influence of governments, privatizations in the U.K. as well as elsewhere have involved greater regulation for firms. More attention to each of these dimensions separately was an obvious learning from the early United Kingdom privatization program. Regulatory issues were not an aside, but were a central part of the privatization transformation. This continues today.[15] The implication of this may well be that greater time is required to get the infrastructure for privatization regulation, competition, and accountability requirements just right. Care and caution, rather than speed, yields public benefits, from experience.[16]

Returning to observations of social aspects of privatization, I concluded that the social contours of inequality appear unfortunately to have deepened. Low-income consumers have generally been affected more than others. Emphasizing growing disparities, employment reductions were witnessed along with simultaneous growth in executive remuneration levels. Indeed, there has been a noticeable theme of winners and losers with privatization. Sure, the spread of individual incomes appears to have widened. But on a national scale, my review also noted cases where a whole country was expected to lose, in contrast to the handsome gains made by international investors. The theme of winners and losers is undeniable.

What are the implications here? In a sense, it is simply a relearning of an old maxim. Identifying the winners and losers of policy decisions as separate groups is part of good policy analysis. Its absence is part of power and political opportunism. Openness to such information is part of achieving a better balance in future privatizations compared to those of the past.

Privatization is obviously a strategy that is inherently political. It brings into relief clashing values. As such, the future of the public-private mix is one in which the community itself will continue to make choices, as well as political leaders. One of the first lessons for any privatization researcher is that there are no accurate economic theories, no equations, and little quantitative guidance as to what belongs inside government and what does not. The role of government is contestable, and as such it boils down largely to a community choice. Thus, we might initially find it surprising that whilst the French buy their water from private companies, Sydney citizens are not likely to consider doing so following a series of water-quality scares in the late 1990s in which water from a recently privatized treatment plant had to be boiled before drinking.[17] Whilst Australian citizens have bought alcohol from private companies, Canadians have traditionally insisted that the government own such outlets. Whilst Australia has been busily privatizing its major airports, the New Zealand government has been paralyzed over the refusal by the New Zealand community to allow such remaining privatizations. Whilst many governments talk of post office privatization, almost none have done so. And so on. The "right balance" of private and public sector activities appears to be as much a community, and hence a political, choice as it is an economic or financial one.

Even if the presumed economic and social benefits of privatization evaporate, or are only marginal, the sale of public enterprises is still likely to be far easier for governments than cutting public expenditure, or announcing tax increases in the short term. Irrespective of the degree to which privatization proceeds are used by governments to meet policy objectives such as public debt reduction or else are used in the pursuit of other recurrent policy directions, it is politically attractive. From the perspective of broad community interests, too, there is also no doubt that unless catastrophic service difficulties or outrageous price increases occur, a change in ownership will continue to be seen by end-user consumers as an issue of little concern. The more that postprivatization service or quality levels are debated with no clear or obvious consensus, the more privatization will continue to be smart politics.

Returning again to the review conclusions, we noted that a common risk with all privatization programs was the allegation of corruption. Further, we concluded that whether such allegations are proven, doubts over corruption and cronyism are likely to linger when reformist governments create an atmosphere of less openness in the availability of information. Citizens will continue to interpret silence as guilt in the midst of sensational media accusations. We aim for a balance of power in accessing information, whether government or business. A democratic society needs a dispersal of power, not one dominated by private business interests (to run government), or powerful governments (to corrupt democratic processes).[18]

CONCLUSIONS

So, where does all this leave us? What are the implications of these empirical findings, theoretical ideas, and discussion points? Clearly, there are real cost savings to be gained on average through establishing competitive contracting arrangements, albeit that savings are likely to be quite different for different services. Contracting either in-house or externally can both be effective. Moreover, in traditional service areas such as cleaning, refuse collection, and maintenance, contracting should already be in place. Expecting contracting to be a panacea for all public sector services, though, would be foolish. Some are difficult to accurately specify and measure, or are infrequent and uncertain. These may attract greater governance costs. In considering current trends in outsourcing and contracting, a bigger question also needs to be addressed. When contracting reforms are applied to governments in a wholesale manner, there is a real danger that the market/contracting model will be emphasized at the expense of sensible alternatives such as "cooperation" or "negotiation" with in-house or external teams. A series of alternative options for establishing the cost effectiveness and relative competitiveness of services exist. These range from the simple establishment of business units (with their own service contracts at specific unit costs, business plans, and competitive comparisons), benchmarking comparisons, the periodic adoption of business-process reengineering for restructuring operations, as well as the more well known competitive tendering and outsourcing options. Formally contracting through the market is only one of the modes of establishing the competitiveness of operations. There is certainly a current trend amongst managers to adopt without question quantitative techniques promising management improvements and believing that these can somehow solve problems and make decisions previously conceived of as political in nature. I should emphasize again that the international literature and empirical findings on privatization as contracting out services do not suggest that competitive contracting is always inappropriate. Neither do they say that competitive contracting always is. Careful application of this strategy with targets based on our learnings to date is likely to yield greater benefits than a blanket application based on ideology.

On the question of enterprise sales, the promised benefits of private ownership appear to have exceeded the measured gains to date. Nonetheless, there has been much to learn from privatizations that have occurred worldwide to date. Perhaps the overwhelming message from measurements taken of past privatizations was the need for a healthy degree of skepticism. Whilst it is now possible to privatize just about anything, it is not necessarily sensible. The recurring theme of "winners and losers" that seems to inevitably follow privatization reforms is worrying, as is the speed and inevitability with which such reforms are sold to the populace. Much of the journey on which we are embarking as we reshape government is being undertaken on faith. We need to recognize that the results are not all one way. In researching the two most common forms of privatization, I have adopted a multidimensional approach to performance, and have attempted to arrive at conclusions in an open and transparent manner. Having used an innovative statistical analysis technique as well as previous findings in the field, our experience teaches us that the impacts of privatization are manifold. There is, no doubt, much to be gained for communities and citizens through the judicious use of privatization as well as other reforms, and through careful structuring of market and regulatory arrangements. But differences between the theory of privatization on the one hand and the reality on the other remain. One size will not usually fit all. A learning approach is needed as we go, in order to get the right balance. We now know that the common question, Does privatization work? requires a supplementary request for clarification before any reliable assessment can be made. "Work? . . . Work for whom?" The research presented in this book has aimed to contribute towards a clearer understanding of the answers to this question.

Appendix A
Key Statistical Tests

Empirical work in this research adopted three main statistical tests. These included, firstly, a test for proportions, secondly, a test for data heterogeneity, and thirdly, a test to ascertain the sensitivity of conclusions to unretrieved findings.

The simple sign test may be adopted to clarify whether the proportion of either positive or negative empirical findings for an hypothesis might have arisen simply by chance. In other words, we are first interested in the question "do the cumulative results suggest that one direction of result occurs more frequently than chance alone would suggest?" (Cooper 1989a, p. 91). If there was no relationship between privatization and performance (however defined) we would expect the number of findings in each direction to be equal. The sign test therefore tests whether the proportion found in our cumulative results is significantly different to an assumed equal split in the population. The binomial test is as follows:

$$Z_{vc} = \frac{N_p - (1/2 \times N_t)}{1/2\sqrt{N_t}}$$

where

Z_{vc} = the standard normal deviate, or Z score, for the overall series of comparisons;
N_p = the number of positive findings;
N_t = the number of comparisons (positive plus negative findings) (Cooper 1989a, p. 92).

An important second issue in meta-analysis work is that of the degree to which the empirical results under consideration are homogeneous, or heterogeneous. The degree to which the results do not exhibit homogeneous characteristics can be determined through the construction of a "Q_t" statistic, based on the interpretation made by Cooper (1989a) of earlier work by Hedges and Olkin (1985) for the case of the "r" effect size index. Such a homogeneity statistic asks the question, Is the variance in effect sizes significantly different from that expected by sampling error? (Cooper 1989a, p. 114). If the answer is yes, then the results are heterogeneous—that is, other potential moderating sources of variation exist. These moderating sources might for example include different service types, the fact that contracting in this sample has included both contracting "out" of the public sector and contracting "in-house," as well as different countries, and so on. This test is applied as follows:

$$Q_t = \sum_{i=1}^{k} (n_i - 3)z_i^2 - \frac{\left[\sum_{i=1}^{k} (n_i - 3)z_i \right]^2}{\sum_{i=1}^{k} (n_i - 3)}$$

where

z_i = corrected effect size
n_i = sample size of group i
k = total number of samples combined.

This Q_t statistic is distributed as χ^2, with $k-1$ degrees of freedom (Cooper 1989a, p. 115). An alternative (equivalent) form of calculation for this statistic is also presented by Rosenthal (1991, p. 74).

The third issue, Rosenthal's "file-drawer" concept, is also relevant. Rosenthal (1991, p. 103) comments that there has long been a concern that published studies in the social sciences are a biased sample of the studies that are actually carried out. In other words, research journals tend to attract and publish studies that find "significant results," whilst other studies not coming up with significant results remain back in the lab—literally in the "file drawer." To estimate the degree of damage that could be done to any research conclusion by such file-drawer studies, an estimate can be made of the number of unreported nonsignificant studies that are needed to reduce the current meta-analytic results to a significance level of p = 0.05 or higher.

The formula adopted for this calculation was as follows:

$$X = \frac{\left(\sum Z \right)^2}{1.645^2} - K$$

where

X = the number of unretrieved studies averaging null results required to bring the new overall p to a significance level of .05 or higher
Z = Equivalent Z for a one tailed p significance level
K = the number of studies (or effect sizes) combined.

Appendix B

TABLE A.B1 Literature Review Search Terms for Databases

Database	Search Period	Major Search Term	Combined with any of the Following Terms
ABI/INFORM-Global	1971–1995 (Sept)		
	1971–1980	privati?	result?, performance, effectiveness, efficiency, statistical analysis, or data analysis
	1980–1986	nationali?	result?, performance, effectiveness, efficiency, statistical analysis, or data analysis
	1987–1989	contracting out	result?, performance, effectiveness, efficiency, statistical analysis, or data analysis
	1989–1995	property rights	result?, performance, effectiveness, efficiency, statistical analysis, or data analysis
		outsourcing	result?, performance, effectiveness, efficiency, statistical analysis, or data analysis
PAIS (Public Affairs information Service)	1972–1995 (Sept)		
	1972–1995	privati?	performance, efficiency, effectiveness, statistic, analysis, data*, or case*
		right of property	performance, efficiency, effectiveness, statistic, analysis, data*, or case*
		service contract	
		outsource*	
		contract out	
DAO (Dissertation Abstracts Online)	1972–1995 (Sept)		
	1861–1981	privati?	result?, effect?, analysis, impact?, or performance
	1982–1987	outsourc?	result?, effect?, analysis, impact?, or performance
	1988–1992	contract? and public	result?, effect?, analysis, impact?, or performance
	1993–1995	property rights	result?, effect?, analysis, impact?, or performance

Appendix C

TABLE A.C1 Summary of Effect Size Derivations for Privatization as Contracting Out

Study	Est.	Sectors	N	Param.	D.F.	t	F	r	Est. r	Zc	Ref / Page	Comments/Assumptions
All Economic Measures			20131									
Cost			20030									
Cleaning			6067									
Berenyi and Stevens (1988)	8	Pub/Pri	20	6	14	2.01			−0.47	−0.51	Table 3, p15	
Berenyi and Stevens (1988)	8	Pub/Pri	20	5	15	3.55			−0.68	−0.82	Table 3, p15	
Domberger, Meadowcroft, and Thompson (1987)	3	Pub/Pri	2947	31	2916	−8.53			−0.16	−0.16	Table 2, p44	Cleaning also includes orderly & housekeeping services.
Domberger, Hall, & Li (1994)	1	Pub/Pri	61	13	48				−0.26	−0.27	Table 2	Commercial & special school effect sizes averaged.
U.K. Audit Office (1987)	2	Pub/Pri	18	1	17	−3.8213			−0.68	−0.83	Tables 9, 11 & Appendix 1	Data reanalyzed using t test (two samples).
Domberger, Meadowcroft, and Thompson (1987)	3	Pub/Pub	2947	31	2916	−2.49			−0.05	−0.05	Table 2, p44	Cleaning also includes orderly & housekeeping services.
U.K. Audit Office (1987)	2	Pub/Pub	54	1	53	−6.3587			−0.66	−0.79	Tables 9, 11 & Appendix 1	Data reanalyzed using t test (two samples).
Corporate			120									
Berenyi and Stevens (1988)	8	Pub/Pri	20	5	15	0.27			0.07	0.07	Table 3, p15	
Carver (1989)	1	Pub/Pri	100	3	97	2.104			0.21	0.21	p32	Property tax assessment categorized as corporate service.
Engineering Works			889									
Greene (1994)	12	Pub/Pri	12	1	11		0.0186		−0.04	−0.04	Table 1, p1308	
Martin and Stein (1993)	7	Pub/Pri	877	13	864	2.61			−0.09	−0.09	Table 7.5, p96	
Fire												
Greene (1994)	12	Pub/Pri	12	1	11		0.758		−0.25	−0.26	Table 1, p1308	
Health												
Martin and Stein (1993)	7	Pub/Pri	877	13	864	0.839			0.03	0.03	Table 7.5, p96	
Maintenance			60									
Berenyi and Stevens (1988)	8	Pub/Pri	20	5	15	2.69			−0.57	−0.65	Table 3, p15	
Berenyi and Stevens (1988)	8	Pub/Pri	20	6	14	2.09			−0.49	−0.53	Table 3, p15	
Berenyi and Stevens (1988)	8	Pub/Pri	20	6	14	1.9			−0.45	−0.49	Table 3, p15	

(continues)

TABLE A.C1 *continued*

Study	Est.	Sectors	N	Param.	D.F.	t	F	r	Est. r	Zc	Ref / Page	Comments/Assumptions
Multiple			523									
Ascher (1987)	2	Pub/Pri	15	1	14	2.61823			-0.57	-0.65	Table 7.6, p239	
Ascher (1987)	2	Pub/Pub	8	1	7	2.52433			-0.69	-0.85	Table 7.6, p239	
Ferris (1988)	1	Pub/Pri	500	17	483	3.33333			-0.15	-0.15	Table 1, p213	
Other			909									
Berenyi and Stevens (1988)	8	Pub/Pri	20	5	15	4.62			-0.77	-1.01	Table 3, p15	
Greene (1994)	12	Pub/Pri	12	1	11		0.8069		0.26	0.27	Table 1, p1308	General Government Services categorized as "Other."
Martin and Stein (1993)	7	Pub/Pri	877	13	864	0.153			0.01	0.01	Table 7.5, p96	General Government Services categorized as "Other."
Parks/Recreation			889									
Greene (1994)	12	Pub/Pri	12	1	11		5.7838		-0.59	-0.67	Table 1, p1308	
Martin and Stein (1993)	7	Pub/Pri	877	13	864	2.11			0.07	0.07	Table 7.5, p96	
Police/Security			889									
Greene (1994)	12	Pub/Pri	12	1	11		0.7442		-0.25	-0.26	Table 1, p1308	
Martin and Stein (1993)	7	Pub/Pri	877	13	864	0.69			-0.02	-0.02	Table 7.5, p96	
Refuse			6045									
Albin (1992)	3	Pub/Pri	58	2	56	-1.466			-0.19	-0.19	Table 1, p14	
Berenyi and Stevens (1988)	8	Pub/Pri	20	6	14	3.88			-0.72	-0.91	Table 3, p15	
Buck and Chaundy (1992)	1	Pub/Pri	329	24	305	-7.31			-0.39	-0.41	Eqn. 24 (Table 4)	White's t adopted.
Domberger, Meadowcroft, and Thompson (1986)	2	Pub/Pri	610	17	593	-7.66			-0.30	-0.31	Table 8.4, p197	
Domberger, Meadowcroft, and Thompson (1986)	2	Pub/Pri	610	17	593	-4.52			-0.18	-0.18	Table 8.4, p197	
Greene (1994)	12	Pub/Pri	12	1	11		0.0972		-0.09	-0.09	Table 1, p1308	
Kemper & Quigley (1976)	1	Pub/Pri	129	4	125				-0.25	-0.26	Table 3.11B, p64	Four effect sizes averaged.
Kitchen (1976)	1	Pub/Pri	48	17	31				-0.80	-1.09	Eqn. 4, p69	Average effect size adopted.
Pommerehne and Frey (1977)	1	Pub/Pri	103	11	92	-7.3473		-0.41	-0.41	-0.44	Eqns 7 & 9 , p235, 236	
Szymanski and Wilkins (1993)	2	Pub/Pri	1460	24	1436	-8			-0.21	-0.21	CPU Equation, Table 2, p120	White standard errors adopted in calculation of t.
Szymanski (1993)	4	Pub/Pri	386	12	374	-4.2			-0.21	-0.22	Table 3, Eqn 2, p12	Pre CCT data.
Szymanski (1993)	4	Pub/Pri	217	16	201	-1.7273			-0.12	-0.12	Table 3, Eqn 5, p12	Post CCT data.
Szymanski and Wilkins (1993)	2	Pub/Pub	1460	24	1436	-6			-0.16	-0.16	CPU Equation, Table 2, p120	White standard errors adopted in calculation of t.
Szymanski (1993)	4	Pub/Pub	386	12	374	-4.1667			-0.21	-0.21	Table 3, Eqn 2, p12	Pre CCT data.
Szymanski (1993)	4	Pub/Pub	217	16	201	-1.7			-0.12	-0.12	Table 3, Eqn 5, p12	Post CCT data.
Training			913									
Berglund (1992)	2	Pub/Pri	36	2	34	0.11433			0.02	0.02	p143	Data reanalyzed using t test (two samples).

Study	k	Pub/Pri	N1	n	N2	t		ES	ES	Source	Notes
Martin and Stein (1993)	7		877 1745	13	864	1.11		−0.04	−0.04	Table 7.5, p96	
Transport											
Bails (1979)	1	Pub/Pri	437	8	429	0.49		−0.02	−0.02	Table 1, p67	Three effect sizes averaged.
Feldman (1987)	1	Pub/Pri	68	25	43		0.238	0.24	0.24	Eqn 1 from pp1, 36 & 110	Two effect sizes averaged.
Harding (1990)	1	Pub/Pri	363	12	351		−0.001	−0.01	−0.01	Table 3, p104, Models 1 & 2	
Martin and Stein (1993)	7	Pub/Pri	877	13	864	1.68		0.06	0.06	Table 7.5, p96	
Water Treatment											
Holcombe (1991)	1	Pub/Pri	32	7	25	2.19		0.40	0.43	Table 1, p38	
Health											
Wheeler, Zuckerman, and Aderholdt (1982)	1	Pub/Pub	60	1	59		5.06	−0.28	−0.29	Table 2, p162	
Productivity			101								
Engineering Greene (1994)	12	Pub/Pri	12	2	10	−0.5768		0.18	0.18	Table 3, p1314	Data reanalyzed using t test (two samples).
Fire Greene (1994)	12	Pub/Pri	12	2	10	−0.4067		0.13	0.13	Table 3, p1314	Data reanalyzed using t test (two samples).
Multiple Folz (1985)	2	Pub/Pri	14	1	13		−0.24	−0.24	−0.24	Tables 28 & 29, pp 164 & 167	Two effect sizes averaged.
Other Greene (1994)	12	Pub/Pri	12	2	10	−0.9085		0.28	0.28	Table 3, p1314	Data reanalyzed using t test (two samples).
Parks/Recreation Greene (1994)	12	Pub/Pri	12	2	10	−0.3617		0.11	0.11	Table 3, p1314	Data reanalyzed using t test (two samples).
Police/Security Greene (1994)	12	Pub/Pri	12	2	10	1.0068		−0.30	−0.31	Table 3, p1314	Data reanalyzed using t test (two samples).
Refuse Greene (1994)	12	Pub/Pri	12	2	10	−0.356		0.11	0.11	Table 3, p1314	Data reanalyzed using t test (two samples).
Transport Hensher (1989)	1	Pub/Pri	15	2	13	−4.8161		−0.80	−1.10	Table 1, p8	Data reanalyzed using t test (two samples).

Appendix D

TABLE A.D1   Summary of Effect Size Derivations for Privatization as Enterprise Sales

Author (Primary)	Ref	Inclusion comments	Ref / Page	Comments/Assumptions	Control Comments	N	Reform	Param's	D.F.	t	r	Est r	Zc
All Economic Measures						2272							
Productivity													
Labor Productivity													
Luders (1993)	44	Reanalyzed the data.	Table 7, p116	CAP (Steel) privatization, 1986	None	8	privatization	2	6	3.06		0.78	1.05
Luders (1993)	44	Reanalyzed the data.	Table 7, p116	Celulosa Arauco privatization, 1980	None	14	privatization	2	12	6.192		0.87	1.34
Luders (1993)	44	Reanalyzed the data.	Table 7, p116	C.T.C. (Telephone) privatization, 1987	None	9	privatization	2	7			0.82	1.14
Hutchinson (1991)	522		Table 6.8, p102	Ferranti, U.K. '81 privatization ownership change analyzed.	Reference group for each sector	306	privatization	6	300	0.82		0.05	0.05
Hutchinson (1991)	522		Table 6.9, p103	British Aerospace & Rolls Royce ownerships analyzed.	Reference group for each sector	306	privatization	6	300	1.01		0.06	0.06
Hutchinson (1991)	522		Table 6.10, p104	National Freight Corporation, U.K. '81 privatization.	Reference group for each sector	306	privatization	4	302	0.656		0.04	0.04
Moussios (1994)	545	Transformed ARIMA.	Tables 1&2, p's146 & 155	British Telecom privatization (1982–1993)	National Productivity & Regulation	46	privatization	8	37		0.3792	0.38	0.40
Labor Prod Growth Rate													
Hutchinson (1991)	522		Table 6.8, p102	Ferranti, U.K. '81 privatization ownership change analyzed.	Reference group for each sector	306	privatization	6	300	-3.37		-0.19	-0.19
Hutchinson (1991)	522		Table 6.9, p103	British Aerospace & Rolls Royce ownerships analyzed.	Reference group for each sector	306	privatization	6	300	-1.44		-0.08	-0.08
Hutchinson (1991)	522		Table 6.10, p104	National Freight Corporation, U.K. '81 privatization analyzed.	Reference group for each sector	306	privatization	4	302	-0.622		-0.04	-0.04
Parker & Martin (1995)	1032	Reanalyzed the data.	Table 3, p209	11 U.K. privatized companies	None	22	privatization	2	20	-0.684		-0.15	-0.15
Parker & Martin (1995)	1032	Reanalyzed the data.	Table 5, p213	11 U.K. privatized companies	Whole U.K. Economy	22	privatization	2	20	-0.597		-0.13	-0.13
Parker (1994)	1075	Reanalyzed the data.	Table 8, p104	British Telecom, 1979/80–1993/94	None	13	privatization	2	11	1.13		0.32	0.33
Total Factor Productivity													
Avishur (1994)	1071		Table 10, p63 (average)	British Telecom, 1959 – 1990	Time, Capital, Labor	90	privatization	7	83			0.04	0.04
Total Factor Productivity Growth Rate													
Parker & Martin (1995)	1032	Reanalyzed the data.	Table 4, p209	11 U.K. privatized companies	None	22	privatization	2	20	-1.149		-0.25	-0.25
Parker & Martin (1995)	1032	Reanalyzed the data.	Table 6, p214	11 U.K. privatized companies	Whole U.K. Economy	22	privatization	2	20	-1.235		-0.27	-0.27
Parker (1994)	1075	Reanalyzed the data.	Table 9, p105	British Telecom, 1979/80–1993/94	None	13	privatization	2	11	-0.398		-0.12	-0.12
Technical Efficiency													
Nuruzzman (1989)	578		Equation 6, Table 19, p86	59 cotton textile mills in Bangladesh	Location, age, size, capacity usage & workers to supervisors ratio	155	privatization	7	148	3.232		0.26	0.26

(continues)

TABLE A.D1 continued

Author (Primary)	Ref	Inclusion comments	Ref / Page	Comments/Assumptions	Control Comments	N	Reform	Param's	D.F.	t	r	r	Est r	Zc
Financial						2278								
Return on Assets														
Megginson, Nash & Van Randenborgh (1994)	298		Table III, p426	Worldwide sample of privatized firms.	None	51	privatization	2	49	1.87			0.26	0.26
Return on Equity														
Hutchinson (1991)	522		Table 6.8, p102	Ferranti, U.K. '81 privatization ownership change analyzed.	Reference group for each sector	306	privatization	6	300	1			0.06	0.06
Hutchinson (1991)	522		Table 6.9, p103	British Aerospace & Rolls Royce ownerships analyzed.	Reference group for each sector	306	privatization	6	300	1.74			0.10	0.10
Hutchinson (1991)	522		Table 6.10, p104	National Freight Corporation, U.K. '81 privatization analyzed.	Reference group for each sector	306	privatization	4	302	0.135			0.01	0.01
Megginson, Nash & Van Randenborgh (1994)	298		Table III, p426	Worldwide sample of privatized firms.	None	55	privatization	2	53	-0.599			-0.08	-0.08
Parker (1994)	1075	Reanalyzed the data.	Table 6, p102	British Telecom, 1979/80–1993/94	None	14	privatization	2	12	1.522			0.40	0.43
Parker & Hartley (1991)	263		Table 4, p638	British Aerospace	Time	8	privatization	4	4	-1.42			-0.58	-0.66
Parker & Hartley (1991)	263		Table 4, p638	National Freight Corporation	Time	8	privatization	3	5	2.48			0.74	0.96
Parker & Hartley (1991)	263		Table 4, p638	British Airways	Time	8	privatization	3	5	4.02			0.87	1.35
Yarrow (1989)	271	Reanalyzed the data.	Table 9, p319	British Aerospace	None	9	privatization	7	2	-1.661			-0.76	-1.00
Yarrow (1989)	271	Reanalyzed the data.	Table 9, p319	Cable & Wireless	None	10	privatization	8	2	0.704			0.45	0.48
Yarrow (1989)	271	Reanalyzed the data.	Table 9, p319	Associated British Ports	None	9	privatization	7	2	0.378			0.26	0.26
Yarrow (1989)	271	Reanalyzed the data.	Table 9, p319	Jaguar	None	6	privatization	4	2	0			0.00	0.00
Meller (1993)	373	Reanalyzed the data.	Table 4.1, p108	CAP (Steel)	None	7	privatization	2	5	1.08			0.44	0.47
Meller (1993)	373	Reanalyzed the data.	Table 4.1, p108	CTC (Telephone)	None	6	privatization	2	4	1.835			0.68	0.82
Meller (1993)	373	Reanalyzed the data.	Table 4.1, p108	ENDESA (Electricity)	None	6	privatization	2	4	1.555			0.61	0.72
Meller (1993)	373	Reanalyzed the data.	Table 4.1, p108	ENTEL (Telecommunications)	None	7	privatization	2	5	1.767			0.62	0.72
Meller (1993)	373	Reanalyzed the data.	Table 4.1, p108	IANSA (Sugar)	None	7	privatization	2	5	4.697			0.90	1.49
Meller (1993)	373	Reanalyzed the data.	Table 4.1, p108	Lab Chile	None	7	privatization	2	5	0.791			0.33	0.35
Meller (1993)	373	Reanalyzed the data.	Table 4.1, p108	SOQUIMICH (Nitrate)	None	7	privatization	2	5	2.153			0.69	0.86
Return on Equity Growth Rate														
Hutchinson (1991)	522		Table 6.8, p102	Ferranti, U.K. '81 privatization ownership change analyzed.	Reference group for each sector	306	privatization	6	300	1.41			0.08	0.08
Hutchinson (1991)	522		Table 6.9, p103	British Aerospace & Rolls Royce ownerships analyzed.	Reference group for each sector	306	privatization	6	300	-1.81			-0.10	-0.10
Hutchinson (1991)	522		Table 6.10, p104	National Freight Corporation, U.K. '81 privatization analyzed.	Reference group for each sector	306	privatization	4	302	-0.828			-0.05	-0.05
Return on Sales														
Domberger (1993)	773	Reanalyzed the data.	Table 4, p 64.	10P'd Cos 1979–1988, U.K.	None	10	privatization	1	9	0.94			0.30	0.31
Megginson, Nash & Van Randenborgh (1994)	298		Table III, p426	Worldwide sample of privatized firms.	None	55	privatization	2	53	3.146			0.40	0.42
Moussios (1994)	545	Transformed ARIMA.	Table 4, p172	British Telecom privatization (1982–1993)	National Productivity & Regulation	48	privatization	8	39	2.613			0.39	0.41
Yarrow (1986)	853	Reanalyzed the data.	Table 3, p337	5 privatized Firms in U.K., 1981–1984	None	25	privatization	2	22	1.12			0.23	0.24
Yarrow (1989)	271	Reanalyzed the data.	Table 9, p319	British Aerospace	None	9	privatization	7	2	-0.447			-0.30	-0.31
Yarrow (1989)	271	Reanalyzed the data.	Table 9, p319	Cable & Wireless	None	10	privatization	8	2	3.353			0.92	1.60
Yarrow (1989)	271	Reanalyzed the data.	Table 9, p319	British Oil	None	9	privatization	7	2	-1.935			-0.81	-1.12
Yarrow (1989)	271	Reanalyzed the data.	Table 9, p319	Associated British Ports	None	9	privatization	7	2	0.281			0.19	0.20
Yarrow (1989)	271	Reanalyzed the data.	Table 9, p319	Jaguar	None	8	privatization	6	2	1.406			0.71	0.88

Study	N	Notes	Table	Sample / Event	Control	Reform	k	n	df	Coef.		r	r
Value Added Growth Rate													
Parker & Hartley (1991)	263		Table 4, p638	British Aerospace	Time	privatization	8	4	4	-0.68		-0.32	-0.33
Parker & Hartley (1991)	263		Table 4, p638	National Freight Corporation	Time	privatization	8	5	3	0.54		0.23	0.24
Parker & Hartley (1991)	263		Table 4, p638	British Airways	Time	privatization	8	5	3	2.54		0.75	0.97
Parker & Martin (1993)	185	Reanalyzed the data.		10 U.K. companies	None	privatization 1	10	9	1	-1.127		-0.35	-0.37
Investor Returns							132						
Aggarwal, Leal & Hernandez (1993)	186		Exhibit 5, Panel B, Year 1	Chile	Market Adjusted	privatization	9	7	2	-5.04		-0.89	-1.40
Menyah, Paudyal, and Inyang (1990)	61		Table 1, Panel A, p53	U.K. privatization IPO returns (wealth transfers)	Market Adjusted & Private IPO	privatization	34	32	2	1.79		0.30	0.31
Sinha (1993)	547		Table 6, p78	40 U.K. privatizations	None	privatization	40	40			0.5152	0.52	0.57
Smith (1994)	359	Reanalyzed the data.	Table , p15	49 U.K. privatizations	Market Adjusted	privatization	49	47	2	6.157		0.67	0.81
Investment Inside Firm							113						
Parker (1994)	1075	Reanalyzed the data.	Table 7, p103	British Telecom, 1979/80–1993/94	None	privatization	99	12	2	-2.007		-0.50	-0.55
Megginson, Nash & Van Randenborgh (1994)	298		Table III, p426	Worldwide sample of privatized firms.	None	privatization	14	35	2	1.237		0.20	0.21
Moussios (1994)	545	Transformed ARIMA.	Table 3, p163	British Telecom privatization (1982–1993)	National Productivity & Regulation	privatization	48	40	7	45.62		0.99	2.67
R&D													
Parker (1994)	1075	Reanalyzed the data.	Table 7, p103	British Telecom, 1979/80–1993/94	None	privatization	14	12	2	-19.08		-0.98	-2.41
Economic							192						
GNP Growth													
Arbey (1993)	548			High Income	None	privatization	49	40	9	-1.048		-0.16	-0.17
Arbey (1993)	548			Low Income	None	privatization	49	40	9	-2.411		-0.36	-0.37
Arbey (1993)	548			Middle Income	None	privatization	49	40	9	0.532		0.08	0.08
Yoder, Borkholder & Friesen (1991)	55		Table 2, p431	Low Income	None	privatization	17	15	2		0.47	0.47	0.51
Yoder, Borkholder & Friesen (1991)	55		Table 2, p431	Middle Income	None	privatization	28	26	2		-0.145	-0.15	-0.15
Other Reforms													
Productivity													
Labor Productivity													
Hutchinson (1991)	522		Table 6.8, p102	Ferranti, U.K. '75 nationalization ownership change.	Reference group for each sector	nationalization	306	300	6	-0.272		-0.02	-0.02
Hutchinson (1991)	522		Table 6.9, p103	British Aerospace & Rolls Royce ownerships analyzed.	Reference group for each sector	nationalization	306	300	6	0.036		0.00	0.00
Hutchinson (1991)	522		Table 6.11, p105	Rover, U.K. '74 nationalization ownership change.	Reference group for each sector	nationalization	306	302	4	0.857		0.05	0.05
Labor Prod Growth Rate													
Hutchinson (1991)	522		Table 6.8, p102	Ferranti, U.K. '75 nationalization ownership change.	Reference group for each sector	nationalization	306	300	6	0.098		0.01	0.01
Hutchinson (1991)	522		Table 6.9, p103	British Aerospace & Rolls Royce ownerships analyzed.	Reference group for each sector	nationalization	306	300	6	-0.19		-0.01	-0.01

(continues)

TABLE A.D1 *continued*

Author (Primary)	Ref	Inclusion comments	Ref / Page	Comments/Assumptions	Control Comments	N	Reform	Param's	D.F.	t	r	Est r	Zc
Hutchinson (1991)	522		Table 6.11, p105	Rover, U.K. '74 nationalization ownership change.	Reference group for each sector	306	nationalization	4	302	-1.18		-0.07	-0.07
Firms Financial Performance													
Return on Equity													
Hutchinson (1991)	522		Table 6.8, p102	Ferranti, U.K. '75 nationalization ownership change.	Reference group for each sector	306	nationalization	6	300	0.004		0.00	0.00
Hutchinson (1991)	522		Table 6.9, p103	British Aerospace & Rolls Royce ownerships analyzed.	Reference group for each sector	306	nationalization	6	300	0.453		0.03	0.03
Hutchinson (1991)	522		Table 6.11, p105	Rover, U.K. '74 nationalization ownership change.	Reference group for each sector	306	nationalization	4	302	0.218		0.01	0.01
Parker & Hartley (1991)	263		Table 4, p638	British Aerospace	Time	8	nationalization	4	4	0.68		0.32	0.33
Parker & Hartley (1991)	263		Table 4, p638	Rolls Royce	Time	8	nationalization	3	5	2.2		0.70	0.87
Return on Equity Growth Rate													
Hutchinson (1991)	522		Table 6.8, p102	Ferranti, U.K. '75 nationalization ownership change.	Reference group for each sector	306	nationalization	6	300	0.146		0.01	0.01
Hutchinson (1991)	522		Table 6.9, p103	British Aerospace & Rolls Royce ownerships analyzed.	Reference group for each sector	306	nationalization	6	300	-0.147		-0.01	-0.01
Hutchinson (1991)	522		Table 6.11, p105	Rover, U.K. '74 nationalization ownership change.	Reference group for each sector	306	nationalization	4	302	-0.193		-0.01	-0.01
Value Added Growth													
Parker & Hartley (1991)	263		Table 4, p638	British Aerospace	Time	8	nationalization	4	4	-1.62		-0.63	-0.74
Parker & Hartley (1991)	263		Table 4, p638	Rolls Royce	Time	8	nationalization	3	5	1.73		0.61	0.71
No Reform (Control Group)													
Return on Sales													
Domberger (1993)	773	Reanalyzed the data.	Table 4, p 64	5 Co's remaining public, 1979–1988, U.K.	None	5	None (Control Group)	1	4	1.225		0.52	0.58
Yarrow (1986)	853	Reanalyzed the data.	Table 4, p338	5 non-privatized firms in U.K., 1981–1984	None	20	None (Control Group)	2	18	0.768		0.18	0.18
Social													
Service Quality													
Moussios (1994)	545	Transformed ARIMA.	Table 5, p207	British Telecom privatization (1982–1993)	Public Accountability, and Regulation	144	privatization	9	134	-0.275		-0.02	-0.02
Moussios (1994)	545	Transformed ARIMA.	Table 6, p212	British Telecom privatization (1982–1993)	Public Accountability, and Regulation	131	privatization	10	120	8.396		0.61	0.71
Moussios (1994)	545	Transformed ARIMA.	Table 7, p218	British Telecom privatization (1982–1993)	Public Accountability, and Regulation	144	privatization	8	135	-1.925		-0.16	-0.16
Moussios (1994)	545	Transformed ARIMA.	Table 8, p227	British Telecom privatization (1982–1993)	Public Accountability, and Regulation	144	privatization	9	134			-0.08	-0.08
Moussios (1994)	545	Transformed ARIMA.	Table 9, p232	British Telecom privatization (1982–1993)	Public Accountability, and Regulation	96	privatization	8	87	0.2		0.02	0.02
Moussios (1994)	545	Transformed ARIMA.	Table 10, p238	British Telecom privatization (1982–1993)	Public Accountability, Regulation & Monetary compensation	96	privatization	9	86	0.59		0.06	0.06

	N		Table	Sample	Controls	Reform							
Disclosures													
Thomson (1993)	27	Reanalyzed the data.	Table 1, p138	12 U.K. electricity suppliers	None		622	1	1		−0.317	−0.32	−0.33
Employment													
Bhaskar & Khan (1995)	1027			Employment (5 categories)	Wages	privatization	93	4	27		−0.491	−0.49	−0.54
Parker & Hartley (1991)	480		Table 3, p412	British Aerospace 3	Outputs, Time, & Lag	privatization	31	7	10		0.643	0.64	0.76
Parker & Hartley (1991)	480		Table 3, p412	National Freight Corporation 1	Outputs, Time, & Lag	privatization	17	7	10		−0.524	−0.52	−0.58
Parker & Hartley (1991)	480		Table 3, p412	British Airways	Outputs, Time, & Lag	privatization	17	7	7	−2.14		−0.63	−0.74
Parker (1994)	1075	Reanalyzed the data.	Table 5, p101	British Telecom, 1979/80–1993/94.	None	privatization	14	2	12	−1.676		−0.44	−0.47
Megginson, Nash & Van Randenborgh (1994)	298		Table III, p427	Worldwide sample of privatized firms	None	privatization	39	2	37	0.956		0.16	0.16
Executive Remuneration													
Haskel &Szymanski (1992)	944	Reanalyzed the data.	Table 17.2, p349	7 U.K. privatized co's, with 5 public sector co's for control.	Averaged Public Sector Exec Remuneration Controls	privatization	12	2	10	2.084		0.55	0.62
Other Reforms													
Nationalization													
Employment													
Parker & Hartley (1991)	480		Table 3, p412	Rolls Royce	Outputs, Time, & Lag	nationalization	22	7	15		−0.862	−0.86	−1.30
Parker & Hartley (1991)	480		Table 3, p412	British Aerospace 1	Outputs, Time, & Lag	nationalization	17	7	10		0.5096	0.51	0.56

Notes

CHAPTER ONE

1. Organisation for Economic Co-operation and Development (1998), p. 65.
2. Galal et al. (1994), pp. 528.
3. Anderson (1989), cited in Emy and Hughes (1988), p. 577.
4. Osborne and Gaebler (1993).
5. Barnekov and Raffell (1990).
6. Letwin (1988), p. 21.
7. Bishop and Kay (1992), p. 194.
8. Leiberman (1993).
9. It should be recognized that of these 6,800 reported privatizations, the great majority of these instances were in Eastern Europe (Kikeri, Nellis, and Shirley 1992).
10. Governments around the world are quoted as receiving £25 billion during 1990 from the sale of assets—about the same as the previous year, but down from £39 billion in 1988, in Mason (1991), p. 31.
11. Proceeds for the United Kingdom are taken from Moore (1992). There is nevertheless some dispute about the size of proceeds from privatizations in the U.K., with Whitfield arguing that proceeds between 1979–80 and 1989–90 were closer to some £60.3 billion (Whitfield 1992, p. 143).
12. Reserve Bank of Australia (1997).
13. Kelsey (1993), p. 57.
14. Reserve Bank of Australia (1997). The most aggressive privatizing state, Victoria, contributed almost 40 percent of this total albeit that this state is only around 24 percent of Australia's population.
15. Ernst (1992).
16. Boston (1988).
17. Letwin (1988), p. 52. "Selling the Family Silver" was also to be the title of later books such as Chapman's (1990) *Selling the Family Silver: Has Privatization Worked?*
18. Whitfield (1992, p. 173) cites a cost of £832.93 million for "fees to outside organisations in the furtherance of privatizations" in the U.K. through the 1980s.
19. See, for example, the two statistical studies of Boyd (1991) and Capon, Farley, and Hoenig (1990).

CHAPTER TWO

1. Drucker (1969, p. 218).
2. Ibid., p. 229.

3. See Ernst (1998, p. 1,742).

4. Savas (1987, p. 3).

5. Heald (1984) lists eleven activities of privatization under four major headings, and Pirie (1985) lists twenty-two possible privatization activities.

6. See Barnekov and Raffel (1990), Dixon (1991), Poole and Fixler (1987), and Ernst (1992).

7. See writers such as Kettl (1988) and Sundquist (1984).

8. Adapted from Hanke (1987, p. 4). Definitions of privatization consistent with this view are also provided in Abelson (1987a), Rigg and Leach (1990), Adam, Cavendish, and Mistry (1992), and Starr (1989). A smaller number of narrower definitions of privatization also exist. Firstly, Kikeri, Nellis, and Shirley (1992) from the World Bank define privatization solely in terms of enterprise sales—as "the sale of SOEs to the private sector by the sale—full or partial—of ongoing concerns, or by the sale of assets following liquidation." Donahue (1989), on the other hand, argues that aside from a strictly limited number of asset sales, privatization in the United States meant and continues to mean "enlisting private energies to improve the performance of tasks that would remain in some sense public."

9. See Adam, Cavendish, and Mistry (1992).

10. See for example Wiltshire (1987), Whitfield (1992), and Foster (1992, p. 116).

11. This objective was perhaps understandable in the early privatization programs, in view of the historically significant debate around the possibility of crowding out private investment and the potential inability of the share market to absorb these sales.

12. The one exception to this in Table 2.2 is from Wiltshire (1987), who notes that the Department of Trade and Industry put forward this objective in the Public Accounts Committee 1985–86 briefing to the U.K. House of Commons. In this case, as Table 2.2 shows, "securing successful transfer of the company to the private sector" was itself an explicit objective.

13. See Florestano and Gordon (1980), and Messiter (1993).

14. See for instance Jones (1993), Ferris and Graddy (1986), Messiter (1993), McDavid (1985), Bendick (1989), Chandler and Feuille (1991), Chi (1989), and Jones (1993).

15. The PA Consulting survey was based on 1,200 questionnaire responses internationally, and 233 responses in Australia during 1997–98.

16. The Deloitte and Touch Consulting Group (1997) survey looked at 120 Australian organizations outsourcing information technology during 1997.

17. This diagram was developed from the early work of the Public Bodies Review Committee of the Victorian Parliament, Australia. It was updated in late 1998 using information obtained through consulates, embassies, and trade missions.

18. The source of this data was Kikeri, Nellis, and Shirley (1992, p. 22). The data included liquidations and any sale that reduced the government share in the firm to less than 50 percent, but excluded reprivatizations.

19. Wolf (1992), commenting on Hax (1992).

20. Of the privatizations listed in OECD (1994), the largest numbers of transactions were from the Russian Federation (representing around one-third of the total number of privatizations) and the Czech Republic (at around one-quarter of the privatizations).

21. The Reserve Bank of Australia (1997) reports that Australia has had one of the larger privatization programs of all OECD countries in the 1990s—second, by value, only to the United Kingdom, and second only to New Zealand in terms of proceeds relative to GDP.

22. See Evatt Research Centre (1990).

23. The Industry Commission (1995, p. 61) of Australia reports averages of between 7 and 18 percent for local government from the research of others between 1988 and 1992, whilst for state governments, it suggests New South Wales and Western Australia contracted 4.0 percent of total current expenditures in 1993–94.

24. This 50 percent of turnover requirement meant effectively that local government bodies were required to undertake competitive tendering for the bulk of their services due to the accrual accounting practices that were also being introduced at the time. Few of Victoria's seventy-eight municipalities had failed to meet the 50 percent target by 1998.

25. Auditor General of Victoria (1998).

26. Although the number and speed of privatizations in these countries were continually the subject of newspaper headlines in the popular press, less prominence was given to the criticisms of authors such as Frydman and Rapaczynski (1993), who argue that "attempts to emulate western privatizations were, by and large, a failure." In more recent times, the privatizations that underpinned reform efforts in the former USSR have come under similar criticism.

27. See Parsons (1995, p. 3).

28. See Hughes (1994, p. 99).

29. See McIntosh, Shauness, and Wettenhall (1997) for an account of contracting in Australia over more than a century.

30. McIntosh, Shauness, and Wettenhall (1997) report that in 1894, the well-accepted practice of competitive contracting for construction works was interrupted by a Royal Commission that found widespread fraud in the contracting-out system, schedule rigging, and dissatisfaction with inferior quality work. In less than a decade, the contracting-out system was replaced by government-supplied day labor as the dominant mode of labor for construction. Improved work quality, better working conditions, and more secure employment was said to have resulted from this. Importantly, McIntosh, Shauness, and Wettenhall recognized also that more swings of this private/public pendulum occurred over subsequent decades.

CHAPTER THREE

1. Donahue (1989, p. 3).

2. Boston (1991).

3. See the analysis of Spicer et al. (1991).

4. See Self (1994), and Stretton and Orchard (1994).

5. Osborne, D., and Gaebler, T. (1993, p. 25).

6. See Lane (1991).

7. Parsons (1995, p. 63), adapted from Colebatch and Larmour (1993).

8. Williamson (1975, 1985).

9. See Boston (1991).

10. Spicer et al. (1991).

11. See for instance the contributions of Considine (1988, 1990) and Paterson (1988) on both sides of this international debate.

12. Boston (1991, p. 9).

13. Pollitt (1993, p. 1).

14. See ibid., p. 49.

15. See Hughes 1994, chapter 3.

16. Spicer et al. (1991).

17. Hodge (1993a).

18. Of course this assumes that the process of subsuming the organization's goals into the financial bottom line does not in any way introduce incentives that improve the organization's financial performance but work against the achievement of the organization's objectives. This itself is a sizable assumption.

19. No doubt many might believe that economic goals would logically follow this redistribution of power, but there is no guarantee of this. The primary issue suggested here is power and influence, not economics.

20. Cited in Wettenhall (1983).

21. Indeed, the ability of capitalist economies to themselves fail for a time was demonstrated through the great depression of 1929–33 (Bishop and Kay 1992).

22. This point was also made independently by Mintzberg (1996) in his *Harvard Business Review* article. He makes the point powerfully, simply stating that "capitalism did not triumph at all; balance did."

CHAPTER FOUR

1. See Hodge (1993a, p. 26).

2. There is an increasingly prevalent argument that traditional models for public administration, dominant for most of this century, are being gradually discredited. Newer models are being adopted throughout the world (Hughes 1995, p. 59). The success of new practices and public management models will in large part depend on the extent to which traditional public sector values can be maintained if this is indeed expected by the voting public.

3. Notice, however, that we have viewed each sector as a whole in our discussion so far. Of course, the reality of modern government is that a large part of its responsibilities involves providing services to clients. This being the case, then rather than comparing the sectors as a whole and noting that different values underpin both, it may well be more productive to debate in which areas of public sector operations private values could better be adopted to underpin the improved provision of public services.

CHAPTER FIVE

1. See, for example, Savas (1987, 1992b, and 1993).

2. See, for example, Whitfield (1992).

3. Hunter and Schmidt (1990, p. 468).

4. For the case of privatization as contracting out, an example of such a "dizzying list" was provided by the Australian Department of Administrative Services in its submission to the 1995 Industry Commission Inquiry into Competitive Tendering and Contracting Out by Public Sector Agencies. Entitled a Selected Bibliography, the presentation, simply of summary concepts and findings from the contracting-out literature reviewed, amounted to some seventy-three pages. The report included only a handful of the empirical studies that were considered in this research project. Moreover, it did not include any significant discussion at all on theoretical, empirical, evaluation methodology, or other issues.

5. Cooper (1989a, p. 142).

6. As well, vote-counting procedures also ignore the fact that different aspects of the subject may be under review and that authors may be writing with inconsistent definitional frameworks.

7. Rosenthal (1991, p. 6).

8. Ibid., p. 10.

9. Cook et al. (1992).

10. Cook et al. (1992, p. viii).

11. Johnson, Mullen, and Salas (1995, p. 94) report in their recent comparison of meta-analytic approaches that "literally hundreds of meta-analyses have been published" in a wide range of disciplines. They furthermore argue strongly that "a growing consensus maintains that this approach is more precise than traditional, or narrative, reviews of research literature." Thus, rather than being a topic of passing interest, these authors see the meta-analytic research approach as one of increasing popularity and acceptance in the mid-1990s.

12. Rosenthal (1991, p. 21).

CHAPTER SIX

1. ABI/INFORM provides abstracts for "articles in the world's most respected business publications" (Proquest 1995a). It is international in scope, with a special emphasis on Canada, Europe, and the Pacific Rim. The coverage of PAIS is also international in scope, but as well as periodical articles, also covers monographs, government documents, pamphlets, reports of public and private agencies, microfiche, and newspapers (PAIS 1995). The DAO (Dissertation Abstracts Online) database presents work from over 1,000 universities throughout the world, including most North American graduate schools and many European universities. It covers humanities, social sciences, science, and engineering (Proquest 1995b).

2. Others, such as, say, the Social Sciences Citation Index, could just as logically have been used. Clearly, the adoption of any one source of references or another runs the risk of not covering completely all of the journals, though accessing all the studies ever completed in an area of study is not physically possible in any case. The real risk is the possibility that the sample of studies obtained for review might be biased from using one source over another. In this study, it was considered that these three databases represented a strong range of information sources over the various major disciplines that were likely to have undertaken quantitative studies on privatization, and that the risk of such bias was likely to be low.

3. Details of search terms and time periods covered for each database search are indicated in Appendix B.

4. A visit was also made to the Competitive Tendering and Contracting Centre at the University of Sydney to increase potential coverage in the area of privatization as contracting out.

5. Information was collected and stored in a Microsoft Access software database for each reference, including: *reference details* (such as title of paper and publication, date, type of publication, country studied); *author details* (such as primary author and other authors, discipline of primary author); *study details* (such as country studied, type of analysis, funding of study, and type of research question addressed, whether an analysis of contracting,

enterprise sale(s), property rights, or general review, etc.); *study conclusions* (such as general conclusions reached, performance dimensions analyzed, and sector favored).

6. Reanalyses of Greene (1994), Berglund (1992), Hensher (1989), and U.K. Audit Office (1987) were all examples of this approach to reanalyze reported data.

7. Stevens's work in the United States, for example, was reported in several places (Berenyi and Stevens 1988, Stevens 1984, Ecodata 1984 as well as several review documents), however, only results from the first of these reports were included in the meta-analysis.

8. In most of the less sophisticated study designs the exact time and duration of the study was not detailed.

9. To the extent that it was possible to test more formally for potential differences in these two distributions, they were found to be not statistically different from each other at the .05 level. This was tested through a chi squared test to assess the hypothesis that both distributions are the same, and that observed differences could have arisen through random chance.

10. For the studies to be included in the meta-analysis, sixteen out of the twenty-eight studies (56 percent) related to the United States. Again, the distributions for all studies and for the meta-analysis studies appeared to be similar. This was formally tested using a χ^2 test, and it was confirmed that the distributions were not different at a level of .05.

11. For the meta-analysis subgroup, nineteen of the twenty-eight studies (i.e., 68 percent) were of local government. In some instances, the level of government was not noted in the report. The two distributions of studies by level of government were again formally tested as not significantly different from each other at the .05 level.

12. To the extent that it was possible to make a formal assessment of this, it was confirmed at the .05 level. The three groups tested here were disappointingly broad, however.

13. The fact that performance is being judged by groups of people other than those at the front line of service delivery is not the issue here. Everyone has the right to make judgments on performance. The values of those judging performance is the critical point, however, and in any judgment of performance it is desirable to make explicit the values of both those undertaking the work being assessed and those making a performance assessment away from the service providers.

14. Likewise, for those studies included in the meta-analysis, the economic dimension dominated.

15. For the meta-analysis studies, the distribution of support for one sector or another was similar, as shown in Figure 6.7b.

CHAPTER SEVEN

1. See Seghers (1986) and Knipe (1993) respectively.

2. Speculation on why so few analyses seemed to be available in the area of outsourcing in the private sector might include several comments. Firstly, this term would only be one of a number of terms appropriate to adopt in a search on this particular topic. Secondly, there may be very few publicly available analyses of this type of decision because of the desire to keep such "competitive" information secret. Thirdly, few statistical analyses may actually have been undertaken on this topic at the time of this research even though it appears to be an increasingly common practice in today's business culture.

3. During the completion of this research work a major parallel investigation was undertaken by the Industry Commission, Australia.

4. The format for these studies is drawn from a review on contracting out by Domberger and Rimmer (1994) and the references come from several sources.

5. This was done using the formula:

$$Z_{ave} = \frac{\sum\limits_{i=1}^{k} (n_i - 3) z_i}{\sum\limits_{i=1}^{k} (n_i - 3)}$$

Where

Z_{ave} = average weighted effect size

n_i = total sample size for the ith comparison (Cooper 1989a, p. 108)

z_i = Effect size (Fisher transformed), and

k = Number of samples.

6. Confidence limits were determined for each weighted mean effect-size estimate based on the guidelines of Cooper (1989a , p. 110). Their calculation was as follows:

$$\text{C.I.}_{z\,95\%} = z_{ave} + \frac{1.96}{\left[\sqrt{\sum_{i=1}^{k} (n_i - 3)} \right]} , \text{ and } \text{C.I.}_{z\,95\%} = z_{ave} - \frac{1.96}{\left[\sqrt{\sum_{i=1}^{k} (n_i - 3)} \right]}$$

7. The (2 tailed) p level for the weighted average effect size from several (k) studies combined was calculated using these confidence limits, knowing that:

$$Z = \frac{z_{ave}}{\left[\sqrt{\sum_{i=1}^{k} (n_i - 3)^{-1}} \right]}$$

For the case of unweighted p levels, the formula provided by Rosenthal (1991, p. 69), for the derivation of significance levels, was adopted:

$$\frac{\left(\sum\limits_{i=1}^{k} w_i \cdot z_i \right)}{\left(\sqrt{\sum_{i=1}^{k} (w_i^2)} \right)} = z$$

Where

w_i = the weight for the ith effect size. (Hence, the denominator therefore involves simply the total number of effect sizes included in making an unweighted mean estimate.)

z_i = the z statistic corresponding to the p level for each study effect size.

8. For the binomial test for all economic effect sizes, $Z = 3.576$, and $p < .0001$.

9. For the binomial test for (cost-based) cleaning effect sizes, $Z = 3.576$, and $p < .0001$.

10. The binomial test for all economic refuse collection effect sizes produced $Z = 3.500$, and hence $p < .0005$.

11. As an example, despite all of the three maintenance (cost-based) effect sizes being negative, the proportion was only significant using the binomial sign test at a level of .08. This proportion was therefore not significant at the .05 level.

12. For all services other than cleaning and refuse collection as a group, the proportion of negative signs found for all economic measures (20/34) yielded $Z = 1.029$, and hence $p < .40$.

13. The statistical significance of the heterogeneity of the Z's can be obtained from a χ^2 distribution computed as follows:

$$\sum_{i=1}^{k} (n_i - 3)(z_{ri} - \bar{z}_r)^2 \text{ is distributed as } \chi2 \text{ with } k-1 \text{ degrees of freedom,}$$

where

z_{ri} = the Fisher corrected effect size r_i,

n_i = the number of sampling units on which each r is based, and

z_r = the weighted mean of z's.

14. The cost-based effect sizes as a group were also significantly heterogeneous, with $\chi^2 = 378.3$, and $p < .005$.

15. For the cleaning weighted average effect size, $Z = 8.870$, and $p < .0001$. The cleaning effect sizes showed a significant $\chi^2 = 62.6$ ($p < .005$).

16. For corporate services, $Z = 2.037$ ($p = .042$). The chi square heterogeneity test was not significant, with $\chi^2 = 0.29$.

17. By definition, the classification of services did involve some degree of arbitrariness. Services such as "general government services" from Greene (1994) and from Martin and Stein (1993) could have also been included in this "corporate" category, rather than in the "other" category. Their inclusion would have further strengthened the conclusion that contracting corporate services increases costs, however. Both of the effect sizes for these "general government services" were positive, indicating that contracting increased service costs.

18. Engineering works yielded $Z = -2.621$ ($p = .009$), and testing heterogeneity, $\chi^2 = 0.02$, $p < .75$.

19. For maintenance services, $Z = -3.974$, and $p = .0001$. The heterogeneity test yielded $\chi^2 = 0.23$, and a file-drawer analysis revealed that a mere eleven positive unretrieved effects sizes (or studies) would be needed to reduce this conclusion to nonsignificance.

20. For the parks and recreation samples, $Z = 1.906$, and $p = .057$, and in terms of heterogeneity, $\chi^2 = 4.94$ and $p < .05$.

21. Formally, for police/security services, $Z = -0.768$ ($p = .44$), and $\chi^2 = 0.49$ ($p < .25$).

22. For refuse collection, $Z = 17.244$ ($p < .0001$), and $\chi^2 = 74.2$, which is significant at a level of $< .005$.

23. Training services yielded $Z = -1.074$ ($p = .28$), and $\chi^2 = 0.10$ ($p < .75$).

24. Formally, for transport services, $Z = +1.273$ ($p = .20$), and $\chi^2 = 5.31$, $p < .25$.

25. The single water treatment sample showed $Z = 2.289$, and $p = .022$.

26. For health, $Z = -2.181$, and $p = .029$.

27. Statistically, $Z = -1.289$, with $p = .20$.

28. For the productivity effect sizes, formally, $\chi^2 = 15.79$, and $p < .05$.

29. In any data collection effort for a primary research study, the detection and interpretation of "outliers" is also an issue of some importance. An outlier is some observation discordant from the majority of the sample. The existence of any outliers in this data set was investigated using the exploratory statistical techniques of Tukey (1962), and both outliers and extreme values were isolated. It was nevertheless decided to include such studies (even though they had poor statistical controls) so that the degree to which such studies with poor controls yielded different effect sizes could be tested empirically. It was also recognized that potential outliers should be excluded as a part of sensitivity tests, so that the sensitivity of conclusions to the inclusion or otherwise of this data point could be established. Ideally, the analyst would not wish conclusions to be dependent on the inclusion of this one value.

30. To test for the possible effect of a moderator variable, a single degree of freedom "contrast" test was adopted. The statistical significance of testing a set of effect sizes can be obtained from a "Z" as follows:

$$Z = \frac{\sum \lambda_j z_{rj}}{\sqrt{\sum \lambda_j^2 / w_j}}$$

Where

λ_j = the contrast weight chosen such that the sum of the λ_j's will be zero

z_{rj} = the Fisher z_r for any one study

w_j = the inverse of the variance of the effect size, which for this case is given as

$w_j = (n_j - 3)$ (Rosenthal 1991, p. 80).

The possible influence of a moderator variable can then be tested by determining the significance of this statistic.

31. The average effect size for contracting with the private sector ($r_{ave} = -0.23$, n = 50) was not significantly different from that contracting with the public sector ($r_{ave} = -0.35$, n = 7), p = .053. These averages are unweighted.

32. This comparison revealed contracting with the public sector ($r_{ave} = -0.27$, n = 5) was associated with a smaller average cost-saving effect compared to that achieved through contracting with the private sector ($r_{ave} = -0.38$, n = 18). This contrast in favor of private sector provision was significant at the .05 level, but was not significant at .01 by a small margin (p = .013). This finding provided at least some support of the existence of a significant difference in relative effect sizes between private and public provision, albeit not strictly significant at the .01 level and also knowing that this latter comparison only related to cleaning and refuse services alone.

33. Whether it is the researcher's discipline per se, or another variable such as the type of service studied, which is the cause of the different reported effect size cannot, unfortunately, be determined.

34. Those with more than eight statistical control variables in the analysis exhibited ($r_{ave} = -0.16$), compared to those with eight or less ($r_{ave} = -0.30$).

35. For those with an interest more in studies having greater sophistication through more control variables, the more sophisticated studies as a group showed an average weighted effect size of $r_{ave} = -0.10$. This was statistically significant at a level of .0000. Results for the unweighted average ($r_{ave} = -0.16$) were also consistent.

36. See Glass, McGaw, and Smith (1981, p. 64).

37. This finding may be contrary to expectations, which might have predicted that local government would yield bigger effect sizes, rather than smaller.

38. Since cleaning and refuse services have reported higher than average savings (i.e., −30.2 percent and −19.3 percent respectively), the inclusion of these twenty cleaning and refuse cost-saving estimates leads to a greater calculated overall average.

39. The simple adjustment calculations were as follows: 87 percent of 15.6 percent = 13.6 percent, and 87 percent of 9.8 percent = 8.5 percent.

40. This cost-reduction estimate does not include any costs that may be associated with the development of the contracting process, getting together tenders, or monitoring of contractor progress, etc. The implications of this are considered in the following section.

41. Rosenthal (1991, p. 134) indicates that in computing the binomial effect size display concept, the experimental group success rate is $0.50 + r/2$ (or $50 + 11/2 = 55.5\%$), whilst the success rate for the control group is $0.50 − r/2$ (or $50 − 11/2 = 44.5\%$). The difference in success rates is therefore 11 percent.

42. The U.K. Audit Office (1987) report presents a savings figure of £73 million, which "represents an average saving of 20% of previous costs for those services put to contract." This £73 million figure "is partly net of redundancy costs" expected to amount to £11.1 million, but is quoted as not taking into account "the costs of tendering estimated by the NAO as broadly of the order of £15m for the whole programme." Thus, the estimated percentage costs of tendering were $(15/73) \times 20\% = 4.1\%$.

43. The importance of properly measuring costs involved in establishing the tendering process rather than simply relying on "planning estimates" is reinforced in Australian case studies such as Mosman Council, as cited by Albin (1992). In this case, he notes that as at the date of his paper, the current costs of implementing the competitive tendering arrangements stood at six times the initial estimate.

44. Few estimates for contract preparation and documentation exist. One further recent Australian estimate is that of 9 percent for the construction industry (Cogno and Hill 1996).

45. If, as the moderator analysis suggests, savings for contracting out are significantly greater for the "traditional" maintenance, cleaning, and refuse collection services compared to the other services, the possible reasons for this deserve attention. Speculatively, reasons might include at least four:

1. These traditional services may have been relatively more constrained by inflexible working practices based on years of industrial relations negotiations and poor work habits. Such procedures may be freed up when subject to contracting. An example here might be the reduction from three-person crews to two- or even one-person crews with refuse collection contracting.

2. Traditional services may be more susceptible to improvements being made through technological innovation and logistics reengineering. Again, using the example of garbage collection, technology has improved remarkably over recent decades.

3. Traditional services may be easier and more straightforward to both specify and measure. This may provide a ready mechanism for review when considering which parts of the service should continue to be provided and which parts should not. Those services that are easier to measure may also receive more attention, and with this greater attention, greater savings may be encouraged.

4. Lastly, more experience may simply have been gained with contracting in traditional service areas, leading to efficiency gains being made through long experience.

46. Carnaghan and Bracewell-Milnes (1993) also quote the U.K. Audit Commission Controller as arguing that such failure rates imply that the council has chosen badly, it has not specified its contracts properly, or else it has not monitored them well enough.

47. Of course, anecdotes may always be provided to "disprove" this conclusion. In Victoria, Australia, compulsory competitive tendering has been introduced, which through legislation requires all councils to put to tender at least 50 percent of their services. Rate reductions, which were separately legislated, also occurred along with the formation of larger councils through forced amalgamations down to one-third of the previous number. Politically, contracting can be claimed to have contributed to rate reductions, although no cause-effect relationship exists. No comprehensive statistical studies independent of government have been undertaken on this to date.

48. A further 4 percent comprised mostly fixed-term contract staff who were terminated after the contracting-out decision.

49. See Industry Commission (1996), Tables B4.2 and B4.1.

50. Escott and Whitfield (1995, p. 150).

51. Ibid., p. 165.

52. For these three weighted service-quality effect sizes, $Z = -0.174$, and $p > .10$. The average unweighted effect size found was $r_{ave} = +0.03$, and was again not significantly different from zero at .10. Here, $Z = -0.224$, and $p > .10$.

53. The chi square heterogeneity test ($\chi^2 = 1.03$) for these three quality findings was nowhere near significant at the .05 level.

54. Furthermore, we might also observe that in most instances where quality has not been maintained, contracting can be a "two-way street," rather than one way. Hence, contractors can be changed or else brought in-house if the need is urgent. Hirsch (1991) specifically addresses this issue of "switching" in his review and notes the degree to which the various service types have been observed to switch based on experience.

55. This weighted average was highly significant with $Z = -5.221$, and $p < .0001$. For the case of the unweighted mean, $r_{ave} = -0.21$, which was again highly significant; with $Z = -5.278$, and $p < .0001$.

56. Here, $Z = -3.166$, and $p = .0029$.

57. See Hughes (1994, p. 237).

58. Hughes (1994).

59. Commonwealth Ombudsman (1997, pp. 1, 59–74).

60. See Hughes (1994), chapter 10.

61. Mulgan (1997).

62. The alternative interpretation of this refusal to supply data as simply a refusal to cooperate with policies of a central government of different persuasion (and not a refusal to supply information due to reasons of commercial-in-confidence) is acknowledged. This alternative interpretation raises to center stage the undesirability of using commercial-in-confidence as a purely political tool.

63. In reviewing Savas's 1987 book, Gormley (1989, p. 356) sees the issue of accountability as one of Savas's blind spots. In support of this, he points out that Savas "has very little to say on the subject," and that, in addition, "Savas very seldom uses the word, which cannot be found in the index."

64. This is the case in California, according to Coghill (1997).

CHAPTER EIGHT

1. The reanalyses of data from Parker and Martin (1993), Parker (1994a), Thomson (1993), Yarrow (1989), and Domberger (1993) are all examples from this category.

2. Research analyzing performance levels following changes in agency status in the U.K., for instance, was reported several times (Parker 1992, Dunsire, Hartley, and Parker 1991, Parker and Martin 1993, Parker and Hartley 1991a, 1991b, Dunsire et al. 1988, and Dunsire 1991), as well as being quoted in other review documents. Results from each of these authors were included in the meta-analysis only once.

3. Formally, there was little difference between the two distributions of studies by publication date. For the proportions up to 1990, and after, $\chi^2 = 0.21$, which was well below the critical χ^2 value of 5.99 for two degrees of freedom, at the .05 significance level.

4. In the case of those studies included in the meta-analysis, some 66 percent analyzed the U.K., less developed countries were the subject of 21 percent of analyses, and 13 percent of studies analyzed multiple countries. From the formal perspective, the distributions for "all studies" and for the "meta-analysis studies" were similar ($\chi^2 = 4.29$, less than the χ^2 critical value of 5.99 for the .05 level with two degrees of freedom).

5. A comparison between the following categories was undertaken: "Economics," "Business/Commerce," and "Other." There was a significant difference between the relative proportions of these disciplines at the .05 level ($\chi^2 = 6.98$), which was less than the critical value for two degrees of freedom.

CHAPTER NINE

1. Of course, such flexibility is often a key element in the attractiveness of buying an enterprise, and has been a major selling point politically.

2. Recall that the costs of service provision were found empirically to be critically dependent on these dozen or so parameters as well as the sector providing the service.

3. In the analysis of British Aerospace in this research, the first sale date (i.e., 1981) was taken as the effective date for privatization. This date was taken as the most logical, as the U.K. government undertook not to interfere with the running of the company after this time (Parker and Hartley 1991b).

4. Parker and Hartley (1991a, p. 406).

5. Parker and Hartley (1991b, p. 634).

6. Such difficulties are likely, in the view of the author, to be magnified even further if one contemplated an analysis of public versus private sector efficiency using the property rights literature. In reviewing property rights studies, constant vigilance would be required to ensure that the above mentioned issues were always recognized. In addition to those parameters that could be captured in an analysis, others also exist. For example, a property rights-based econometric analysis of the provision of a bus service may well capture many variables considered to influence the costs of the service including the level of passenger demand, the pickup density, the types of passengers, and so on. It is unlikely, in the view of this author, for the analysis to be able to capture all parameters that would properly reflect the inherently different process of decisionmaking that historically led to the provision of a private, as com-

pared to a public, bus service along a particular route. All other things being equal, therefore, one might expect private bus companies to establish bus services in those areas that are inherently more attractive from the perspectives of demand, greater density, better competitive factors, lower regulation, and even better topography, and so on. The point is that it may well not be possible to capture all of the factors influencing the inherently different conditions of the various production tasks undertaken through the private and the public decisions. This is a significant issue. In any event, the property rights body of data was not analyzed in this research. Data analysis was limited to actual sales of enterprises.

7. Of course, we might also suspect the same tainting with a narrative analysis of enterprise sales performance findings, as well. Concerns about the imperfect data would be in addition to the concerns noted in Chapter 5 about the degree to which narrative reviews can be skewed by the reviewer.

8. The amount of literature on privatization as the sale of enterprises is massive, and yet surprising. An extensive array of reports on the subject certainly exists. Most are discussions, case studies, and commentaries, providing a high level of appreciation of the various threads of history and political events surrounding sales throughout the world. The actual body of evaluation evidence purporting to present quantitative empirical results is relatively small, however. This limited empirical evidence also covers a variety of performance dimensions, so that the evidence relating to any one specific area can actually be relatively thin.

9. The initial finding that labor productivity improvements were generally observed throughout the 1980s is probably not surprising from first principles. It was a time of increasing computerization and technological change affecting all employees in a firm. For managers, it was the decade for placing a personal computer on every corporate desk. It was also the decade in which middle managers were increasingly under pressure as organizations became flatter. Middle-management numbers were being trimmed, in recognition of the need for all employees to add value to the corporation's services, rather than the traditional hierarchical public sector orientation of administrating, processing, and controlling.

10. See for example Anonymous (1995), Miller (1994), Meller (1993), Hutchinson (1991), and Megginson, Nash, and Van Randenborgh (1994).

11. The relatively high frequency of this finding is interesting. It is particularly so in view of the warning by the World Bank report (Galal et al. 1994, p. 13) that "profit measures typically favor private firms" due in part to "the public enterprises operating in different sectors" but more importantly, "due to differences in pricing behavior" of private firms.

12. See Hutchinson (1991), Megginson, Nash, and Van Randenborgh (1994), Moussios (1994), and Parker and Hartley (1991b).

13. Aggarwal, Leal, and Hernandez (1993) notes that in the case of Chile, the 8 percent gains after the first day of the float (relative to the market) were followed subsequently by 32 percent lower returns than the rest of the stock market. Shareholder losses also occurred in a privatization float in Japan according to Okumura (1994). He reports that the share price set for the float of the East Japan Railways Company was set artificially high by the Japanese government "just to make a profit." This scandalous sale resulted in massive losses to unaware and overly trusting new shareholders.

14. An average effect size can be calculated when it assists one's understanding of an area of performance. For this data on enterprise sales, an overall average of effect sizes for all areas of performance was not determined. Such a calculation would not have

contributed towards a better understanding of the performance impacts of enterprise sales. An overall "grand average" effect size would have no real meaning. Average effect sizes were therefore only calculated for each of the specified performance categories.

15. Consistent with our analysis of contracting out, weighted mean effect sizes were determined by weighting all effect sizes by their respective sample sizes less three (i.e., n − 3).

16. Conclusions reached for productivity improvements were robust and were reached consistently adopting both weighted and unweighted averages.

17. For this sign test, $Z = 3.000$, $p < .001$.

18. The average effect size for the six labor productivity growth-rate estimates following privatization was significantly negative with $r_{ave} = -0.10$, and confidence limits (-0.16 to -0.04), with $p < .002$. The average effect size for the total factor productivity growth rate was not different from zero ($p < .11$), however, with $r_{ave} = -0.23$ for the two studies using this measure (producing three estimates), and wide confidence limits of -0.52 to $+0.05$.

19. For this category, $\chi^2 = 71.09$, and $p < .005$ for 17 degrees of freedom.

20. As in the previous analysis of contracting, a standard statistical contrast test was adopted for the analysis of moderator variables (Rosenthal 1991, p. 80; Johnson, Mullen, and Salas 1995).

21. Looking at whether the country studied may have moderated the results, it was found that only the U.K. provided studies with controls, and only studies in other countries were without controls. This yielded the identical contrast test, with the unweighted average effect size for U.K. studies ($r_{ave} = +0.11$) being much smaller than studies from countries including Chile and Bangladesh ($r_{ave} = +0.95$), at a significance level of $p < .0000$. Clearly, we cannot be sure whether the presence of controls moderated the effect sizes, or the country. Looking only at the more sophisticated (absolute) productivity studies with controls as a single group, these exhibited a weighted average effect size of $r_{ave} = 0.06$. This group of five effect sizes yielded $Z = 2.00$, significant at a level of .05. Consistent results were also found for the unweighted average effect size. For labor productivity studies with controls taken as a group, the average effect size was also significant at the .05 level for both weighted and unweighted estimates.

22. Here, $\chi^2 = 106.14$, and $p < .005$ for the whole financial performance category. Return on sales estimates ($\chi^2 = 28.70$, and $p < .005$) and return on equity estimates ($\chi^2 = 41.83$, and $p < .005$) were also each heterogeneous when tested separately.

23. No significant differences were found between the various absolute financial performance measures. The unweighted average effect sizes for improvements in RoE ($r_{ave} = +0.39$), RoS ($r_{ave} = +0.29$), and RoA ($r_{ave} = +0.26$) were not significantly different from each other at a level of .10.

24. Again, looking only at the more sophisticated (absolute) financial performance studies with controls as a single group, these exhibited an average weighted effect size of $r_{ave} = +0.08$, significant at a level of $p = .014$. For this group, $Z = 2.47$. The unweighted average effect size was consistent with this.

25. This was also the case for performance improvements judged solely on the basis of return on equity. Privatized firms showed $r_{ave} = +0.39$ compared to nationalizations, $r_{ave} = +0.25$. Again this was not significant at .10. Consistent conclusions were again reached contrasting privatization and nationalization measurements for growth in return on equity and growth in value added.

26. For this contrast, return on sales data was adopted, providing nine effect sizes for privatization, and two for the no-reform category.

27. Several anecdotes of reductions in long-term research and development work were communicated to the author during the course of this analysis. One example of this was in a recently privatized electricity supply company in Australia where groups working in the area of electricity demand management were steadily disbanded, and the duties of these staff progressively changed to sales promotional positions. "The job is now to sell more electricity, not reduce demand" was the explanation offered by the staff member. Such evidence, although only anecdotal, indicates the need for careful analysis of research and development questions.

28. Consistent conclusions were reached here whether weighted and unweighted averages were adopted. All Z scores were high, with a strong degree of discrimination. This may have accurately reflected the data or may have been due to two alternative reasons. Firstly, assumptions made in deriving effect sizes from Moussios's work may have been questionable. (Effect size estimates could not be calculated directly from his work, which was based on auto regressive integrated moving average [ARIMA] transfer function techniques. Equivalent expressions were therefore derived for effect sizes as shown in Hodge 1996b.) Alternatively, it may be that the ARIMA technique itself has a high capacity to discriminate different associations.

29. For the investment behavior category, $\chi^2 = 301.2$ and $p < .005$ for the four effect size estimates.

30. The sample of four effect sizes for shareholder financial performance showed $\chi^2 = 27.30$, $p < .005$.

31. Looking at both the weighted and unweighted averages, both were negative, however neither was significant.

32. For these five estimates of economic growth, $\chi^2 = 10.43$, $p < .05$.

33. Readers should note that the judicious use of language, of course, can easily turn the tables towards one's own convictions here. The World Bank team found domestic consumers gaining in four cases, losing in five, and having no benefits in the remaining three. Strong supporters of privatization would therefore reword our summary. They would be quick to adopt a phrase such as "consumers lost in only a minority of cases" (i.e., five out of twelve). Whilst this statement is also technically correct, it is still clear that consumers were not major winners in the majority of cases. The promise of consumers winning from privatization was therefore not delivered, based on this analysis.

34. See Ernst (1993a), Yarrow (1989), Marsh (1991), Miller (1994).

35. Ernst (1993a).

36. See Caulkin (1986).

37. Beardwell and Holden (1997) cite the *Guardian* newspaper and present a few colorful examples of salary rises for senior executives that well illustrate the point. Cedric Brown at British Gas had an annual salary increase of 75 percent to £475,000 following privatization, as well as receiving £330,000 in share options. In December 1995, it emerged that he had also arranged for extra pension payments worth £2,000,000. The British Gas Pensioners' Christmas Party was cancelled to reduce company costs. David Moss, the Chief Executive Officer of the Southhampton Hospitals Trust had his pay doubled. Colin Webster of Powergen reaped, in one single day, a £250,000 share option profit for himself. The contrast is stark between the promised consumer benefits that largely failed to materialize and the "fat cats and cream" behavior of senior executives reported in the *Guardian*.

38. The unweighted average for service quality measurements was almost the same at $r_{ave} = +0.09$, and was again significant at .05.

39. For the six service quality measurement effect sizes, $\chi^2 = 64.04$, indicating heterogeneity at a significance level of .01.

40. The public accountability variable in Moussios's work reflected the status of public accountability during three periods. The first period was in each month during 1982 through April 1983, when BT published monthly quality of service indicators, and the second from April 1983 to September 1987, where "BT ceased the release of systematic information on quality, on the grounds of commercial sensitivity even though it remained state-owned and encountered no competitive threats." The third period was after September 1987, when BT resumed the monthly publication of quality service indicators "after extensive prodding by OFTEL that continues to this day" (Moussios 1994, p. 101).

41. The variable for regulatory intensity in Moussios's work measured the relative impact of price controls. Four time periods were included here. The first period analyzed was between 1982 and August 1984, when BT's pricing regime was established legislatively, and the second was from that point until July 1989, when price controls were set covering local and national calls. The third period was a subsequent term until end July 1991, when OFTEL moderately extended the range of services covered by the price controls. Lastly, the final period continued until 1993, during which OFTEL concluded a duopoly review and both the scope and stringency of price controls was extended.

42. The six effect sizes for employment yielded $\chi^2 = 23.14$, which was significant at the .01 level.

43. It is reasonable to consider that much of this improvement in financial performance accountability compared to past public administration practices is also achievable through corporatization and regulation processes—without a change in ownership.

44. World Bank Policy Research Report (1995).

45. McKay (1996).

46. Strong similarities have also been recently observed throughout privatization processes in Victoria, Australia, where the Administrative Appeals Tribunal, the office of the auditor general and other independent offices have all been attacked and weakened by the privatizing government.

47. Anonymous (1995).

48. See Marsh (1991).

49. Reserve Bank of Australia (1997).

50. Shallcrass (1993, p. 173), as cited in De Vries, O'Reilly, and Scoular (1998).

51. See De Vries, O'Reilly, and Scoular (1998).

52. Roarty, M. (1998).

53. No independent rigorous evaluation of the relative success of these arrangements has been undertaken to date.

54. Hendley (1992, p. 154).

CHAPTER TEN

1. The Australian Department of Defence is, for instance, up to the fifth edition of its market-testing Commercial Support Program (CSP) guidelines, these having been shaped by eight years of learning and development, decades of experience overseas and following reviews such as that of the National Audit Office. Likewise, there are several comprehensive sets of guidelines around, such as those for outsourcing issued by the Victorian gov-

ernment. These guidelines (Department of Treasury and Finance 1996), which amount to some 612 pages, detail around 470 steps in what surely must be regarded as the ultimate comprehensive and rational outsourcing process. Blissfully unaware of Simon's famous contributions to the concept of boundedness to rationality, the big question with these guidelines is not how close they are to rational perfection from the economist's perspective, but the extent these guidelines and the process prescribed is ever actually going to be used in practice given their size. Furthermore, a second relevant question arises from the fact that the guidelines appear to treat government as if it were the same as a McDonald's corporation or a retail store. Government may well be just like a business in the loose spin of political rhetoric, but it is doubtful even with the pressures of globalization whether we have yet reached a stage where most of the community genuinely believe that if only public sector services were somehow "McDonaldized" or "Nike'd" then government would be magically transformed for the better.

2. To some, the notion of competition as a panacea for all is currently being pursued with religious zeal. In 1994, Australia enacted legislation that required the Acts underpinning all government agency services to be reviewed. The principal objective of this review was to ensure that no public sector organization enjoyed advantages by virtue of its public ownership status. A requirement was on the review to prove that the benefits flowing from the agency's services could only be achieved through monopoly arrangement, and that the costs of this were not exceeded by the benefits. Many services have been opened up to competition. Australia has also witnessed a strong reaction from rural voters against the dominant idea of pursuing competition without question, however, following the rationalization of services from rural banks, the removal of government service delivery in many regional areas, and questionable rural service quality in telecommunications after the initial privatization of one-third of Telstra. Certainly, the rhetoric on competition has begun to change, with proclamations that "we will put competition policy under the microscope!" (Tim Fisher, Federal National Party leader, ABC 3LO Radio, September 19, 1998). The shape of new or alternative policy directions are not yet apparent.

3. Recall that, averaged over all available international measurements (most of which related to local government garbage collection, cleaning, and maintenance services), a mean cost saving of around 12 percent was found, but averaged over services (equally weighted) a mean of around 6 percent was found.

4. Not listed in the findings above was the strongest (and obvious) statistical observation continually found in studies between the amount of work done and the cost of that work.

5. Sources for cost savings were as follows: NSW Treasury (1993) reported a cost saving of 20 percent, CTC Consulting (1994) likewise found a cost saving of 20 percent, and Williamson (1998) reported a cost saving of 26 percent.

6. The standing of these cost-savings estimates is likely to have been increased by the Australian Industry Commission's comprehensive report on this subject as well (Industry Commission 1996).

7. In the case of the Defence Department's Commercial Support Program, it reported cost savings of "one-third," for instance. The Australian National Audit Office (1998, pp. 32–33), however, came to the conclusion that "the level of reported savings . . . has limited value as an indicator of performance" and although this CSP estimate may be a rough guide to overall costs, it "does not have sufficient verifiable support to be used as a benchmark."

8. One exception to this has been the Department of Treasury and Finance (1997) survey noted in Chapter 7, which reported the costs of managing outsourced contracts at between 1.6 and 11.3 percent, with an average of 1.9 percent.

9. Such criticisms include limited predictive and explanatory power, the looseness of the definition of "transaction cost," and the fact that the actual growth of large firms over the past century can be attributed mainly to the pursuit of market power and to the various mechanisms of government support. It suffers from the criticisms leveled at the key assumption of the self-interested individual, as well.

10. Interestingly, this figure of 29 percent from PA Consulting (1997) is identical to the proportion of IT activities presently outsourced in Australian public sector organizations.

11. See PA Consulting (1997, p. 9).

12. See ibid., p. 4.

13. It is also the need to somehow wrestle with the tension between rigid public sector tendering processes, in which a rock solid specification is developed, for instance, with the reality that the majority of complex outsourcing contracts may well need to be renegotiated partway through the contract period. Some 80 percent of companies that had outsourced IT activities for contract periods of five years apparently renegotiated their contracts after only one year, according to one recent report (Robertson 1998, p. 5).

14. Perhaps the most striking recent example of the potential for a "hollowed-out" government was given by a major central Victorian government department, who when asked by the auditor general to document the government's objectives for outsourcing, replied that it could not do this by the date requested, but that it would do so a few weeks later. "That job," the department explained, "has been outsourced, and we need to ring up the contractor to get them to document why we outsourced"!

15. Even the infamous light-handed (deregulated) approach to privatization demands a greater attention to regulation. Australia's Consumer and Competition Commission head, Professor Alan Fels, for instance states that "it's a paradox but the greater the degree of deregulation, the greater the need for regulation by competition law, otherwise you just replace a public monopoly with a private one." Mottram (1999, p. 2).

16. The case for care and caution is even stronger for developing countries pursuing a transition towards a stronger mixed economy, and recognizing the difficult balance required between local ownership versus overseas investment.

17. The speed at which both the media and the public can jump to conclusions (whether fair or not) as to the cause of such water-quality reductions is indicative of the sensitivity of the privatization issue and the sensitivity to the removal of such basic services.

18. Simon, H. A. (1997). Keynote Address presented to the American Society of Public Administration Annual Conference, Pittsburgh, July.

References

Abdala, M. A. 1992. Distributional Impact Evaluation of Divestiture in a High Inflation Economy: The Case of Entel Argentina, Ph.D. Thesis, Boston University.

Abelson, P. 1987a. Introduction. In *Privatization: An Australian Perspective*, edited by P. Abelson, pp. 1–9. Mosman, NSW: Australian Professional Publications.

_____. 1987b. Privatization: A Point of View. In *Privatization: An Australian Perspective*, edited by P. Abelson, pp. 294–316. Mosman, NSW: Australian Professional Publications.

Adam, C., Cavendish, W., and Mistry, P. 1992. *Adjusting Privatization: Case Studies from Developing Countries*. James Currey, London: Heinemann, N.H.

Adonis, A. 1992. Compulsive Competitive Tendering: The State of Play in British Local Government. University of Sydney, *CTC Newsletter* 2 (September), pp. 1–2.

Aggarwal, R., Leal, R., and Hernandez, L. 1993. The Aftermarket Performance of Initial Public Offerings in Latin America, *Financial Management* 22(1), Spring, pp. 42–53.

Aharoni. 1988. Why do Governments Privatize? *Technovation* 8(3), pp. 7–22.

Albin, S. 1992. Bureau Shaping and Contracting Out: The Case of Australian Local Government, Public Policy Discussion Paper 29, Australian National University, Canberra.

Alchian, A. 1965. Some Economies of Property Rights, *Il Politico* 30, pp. 816–829.

Alderfer, C. P. 1972. Existence, Relatedness, and Growth: Human Needs in Organisational Settings. New York: Free Press.

Ambrosio, J. 1992. PaineWebber Takes on New Outsourcing Role. *Computer World* 26(43), Oct. 26, p. 4.

ANAO. 1998. *Commercial Support Program: Department of Defence, Audit Report Number 2*. Australian National Audit Office: Canberra, pp. 32–33.

Anderson, I. M., and Tomenson, B. M. 1994. The Efficacy of Selective Re-Uptake Inhibitors in Depression: A Meta-Analysis of Studies Against Tricyclic AntiDepressants. *Journal of Psychopharmacology* 8(4), pp. 238–249.

Anderson, J. E. 1989. Government and the Economy: What is Fundamental? In *Fundamentals of the Economic Role of Government*, edited by W. J. Samuels, pp. 19–22. New York: Greenwood Press.

Anonymous. 1993. Outsourcing Can Cut Inefficiencies, Improve Planning. *Employee Benefit Plan Review* 48(2), August, pp. 52.

_____. 1995. Disgusted. *The Economist*. March 11, pp. 61–62.

Arbey, B. M. 1993. Privatization: A Process of Economic Transformation in Modern Economies. M.A. dissertation, Florida Atlantic University.

Ascher, K. 1987. The Politics of Privatization: Contracting Out Public Services. New York: St. Martin's Press.

Ashton, T. 1998. Contracting for Health Services in New Zealand: A Transaction Cost Analysis. *Social Science Medicine* 46(3), pp. 357–367.

Auditor General of Victoria. 1998. Report on Ministerial Portfolios, May. Melbourne.

Australian National Audit Office. 1998. Performance Audit Commercial Support Program, Audit Report No. 2. Department of Defence, Australian National Audit Office, Canberra.

Avishur, A. 1994. The Effect of the Privatization of British Telecom on Efficiency: A Dual Approach. Ph.D. Thesis, University of Chicago.

Badelow, C. 1998. Discussion in *Commercial Support Program Benchmarking Seminar*. Canberra, September 29–30.

Baer, T. 1991. Hidden Costs Can Undermine Savings from Outsourcing. *Computer World*. November 18, p. 109.

Bails, D. 1979. Provision of Transportation Services, *Public Choice* 34(1), pp. 65–68.

Baquet, D., and Gottlieb, M. 1991. Without Competing Bids, New York Pays the Price, The Contract Game: How New York Loses. *New York Times*. February 19, pp. A1, B4.

Barnekov, T. K., and Raffell, J. A. 1990. Public Management of Privatization. *Public Productivity and Management Review*. 14(2), Winter, pp. 135–152.

Basu, P. K. 1994. Demystifying Privatization in Developing Countries. *International Journal of Public Sector Management* 7(3), pp. 44–55.

Beardwell, I., and Holden, L. 1997. *Human Resource Management: A Contemporary Perspective*. London: Pitman Publishing.

Beauris, V. 1993. Probity and Pitfalls: Tendering and Purchasing Case Studies. In *Doing More with Less: Contracting Out and Efficiency in the Public Sector*, edited by Jane Coulter, pp. 5–10. Kensington, NSW: Public Sector Research Centre.

Becker, E. R., and Sloan, F. A. 1985. Hospital Ownership and Performance. *Economic Inquiry* 23(1) (January), pp. 21–37.

Bendick, M. 1989. Privatizing the Delivery of Social Services: An Idea to be Taken Seriously. In *Privatization and the Welfare State*, edited by S. B. Kamerman and A. J. Kahn, pp. 97–120. Princeton, N.J.: Princeton University Press.

Bennett, J. T., and Johnson, M. H. 1979. Public Versus Private Provision of Collective Goods and Services: Garbage Collection Revisited. *Public Choice* 34, pp. 55–63.

Berenyi, E. 1981. Contracting Out Refuse Collection, The Nature and Impact of Change. *Urban Interest* 3 (Spring), pp. 30–42.

Berenyi, E. B., and Stevens, B. 1988. Does Privatization Work? A Study of the Delivery of Eight Local Services. *State and Local Government Review* 20, pp. 11–20.

Berglund, D. D. 1992. Job Corps and the Public-Private Debate. Ph.D. Thesis, Virginia Polytechnic Institute and State University.

Bhaskar, V., and Khan, M. 1995. Privatization and Employment: A Study of the Jute Industry in Bangladesh. *American Economic Review* 85(1)(March), pp. 267–273.

Bice, K., and Salmons, R. 1995. Price Rigging Fines Not Set in Concrete. *Australian Financial Review* December 5, p. 1.

Biggs, B. L., Kralewski, J., and Brown, G. 1980. A Comparison of Contract Managed and Traditionally Managed Nonprofit Hospitals. *Medical Care* 18, pp. 585–596.

Bishop, M., and Kay, J. 1989a. Privatization in the United Kingdom: Lessons from Experience. *World Development* 17(5), pp. 643–657.

_____. 1989b. Does Privatization Work? Lessons from the U.K. London: London Business School.

_____. 1992. Privatization in Western Economies. In *A Symposium in Honour of Herbert Giersch*, edited by Horst Siebert, pp. 193–209. Tubingen Mohr: Institut fur Weltwirtschaft an der Universitat Kiel.

Bishop, M., Kay, J., and Mayer, C. 1994. *Privatization and Economic Performance*. Oxford: Oxford University Press.

_____. 1995. *The Regulatory Challenge*. Oxford: Oxford University Press.

Bishop, M., and Thompson, D. 1992. Regulatory Reform and Productivity Growth in the UK's Public Utilities. *Applied Economics* 24(11), pp. 1180–1190.

Boardman, A., and Vining, A. 1988. The Behaviour of Mixed Enterprises. Working paper, University of British Columbia, Faculty of Commerce and Business Administration.

Borcherding, T. E., Pommerehne, W. W., and Schneider, F. 1982. Comparing the Efficiency of Public and Private Production: The Evidence from Five Countries. *Journal of Economics* (Zietschrift fur Nationalokonomie), Supplement 2, pp. 127–156. New York: Springer-Verlag/Wien.

Boston, J. 1988. From Corporatisation to Privatization: Public Sector Reform in New Zealand. *Canberra Bulletin of Public Administration* 57 (December), pp. 71–86.

_____. 1991. The Theoretical Underpinnings of Public Sector Restructuring in New Zealand. In *Reshaping the State: New Zealand's Bureaucratic Revolution,* edited by J. Boston, J. Martin, J. Pallot, and P. Walsh, pp. 1–26. Auckland, NZ: Oxford University Press.

Boyd, B. K. 1991. Strategic Planning and Financial Analysis: A Meta-Analytic Review. *Journal of Management Studies* 28(4)(July), pp. 353–374.

Browne, A., and Wildavsky, A. 1984. Should Evaluation become Implementation? In *Implementation,* edited by J. Pressman and A. Wildavsky. 2nd Ed. Berkeley: University of California Press.

Buck, D., and Chaundy, D. 1992. Competitive Tendering and Refuse Collection Revisited. Paper in preparation for Fiscal Studies.

Burnett, M. 1984. Privatization: The Wandsworth Experience. *Accountancy* 95 (1087) (March), pp. 143–144.

Capon, N., Farley, J. U., and Hoenig, S. 1990. Determinants of Financial Performance: A Meta-Analysis. *Management Science* 36(10) (October), pp. 1,143–1,159.

Carnaghan, R., and Bracewell–Milnes, B. 1993. Testing the Market: Competitive Tendering for Government Services in Britain and Abroad. London: Institute of Economic Affairs.

Carney, S. 1993. Asset Sales Not the Key Issue: Stockdale. *The Age.* August 9, p. 3.

Carver, R. H. 1989. Examining the Premises of Contracting Out. *Public Productivity and Management Review* 8(1), pp. 27–40.

Caulkin, S. 1986. BCAL's Blues. *Management Today* (November), pp. 46–53.

Centre for Public Services. 1995a. Corruption Increases with Spread of CCT. *Public Service Action* 49/50.

_____. 1995b. Calculation of the National Costs and Savings of CCT. Research Paper, Supplement to *The Gender Impact of CCT In Local Government,* Equal Opportunities Commission, United Kingdom, March.

Chandler, T. D. 1994. Sanitation Privatization and Sanitation Employees' Wages. *Journal of Labour Research* 15(2) (Spring), pp. 137–153.

Chandler, T., and Feuille, P. 1991. Municipal Unions and Privatization. *Public Administration Review* 51 (Jan/Feb), pp. 15–22.

Chapman, C. 1990. Selling the Family Silver: Has Privatization Worked? London: Hutchison Business Books-Random Century.

Chi, K. S. 1989. Prison Overcrowding and Privatization: Models and Opportunities. *Journal of State Government* 62(2), pp. 70–76.

Chin, O., and Webb, G. 1987. Privatization: A View from the Private Sector. In *Privatization: An Australian Perspective*, edited by P. Abelson. Sydney: Australian Professional Publications.

Chittendon, M. 1996. Rail Fraud Inquiry Halts First Sell-Off. *The Sunday Times* (London), February 4.

Coase, R. 1937. The Nature of the Firm, *Economica N.S.* 4, pp. 386–405.

Coghill, K. 1997. Personal Communication, Melbourne.

Cogno, L., and Hill, S. 1996. Builder Calls for Overhaul of Tender Costs. *The Australian.* July 31, p. 28.

Colebatch, H., and Larmour, P. 1993. *Market, Bureaucracy and Community.* London: Pluto Press.

Commonwealth Ombudsman. 1997. Annual Report 1996–97. Canberra.

Confederation of British Industry. 1988. The Competitive Advantage. Report to the CBI Public Expenditure Task Force, London.

Considine, M. 1988. The Corporate Management Framework as Administrative Science: A Critique. *Australian Journal of Public Administration* 47(1) (March), pp. 4–18.

_____. 1990. Managerialism Strikes Out. *Australian Journal of Public Administration* 49(2) (June), pp. 166–178.

Cook, T. D., Cooper, H., Cordray, D. S., Hartmann, H., Hedges, L. V., Light, R. J., Louis, T. A., and Mosteller, F. 1992. Meta-Analysis for Explanation: A Case Book. New York: The Russell Sage Foundation.

Cooper, H. M. 1984. *The Integrative Research Review: A Systematic Approach.* Applied Social Research Methods Series, vol. 2. Beverly Hills, Calif.: Sage Publications.

_____. 1989a. *Integrating Research: A Guide for Literature Reviews,* 2d Ed. Applied Social Research Methods Series, vol. 2. Newbury Park, Calif.: Sage Publications.

_____. 1989b. *Homework.* New York: Longman.

Cooper, H. M., and Rosenthal, R. 1980. Statistical versus Traditional Procedures for Summarising Research Findings. *Psychological Bulletin* 87, pp. 442–449.

Corbett, D. 1992. Australian Public Management. St Leonards, NSW: Allen and Unwin.

Crouch, G. I. 1992. Marketing International Tourism: A Meta-Analytic Study of Demand. Ph.D. Thesis, Monash University.

Cubbin, J., Domberger, S., and Meadowcroft, S. 1987. Competitive Tendering and Refuse Collection: Identifying the Sources of Efficiency Gains. *Fiscal Studies* 8(3) (August), pp. 49–58.

CTC Consulting 1994. *Competitive Tendering and Contracting in the West Australian Public Sector.* Sydney: University of Sydney.

Davidson, K. 1996a. Auditor Qualifies United Energy's Pre-Sale Accounts. *The Age,* 18 May, pp. 1, A4.

_____. 1996b. Auditing the Truth on Accountability. *The Age.* 30 May, p. A17.

Davies, D. G. 1981. Property Rights and Economic Behaviour in Private and Government Enterprises: The Case of Australia's Banking System. *Research in Law and Economics* 3, pp. 111–142.

Davis, G., Wanna, J., Warhurst, J., and Weller, P. 1993. Public Policy in Australia, 2d Ed. Sydney: Allen & Unwin Pty Ltd.

De Alessi, L. 1980. The Economics of Property Rights: A Review of the Evidence. *Research in Law and Economics* 2, pp. 1–47.

_____. 1987. Property Rights and Privatization. In Prospects for Privatization, edited by S. H. Hanke. New York: Academy of Political Science, pp. 24–35.

DeHoog, R. 1990. Human Services Contracting: Environmental, Behavioural and Organisational Conditions. *Administration and Society* 16 (February), pp. 427–454.

Deloitte and Touche Consulting Group 1997. *Information Technology Outsourcing Survey: A Comprehensive Analysis of IT Outsourcing in Australia*, Version 3.1, November.

Demsetz, H. 1967. Toward a Theory of Property Rights. *American Economic Review* 57, pp. 347–359.

Department of Administrative Services. 1995. Submission to the Industry Commission Inquiry into Competitive Tendering and Contracting by Public Sector Agencies 1995, April, Australia.

Department of Treasury and Finance. 1995. *Government Business Enterprises Reform in Victoria: A Guide to the First Three Years October 1992–September 1995*. Privatizations and Industry Reform Division, Department of Treasury and Finance, State Government of Victoria, December.

_____. 1996. *Outsourcing and Contract Management Guidelines*, Outsourcing and Contract Management Unit, Melbourne, February.

_____. 1997. *Victorian Outsourcing Activity Survey: 1995–96*. Outsourcing and Contract Management Unit, Melbourne, December.

DeVries, K., O'Reilly, C., and Scoular, R. 1998. The New Zealand Privatization Experience. Internal Report, Monash Mt. Eliza School of Business and Government, Melbourne, November.

Dinavo, J. V. 1995. Privatization in Developing Countries: Its Impact on Economic Development and Democracy. Westport, Conn.: Praeger Publishing.

Dixon, R. B. 1991. Privatization and Local Government. In *The Future of the Public Sector*, edited by E. W. Russell, pp. 80–97. Melbourne: Public Sector Management Institute.

_____. 1992. Reducing Service Delivery Costs Through Public/Private Partnerships. *Government Finance Review* 8(3), pp. 31–33.

Doherty, E. 1989. Alternative Delivery of Services in Rochester, New York. In *Public Sector Privatisation: Alternative Approaches to Service Delivery*, edited by E. Finley, pp. 25–34. New York: Quorum Books.

Domberger, S. 1993. Privatization: What Does the British Experience Reveal? *Economic Papers* 12(2), pp. 58–68.

_____. 1994. Public Sector Contracting: Does It Work? *The Australian Economic Review*, 3rd qtr., pp. 91–96.

Domberger, S., and Rimmer, S. 1994. Competitive Tendering and Contracting Out in the Public Sector: A Survey. *International Journal of the Economics of Business* 1(3), pp. 439–453.

Domberger, S., Hall, C., and Li, E. 1994. The Determinants of Quality in Competitively Tendered Contracts. Working Paper Series, Graduate School of Business, University of Sydney.

_____. 1995. Competitive Tendering and Contracting in the NSW Public Sector: The 1995 Survey Findings, Graduate School of Business, University of Sydney, September.

Domberger, S., Meadowcroft, S. A. and Thompson, D. J. 1986. Competitive Tendering and Efficiency: The Case of Refuse Collection. *Fiscal Studies* 7(4) November, pp. 69–87.

_____. 1987. The Impact of Competitive Tendering on the Costs of Hospital Domestic Services. *Fiscal Studies* 8(4), pp. 39–54.

_____. 1988. Competition and Efficiency in Refuse Collection: A Reply. *Fiscal Studies* 9(1), pp. 80–90.

Domberger, S., Farago, S., Hall, C., and Li, E. 1993. Competitive Tendering and Contracting in the NSW Public Sector: The 1993 Survey Findings. Graduate School of Business, University of Sydney, December.

Donahue, J. D. 1989. *The Privatization Decision: Public Ends, Private Means.* New York: Basic Books.

Douglas, M. 1994. New Zealand Paths to Competitive Tendering: The Dunedin City Council Case Studies. Address to a Seminar on Competitive Tendering in Local Government, 29–30 June, Australia.

Douglas, R. 1994. Privatization: Lessons from New Zealand. In *Does Privatization Deliver? Highlights from a World Bank Conference,* edited by Ahmed Galal and Mary Shirley, pp. 19–23. Washington, D.C.: EDI Development Studies, World Bank.

Drucker, P. 1969. *The Age of Discontinuity: Guidelines to Our Changing Society.* London: Heinemann.

Duncan, I., and Bollard, A. 1992. *Corporatisation and Privatization.* Auckland, NZ: Oxford University Press.

Dunleavy, P. 1986. Explaining the Privatization Boom: Public Choice Versus Radical Approaches. *Public Administration* 64 (Spring), pp. 13–34.

Dunsire, A. 1991. Organisational Status Change and Performance: The Significance of Internal Structure. In *Privatization and Economic Efficiency: A Comparative Analysis of Developed and Developing Countries,* edited by Attiat F. Ott and Keith Hartley, pp. 126–160. Aldershot, England: Edward Elgar.

Dunsire, A., Hartley, K., and Parker, D. 1991. Organisational Status and Performance: Summary of the Findings. *Public Administration* 69 (Spring), pp. 21–40.

Dunsire, A., Hartley, K., Parker, D., and Dimitriou, B. 1988. Organisational Status and Performance: A Conceptual Framework for Testing Public Choice Theories. *Public Administration* 66(4) (Winter), pp. 363–388.

Ecodata Inc. 1984. *Delivering Municipal Services Efficiently: A Comparison of Municipal and Private Service Delivery.* Technical Report. Washington, D.C.: U.S. Department of Housing and Urban Development, Office of Policy Development and Research, June.

Edwards, B., and Moch, A. 1992. From Water to Public Works: One City's Privatization Success Story. *American City and County* 107(2), pp. 38–39.

Edwards, F. R., and Stevens, B. J. 1978. The Provision of Municipal Sanitation Services by Private Firms: An Empirical Analysis of the Efficiency of Alternative Market Structures and Regulatory Arrangements. *Journal of Industrial Economics* 27 (December), pp. 133–147.

Emy, H. V., and Hughes, O. E. 1988. *Australian Politics: Realities in Conflict.* South Melbourne: Macmillan.

Engen, J. R. 1994. Knowing Better. *World Trade* 7(2), pp. 42–46.

Ernst, J. 1991. The British Experiment in Privatizing Essential Services. *Policy Issues Forum* (November) pp. 11–16.

_____. 1992. Whose Utility? The Social Impact of Public Utility Privatization and Regulation in Britain. Ph.D. Thesis, University of York.

_____. 1993a. The Seven Deadly Myths of Public Utility Privatization. Public Presentation, Melbourne, March.

_____. 1993b. Public Utility Regulation in Britain and Its Relevance to Australia. Consumer Law Centre of Victoria Forum, Melbourne.

_____. 1994a. *Whose Utility? The Social Impact of Public Utility Privatization and Regulation in Britain.* Public Policy and Management Series. Buckingham: Open University Press.

_____. 1994b. Privatization, Competition and Contracts. In *The Contract State*, edited by John Alford and Deidre O'Neill, pp. 101–135. Deakin Series in Public Policy and Administration no. 6. Geelong, Victoria: Centre for Applied Social Research.

_____. 1995. The Impact of Compulsory Tendering on Government Business. Presentation to the Annual State Conference of the Royal Institute of Public Administration Australia, Victorian Division.

_____. 1998. Privatization. In *International Encyclopedia of Public Policy and Administration*, edited by Jay M. Shafritz, pp. 1,741–1,745. Boulder, Colo.: Westview Press.

Escott, K., and Whitfield, D. 1995. The Gender Impact of CCT in Local Government. UK Equal Opportunities Commission, Research Discussion Paper no. 12.

Evatt Research Centre. 1990. *Breach of Contract: Privatization and the Management of Australian Local Government.* Sydney: Evatt Foundation, Pluto Press.

Farago, S., and Domberger, S. 1994. Competitive Tendering and Contracting in NSW Government Trading Enterprises: A Survey. Working Paper Series, Number 2-94. Graduate School of Business, University of Sydney, February.

Farago, S., Hall, C., and Domberger, S. 1994. Contracting of Services in the Western Australian Public Sector. Graduate School of Business, University of Sydney, CTC Research Paper.

Feldman, T. R. 1987. Efficiency and the Provision of Municipal Services. Ph.D. dissertation, Harvard University.

Fels, A., and Xavier, P. 1990. Corporate Power with Public Purpose: Monitoring the GBE's. In *Telecommunications Law: Australian Perspectives*, edited by Mark Armstrong, pp. 310–334. Melbourne: Media Arm Pty Ltd.

Ferris, J. M. 1988. The Public Spending and Employment Effects of Local Service Contracting. *National Tax Journal* 41(2), pp. 209–217.

Ferris, J., and Graddy, E. 1986. Contracting Out: For What? With Whom? *Public Administration Review* 46(4) (July/August), pp. 332–344.

Field, N. 1995. Watchdog Strains at the Leash. *Australian Financial Review*. December 5, p. 8.

Finder, A. 1993. Dangerous Parking: New York's Biggest Scandal of 1980s Bubbles Up to Embarrass Inspectors. *New York Times* April 11, p. 25.

Fisher, R. A. 1932. *Statistical Methods for Research Workers.* 4th Ed. London: Oliver and Boyd.

Florestano, P. S., and Gordon, S. B. 1980. Public vs. Private: Small Government Contracting with the Private Sector. *Public Administration Review* 40(1) (January/February), pp. 29–34.

Folz, D. H. 1985. Municipal Productivity and Service Quality: A Regression-Based Fiscal Analysis. Ph.D. Thesis, University of Tennessee.

Foster, C. D. 1992. *Privatization, Public Ownership and the Regulation of Natural Monopoly.* Oxford: Blackwell Publishers.

Freund, D. 1988. Has Public Sector Contracting with Health Maintenance Organisations in the United States Saved Money? In *Economics and Health 1988,* Proceedings of the 10th Australian Conference of Health Economists, edited by Chris Selby-Smith. Melbourne: Public Sector Management Institute, Monash University.

Frydman, R., and Rapaczynski, A. 1993. Privatization in Eastern Europe: Is the State Withering Away? *Finance and Development* (June), pp. 10–13.

Fryklund, I. 1994. Privatization: American Style. *Business Forum* 19(1/2) (Winter/Spring), pp. 4–8.

Furubotn, E. G., and Pejovich, S. 1972. Property Rights and Economic Theory: A Survey of Recent Literature. *Journal of Economic Literature* 10, pp. 1,137–1,162.

_____. 1974. *The Economics of Property Rights.* Cambridge, Mass.: Ballinger.

Galal, A., Jones, L., Tandon, P., and Vogelsang, I. 1994. *Welfare Consequences of Selling Enterprises: An Empirical Analysis.* International Bank for Reconstruction and Development, The World Bank. Oxford: Oxford University Press.

Gewirtz, N. 1987. Testing the Promise of Private Contracting: An Evaluation and Policy Analysis of Public and Private Social Services for Pregnant and Parenting Teenagers. Ph.D. Thesis, University of Connecticut.

Gilmour R. S., and Jensen, L. S. 1998. Reinventing Government Accountability: Public Functions, Privatization, and the Meaning of "State Action." *Public Administration Review* 58(3) (May/June), pp. 247–258.

Glass, G. 1976. Integrating Findings: The Meta-Analysis of Research. *Educational Researcher* 5(10), pp. 3–8.

Glass, G. V., and Smith, M. L. 1979. Meta-Analysis of Research on the Relationship of Class Size and Achievement. *Evaluation and Policy Analysis* 1, pp. 2–16.

Glass, G. V., McGaw, B., and Smith, M. L. 1981. *Meta-Analysis in Social Research.* PLACE: Sage Publications Inc.

Gormley, W. T. 1989. Book Review of Savas 1987. *Policy Analysis and Management* 8(1), pp. 354–356.

Green, R., and Vogelsang, I. 1994. British Airways: A Turnaround Anticipating Privatization. In *Privatization and Economic Performance,* edited by M. Bishop, J. Kay, and C. Mayer, pp. 89–111. Oxford: Oxford University Press.

Greene, J. D. 1994. Does Privatization Make a Difference? The Impact of Private Contracting on Municipal Efficiency. *International Journal of Public Administration* 17(7) (August), pp. 1,299–1,325.

Hall, J., and Rosenthal, R. 1991. Testing for Moderator Variables in Meta-Analysis: Issues and Methods. *Communication Monographs* 58 (December), pp. 437–448.

Hall, T. 1994. Politics Stalls More Asset Sales. *Asiamoney* 5(3) (April), pp. 39–40.

Halper, M. 1993. Outsourcers: Saviours or Charlatans? *Computer World* 27(31) (August 2), p. 63.

Hanke, S. H. 1987. Privatization in the Developing World: Introduction. In *Privatization and Development,* edited by S. H. Hanke, pp. 3–5. International Center for Economic Growth, Institute for Contemporary Studies, California.

Harding, R. W. 1990. Contracting Out the Bussing of School Children: An Industrial Organisation Analysis. Ph.D. Thesis, University of California, Los Angeles.

Hartley, K., and Huby, M. 1986. Contracting Out Policy: Theory and Evidence. In *Privatization and Regulation: The UK Experience,* edited by J. Kay, C. Mayer, and D. Thompson, pp. 284–296. Oxford: Clarendon.

Hartley, K., and Parker, D. 1991. Privatization: A Conceptual Framework. In *Privatization and Economic Efficiency: A Comparative Analysis of Developed and Developing Countries,* edited by Attiat F. Ott and Keith Hartley, pp. 11–25. Aldershot, England: Edward Elgar.

Hartley, K., Parker, D., and Martin, S. 1991. Organisational Status Ownership and Productivity. *Fiscal Studies* 12(2) (May), pp. 46–60.

Haskel, J., and Szymanski, S. 1992. Privatization and the Labour Market: Facts, Theory and Evidence. In *Privatization and Regulation: The UK Experience,* edited by M. Bishop, J. Kay, C. Mayer, and D. Thompson, pp. 336–351.

Hatry, H. P., Brounstein, P. J., and Levinson, R. B. 1993. Comparison of Privately and Publicly Operated Correctional Institutions. In *Privatizing Correctional Institutions,* Edited by G. Bowman, S. Hakim, and P. Seidenstat, pp. 193–212. New Brunswick, N.J.: Transaction Publishers.

Hax, H. 1992. Privatization Agencies: The Treuhand Approach. In *Privatization: A Symposium in Honour of Herbert Giersch,* edited by H. Siebert, pp. 143–155. Tubingen Mohr: Institut fur Weltwirtschaft an der Universitat Kiel.

Heald, D. 1984. Privatization: Analysing its Appeal and Limitations. *Fiscal Studies* 5(1), pp. 98–105.

———. A Financial Autopsy on the CEGB. *Energy Policy* 17(4) (August), pp. 337–350.

Hedges, L. V., and Olkin, I. 1985. *Statistical Methods for Meta-Analysis.* Orlando, Fla.: Academic Press.

Hendley, K. 1992. Legal Development and Privatization in Russia: A Case Study. *Soviet Economy* 8 (April/June), pp. 130–157.

Hensher, D. 1987. Productive Efficiency, Ownership and Contracting Out of Transport Services. In *Privatization: An Australian Perspective,* edited by P. Abelson, pp. 154–167. Mosman, NSW: Australian Professional Publications.

———. 1989. Competitive Tendering in the Transportation Sector. *Economic Papers* 8(1) (March), pp. 1–11.

Herzberg, F. 1966. Work and the Nature of Man. Cleveland, Oh.: World.

Hirsch, W. Z. 1965. Cost Functions of an Urban Government Service: Refuse Collection. *The Review of Economics and Statistics* 47 (February), pp. 87–92.

———. 1991. *Privatizing Government Services: An Economic Analysis of Contracting Out by Local Governments.* Institute of Industrial Relations, University of California, Los Angeles.

Hodge, G. A. 1993a. *Minding Everybody's Business: Performance Management in Public Sector Agencies.* Public Sector Management Institute, Monash University.

———. 1993b. Measuring the Effectiveness of Privatization and Contracting Out. Presentation to the RIPPA/PSMI Seminar, Privatization/Contracting Out—Passing Fad or Permanent Reform? Melbourne, September 22.

———. 1996. *Contracting Out Government Services: A Review of International Evidence.* Melbourne: Montech Pty. Ltd.

———. 1997. Contracting Out: Just Another Fad or Fundamental Reform? *Journal of Economic and Social Policy* 2(1), pp. 54–65.

Holcombe, R. G. 1990. The Tax Cost of Privatization. *Southern Economic Journal* 56(3), pp. 732–742.

———. 1991. Privatization of Municipal Wastewater Treatment. *Public Budgeting and Finance* 11(3), pp. 28–42.

Holmes, P. A. 1985. Taking Public Services Private: A Growing Trend Cuts Government Costs. *Nation's Business* 73(8), pp. 18–24.

Howard 1998. *The Canadian Alternative Service Delivery Program*, Presentation to the Commercial Support Program Benchmarking Seminar, September 29–30, 1998, Canberra.

Hubbard, G. 1993. How to Make that Tough Outsourcing Decision Work for You. *Facilities Design and Management* 12(7) (July), pp. 46–49.

Hughes, O. 1992. Public Management or Public Administration? *Australian Journal of Public Administration* 51(3) (September), pp. 286–296.

———. 1994. *Public Management and Administration: An Introduction.* New York: St. Martin's Press.

Hunter, J. E., and Schmidt, F. L. 1990. *Methods of Meta-Analysis: Correcting Error and Bias in Research Findings.* Newbury Park, Calif.: Sage Publications.

Hunter, J. E., Schmidt, F. L. and Jackson, G. B. 1982. *Meta-Analysis: Cumulating Findings Across Research.* Beverly Hills, Calif.: Sage.

Hutchinson, B. 1994. Free At Last. *Canadian Business* 67(11) (November), pp. 21–28.

Hutchinson, G. A. 1991. Efficiency Gains Through Privatization of UK Industries. In *Privatization and Economic Efficiency: A Comparative Analysis of Developed and Developing Countries,* edited by Attiat F. Ott and Keith Hartley, pp. 87–107. Aldershot, England: Edward Elgar.

Hyndman, R. 1996. Personal Communication. Monash University, Clayton. May.

Industry Commission. 1995. Competitive Tendering and Contracting by Public Sector Agencies. Draft Report. Australia, 24 October.

Industry Commission. 1996. Competitive Tendering and Contracting by Public Sector Agencies. Australia. January.

Inotai, A. 1992. Experience with Privatization in East Central Europe. In *Privatization: A Symposium in Honour of Herbert Giersch,* edited by Horst Siebert, pp. 163–182. Tubingen Mohr: Institut fur Weltwirtschaft an der Universitat Kiel.

Jackson, G. B. 1978. Methods for Reviewing and Integrating Research in the Social Sciences. Final Report to the National Science Foundation for Grant No. DIS 76-20309. Washington, D.C.: Social Research Group, George Washington University, April.

Jenkinson, T., and Mayer, C. 1994. The Costs of Privatization in the UK and France. In *Privatization and Economic Performance,* edited by M. Bishop, J. Kay, and C. Mayer, pp. 290–298. Oxford: Oxford University Press.

Jensen, P., and Fernandez, P. 1994. Competitive Tendering and Contracting—Cultural Change. CTC Research Paper, Graduate School of Business, University of Sydney.

Jensen, R. 1990. Privatization Issues: Experience in Phoenix, Arizona. 46th Conference of Local Government Engineering, Melbourne, 19–20 February.

Johnson, B. T., Mullen, B., and Salas, E. 1995. Comparison of Three Major Meta-Analytic Approaches. *Journal of Applied Psychology* 80(1), pp. 94–106.

Johnson, M. 1994. Water Privatization in the UK and the Effects on Consumers. Public Sector Report. Newsletter of the Public Sector Research Centre, University of NSW.

Jones, M. 1993. Local Authority Contracting Out: A Review of World Experience. Memo. February, pp. 41–47.

Juneau, L. 1992. Maxus' Miracle of a Deal. *Network World* 9(7) February 17, p. 35.

Kay, J. 1985. Who Benefits From Privatization? The City-Association Lecture, November. London: Certified Accountants Educational Trust and the City of London Polytechnic. Cited in Davis et al. 1993, p. 120.

Kay, J. A., and Thompson, D. J. 1986. Privatization: A Policy in Search of a Rationale. *The Economic Journal* 96 (March), pp. 18–32.

Kelsey, J. 1993. *Rolling Back the State: Privatization of Power in Aotearoa/New Zealand.* Wellington, NZ: Bridget Williams Books Limited.

Kemper, P., and Quigley, J. M. 1976. *The Economics of Refuse Collection.* Cambridge, Mass.: Ballinger Publishing Co.

Kerin, J. 1996. Judge Rejects Brown Secrecy on Water Poll. *The Australian.* June 12, p. 8.

Kettl, D. F. 1988. Performance and Accountability: The Challenge of Government by Proxy for Public Administration. *American Review of Public Administration* 18(1), pp. 9–28.

Kikeri, S., Nellis, J., and Shirley, M. 1992. *Privatization: The Lessons of Experience.* Washington, D.C.: The World Bank.

Kitchen, H. M. 1976. A Statistical Estimation of an Operating Cost Function for Municipal Refuse Collection. *Public Finance Quarterly* 4(1) (January), pp. 56–76.

Knipe, D. 1993. Corporatisation of Melbourne Water. International Public Sector Workshop, Monash University, Geelong, July 12–22.

Kobrak, P. 1995. Privatization and Cozy Politics: Can We Have One Without the Other? Paper presented to the 56th Annual Conference of the American Society for Public Administration, Texas. July 22–26.

Kostro, C. 1994. The Road to Cheaper Services. *American City and County* 109(9), pp. 16.

Kotz, S., and Johnson, N. L. 1985. *Encyclopedia of Statistical Sciences,* vol. 6. New York: Wiley.

Kramer, R., and Terrell, P. 1984. *Social Services Contracting in the Bay Area.* Berkeley Calif.: Institute of Governmental Studies, University of California.

Kunda, A. 1994. Web of Intrigue Over WCCM Privatization. *African Business* 194 (December), p. 23.

Lane, R. 1991. *The Market Experience.* Cambridge: Cambridge University Press.

Leeds, R. S. 1991. Privatization Through Public Offerings: Lessons from Two Jamaican Cases. In *Privatization and Control of State-Owned Enterprises,* edited by R. Ramamurti and R. Vernon, pp. 86–125. Washington, D.C.: World Bank.

Leiberman, I. W. 1993. Privatization the Theme of the 1990s: An Overview. *The Columbia Journal of World Business* (Spring), pp. 8–17.

Lensing, W. C. 1994. A Case Study of Social Transformation in Medical Care at the Community Level. Ph.D. Thesis, University of North Texas.

Letwin, O. 1988. *Privatizing the World: A Study of International Privatization in Theory and Practice.* International Privatization Unit, N. M. Rothschild & Sons Ltd. London: Cassell Educational Ltd.

LGIU (Local Government Information Unit). 1994. CCT On the Record: A Review of Experience of Compulsory Competitive Tendering Under the Local Government Act 1988. London: LGIU London.

Liberal and National Parties. 1996. Privatization: In The Public Interest and For The Public Benefit. Liberal and National Parties' Policy, Melbourne.

Loh, L., and Venkatraman, N. 1992. Determinants of Information Technology Outsourcing: A Cross Sectional Analysis. *Journal of Management Information Systems* 9(1), pp. 7–24.

Lorch, K. 1991. Privatization Through Private Sale: The Bangladeshi Textile Industry. In *Privatization and Control of State-Owned Enterprises,* edited by R. Ramamurti and R. Vernon, pp. 126–151. Washington, D.C.: World Bank.

Luders, R. J. 1993. The Success and Failure of State Owned Enterprise Divestitures in a Developing Country: The Case of Chile. *The Columbia Journal of World Business* 28(1) (Spring), pp. 98–121.

Majone, G., and Wildavsky, A. 1978. Implementation as Evolution. In *Policy Studies Review Annual*, edited by H. Freeman Beverly Hills, Calif.: Sage. Reprinted in *Implementation*, edited by J. Pressman and A. Wildavsky. 2nd Ed. Berkeley: University of California Press.

Malka, S. 1990. Contracting for Human Services: The Case of Pennsylvania's Subsidized Child Day Care Program—Policy Implications and Prospects. *Administration in Social Work* 14(1), pp. 31–46.

Mangan, T., and Carlini, J. 1991. Is Outsourcing a Savvy Move for Users? *Network World* 8(30) July 29, p. 29.

Marsh, D. 1991. Privatization Under Mrs Thatcher: A Review of the Literature. *Public Administration* 69, pp. 459–480.

Martin, D. L., and Stein, R. M. 1993. An Empirical Analysis of Contracting Out Local Government Services. In *Privatizing the United States Justice System: Police, Adjudication, and Corrections Services from the Private Sector*, edited by G. Bowman, S. Hakim, and P. Seidenstat, pp. 82–106. Jefferson, N.C.: McFarland & Co.

Mascarenhas, R. C. 1991. State-Owned Enterprises. In *Reshaping the State: New Zealand's Bureaucratic Revolution*, edited by J. Boston, J. Martin, J. Pallot, P. and Walsh, pp. 27–54. Auckland, NZ: Oxford University Press.

Maslow, A. H. 1954. *Motivation and Personality*. New York: Harper and Row.

Mason, J. 1991. Europe's Privatization Party. *International Management* (December), pp. 30–33.

McDavid, J. C. 1985. The Canadian Experience with Privatizing Residential Solid Waste Collection Services. *Public Administration Review* 45(19) September/October, pp. 602–608.

McDavid, J. C., and Schick, G. K. 1987. Privatization versus Union Management Cooperation: The Effects of Competition on Service Efficiency in Municipalities. *Canadian Public Administration* 30(3) (Fall), pp. 472–488.

McEntee, G. W. 1985. City Services: Can Free Enterprise Outperform the Public Sector? *Business and Society Review* 55 (Fall), pp. 43–47.

McIntosh, K., Shauness, J., and Wettenhall, R. 1997. *Contracting Out In Australia: An Indicative History*. Centre for Research in Public Sector Management, University of Canberra.

McKay, S. 1996. HRL Rescue Benefits Kennett's Wife, Sons. *The Age* (June 1), p. 4.

Megginson, W. L., Nash, R., and Van Randenborgh, M. 1994. The Financial and Operating Performance of Newly Privatized Firms: An International Empirical Analysis. *The Journal of Finance* 49(2), pp. 403–452.

Mehay, S. L., and Gonzalez, R. A. 1985. Economic Incentives Under Contract Supply of Local Government Services. *Public Choice* 46, pp. 79–86.

———. 1993. Direct and Indirect Benefits of Intergovernmental Contracting for Police Services. In *Privatizing the United States Justice System*, edited by G. Bowman, S. Hakim, and P. Seidenstat, pp. 67–81. Jefferson, N.C.: McFarland & Co.

Meller, P. 1993. A Review of Chilean Privatization Experience. *Quarterly Review of Economics & Finance* 33, pp. 95–112.

Mennemeyer, S. T., and Olinger, L. 1989. Selective Contracting in California: Its Effect on Hospital Finances. *Inquiry* 26, pp. 442–457.

Menyah, K., Paudyal, K., and Inyang, C. 1990. The Pricing of Initial Offerings of Privatized Companies on the London Stock Exchange. *Accounting and Business Research* 21(81), pp. 51–56.

Messiter, G. 1993. Contracting Out in the NSW Public Sector: Commercial Services Group as a Case Study. In *Doing More with Less? Contracting Out and Efficiency in the Public Sector*, edited by J. Coulter. Kensington, Australia: Public Sector Research Centre, pp. 52–61.

Miller, A. N. 1994. Privatization: Lessons from the British Experience. *Long Range Planning* 27(6), pp. 125–136.

Miller, T. I. 1976. The Effects of Drug Therapy on Psychological Disorders. Ph.D. Dissertation, University of Colorado.

Miller, T., Dickerson, H., and Greenstein, I. 1984. Private Management: A Comparative Analysis. *Journal of Housing* 41(6), pp. 109, 202–204.

Millward, R. 1986. The Comparative Performance of Public and Private Ownership. In *Privatization and Regulation*, edited by J Kay, C. Mayer, and D. Thompson, pp. 119–144. Oxford: Clarendon Press.

Millward, R., and Parker, D. 1983. Public and Private Enterprise: Comparative Behaviour and Relative Efficiency. In *Public Sector Economics*, by R. Millward, D. Parker, L. Rosenthal, M. T. Sumner, and N. Topham, pp. 199–274. London: Longman.

Milne, R. 1987. Competitive Tendering in the NHS: An Economic Analysis of the Early Implementation of HC (83) 18, *Public Administration* 65 (Summer), pp. 145–160.

Mintzberg, H. 1996. Managing Government—Governing Management. *Harvard Business Review* (May–June), pp. 75–83.

Montoya-Weiss, M. M., and Calantone, R. 1994. Determinants of New Product Performance: A Review and Meta-Analysis. *Journal of Product Innovation and Management* 11, pp. 397–417.

Moore, J. 1990. Privatization: The Liberals View to Improving Efficiency and Performance of Industry. In *Profiting from Opportunities in Privatization*, n.p. Sydney: I.I.R. Pty. Ltd.

———. 1992. British Privatization—Taking Capitalism to the People. *Harvard Business Review* (January–February), pp. 115–124.

Moore, S. 1986. Contracting Out: A Painless Alternative to the Budget Cutter's Knife. In *Proceeding of the Academy of Political Science* 36(3), Prospects for Privatization, edited by S. H. Hanke, pp. 60–73.

Morgan, D. R. 1992. The Pitfalls of Privatization: Contracting Without Competition. *American Review of Public Administration* 22 (December), pp. 251–269.

Mottram, M. 1999. The Corporate Umpire. *The Age*, News Extra (July 17), p. 2.

Moussios, A. 1994. "Hybrid" Status, Regulation and Performance: An Empirical Analysis of the Denationalisation of British Telecom. DPA Thesis, University of Georgia.

Mulgan, R. 1997. Contracting Out and Accountability. *Australian Journal of Public Administration* 56(1) (December), pp. 106–116.

Musgrove, K. E. 1988. A Comparative Study of District Owned Versus Contracted Pupil Transportation Systems in Missouri. EDD Thesis, University of Missouri, Columbia.

Narby, D. J., Cutler, B. L., and Moran, G. 1993. A Meta-Analysis of the Association Between Authoritarianism and Juror's Perceptions of Defendant Culpability. *Journal of Applied Psychology* 78(1), pp. 34–42.

National Center for Policy Analysis. 1985. *Privatization in the U.S.: Cities and Counties*. NCPA Policy Report No. 116, Dallas, Texas, June.

Nellis, J. 1991. Privatization in Reforming Socialist Economies. In *Privatization in Eastern Europe: Current Implementation Issues*, edited by A. Bohm and V. Kreacic, pp. 15–23. Ljublijana, Yugoslavia: International Centre for Public Enterprises in Developing Countries.

Nelson, L., and Kuzes, I. Y. 1994. Evaluating the Russian Voucher Privatization Program. *Comparative Economic Studies* 36(1), pp. 55–67.

NSW Treasury. 1993. Competitive Tendering and Contracting in the NSW Budget Sector: Survey Findings. NSW Treasury, December.

Nuruzzman, S. A. M. 1989. Public and Private Production of a Private Good: The Case of Cotton Textile Manufacturing Industry in Bangladesh. Ph.D. Thesis, University of Hawaii.

Okumura, H. 1994. The ¥600,000 Dream. *Tokyo Business* 62(2), pp. 16–17.

Organisation for Economic Co-operation and Development. 1994. *Trends and Policies in Privatization* 1(3). Paris: Centre for Co-operation with the Economies in Transition.

_____. 1998. *Public Management Reform and Economic and Social Development*. Public Management Services, Public Management Committee.

Osborne, D., and Gaebler, T. 1993. Reinventing Government: How the Entrepreneurial Spirit is Transforming the Public Sector. Reading MASS.: Addison-Wesley Publishing Co.

Ottenbacher, K., and Cooper, H. 1983. Drug Treatments of Hyperactivity in Children. *Developmental Medicine and Child Neurology* 25, pp. 353–357.

Owen, A. 1995. Public Sector Ethics—Some Practical Implications. Presentation to Public Sector Ethics Seminar, Graduate School of Government, Monash University, 22 September.

PA Consulting Group. 1997. *Strategic Sourcing Survey 1998: Australia in the International Context*, Melbourne.

Pack, J. 1989. Privatization and Cost Reduction. *Policy Sciences: An International Journal Devoted to the Improvement of Policy Making* 22, pp. 1–15.

Pack, R. 1992. Reliability Analysis of Vendor Managed Corporate Telecommunications Networks: A Study on the Impact of Network Availability Levels When Network Management is Outsourced. Ph.D. Thesis, Golden Gate University.

Paddon, M. 1993a. Taking Contracting Seriously: The Current Debate in the UK and Europe. In *Doing More With Less? Contracting Out and Efficiency in the Public Sector*, edited by J. Coulter, n.p. Kensington, NSW: Public Sector Research Centre, University of New South Wales.

_____. 1993b. Competitive Tendering and Contracting Out in UK Local Government. *Administrative and Managerial Reform in Government: A Commonwealth Portfolio of Current Good Practice*, Proceedings of a Pan Commonwealth Working Group Meeting, Kuala Lumpur, Malaysia, 19–22 April, pp. 115–161.

PAIS. 1995. Provisional List of Periodicals. PAIS International Database. New York: Public Affairs Information Services, Inc.

Parker, D. 1990. The 1988 Local Government Act and Compulsory Competitive Tendering. *Urban Studies* (October), pp. 653–668.

_____. 1992. Agency Status, Privatization and Improved Performance: Some Evidence from the UK. *International Journal of Public Sector Management* 5(1), pp. 30–38.

_____. 1994a. A Decade of Privatization: The *Effect of Ownership Change and Competition on British Telecom*. *British Review of Economic Issues* 16(40), pp. 87–113.

_____. 1994b. International Aspects of Privatization: A Critical Assessment of Business Restructuring in the UK, former Czechoslovakia and Malaysia. *British Review of Economic Issues* 16, pp. 1–32.

Parker, D., and Hartley, K. 1991a. Organisational Status and Performance: The Effects on Employment. *Applied Economics* 23(2) (February), pp. 403–416.

_____. 1991b. Do Changes in Organisational Status Affect Financial Performance? *Strategic Management Journal* 12(8) (November), pp. 631–641.

_____. 1991c. Status Change and Performance: Economic Policy and Evidence. In *Privatization and Economic Efficiency: A Comparative Analysis of Developed and Developing Countries*, edited by Attiat F. Ott and Keith Hartley, pp. 108–125. Aldershot, England: Edward Elgar.

Parker, D., and Martin, S. 1993. Testing Time for Privatization. *Management Today* (August), pp. 44–47.

_____. 1995. The Impact of UK Privatization on Labour and Total Factor Productivity. *Scottish Journal of Political Economy* 42(2), pp. 201–220.

Parsons, W. 1995. *Public Policy: An Introduction to the Theory and Practice of Policy Analysis*. Cheltenham, England: Edward Elgar, 1995.

Paterson, J. 1988. A Managerialist Strikes Back. *Australian Journal of Public Administration* 47(4) (December), pp. 287–295.

Peak, D. A. 1994. The Risks and Effects of Outsourcing on the Information Systems Function and the Firm. Ph.D. Dissertation, University of North Texas.

Pearson, K. 1933. On a Method for Determining Whether a Sample of Size n Supposed to Have Been Drawn from a Parent Population Having a Known Probability Integral Has Probably Been Drawn at Random. *Biometrika* 25, pp. 379–410.

People Together Project. 1998. *Turning People Into Commodities–Report of the Public Hearings on Competitive Tendering in Human Services*, March.

Perry, J. L., and Babitsky, T. T. 1986. Comparative Performance in Urban Bus Transit: Assessing Privatization Strategies. *Public Administration Review* 46(1), pp. 57–66.

Peterson, N. M. 1984. *Solid Waste Collection, This Way Up: The Local Official's Handbook for Privatization and Contracting Out*, edited by R. Q. Armington and W. D. Ellis. Lake Bluff, Ill.: Regney Books.

Pirie, M. 1985. *Privatization in Theory and Practice*. London: Adam Smith Institute.

_____. 1986. *Privatization in Theory and Practice*. Sydney: Adam Smith Institute and Centre 2000 Limited.

Pollitt, C. 1993. *Managerialism and the Public Services*. 2d Ed. Oxford: Blackwell Publishers.

Pommerehne, W., and Frey, B. 1977. Public versus Private Production Efficiency in Switzerland: A Theoretical and Empirical Comparison. In *Comparing Urban Service Delivery Systems*. Urban Affairs Annual Review, edited by Vincent Ostrom and Robert Bish, pp. 221–241. Beverly Hills, Calif.: Sage Publications.

Poole, R. W., and Fixler, P. E. 1987. Privatization of Public-Sector Services in Practice: Experience and Potential. *Journal of Policy Analysis and Management* 6(4), pp. 612–625.

Proquest. 1995a. *How to Use Proquest Searchware*. Ann Arbor: UMI.

_____. *Proquest Database Documentation for Dissertation Abstracts*. Ann Arbor: UMI.

Proust, E. 1995. Competitive Government in Victoria. Presentation to the Annual State Conference of the Royal Institute of Public Administration Australia, Victorian Division.

Public Bodies Review Committee. 1991. Report to the Parliament on the Appropriate Model for Corporatisation of the State Electricity Commission, Melbourne, June.

Punch, G. 1990. A Short Introduction on Performance Measurement and the Implementation Process. Presentation to the Public Sector Performance Management Conference, December 6.

Ralston Saul, J. 1997. *The Unconscious Civilisation*. Ringwood, Melbourne: Penguin Books.

Rance, C. 1999. New Tender System 'Hasn't Helped' Aged, Disabled. *The Age* (30 January), p. F44.

Rees, R. 1994. Economic Aspects of Privatization in Britain. In *Privatization in Western Europe: Pressures, Problems and Paradoxes*, edited by V. Wright, pp. 44–56. London: Pinter Publishers.

Rehfuss, J. A. 1991. A Leaner, Tougher Public Management? Public Agency Competition with Private Contractors. *Public Administration Quarterly* (Summer), pp. 239–250.

Reserve Bank of Australia. 1997. Privatization in Australia. *Reserve Bank of Australia Bulletin* (December), pp. 1–10.

Rhodes, R. 1997. The Transformation of British Public Administration. Paper presented to the American Society of Public Administration Conference, Philadelphia, July 26–30.

Richardson, J. 1987. Ownership and Regulation in the Health Care Sector. In *Privatization: An Australian Perspective*, edited by P. Abelson, pp. 249–274. Mosman, NSW: Australian Professional Publications.

Rigg, J., and Leach, G. 1990. Futures Issues: After Privatization—Economic Ideas and the Business Environment. *Long Range Planning* 23(1), pp. 151–156.

Rimmer, S. 1991a. Estimated Savings from Competitive Tendering. Assistance Evaluation Branch Staff Working Paper No. 1, April.

_____. 1991b. Competitive Tendering, Contracting Out and Franchising: Key Concepts and Issues. *Australian Journal of Public Administration* 50(3), pp. 292–302.

_____. 1993. Aspects of Competitive Tendering and Contracting in Local Government Administration. Ph.D. Dissertation, University of New England, Armidale.

Rimmer, S., and Webb, G. 1990. Greater Efficiency Through Competitive Tendering: Fact or Fiction? *Economic Papers* 9(4), pp. 51–60.

Ring, P. S., and Van De Ven, A. H. 1992. Structuring Co-operative Relationships Between Organisations. *Strategic Management Journal* 13, pp. 483–498.

Roarty, M. 1998. Electricity Industry Restructuring: The State of Play. Research Paper 14, Parliamentary Library of Australia. Science, Technology, Environment and Resources Group, May.

Robertson, R. 1998. Contract Details are the Secret to Success. *Australian Financial Review*, Outsourcing Special Report, p. 5.

Robinson, M., and Wilson, S. 1994. Privatization in Massachusetts: Getting Results. *Government Union Review* 15(1) (Winter), pp. 1–55.

Robson, P. 1993. Sky High—and Dry! *Credit Management* (January), pp. 33–36.

Rodriguez, F. 1992. The Mexican Privatization Programme: An Economic Analysis. *Social and Economic Studies* 41(4), pp. 149–171.

Roehm, H. S., Castellano, J., and Karns, D. A. 1989. Contracting Services to the Private Sector: A Survey of Management Practices. *Government Finance Review* 5(1), pp. 21–25, 52.

Rose. P. 1994. Costing Government Services: Benchmarks for Making. *Government Finance Review* 10 (June), pp. 7–11.

Rosenthal, R. 1991. *Meta-Analytic Procedures for Social Research*. Rev. Ed. Applied Social Research Methods Series, vol. 6. Newbury Park, Calif.: Sage Publications.

Rosenthal, R., and Rubin, D. B. 1978. Interpersonal Expectancy Effects: The First 345 Studies. *The Behavioural and Brain Sciences* 3, pp. 377–415.

_____. 1982. A Simple, General Purpose Display of Magnitude of Experimental Effect. *Journal of Educational Psychology* 74, pp. 166–169.

Roth, G. 1987a. *The Private Provision of Public Services in Developing Countries.* New York: Oxford University Press.

_____. 1987b. Privatization of Public Services. In *Privatization and Development,* edited by S. H. Hanke, pp. 129–140. International Centre for Economic Growth, Institute for Contemporary Studies, California.

Rothenburg Pack, J. 1989. Privatization and Cost Reduction. *Policy Sciences* 22(1) (March), pp. 1–25.

Russell, E. W. 1994. Personal Communication. Monash University, Clayton. July.

Sakita, M. 1989. Restructuring of the Japanese National Railways: Review and Analysis. *Transportation Quarterly* 43, pp. 29–45.

Saunders, P., and Harris, C. 1994. *Privatization and Popular Capitalism.* Buckingham, England: Open University Press.

Savas, E. S. 1974. Municipal Monopolies versus Competition in Delivering Urban Services. In *Improving the Quality of Urban Management,* edited by W. D. Hawley and D. Rogers. Beverly Hills, Calif.: Sage.

_____. 1977a. An Empirical Study of Competition in Municipal Service Delivery. *Public Administration Review* 37 (Nov./Dec.), pp. 717–724.

_____. 1977b. Policy Analysis for Local Government: Public vs Private Refuse Collection. *Policy Analysis* 3(1) (Winter), pp. 49–74.

_____. 1980. Comparative Costs of a Public and Private Enterprise in a Municipal Service. In *Public and Private Enterprise in a Mixed Economy,* edited by W. J. Baumol, pp. 253–269. London: Macmillan.

_____. 1981. Intra-City Competition Between Public and Private Sector Delivery. *Public Administration Review* 41 (Jan/Feb), pp. 46–52.

_____. 1987. *Privatization: The Key to Better Government.* Chatham, N.J.: Chatham House Publishers.

_____. 1992a. Privatization and Productivity. In *Public Productivity Handbook,* edited by Mark Holzer, pp. 79–98. New York: Marcel Dekker.

_____. 1992b. A Comparative Study of Private and Public Bus Operations in New York City. Report to the U.S. Department of Transportation, Washington, FTA-NY-11-0049-91-1.

_____. 1993. It's Time To Privatize. *Government Union Review* 14(1), pp. 37–52.

Savas, E. S., Grava, S., and Sparrow, R. 1991. The Private Sector in Private Transportation in New York City: A Policy Perspective. U.S. Department of Transportation, January.

SCAT (Services to Community Action and Trade Unions). 1988. *Taken to the Cleaners: The Lincolnshire Experience (Dirty Schools, Exploited Cleaners, Contract Failures).* Written for East Midlands NUPE NALGO, November.

Schmidt. L. 1999. Vitamin Cheats Cough Up Millions. *Business Review Weekly,* Melbourne (June 4), p. 49.

Schneider, K. 1992. U.S. Cites Waste in Its Contracts: Study Suggests Privatization Isn't Necessarily a Cure. *New York Times* December 2, p. A1.

Seear, R. 1994. Contracting Out of Asset Maintenance—Melbourne Water "A Contractors Perspective." ICOMS Conference, 1994, Australia.

Seghers, F. 1986. Computerising Uncle Sam's Data: Oh How the Public is Paying. *Business Week* (December 15), pp. 67–68.

Self, P. 1994. Public Choice and Public Benefit: Politics, Public Service and Markets. Presentation to the annual RIPPA Conference, Melbourne.

Senge, P. M. 1992. *The Fifth Discipline: The Art and Practice of the Learning Organization.* London: Century Business.

Shallcrass, R. 1993. Privatisation: The New Zealand Experience. In *Privatisation: The Financial Implications,* edited by Kevin Davis and Ian Harper, pp. 163–174. Sydney: Allen and Unwin.

Shannon, A. G., and Athanasou, J. A. 1992. Using Meta-Analysis Techniques as an Evaluation Tool. Proceedings of the Australasian Evaluation Society International Conference, 1992, pp. 93.1–93.23.

Simmons, J. 1995. Rudy to Can Mob Garbage Haulers. *New York Post* (October 25), p. 9.

Simms, M. 1982. The Dilemmas and Paradoxes of Public Bodies Performing Commercial Tasks: Politics. *Journal of the Australasian Political Studies Association* 21(2), pp. 32–40.

Sinha, P. K. 1993. Analysis of Privatization Through Public Offerings. Ph.D. Dissertation, University of Pennsylvania.

Slater, R. B. 1992. What's Driving the Outsourcing Bandwagon? *Bankers Monthly* 109(6), p. 23–24.

Smith, P. 1994. The Stunning Success of Privatization Shares. *Investors Chronicle* 107(1363), pp. 14–15.

Snedecor, G. W. 1946. *Statistical Methods,* 4th Ed. Ames: Iowa State University Press.

Spicer, B., Bowman, R., Emanuel, D., and Hunt, A. 1991. *The Power to Manage: Restructuring the New Zealand Electricity Department As a State Owned Enterprise—The Electricorp Experience.* Auckland, NZ: Oxford University Press.

Spiegel, M. R. 1961. *Theory and Problems of Statistics.* Schaums Outline Series. New York: McGraw-Hill Book Company.

Spindler, S. 1996. Whose Mandate? Presentation to the "Whose Mandate" Seminar, Parliament House, Spring Street, Melbourne, May 17.

SPSS. 1993. SPSS for Windows Base System User's Guide, Release 6.0.

Starr, P. 1989. The Meaning of Privatization. In *Privatization and the Welfare State,* edited by S. B. Kamerman and A. J. Kahn, pp. 15–48. Princeton, N.J.: Princeton University Press.

Stein, L. 1994. Privatization, Workforce Cutbacks, and African-American Municipal Employment. *American Review of Public Administration* 24(2), pp. 181–191.

Stevens, B. J. 1977. Service Arrangement and the Cost of Residential Refuse Collection. In *The Organisation and Efficiency of Solid Waste Collection,* edited by E. S. Savas, pp. 121–138. Lexington, Mass.: Lexington Books.

Stevens, B. J. 1984. Comparing Public and Private Sector Productive Efficiency: An Analysis of Eight Activities. *National Productivity Review* 3 (Autumn), pp. 395–406.

Stone, B. 1995. Administrative Accountability in the Westminster Democracies: Towards a New Conceptual Framework. *Governance* 8 (October), p. 8.

Stretton, H. 1994. Old Thoughts and Young Theories. Presentation to the RIPPA Annual Conference, Professional Day, 26 November, Flinders University, South Australia.

Stretton, H., and Orchard, L. 1994. *Public Goods, Public Enterprise, Public Choice: Theoretical Foundations of the Contemporary Attack on Government.* New York: St. Martin's Press.

Sundquist, J. L. 1984. Privatization: No Panacea for What Ails Government. In *Public-Private Partnerships: New Opportunities for Meeting Social Needs*, edited by H. Brooks, L. Leibman, and C. S. Schelling, pp. 303–318. Cambridge, Mass.: Ballinger.

Szymankiewicz, J. 1994. Contracting Out or Selling Out?: Survey Into the Current Issues Concerning the Outsourcing of Distribution. *Logistics Information Management* 7(1), pp. 28–35.

Szymanski, S. 1993. Garbage In, Garbage Out: Cost Reductions in Refuse Collection Since Compulsory Competitive Tendering. Unpublished manuscript, London Business School.

Szymanski, S., and Wilkins, S. 1993. Cheap Rubbish? Competitive Tendering and Contracting Out in Refuse Collection—1981–88. *Fiscal Studies* 14(3), pp. 109–130.

Taggart, M. 1992. The Impact of Corporatisation and Privatization on Administrative Law. *Australian Journal of Public Administration* 51(3) (September), pp. 368–373.

Thobe, D. 1992. Who's Minding the Shop? BCR's Survey on Outsourcing. *Business Communications Review* 22(5), pp. 22–26.

Thomas, C. W. 1991. Prisoners' Rights and Correctional Privatization: A Legal and Ethical Analysis. *Business and Professional Ethics Journal* 10, pp. 3–45.

Thompson, D. J. 1987. Privatization in the UK: Deregulation and the Advantage of Incumbency. *European Economic Review* 31, pp. 368–374.

Thomson, L. 1993. Reporting Changes in the Electricity Supply Industry. *Financial Accountability and Management* 9(2), pp. 131–135.

Treasury of Australia. 1990. Budget Papers: 1990–91. Budget Paper 1, Canberra, AGPS, 1990.

Tucker, W. 1992. Foot in the Door. *Forbes* (February 3), pp. 50–51.

Tukey, J. W. 1962. The Future of Data Analysis. *Annals of Mathematical Statistics* 33(22).

U.K. Audit Office. 1987. Competitive Tendering for Support Services in the National Health Service, HC 318. London: HMSO.

U.S. General Accounting Office. 1991. OMB Circular A-76: Expected Savings Are Not Being Realized in Ft. Sill's Logistics Contract. Report to the Chairman, Subcommittee on Federal Services, Post Office and Civil Service, Committee on Governmental Affairs, US Senate.

_____. 1994a. Public-Private Mix: Extent of Contracting Out for Real Property Management Services in GSA. Briefing Report to the Ranking Minority Member, Subcommittee on Investigations and Oversight, Committee on Public Works and Transportation, House of Representatives, May, GAO/GGD-94-126BR.

_____. 1994b. Government Contractors: Measuring Costs of Service Contractors versus Federal Employees, Report to the Chairman, Subcommittee on Federal Services, Post Office and Civil Service, Committee on Governmental Affairs, US Senate, March.

Van Horn, C. E. 1991. The Myths and Realities of Privatization. In *Privatization and Its Alternatives*, edited by William T. Gormley, Jr., pp. 261–280. Madison, Wisc.: University of Wisconsin Press.

Veljanovski, C. 1987. Selling the State—Privatization in Britain. London: Weidenfeld and Nicholson.

Vickers, J., and Yarrow, G. 1988a. *Privatization: An Economic Analysis.* Cambridge, Mass.: MIT Press.

_____. 1988b. Regulation of Privatized Firms in Britain. *European Economic Review* 32, pp. 465–472.

Walsh, K. 1990. One Year On. *Local Government Chronicle* 24 (August), p. 11.

_____. 1991. *Competitive Tendering for Local Authority Services: Initial Experiences.* London: Department of the Environment. February.

Walsh, K., and Davis, H. 1993. Competition and Service: The Impact of the Local Government Act 1988. Department of the Environment. London: HMSO.

Ward, J. D. 1992. Privatization and Political Culture: Perspectives from Small Cities and Towns. *PAQ* (Winter), pp. 496–522.

Weimer, D. L., and Vining, A. R. 1989. *Policy Analysis: Concepts and Practice.* Englewood Cliffs, N.J.: Prentice-Hall Int.

Weis, K. A. 1991. Influence of Economic Incentives on the Clinical Performance of the Physician Agent. DRPH dissertation, University of North Carolina.

West, M. L. 1993. Get A Piece of the Privatization Pie. *Security Management* 37(3) (March), pp. 54, 59, 60.

Wettenhall, R. 1983. Privatization: A Shifting Frontier Between Private and Public Sectors. *Current Affairs Bulletin* 69(6) November, pp. 114–122.

_____. 1993. Australian Statutory Corporations and the American Public Authority Tradition. *Canberra Bulletin of Public Administration* 75, pp. 40–50.

Wheeler, J. R., Zuckerman, H. S., and Aderholdt, J. 1982. How Management Contracts Can Affect Hospital Finances. *Inquiry* 19, pp. 160–166.

Whitehead, B., and O'Sullivan, B. 1991. When to Say "Yes" or "No" to Outsourcing. *ABA Banking Journal* 83(6) June, pp. 65, 68.

Whitfield, D. 1992. *The Welfare State—Privatization, Deregulation, Commercialisation of Public Services: Alternative Strategies for the 1990s.* London: Pluto Press.

Willcocks, L. 1998. Personal Communication, following *Australian Financial Review* article "Warning: Outsourcing Can Blow Your Budget," November 3, p. 27.

Williamson, B. 1998. The Victorian Government Experience with Market Testing. Presentation to the Commercial Support Program Benchmarking Seminar, Department of Defence, Canberra, September 29–30, 1998.

Williamson, O. 1975. *Markets and Hierarchies.* New York: The Free Press.

_____. 1985. *The Economic Institutions of Capitalism: Firms, Markets, Relational Contracting.* New York: The Free Press.

Wilson, J. Q. 1989. *Bureaucracy: What Government Agencies Do and Why They Do It.* New York: Basic Books.

Wiltshire, K. 1987. *Privatization: The British Experience—An Australian Perspective.* Committee for Economic Development, Melbourne: Longman Cheshire.

_____. 1990. The Paradox of Privatization. Review Article, *Australian Journal of Public Administration* 49(2) (June), pp. 195–199.

Wolf, F. M. 1986. *Meta-Analysis: Quantitative Methods for Research Synthesis.* Quantitative Applications in the Social Sciences Series. Beverly Hills, Calif.: Sage Publications.

Wolf, M. 1992. Comment on Herbert Hax, "Privatisation Agencies: The Treuhand Approach." In *A Symposium in Honour of Herbert Giersch,* edited by H. Siebert, pp. 160–162. Tubingen Mohr: Institut fur Weltwirtschaft an der Universitat Kiel.

World Bank Policy Research Report. 1995. *Bureaucrats in Business: The Economics and Politics of Government Ownership.* World Bank, Oxford University Press.

Yarrow, G. 1986. Privatization in Theory and Practice. *Economic Policy* 2, pp. 324–377.

_____. 1989. Privatization and Economic Performance in Britain. *Carnegie-Rochester Series on Public Policy* 31, pp. 303–344.

_____. 1994. Privatization, Restructuring and Regulatory Reform in Electricity Supply. In *Privatization and Economic Performance*, edited by M. Bishop, J. Kay, and C. Mayer, pp. 62–88. Oxford: Oxford University Press.

Yoder, R. A., and Borkholder, P. 1991. Privatization and Development. *The Journal of Developing Areas* 25 (April), pp. 42.

Zwanziger, J., and Melnick, G. A. 1988. The Effects of Hospital Competition and the Medicare PPS Program on Hospital Cost Behavior in California. *Journal of Health Economics* 7, pp. 301–320.

Index